THE MYSTERIOUS
MRS. NIXON

ALSO BY HEATH HARDAGE LEE

Winnie Davis: Daughter of the Lost Cause

The League of Wives: The Untold Story of the Women Who Took on the U.S. Government to Bring Their Husbands Home

THE MYSTERIOUS
MRS. NIXON

THE LIFE AND TIMES *of* WASHINGTON'S MOST PRIVATE FIRST LADY

HEATH HARDAGE LEE

ST. MARTIN'S
PRESS
NEW YORK

First published in the United States by St. Martin's Press,
an imprint of St. Martin's Publishing Group

www.stmartins.com

Designed by Steven Seighman

Library of Congress Cataloging-in-Publication Data

Names: Lee, Heath Hardage, author.
Title: The mysterious Mrs. Nixon : the life and times of Washington's
    most private first lady / Heath Hardage Lee.
Description: First edition. | New York : St. Martin's Press, 2024. | Includes
    bibliographical references and index.
Identifiers: LCCN 2024013595 | ISBN 9781250274342 (hardcover) |
    ISBN 9781250274359 (ebook)
Subjects: LCSH: Nixon, Pat, 1912–1993. | Nixon, Pat, 1912–1993—
    Influence. | Presidents' spouses—United States—Biography. | Nixon,
    Richard M. (Richard Milhous), 1913–1994.
Classification: LCC E857.N58 L44 2024 | DDC 973.924/092 [B]—dc23/
    eng/20240326
LC record available at https://lccn.loc.gov/2024013595

Our books may be purchased in bulk for promotional, educational, or business use.
Please contact your local bookseller or the Macmillan Corporate and Premium Sales
Department at 1-800-221-7945, extension 5442, or by email at
MacmillanSpecialMarkets@macmillan.com.

First Edition: 2024

10 9 8 7 6 5 4 3 2 1

This book is dedicated with special thanks and admiration to Pat Nixon's "East Wingers," to the Honorable Barbara Hackman Franklin, who worked in the Nixon West Wing and later became the 29th U.S. Secretary of Commerce, and in memory of Helene Colesie Drown, Pat's dearest friend and the one who perhaps knew her best of all.

CONTENTS

PART III: LEADING LADY

THE MYSTERIOUS MRS. NIXON

August 9, 1974

Spotlit under blinding camera lights and accompanied by the sound of thunderous applause, Richard and Pat Nixon, the soon-to-be ex-president and First Lady of the United States, walked wearily toward a raised platform in the East Room of the White House. Following close behind them were the two Nixon daughters, Tricia and Julie, accompanied by their husbands, Edward Cox and David Eisenhower. No one had slept well the night before, knowing what was to come.

Pat, a spouse who had always devoted herself to her husband's interests, had been powerless to help him during the Watergate scandal. After facing formal impeachment inquiries from the House of Representatives, President Nixon ultimately chose to resign. Americans, still in shock, would soon watch Nixon's farewell address to his staff on live television. Pat had balked at the idea of having their exit recorded. "Oh, Dick, you can't have it televised," she said, but in the end she acquiesced to his wishes.

On camera, many of Nixon's best-known White House staffers can be seen observing the event as if watching a train wreck. Henry Kissinger, Nixon's secretary of state and national security advisor, looked nauseated. A young Ben Stein, one of Nixon's speechwriters (later to become a famous comedian), was chewing gum and crying at the same time. Secretary of Defense James R. Schlesinger nervously puffed on his signature pipe, surrounded by swirls of tobacco smoke. Wearing dark sunglasses, the First Lady's social secretary, Lucy Winchester, dabbed her nose discreetly with a handkerchief.

Up on the stage, a pale Julie Eisenhower, who had publicly defended her father for months, wore a strained smile. Her sister, Tricia, famously more private than her younger sister, looked anguished, but it was Pat Nixon who appeared the most stricken. She looked painfully thin in her pink geometric-patterned dress with its wide collar and white belt, an outfit that she had worn on a recent trip to the Middle East—her last foreign trip as First Lady. She seemed to be willing herself not to cry, to keep up appearances for just a few hours more. Despite her fine-boned beauty and legendary poise, Pat had always hated being on camera. And yet here she was, America's most private public person, thrust once again into the spotlight.

Even after the First Family reached the platform, the applause continued. It was perhaps the most painful standing ovation in the history of any presidency. Finally the clapping subsided, and a tearful Richard Nixon gave a fifteen-minute farewell speech, in which he praised his adored mother, Hannah, saying, "She will have no books written about her, but she was a saint." He would be criticized ever after for not mentioning Pat.

Members of Nixon's own cabinet, including Caspar Weinberger, could not comprehend how he "never once made mention of his wife, who had stood by him and supported him throughout the whole ordeal, indeed through his entire career." Daughter Julie Nixon said later that the president could not have kept his composure if he had mentioned her onstage that day. The First Lady's press secretary, Helen Smith, speculated that the president "knew that there is a limit to what Pat can endure—and still keep her head high." Still, it was an unfortunate omission in the eyes of the nation.

The president continued: "Greatness comes not when things go always well for you, but the greatness comes when you are really tested, when you take some knocks, some disappointments, when sadness comes because only if you've been in the deepest valley can you ever know how magnificent it is to be on the highest mountain."

Pat knew these highs and lows well. She had stood beside her husband throughout his tumultuous career, including when Dick lost in the 1960 election to Jack Kennedy and during his incredible comeback win with the election of 1968. She was acutely aware of what her husband described. She had fought the same battles, taking them much more personally than he ever did. The emotional toll public life had taken upon her and her family produced deep scars, but by now she had trained herself to suppress her feelings.

After the speech, the president and the First Lady, along with their daughters and sons-in-law, walked quickly down the aisle and descended the stairs to the Diplomatic Reception Room, where the new president-to-be and his wife, Gerald and Betty Ford, were waiting. The Fords then escorted the Nixons and their entourage to a red carpet, which led not to a lavish diplomatic reception but to their exit from American politics.

As East Wing staffer Patti Matson recalled, the weather outside reflected the somber mood. "It was a day out of central casting. You could not believe all the clouds and the darkness." When the Nixons took their final walk down the White House lawn to their waiting helicopter, Pat whispered to her old friend Betty Ford, now the new First Lady, "Well, Betty, you'll see many of these red carpets, and you'll get so you hate 'em."

Betty Ford, reportedly already in the throes of addiction, awkwardly blurted out, "Have a nice trip, Dick!" as they climbed into the Army One helicopter.

As Pat later recalled: "Our hearts were breaking and there we are smiling." Wasn't that so often the story of her life?

———

It must have taken all Pat had to hold herself together that last day as First Lady. She had never craved center stage. She had a horror of self-promotion that often worked against her. Pat refused to allow the press into her inner life, guarding her private thoughts fiercely. In the absence of hard copy, the media constructed an image of Pat Nixon as "Plastic Pat," a silent, mysterious doll. Journalists created a wind-up automaton as a substitute for the real woman, to whom no one could get close enough to write about accurately.

This was partially a problem of Pat's own making, but she couldn't escape her present circumstances, determined not by her own actions but by those of her husband. This was a fate typical of women who came of age in the 1950s, whether they were First Ladies or not. Her job was to help her husband do his job, but she also had her own individual convictions and interests. Though she had been Second Lady from 1953 to 1961, her biggest trials came as First

Lady during the chaotic late 1960s and 1970s, when civil rights, feminism, and the Vietnam War turned American apple pie into an upside-down tarte Tatin.

The Mysterious Mrs. Nixon is a historical reexamination of America's least-known and most misunderstood First Lady. The real Pat Nixon was nothing like her media-constructed persona. She was warm, generous, and above all interested in people. She was elegant but not aloof, accomplished but down to earth. She was in fact the *opposite* of what Americans thought her to be. She was immune to the power and status that the presidency gave her. In fact, she would have preferred a quiet life raising her two daughters out of the spotlight.

While not a feminist, this First Lady was strongly pro-women, supporting the Equal Rights Amendment, a woman's right to choose, and the placement of more women in high-level government roles (Pat pushed very publicly for a woman to join the Supreme Court). Pat thought women could do anything they set their minds to, including running for president, as she proclaimed in a now-forgotten interview with Barbara Walters. She received little credit for these stances, but she moved the needle substantially forward for women's issues both in public and behind the scenes.

Instead of encouraging her to pursue these agendas, along with her many other interests, Nixon's longtime chief of staff, Bob Haldeman, and others in the West Wing tried to isolate the First Lady and minimize her influence on the president. Some of these male staffers refused to see Pat as the practiced political partner she was, instead attempting to place the First Lady in a cellophane-sealed box like a 1960s Barbie doll: she was to be seen and admired, but not heard. Pat innately recognized and recoiled from the artificiality of political life and deeply resented efforts to package and commodify her in a *Mad Men*–like advertising mode.

So, who was she? *The Mysterious Mrs. Nixon* unravels that mystery by putting Pat back in control of her own story as a strong individual at the very center of American power and influence, with her own distinct personality and accomplishments. She was no victim. Her true story—the *real* story, based on archival accounts and scores of interviews with her friends, family, and former staffers—is much more compelling than the artificially constructed image of the First Lady that most Americans know.

Pat's long journey to the White House begins in 1912 in desolate Ely, Nevada. Her western spirit has often been overlooked in previous portrayals, but it is perhaps her most defining characteristic. As Pat's son-in-law David Eisenhower explained, his mother-in-law came from a "kind of Annie Oakley background. She fits nicely into the political sphere . . . but her spirit is Western and California. She's not someone who's molded by the image-makers."

PART I

A FARMER'S DAUGHTER

1

THE LONELIEST ROAD IN AMERICA

U S Highway 50 is a three-thousand-mile route running from the East
Coast to the West. It begins in Ocean City, Maryland, and ends in West
Sacramento, California. The western part of the highway snakes through
swaths of desolate countryside, including a section in Nevada dubbed "the
Loneliest Road in America." Built in 1926, this asphalt road overlays what
originally was the Central Overland Route and the Pony Express trail.

This treacherous path crosses several of the state's mountain ranges at
high altitudes, winding through four old mining towns. One of these settlements, Ely, lies on the eastern edge of Highway 50 about 320 miles east
of Reno. In 1912, when future First Lady Thelma Catherine "Pat" Ryan was
born in this remote area, not even the Loneliest Road in America existed. Located in White Pine County, Ely was a hardscrabble frontier town surrounded
by snowy, rugged mountains, scraggly pine trees, and a rocky, forbidding
landscape.

The area's first residents were Shoshone Indians. By 1860, a Pony Express
post office and telegraph and the Central Overland Route stagecoach stop
were among the few signs of formal settlement a traveler could find there.
Mining boomtowns for gold, silver, and lead blossomed and then withered
in the region like desert flowers. Vermonter J. W. Long arrived in White
Pine County in 1878, founding the township of Ely after he discovered
gold in the area. In 1887, the state legislature made Ely the county seat,
spurring further development. A Wells Fargo office, a newspaper publisher,
drinking establishments, businesses, and homes began to dot the sparse
landscape.

In 1906, the town's fortunes improved dramatically. Copper was discovered in the area, and the Nevada Northern Railway arrived the same year to transport the precious metal to market. "The Nevada Northern Railway single-handedly made the development of the copper industry possible in White Pine County. Without the railroad, there would be no way to move the ore from the mines to the mill." Copper was crucial for the latest technology: the metal was utilized in telephone wire and for electrical wiring.

Miners soon came in droves to Ely to seek their fortunes, including William "Will" Ryan. Will was an easterner by birth, born January 7, 1866, in Ridgefield, Connecticut. He was a good-looking man, tall, rangy, and blue-eyed, whose parents hailed from County Mayo in Ireland. The young man had a serious case of wanderlust, and "early in life . . . developed an itch for travel and adventure." Will worked as a deckhand on a whaling ship, a surveyor in the Philippines, and a gold prospector in the Yukon.

Though he found no gold in Alaska, he continued his mining career, searching for his fortune in South Dakota's silver mines. It was here he met Kate Halberstadt Bender, a German immigrant from Hesse. When Will met her, Kate was a widow with two young children. Kate's previous husband, Matthew Bender, had been a mining shop foreman who died in a flash flood while Kate was pregnant with their second child, daughter Neva. The couple also had an older son named Matthew.

———

Will was forty-three when he married the twenty-nine-year-old Kate in 1909. The couple had heard enticing tales of rich gold, silver, and copper deposits in Ely, Nevada, and soon moved there to try their luck yet again in the mines. Many before them, including writer Mark Twain, had been drawn to Nevada for the same reason. Twain's classic 1872 book *Roughing It* is a satirical chronicle of the get-rich-quick dreams of those like Will. However, these dreams of massive wealth were almost always chased away by the daily realities of mining. The profession was defined by its dangerous and backbreaking work. Those who chose this career were not only betting against the odds that the mine would yield riches but also gambling with their lives. "The miserable living conditions, the poor sanitation and terrible food, the inadequacy of medical care and the high-risk work of mining created an alarmingly high mortality rate."

Despite their firsthand knowledge of the dangers of the mining profession, the newly married Ryans arrived in Ely and lived first in a tent city. By 1910, the Ryans' eldest, William (known as Bill), was born, followed by son Thomas (called Tom) in 1911. At some point during the Ryans' time in Ely, young Matthew Bender was sent to live with his well-off grandparents in Los Angeles. While this must have been heartbreaking for Kate, she had her hands full caring for Neva, Bill, and Tom in a tiny unheated cabin. She may have welcomed the opportunity for a better life for her oldest child.

By 1912, the family was living in a rented two-room miner's shack on the south side of Campton Street between Fifth and Sixth Streets. Ely remains one of the coldest cities in the United States, with temperatures in March sometimes falling below zero. The early morning of March 16, 1912, was frigid. On this day, Thelma Catherine Ryan arrived at 3:25 a.m. When Will arrived home, delighted with his little girl, he affectionately called her his "St. Patrick's Day Babe in the Morn," and ever after insisted on celebrating her birthday on St. Patrick's Day. He also added Patricia to her given names, but she was always "Babe" to him. She herself would not go by Pat until her college days, preferring to use Thelma or her childhood nickname, Buddy, as a young girl.

The weekend of Pat's birth, a local movie theater, the Bijou, was showing *The Broken Spur*, while a rival theater, the Empire, was showing *A Frontier Girl's Courage*. The local dry-goods store was selling children's clothes for 48 cents and ladies' house dresses for 98 cents. Nationally, the biggest news story of the spring of 1912 would be the loss of the newly built, state-of-the-art luxury ocean liner *Titanic*, which sank after hitting an iceberg on April 15. Fifteen hundred passengers and crew lost their lives that night.

A few days prior to Pat's arrival, on March 12, Juliette Gordon Low established the Girl Guides in Savannah, Georgia. This organization would later acquire its current name, the Girl Scouts. The organizational principles of the Girl Scouts "focused on the outdoors, inclusiveness, volunteerism, and self-reliance." Both the young Thelma Ryan and the older Pat Nixon would connect deeply with the Girl Scout mission: the core principles of independence and self-reliance meshed well with the tough lessons Pat learned in her childhood from her hardworking parents and their harsh life on the still untamed western frontier.

————

In the early 1900s, life in the West was a wild card that could play out in different ways. Here a person could gain or lose a fortune in a matter of months or even weeks. An individual (even a woman) could stake a claim to a homestead and make a go of it. Newcomers could elevate themselves socially with few restrictions if fortune smiled upon their endeavors. Men and women often worked equally hard under harsh conditions. Intense labor from both halves of a couple was required to make their joint risk pay off.

Partially due to the more equal partnership demanded within the frontier culture, western women had more rights during the settlement era than their sisters back east. Women achieved enfranchisement in the western states of Arizona, Kansas, and Oregon in 1912, the same year Pat was born. Her home state of Nevada was not far behind, recognizing women's right to vote in 1914, six years prior to the passing of the national suffrage amendment in 1920. As Anne Martin, president of the Nevada Equal Franchise Society, described it in an article in *Suffragist* magazine in November 1914, "The most important educative factor in our campaign was personal contact with the voter." This kind of door-to-door campaigning is a skill Nevada-born Pat would become proficient at later in her life.

The mining community Pat was born into was especially supportive of giving its women the vote. "Nevada owed much to the progressive-minded, often transient miners of the eastern region." Mining couples like Will and Kate Ryan well understood what Montana congresswoman Jeannette Rankin meant when she said, "Men and women are like right and left hands. It doesn't make sense not to use both."

However, Will, Kate, and their brood didn't remain in Ely for long. "Kate, who hated and feared mining, pleaded with her husband to give up the perilous business." Though Will was reluctant to leave a profession he knew so well, the couple jointly decided to seek the greener pastures and much improved weather of southern California.

———

Will, Kate, and the children traveled by train to Los Angeles and then arrived in the tiny town of Artesia (now Cerritos) by buckboard wagon. Although the town was less than twenty miles southwest of urban Los Angeles, it was mostly farmland when the Ryans arrived in 1913. The business section of town consisted of both sides of a single street. The unspoiled landscape showcased two very different microclimates, as "ten months out of the year you could see snow on the mountains and on either side of the highway were beautiful orange groves" that perfumed the air in spring.

Will and Kate soon bought a "ranch," a small one-story home on a flat ten-and-a-half-acre lot on Pioneer Boulevard. The small home had no running water or electricity. The house initially had only five rooms and no indoor bathroom. Eventually the family added a wing, tore down walls, and extended the living room to include a separate bedroom for Pat. The pride of the house was a baby grand piano—though none of the Ryans played.

Will knew nothing about farming prior to buying the land in Artesia. However, he committed himself to his new vocation and read voraciously about agriculture, soil, and farming techniques. "All of this study paid off, and he eventually became known as the 'cabbage king,' because he raised the biggest cabbages in the county." Kate, Pat, and Pat's brothers all worked together to help Will make the farm a success. But Will didn't give up completely on mining and the siren call of riches. "He invested in oil wells or mines whenever he could spare the cash."

Pat loved stories, reading, and books from an early age, a trait she shared with her father. Louise Raine Borden, Pat's childhood friend, claimed that Pat also inherited her father's deadpan sense of humor. She recalled: "He [Will] was quiet, and he was quite a humorist. He'd tell funny jokes and never crack a smile . . . he always had a yarn to tell, funny story of some kind." Pat "has quite a sense of humor and always did. Now, she probably did get it from her dad."

While Will was widely read and well traveled, Kate connected more to home and hearth. She was "heavy set" and spoke in broken English, but she was sweet to children and "always made real good cinnamon rolls." Pat was especially close to her mother, who taught her how to keep house, sew, and cook. Another family friend, Morton Morehouse, remembered that Kate was very much a woman of her time and place. She "was like many women in those days; she was pretty much of a housewife, and she didn't go out much."

Louise's sister, Myrtle Raine Borden, was also a close childhood friend of Pat's. A favorite pastime that already showed Pat's growing interest in the theater was putting on plays on top of an old water tank on the Raine property. Pat reigned as the director and organizer of the productions. Louise recalled: "She'd make them up and we'd dig out old clothes and sheets. There was nobody at home to tell us we couldn't have them. . . . We'd put on those little old plays out there on top of the tank house" for the neighborhood kids. Myrtle characterized Pat as having "a mind of her own" and a bit of a hot temper as a child, "but she never showed too much of it." She may have had an innate tendency to let her resentments simmer, as her childhood friend noted: "I don't know if she carried a grudge or not, but she wouldn't get right over it."

Artesia and the countryside around it would soon become known as one of the centers of the American dairy industry. This business in Artesia attracted a diverse group of farmers and agricultural workers. At Artesia Grammar School, Pat and her friends mixed easily with children of Portuguese, Dutch, Mexican, and Japanese backgrounds. There was a marked lack of segregation within area schools at this time. According to Pat's childhood friend Myrtle, "Everybody mixed together." Growing up in such an international community may have contributed to Pat's later ease with global travel and her lifelong fascination with cultures different from her own.

Pat, her brothers, and the Raine children all walked to school, since there were no school buses in those days out in the country. Only if it was raining hard would area parents drive the children. The school was a substantial red-brick building located across from the Methodist church in town on Pioneer Boulevard. Each grade had its own large classroom. Pat was a diligent student. She was mature and motivated, skipping two grades in elementary school. She and her brothers Bill and Tom would all graduate in the same class, despite their age differences.

Life on the farm could be hard. Money was often scarce, and much was expected of the three Ryan children at home. Pat learned early on to keep her chin up, not to complain, and not to expect too much from life. However, there were pleasures to be had both outdoors in the beautiful Southern California sunshine and inside reading books or dreaming up plays to perform for the neighborhood. The young girl did have dreams beyond the farm, and a spark within her to make things happen and to see a bigger world. As her friend Myrtle recognized early on: "She's got that push in there that she's always had, ever since she was a little child. I mean she really strives for something and goes out and gets it."

2

SOMETHING MORE THAN JUST AN ORDINARY COUNTRY GIRL

Not every childhood is perfect. Pat's was occasionally marred by her father's drinking binges. Usually an attentive and caring father, every once in a while Will would return from a night out, smelling of alcohol and in a combative mood. Pat saw Kate reprimand her husband in front of the children, leading to scenes that Pat was determined to avoid in her own life. "I detest temper. I detest scenes. I just can't be that way. I saw it with my father," she would tell daughter Julie later in her life. Simply put, Pat was not pliant or subservient. She always had her own dreams and goals in mind. Instead of being defiant or brash to get what she wanted, Pat's style was traditional, conservative. She learned early on to fly under the radar.

Far more upsetting than these occasional fights between her parents was her mother's serious illness, which began toward the end of the 1925 school year. Kate was often in pain and bedridden when Pat came home from school. Because Kate was a Christian Scientist and did not believe in medical intervention, she put off seeing a doctor until her illness had become untreatable. She died on January 18, 1926, from a combination of Bright's disease and liver cancer. Her daughter was only thirteen and a freshman at Excelsior Union High School in Artesia.

Pat's high school friends, including Marcia Elliott Wray, recalled her tightly controlled calm after her mother's funeral. "It was the first time any of us had lost a parent. We were all kind of nervous, I remember, and we were wondering how to treat her when she came back to school. . . . I remember after the service was over at the little funeral parlor, a group of us girls, maybe four or five, were standing out there wondering what to say to

Pat when she came out. She came out smiling and walked directly to us and she said, 'Didn't she look beautiful?'" The bright face the young teenager put on for others and her strenuous effort to keep up appearances surely masked her deep grief. It was an early sign of how she would act when she was in the public eye and life was rocky.

Though Pat did participate in events at the Christian Science and Methodist churches near her growing up, she was not considered particularly religious by her peers. Pat may have learned from her early personal experience with her mother that praying for miracles rarely brought results. As Richard Nixon's famous cousin Jessamyn West, the novelist, later noted of Pat, her fortitude did not surface thanks to religious convictions or upbringing. "It wasn't Christian Science, of any formal kind . . . rather a frontier hardihood. . . . Perhaps it was an early acquaintance with sickness and death. The way Ernest Hemingway put it was: 'Live and get your job done.'"

———

Pat took on a new persona after her mother died. She rarely went by Thelma anymore, preferring to be known by the nickname Buddy. She was plumper at this point than she would be later in her life, weighing about 132 pounds in high school at five feet five and a half inches tall. She was becoming a beautiful young woman with a "very pretty complexion, sort of rosy."

As was typical of this era, household management was seen as "woman's work" and fell almost entirely on Pat when her mother passed away. Her father and brothers counted on her to cook, clean, and do the laundry while still juggling her farm chores with schoolwork and other activities. Pat was now faced with an exhausting daily schedule at a critical developmental juncture. Pat's childhood ended prematurely. Instead, she became a second mother, not only to her brothers but also perhaps to her father as well.

Consequently, Pat was sometimes perceived by her Excelsior Union High School classmates as aloof. "We thought she was pretty stand-offish," her classmate Marcia Elliott Wray recalled, "but now I see it entirely differently. I think she was a lonely child who needed friendship. . . . I suppose we thought that she thought she was better than us. . . . And now I know it wasn't true at all. It was just our reaction to her aloofness, perhaps pride, because her family was having trouble." The young woman did not date much, though she did enjoy going to dances as part of a group, as many in her crowd tended to do. But she wasn't a carefree teenager; she was now a young adult with grown-up duties to fulfill.

Pat had a somewhat distant relationship with her half-sister, Neva, who was seven years her senior. Neva always felt second-best to her brother Matthew, who had received the bulk of their Bender grandparents' attention and resources, probably due to being male and somewhat of a replacement for their deceased son, Kate's first husband. When Kate was alive, she realized this and felt guilty she could not provide the extra items her older daughter craved.

Neva and Pat were both strikingly pretty and resembled each other with their flawless complexions. Neva acted more like an aunt than a sister to Pat, Bill, and Tom. She had left the Ryan residence in Artesia in 1924 after graduation from high school. Her grandparents had bequeathed her a small inheritance, which allowed her to attend Fullerton Junior College and keep her own apartment in Los Angeles.

After Kate died, Neva returned to Artesia occasionally on the weekends. However, she was training to be a nurse, despite (or perhaps because of) her mother's disdain for traditional medicine. Neva would often take a streetcar from L.A. to Artesia to visit. Due to the age difference between Neva and Matthew and their half siblings, they were not particularly close to the Ryan children. It was thirteen-year-old Pat, not twenty-year-old Neva, who took charge of the daily management of the household.

———

On June 7, 1929, Pat, Tom, and Bill graduated from high school together, as noted earlier. "Among the top students in her class, Pat was advanced two grades and eventually graduated the same year as her brother Tom and the eldest, Bill, who had been held back a year." Although all three Ryan children were offered college scholarships, there still wasn't enough money for all of them to attend college at the same time. Tom would go first; it was hoped that the other two children would follow him and continue their education.

Their father, Will, was slowly dying from tuberculosis. Bill took over the farm, while Pat would be assigned the toughest task of all: being a nurse to

her dying father. Tom promised her he would help her get the college education she craved down the road when he finished college and could help her
financially.

Will's illness was only the beginning of more adversity for the Ryans. In
October 1929, the American stock market crashed, and the Great Depression
began. The Roaring Twenties with their postwar excess gave way to Doro-
thea Lange's photos of the desperate poor and the Dust Bowl. A decade of
hardship would follow, affecting almost all who lived through this time, including Pat and her family. "The unemployment rate climbed from 9 percent
in 1930 to 16 percent in 1931, to 23 percent in 1932, by which time nearly
twelve million Americans—a number equal to the entire population of the
state of New York—were out of work. . . . [I]n many homes income fell to
zero. One in four Americans suffered for want of food."

Between 1929 and 1932, one in five American banks failed. Even so, after
her high school graduation, Pat began working for Artesia First National Bank,
a small establishment on the corner of 187th Street and Pioneer Boulevard. Pat
took the job to help pay for her father's hospitalization and medical treatment. Her job was to post the checks each day and to help with the bookkeeping. The staff was small, mostly female, and hardworking; friendly Pat
fit in well with the group.

Pat's friend Blanche Potter Holmes had an older sister, Frances, who
worked at the bank with Pat. One day both Pat and Frances were working
behind the teller window. Blanche recalled, "A young man came to the window. He had a gun in his hand; a note, and he demanded all of the cash.
Frances said that Pat was standing by her and they just froze on the spot and
gave him the money. . . . Later he was found and they had to go to court."
The young women's testimony helped convict the thief. Their calmness and
good memory for the robber's physical features saved the day. Pat didn't ever
allow herself to fall to pieces. And she would never be a damsel in distress.
She couldn't afford such luxuries.

———

On May 5, 1930, Will Ryan died of tuberculosis at the age of sixty-four. Now
Pat, Bill, and Tom were orphans and had only each other to depend on; they
drew together even more tightly than before. It was the three Ryan siblings

against the world. Sorrowful though she was about her father's death, at least now Pat was relieved of the burden of nursing him. Finally she could begin to work toward her dream of a college education.

Pat enrolled under the name Patricia Ryan at Fullerton Junior College in fall 1931 while still working at the bank. The name Thelma and the nicknames Buddy and Babe were left home in Artesia. Now the ambitious young woman went only by Patricia or Pat. Pat would later tell her daughters that the choice of a new name was a tribute to her father. The young woman still had to keep her part-time job to fund her first foray into college life. "Daily at 6 a.m. she dusted, swept, and washed the floors and then returned home in time for her carpool ride to college."

This collegiate Cinderella would return in the afternoons to work as a teller and bookkeeper for the bank. Due to her grueling schedule, Pat was not able to enter fully into the social life at Fullerton College that year. Still, she managed to snag the lead role in the school play *Broken Dishes*, a part played by Bette Davis onstage in New York.

Mabel Myers, one of Pat's professors, remembered her as a good, responsible student, friendly but without many close friends. She noted Pat's good taste in clothes and her ambition to move up in the world. To Myers, it appeared that Pat was "a very personable, attractive girl who knew where she was going and who was intent on getting there because of what it would do for the rest of her family." A college degree not only would unlock better jobs for the young woman but also would give her the social polish she needed to move up in the world. Perhaps more important, Pat loved to learn and wanted to keep learning; otherwise she could not or would not have been able to shoulder such a daunting schedule.

However, Pat did not return to college in the fall of 1932. Instead, she had a chance to see the East Coast and to leave California for the first time since her move there from Nevada. Friends of her aunt Annie (Will's sister) in Connecticut needed someone to drive them from California, where they spent several months a year, back east. The elderly couple, Mr. and Mrs. Beers, interviewed Pat and immediately offered her the job. It was her turn to explore the wider world.

As Pat would soon learn, adventures often involved some adversity. At barely twenty, Pat took charge of the Beerses' ancient boatlike Packard automobile. She changed flat tires, navigated dirt roads through inclement weather, and dealt with failing brakes and broiling temperatures. When the car almost lurched down a steep hill, Pat kept a cool head and was able to steer masterfully, bringing the automobile to a safe stop. Grace under pressure was fast becoming Pat's specialty. But the dangerous road conditions were not what made Pat shudder later in life when she recalled the grueling journey. In 1971, she recounted that Mr. Beers "sat beside me up front. And for three thousand miles he made a clicking sound with his teeth. Flat tires, mud, rain—I could take them all, but that day-long sound of clicking stays with me yet."

Once Pat safely delivered the couple to Ridgefield, she was promised a bus ticket home as payment. However, after spending time with her aunt Annie and her aunt Kate in New York, she decided to remain on the East Coast. Aunt Kate was a nun, known also as Sister Thomas Anna. She worked for Seton Hospital, a Catholic-run facility specializing in the treatment of tuberculosis patients, as the head of the X-ray and pharmacy departments. When Pat was offered a secretarial job there, she was thrilled. She would spend two years of her life here, working in numerous areas of the hospital and even training as a radiology technician.

Not once did it occur to the young woman to fear TB despite her own father's death from the disease. Tuberculosis or "consumption" had been rampant in the nineteenth century, killing one in seven of all people. Good hygiene could help prevent TB, and the United States launched massive public health campaigns to educate the public on tuberculosis prevention and treatment.

Even so, those who caught the disease were stigmatized and seen as invalids who bore—and spread—a dread disease. Perhaps due to Pat's lengthy experience nursing her father, she didn't view those with TB as a health risk. She saw them as people who needed attention and care. Pat often went sledding with patients, in violation of the hospital rules. "I wanted to reach out and help them. . . . That is what gives me the deepest pleasure in the world—helping someone."

While working at Seton Hospital she met and dated several eligible young men, including Dr. Francis Vincent Duke, who oversaw the hospital. A handsome Irishman, the thirty-five-year-old doctor was single and available.

He pursued the beautiful Pat seriously, at one point hinting at marriage, but her head was barely turned. She wanted to enjoy her freedom and her time on the East Coast without any serious romantic entanglements. Associating with nuns certainly helped the young woman keep her distance. She told her daughter Julie many years later, "I didn't want to marry because I had been so busy all my life. I felt I had not lived yet."

Pat also had the chance for some paid travel courtesy of Seton Hospital. One highlight of her job was being Seton's representative at a medical conference held in New York City at the Waldorf Astoria Hotel. Pat playfully wrote "Some dump!" on Waldorf Astoria stationery next to an image of the iconic hotel. Thrilled to be in the big city, she attended lectures and luncheons, and even briefly met President and Mrs. Franklin Roosevelt, who attended a formal dinner at the conference.

Many of Eleanor Roosevelt's comments in her 1933 book *It's Up to the Women* could have been written about Pat herself. As historian Jill Lepore writes, Roosevelt's book made the point that "only women could lead the nation out of the Depression . . . by frugality, hard work, common sense, and civic participation. The 'really new deal for the people' . . . had to do with the awakening of women." Although later, as First Lady, Pat would not look upon Eleanor Roosevelt as one of her role models, as a young independent woman of the Depression era, Pat fit Roosevelt's description to a T. Indeed, Pat started her voting life as a Democrat, even campaigning for presidential candidate Al Smith in high school.

Pat's time off from work also brought excitement. Though Pat never sought attention, she couldn't help but attract it with her slim figure, tailored but chic style, red-gold hair, and chiseled features. On a boat trip to Bear Mountain, she was noticed by a Paramount Pictures talent scout and went to the Paramount Theater in New York for tryouts. Ultimately Pat decided against pursuing this career avenue. Pat never had stars in her eyes and showed pragmatic judgment in the matter. She wrote her brother Bill "that [Hollywood] life is too tough, and unless you are featured the pay is low—one of the reasons why girls are tempted to accept presents and attentions—sheer necessity." Even so, this wouldn't be the last time Hollywood came calling for her.

In the spring of 1934 Tom wrote to his sister with some welcome news.

He had saved enough to help her return home and help her finish college in California. Pat was thrilled, but she still worried how she and her brothers would make ends meet. Despite working for two years in New York, she had not been able to save much. Tom reassured her and suggested that the three siblings share an apartment near the University of Southern California (USC) campus. Pat happily agreed and returned home to California that August.

Pat was granted a research scholarship that fall. In exchange for working twenty hours a week for a USC psychology professor, her tuition was paid, and she also received a small amount toward living expenses. This still wasn't enough to cover all her needs, so she took another part-time secretarial position. During her time at USC, she would work many different odd jobs. Years later, her former English professor Dr. Frank Baxter recalled how he saw her working tirelessly on campus at all hours of the night and day. "He recalled that despite her exhausting schedule, 'she was a good student, alert and interested. She stood out from the empty-headed, overdressed little sorority girls of that era like a good piece of literature on a shelf of cheap paperbacks.'"

Still, Pat had fun. She became lifelong friends with Virginia Shugart, a young woman from Los Angeles she met in an education class. Going to sporting events, they became friendly with many of the USC athletes, who often were called by the Hollywood studios to be extras in films. Virginia later recalled that "THEY usually got first call for the special jobs. And they would say, 'Hi Virginia, there's a call for a movie job.' So, we would rush down to the employment office so that we'd be first there to get the call, and we loved those particular jobs." At $7 a day, these jobs were the best-paying ones the women could obtain.

Pat did live the life of a young woman in an exciting city that was the center of the movie industry in the United States. She had an uncredited dancing scene in the 1935 film *Becky Sharp*, as well as appearances in *The Great Ziegfeld*, *Small Town Girl*, and *Ben Hur*, but the sparkle of Hollywood faded quickly in the face of long, boring days of filming and casting couch politics. Pat was no Eve Harrington and looked around for other employment. By her junior year, Pat was working as a model and personal shopper for Bullocks, "Los Angeles' most deliriously art deco department store for generations." The flagship store on Wilshire Boulevard, where Pat worked and developed a sense of style that served her well once she was constantly in the public eye, opened in 1929 and would almost instantly become a beacon of fashion and glamour in an already glamorous city.

But Pat was practical and had completed education hours and a semester of teacher training at USC. Because of the many different jobs she had held both at and outside the college while she was a full-time student, Pat earned a "Special Credential" from USC that would equate today to a master's degree. This all helped her when she applied for a teaching job through USC's Bureau of Teacher Placement. She was soon notified that she had been chosen to teach business-related subjects, including typing, bookkeeping, stenography, and business principles, at Whittier Union High School in Whittier, California.

Pat, Tom, and Bill again graduated as a trio, this time from USC in June 1937. Tom would be working for Twentieth Century Fox movie studios in the lighting department, while Bill graduated with a master's degree and would be teaching high school in Burbank. Like Bill, Pat began to gear up for the fall teaching semester and a move to a new town.

3

A MAGIC LITTLE CITY

After working in Hollywood film and at Bullocks in high-end clothing sales, Pat must have found Whittier a bit dull initially. Whittier was first and foremost a Quaker town, founded in 1897 by Aquila Pickering, a Quaker elder from Chicago.

Pickering's Land and Water Company swooped in and bought up former ranch land, selling lots to establish a "Quaker Colony." Twenty acres of land were set aside for a future college, first named Whittier Academy, now known as Whittier College. Whittier was incorporated in 1898, and Whittier Academy was established in 1891.

The citrus, walnut, and oil industries drove Whittier's early economy along with the arrival of the Southern Pacific, Pacific Electric, and Santa Fe Railroads. Thanks in large part to the railroads, the new town flourished and acquired the local nickname "the magic little city." By the time Pat arrived in Whittier in the fall of 1937, the population had grown from eight hundred at its founding to close to sixteen thousand. Resident Elizabeth Cloes described the small town as a charming, close-knit community: "Whittier was very much like a little village; a friendly Quaker village. You would walk downtown, and, in every block, you would meet two or three people you knew."

Phil Studebaker, who attended Whittier Union High School during Pat's time there, recalled: "Whittier was a real, small quiet town. . . . Kids all thought they rolled up the sidewalks at nine o'clock." The Quaker influence was strong. Lura Waldrip, a student of Pat's at Whittier High, noted the strict religious rules of the town: "For many, many years there were absolutely no bars within the city limits of Whittier. They were forbidden! And on Sunday, the streetcar did not run to the center of town." Theaters also were not permitted inside the city limits. Many people still used horses and buggies as transportation to and from Sunday church services. Dancing remained forbidden at the high school when Pat began her teaching career there; dances were held instead at the local women's club.

Pat must have had moments where she regretted making the jump from sophisticated big-city life in L.A. to this old-fashioned Quaker enclave. She would later famously say that the only reason she took the job was because she was destined to meet Dick Nixon there in his hometown.

Pat first rented a room from Raymond Collins and his wife, but it would not be long before she would get to know a fellow teacher who would become her roommate and fast friend. Pat and Margaret O'Grady met at Whittier High in the fall semester of 1937. The country was nearing the end of the Great Depression, but hiring was still sluggish. Both young women felt lucky to obtain teaching work. Margaret taught history, while Pat taught business subjects. The two women soon decided to lease a bungalow apartment in the McNees Park area, across from a noisy bowling alley. They shared the rent, the cooking, and the cleaning.

Margaret recalled Pat as a highly organized hard worker who required little sleep. Pat was a natural disciplinarian and wasn't intimidated by teaching. In fact, she excelled at it. One of Pat's former students, Betty Jean Kenworthy, remembered her in the classroom: "She was very businesslike. There was no nonsense about the things she felt we were there to learn, and her purpose was to teach us, but she was very enthusiastic about her subject and the possibilities of jobs, and so forth, if you mastered these business skills. . . . She ALWAYS had this beautiful, pleasant smile . . . and she has so much poise, because she always seemed to be very well in control of any situation. She could have done, really, most anything that she wanted to do."

Mildred Eason Stouffer, Pat's typing student and the daughter-in-law of the district superintendent who hired Pat, also noted Pat's steely ability to control naughty teenage boys. "She had to be a strict disciplinarian in class because of the boys and had good control over the class always." She seemed to have a particular rapport with many of the girls in her classes, however.

Her connection to young people was a talent, a gift she had all her life. Gerry Anderson, one of Pat's fellow teachers at Whittier, immediately noticed this trait in Pat. "All the young people enjoyed her because she enjoyed working with them so that she was a most successful teacher. The students would tell me that she encouraged and inspired them to work hard to do more than they thought they could."

Pat's attractive face and figure were noted by her male students. Future ambassador to Japan Robert Blake, also a typing student of Pat's at Whittier High, recalled: "Miss Ryan was quite a dish, a sweater girl, with beautiful auburn hair."

Just as Pat's friend Blanche had noted in Artesia, Pat continued to love clothes and fashion—only now she had a little pocket money to spend. Margaret noted: "We were both interested in clothes. We would go shopping together on Saturdays and buy new clothes for school. . . . We thought we had lots of money. It was $100 a month."

Despite her popularity with the teachers and students in Whittier during the week, Pat scrupulously guarded both her weekends off and her privacy. Every Friday, she would head out of town to stay with her half sister, Neva, now married to Mark Renter and living in Los Angeles. L.A. was where Pat socialized and dated, not in the small town of Whittier, which was too full of prying eyes. Pat later told daughter Julie Eisenhower: "'I never spent a weekend in Whittier the entire time I taught there.' She seemed proud to have thwarted those who tried to scrutinize her private life."

Pat had a job, money, friends . . . and boyfriends. Her life was completely her own, with the freedom to do and act just as she pleased. Her personal life was a mystery to most in the Whittier community, as she was a reserved and shy person. Carol Gordon, who knew Pat from her early days in Whittier, wrote: "She didn't ever talk about herself at all. She was always very calm and an inward sort of person." A stable, controlled, and independent existence was what Pat preferred. But this way of life was not destined to last much longer for her.

After the holidays, the spring semester at the high school began. In addition to her daytime classroom duties, Pat also taught an evening shorthand class. Her former student Elizabeth Cloes would be the one to change her teacher's life. Cloes was now an elementary school teacher at Lowell Joint Elementary School and a friend of a local lawyer named Dick Nixon, who was from a prominent Whittier family. Cloes had gone to school with Dick's younger brother Eddie, and she was also a fan of Dick's mother, Hannah Nixon, and her famous fruit pies, which she sold at the Nixon family's grocery store in Whittier.

Cloes was active in a local theater group, the Whittier Community Players, and in the winter of 1938 had signed on as the lead actress in a production of George Kaufman and Alexander Woolcott's play *The Dark Tower*. A small part for a pretty girl remained uncast, and Cloes immediately thought of her beautiful young teacher Pat Ryan for the role; she convinced Pat to try out. She recalled, "Pat was a very attractive person. Her eyes are always so impressive because they're dark and flashing. She's always been very, very slender, with rather high cheekbones, lovely hair, and a quiet vivaciousness about her."

After dinner together at the Hoover Hotel, where Cloes resided, the two young women went over to play rehearsal at St. Matthias Church. The church allowed the Whittier Community Players use of its Sunday school space for their rehearsals. Grant Garman, who owned the Poinsettia, a popular local restaurant on Philadelphia Street, had a role in *The Dark Tower*. Garman knew Pat through his wife, Phyllis, and also had known Dick for many years. He recalled that evening: "Pat was there, and Dick came in, and it was like just knowing two people. 'Dick Nixon I'd like to present Pat Ryan,' and then we started going about our work.'"

Garman noticed immediately how smitten Dick was with Pat. She was "a striking and beautiful girl, pleasant and animated. Dick, I think, just took one look at her, at the time she came for the reading of the show and that was it." When Pat and Elizabeth went home that evening, Dick gave them a ride in his Model A Ford. Years later, Elizabeth still remembered: "I sat in the middle; Pat sat on the outside. And he said to her, 'I'd like to have a date with you.' She said, 'Oh, I'm too busy.' So, he laughed and drove us home."

The second and third days, Nixon again brought the young women home. Elizabeth told Pat, "'You sit next to him. He doesn't want to sit next to me.' She said, 'I don't want to sit next to him.' So, I was again in the middle, and he leaned across me and said to her, 'When are you going to give me that date?' She laughed. He said, 'Don't laugh. Someday I'm going to marry you.' He pointed his finger at her, and then she did laugh!" Years later, Virginia Shugart clearly recalled Pat's remark to her that evening: "I met this guy tonight who says he is going to marry me." While bewildered by Dick's forthright approach, Pat was intrigued. Who was this persistent young man, and where did he get such confidence?

Richard Milhous Nixon was born in Yorba Linda, California, on January 9, 1913. Dick's mother, Hannah, came from a prominent Whittier family, the Quaker Milhous clan. She arrived in Whittier at thirteen in 1897 and married another midwesterner, Frank Nixon, from Columbus, Ohio, in 1908.

At its founding, Yorba Linda was a dusty, isolated dot on the map. It was in the middle of nowhere, a barren piece of land where Frank battled the earth to raise citrus. Dick's cousin Jessamyn West recalled, "Frank was a tempestuous man and filled with anger."

Indeed, Richard's later "description of his father Frank Nixon's hot temper reminded Pat sharply of her father Will." In contrast, Hannah had a cool reserved nature. While she clearly adored her children, she was not emotional or outwardly demonstrative toward them. Dick later recalled, "In her whole life, I never heard her say to me or to anyone else, 'I love you.'" The couple soon had four sons: Harold arrived in 1909, Richard in 1913, Francis Donald in 1914, and Arthur in 1918 (the fifth, Ed, would not arrive until 1930). Hannah deliberately named Harold, Richard, and Arthur after medieval English monarchs. Richard was named specifically for Richard I, often known as "Richard the Lionheart," who personified "the epitome of military chivalry as far as Hannah was concerned." By placing fictional crowns on their heads, the stern Hannah also placed the weight of expectation on her young boys. Richard seemed particularly sensitive to her parental pressure. He tended to force himself to perform well in all arenas, even in those he had little talent for.

Frank's farming venture eventually failed in the arid soil of Yorba Linda. In 1922, he moved his young family back to Whittier, closer to Hannah's relatives and to three of his own siblings. He soon opened a filling station with an attached grocery on the outskirts of town. The Nixon boys worked long hours at the gas station even as children—a common practice at that time. The family eventually moved firmly into lower-middle-class prosperity.

Young Dick's worldview was shaped by his Quaker background and deep faith. One aspect was that "women were recognized by Quakers equally with men." The religion also allowed women preachers. The Milhous family was replete with women who were preachers, teachers, and heads of Sunday schools. As Nixon cousin Jessamyn West laughingly put it, "So for QUAKER women—Women's Lib—we've had it! Our men were fetching our slippers long ago!"

Dick graduated from Whittier High in June 1930 as "Outstanding Male Student" of his senior class. He had offers from both Harvard and Yale, but with brother Harold ill with tuberculosis and medical expenses mounting, he felt bound to stay home and help his parents with their business. He continued to work at their grocery store and enrolled in local Whittier College. Dick graduated second in his college class, earning a scholarship to Duke Law School. After completing his law degree he returned to Whittier to a job at Wingert & Bewley. Then, one winter evening, his life took a different turn.

For some reason, the young man was drawn to the theater tryouts that winter evening as an escape from the reality of the daily grind at the law firm. Whatever led him into St. Matthias Church that night, Dick's life was about to brighten up significantly.

Dick took the role of Barry Jones in the play, while Pat took the part of Daphne Martin. The two were thrown together for five weeks of constant rehearsals and got to know each other quickly. On February 17, *The Dark Tower* had its debut performance at the Woman's Club House. After the play, Dick brought Pat by to meet his parents. Clearly Dick was knocked out by Pat's vivacious personality, her looks, and her poise.

Pat liked this guy, but she was not completely smitten. This might have had more to do with circumstances than with Dick himself. She had her freedom and her independence. She had been pursued before seriously in New York by a doctor but had parried his advances. She had no one now she had to take care of besides herself. Why would she give up what it had taken her so long to achieve? Her new suitor was going to have to work hard to convince her that relinquishing such hard-won independence was worth it.

4

MISS VAGABOND

Dick was single-minded when it came to pursuing Pat. She was elusive and mysterious, which may have added to her appeal. She was not going to settle for anything less than the marriage she wanted, and she needed to make sure that Dick was "the one." As he would soon learn, this quest would involve a lengthy courtship, many double dates, and even enduring her dates with other men.

Just one month after their play *The Dark Tower* opened, Dick thoughtfully remembered Pat's birthday with flowers. He began wooing her with more intensity, sending her poems and songs he composed. It is interesting to note that while many letters Dick wrote survive, only a few replies from Pat remain.

Pat told Dick she would never settle down, and that she wanted to travel and see exotic places. He said he would go with her and took to calling her "My Irish Gypsy" and "Miss Vagabond."

Patricia—

Somehow on Tuesday there was something electric in the usually stifling air of Whittier.

And now I know. An Irish gypsy who radiates all that is happy and beautiful was there.

She left behind her a note addressed to a struggling young barrister who looks from a window and dreams.

And in the note, he found sunshine and flowers, and a great spirit which only great ladies can inspire.

Though the letter itself was poetic and dreamy, it was balanced with signs of his active pursuit of Pat. In this letter and others, Dick often drew small boxes around questions, usually asking when he could see her again. Here he wrote: "Someday, let me see you again? In September? Maybe? You're pretty swell regardless!" He would not leave her alone; Pat even tried pretending she was not home when he stopped by unannounced. But Dick knew she was there when he saw that her door was bolted. He slipped a note under her door all the same, writing her about the time she missed with him:

I took the walk tonight and it was swell because you were there all the time. Why? Because a star fell right in front of me . . . the Dipper was turned upside down right over where your house should be and was pouring down on you all the good things, I've wished looking up at it in the past . . . Yes—I know I'm crazy and this is old stuff and that I don't take hints, but you see Miss Pat, I like you!

If Pat felt guilty for missing the walk, she didn't show it. And while she didn't completely shut Dick down, she proposed a very unorthodox arrangement if he wanted to continue seeing her. "Unaccustomed to dealing with someone whose willpower bested her own, she made him a humiliating deal: if he promised not to make any more marriage proposals or avowals of love, she would allow him to drive her up Whittier Boulevard into Los Angeles on Friday evenings and to pick her up on Sunday afternoons after she had enjoyed her weekend dates." Pat would stay at her sister Neva's in Los Angeles on these weekends so she could date the young men from the big city. Dick would kill time while waiting for her by seeing movies, roaming around the city, or reading. It must have been agonizing for the intense young lawyer to play second fiddle to his sweetheart's other beaux.

Years later Dick would tease Pat about the hoops he'd had to jump through to win her love: "Remember how I used to take you to Neva's for your dates??"

Pat hated to hurt anyone's feelings and avoided confrontation at all costs. One evening when Dick dropped by unexpectedly, Pat showed him the door and he left in a huff. He wrote her a few days later:

Dear Patricia:

Please forgive me for acting like a sorehead when you gently ushered me out the other night. You must have thought I was trying to put on the attitude but that I really didn't give a darn—i.e., the school-boy bluff!

But really Patricia—may I make just one comment. I know that you hate like anything to hurt people. I can imagine that many people come to grief over you. But remember that there are some people who are still honest in this world—and that they would rather be told off frankly rather than subtly . . . I believe you just figured I needed a little stepping ego, etc. But I still believe you could tell us boring men where to go—a little more frankly and thus avoid a lot of bother for yourself.

Pat would always go to great lengths not to offend, to make others feel welcome. Uncomfortable social situations, especially those involving confrontation of any sort, were to be avoided at all costs. Dick was much the same in this regard and shared Pat's same dread of "making a scene." Perhaps his tempestuous prior romance with Ola Florence Welch, Dick's first serious girlfriend, had taught him the emotional cost of such drama. In this regard, he and Pat were on the same page.

———

Pat loved to ice-skate, a new sport for Dick. Dick's friend Ken Ball, a fellow debater from Whittier College, remembered that Dick had no talent for it, but he was determined to keep up with the more graceful Pat. Ball recalled how Nixon practiced ice-skating for three afternoons in a row at Artesia's new indoor Iceland Rink until he was bruised and bloodied with effort: "I remember him flying out of control and hitting his face so hard on the ice, he was all covered in blood." Ball, who was a proficient skater himself, took pity on Dick and helped pick him up. He questioned his old debating partner, "'Dick, why do you keep doing this?' His answer was, 'I've got a great date to go ice-skating with on Saturday night, and I *must* be able to keep up with her!'"

Ball, who knew Dick well, noted, "I think you have to recognize that he was intensely competitive." This keen sense of competition extended to all things, including and especially within the context of his pursuit of the young teacher. As Ball noted regarding Dick's attempts to learn to ice-skate, "Richard was a person that anything he tackled he went into with great vigor." This would be especially true of his extended courtship of Pat Ryan. The fact he had to work so hard for her love perhaps made her seem even more attractive.

While he was so enthralled with her, Pat took the opportunity to do a minor "makeover" on her suitor. Upon trying out for the basketball team at Whittier College, his freshman year, Dick suffered an accidental blow that broke a front tooth. The dentist put a gleaming gold cap on. "Pat insisted that I get it changed and put a porcelain (sp) cap on." Dick would later jokingly credit Pat's "obsession about good dentistry" for his political success. Appearances were important to Pat, and her instincts here were correct.

In this respect and many others, Pat reflected Dick's aspirations. She meant to work hard and not settle for anything or anyone until she was sure of her decision. Like the young attorney, she was also a striver, wanting to lead an accomplished, successful, and useful life. At this point, Pat had a thriving career she enjoyed and knew she could support herself.

That summer Pat made a pointed effort to visit more with the Nixon family, spending time with Hannah learning to make her famous fruit pies. She even got up several times at 5 a.m. to help Hannah bake pies to be sold in the market that day. Pat never made the mistake of trying to show up her boyfriend's mother in this area. After her marriage, daughter Julie noted, her mother "never attempted to compete with pies of her own, but baked cakes and biscuits instead."

According to Flora Rheta Schreiber, a best-selling author and good friend of Hannah Nixon's, "Hannah was convinced Pat was chasing Dick." Instead of appreciating Pat's hardworking nature and early-morning assistance, Hannah seemed to initially regard Pat as a social climber. "Hannah convinced herself that Pat was aggressively pursuing her son, not the other way around. The matrons of Whittier agreed with Hannah. After all, wouldn't it be just like an orphaned working-class girl to chase such an eligible boy, and from such an upstanding family?" Pat was also not a Quaker; this alone made her suspect in Hannah's eyes.

Pat would always make great efforts to get along with Hannah, studiously avoiding conflict with her just as she did with everyone else. Still, she would later admit to Julie that she and Hannah had little to tie them together: "She really wasn't a modern person. We did not have much in common." Even so, she respected and admired Hannah's fortitude and strength. Hannah also gradually warmed up to Pat as she got to know her better. Though slender Pat might look delicate, she came from sturdy pioneer stock and had to work hard for everything she had. Pat's iron discipline and work ethic were things Hannah could relate to and appreciate.

While Hannah might have had some initial reservations about Pat, the rest of the family liked her immediately. Ed Nixon, the youngest of the five Nixon brothers, was only nine when he first met Pat. "When my family and I first met her, she was so full of energy and enthusiasm that all of us were immediately drawn to her. Pat fascinated me with her beauty, kindness, and athletic prowess." Pat always had a soft spot in her heart for children, and so because of his age, Ed received extra-special attention from the young woman. She would drive Ed to Huntington Beach and run races with him on the beach. Ed thought he would surely be able to beat her with his long legs, but she consistently outran him. "That fact alone qualified her to be my brother's wife, so I gave Dick my approval, telling him, 'You can marry her if you want.'"

Despite continuing to grow closer to Dick and his family, Pat loved her autonomy. In August 1939, Pat and two of her friends, Virginia Shugart and Margaret O'Grady, decided to take a road trip lasting several weeks to the Pacific Northwest. Pat volunteered to drive. A letter written during the trip on stationery from the Hotel Whitcomb in San Francisco and addressed to Dick begins simply, "Hi." Pat goes on to write wistfully, "I felt so sorta' lonesome—like Thurs. 'cause I didn't get to say goodbye—but anyhoo thanks for hospitality." She signs off with "Lotta luck[,] Pat." Indeed, luck was exactly what Dick would need to catch her.

Despite her strong desire for independence, Pat was fully aware that having a husband and children was regarded by society as the ultimate accomplishment for most women. Though she clearly liked Dick, she still didn't seem eager to be tied down by any man. Even so, Dick's rapt attention to her, his tenacity, and his ambition told her not to dismiss him too quickly. Something appealed to her about the young man, a spark she saw and believed in long before others did.

Pat's friend and roommate Margaret recalled Dick's thoughtful and attentive nature toward Pat while they were dating: "I can remember during the time he was going with Pat before they were married that he was extremely thoughtful and that he would bring her little gifts and notes and so forth, even though he didn't have very much money at the time."

By January 1939 the relationship had taken a more serious turn. Dick wrote up a mock will on January 11, 1939. In this "Straight Note," he promised Pat a sum of "$1,000,000,000,000,000,000" payable to "Patricia Ryan, only, whenever she wants it with interest always at the rate of 100 per cent per annum, payable every day, hour, minute, second or what you will!" The document was "sealed with—(one guess)!" and signed "R. Nixon."

———

Alyce Geiger (later Alyce Koch) met Pat in 1938 when both were teaching at Whittier High School. Alyce commented years later that she always felt the presence of a certain emotional boundary with her friend beyond which no one was allowed. "I never really KNEW Pat, but then, no one did, No one EVER REALLY KNEW PAT." Alyce went on many double dates with Pat and Dick and described the couple:

> Dick was like an open-faced sandwich. Just as EASY to know, as old shoe
> as real as basic! He was himself every moment of the time. There was not
> a single thing about himself he tried to embellish. I cannot say this about
> Pat, as much as I liked her. I understood her background. . . . She was left
> alone without a mother, with two younger brothers to help support. She
> was forced into maturity. . . . She was a lady, a very dignified, happy, and
> outgoing person, TO A DEGREE. But no one ever really "moved in." She
> loved people; she had a warm jolly nature, but she kept a bit removed.

Pat's emotional remove allowed her the time and space to weigh her marital options objectively. She wasn't about to settle for less than she deserved. She had worked hard to have a better life than her parents; she had done without, scrimped, and saved to put not only her brothers but also herself through college at a time when many women didn't even think about higher education. Like her boyfriend Dick, she had her eye on a broader, bigger, more modern life. As a team, perhaps they could truly conquer the world.

5

FULL AND EQUAL PARTNERS

Dick was burning the candle at both ends in the spring of 1940. He was not only a young up-and-coming attorney, involved in numerous civic organizations, but he also had recently formed a frozen orange juice business, Citra-Frost, with two local businessmen. Now, Pat might have been the one urging him to slow down and look at the clock she had given him as a gift to remind him to eat, sleep, and take a break. But she also clearly admired his ambition, enthusiasm, and energy. She couldn't have helped but notice that Dick Nixon was going places.

As their relationship grew more and more serious, the couple took many day trips together to Laguna Beach, Seal Beach, San Clemente, and Dana Point, often bringing Dick's beloved Irish setter, King, with them. Pat and Dick seemed happy to be alone together. They were voracious readers who loved to sit side by side on the beach reading their own books.

On one of their weekend rambles, the couple discovered the charming small town of San Clemente, a "1920s vision of a Spanish Village by the Sea." The town's founder, Ole Hanson, had insisted that all houses be constructed to resemble Spanish haciendas, with white adobe walls and red tiled roofs. Though San Clemente was less than sixty miles from Whittier, it felt like a fairytale Moorish village, all sun-bleached white walls splashed with vibrant flowers and shaded by feathery palm trees.

As they explored sunny California beach towns together, the two young people realized how much they had in common: a shared wanderlust, an appreciation of different cultures and people, a deep sense of ambition. Though they both hailed from small towns, they didn't necessarily want to live in one forever. Both had sought out superior educations and were civic-minded.

Both halves of the couple wanted to lead a broader existence than their parents had before them.

Pat had a strength of character and a level of confidence that attracted Dick but also may have reminded him of the other strong women he admired within his own family: his mother, Hannah, and his grandmother Almira in particular. Unlike many men of his generation, he wasn't put off by female intelligence—he had grown up with Quaker women in charge.

With all these attributes and her striking good looks, Pat could have married anyone. Yet she had held back, unwilling to let go of the pleasant, predictable world she had worked so hard to build. After so many responsibilities as a young motherless girl—cooking, cleaning, keeping house for her father and her two brothers—to finally be in control of her own fate must have been a glorious experience.

Even so, according to her friend Alyce Koch, Pat had been seriously considering the idea of marrying Dick for months. Alyce claimed Pat had come to her in confidence and asked her if she should marry Dick. Alyce responded she could not possibly make that decision for her, as only Pat could know the answer. Alyce then related that Pat "said something I shall never forget. Now this was before her marriage, remember, and I swear this is the truth. 'Alyce, I don't know if I could stand living in Washington.' And I looked at her with an incredible expression, and I said, 'Are you crazy? What in the world are you talking about?' She said, 'Well. Dick's going to be President someday.'" Alyce's husband, Gene, added, "As if he would have had prescience about the role Pat would play in his future career, he went about winning her with the same dexterity with which he later won elections."

There is plenty of evidence that Pat knew politics might be Dick's calling even at this early stage. Dick was president of the Young Republicans Club in Whittier, and he had even considered a run for California's State Assembly in 1939, although that campaign never came to fruition. Historian Will Swift notes: "By the time of her engagement, Pat was well aware that she could become a politician's wife, even though neither she nor Dick yet had an idea of the commitment and sacrifice that public life required."

Another consideration that may have entered Pat's marriage calculus was her age. Pat was now in her late twenties, and in that era her shelf life as a marriageable woman was shrinking. Indeed, by the standards of her era, she was getting precariously close to being called an "old maid." Pat had defied this stereotype longer than most women of her era dreamed of doing. But she did want children. She also would have been drawn to the idea of the close-knit, respectable Quaker family Dick offered. Perhaps with this young man she really could have it all: marriage, children, a stable family life, and a teaching career as well as the romance and travel she craved. Was the tall, dark handsome young lawyer the one? Or was marriage a trap, an end to her solo ambitions? She still wasn't sure.

———

One starry evening in March 1940, Dick drove Pat to Dana Point, one of their favorite haunts overlooking the beach at San Clemente. The couple sat in the moonlight, the top of Dick's new Oldsmobile open to the sky. It was the perfect evening for a proposal, and Dick had set the stage perfectly. He proposed, and Pat happily accepted. But even in this romantic moment, her doubts crept in. According to her daughter Julie Eisenhower, "She loved Dick's romantic nature, which had brought them to Dana Point, and his visions of a great future. But even as she consented, she was not sure she wanted to marry. She was twenty-eight years old and had been independent for a long time."

Thrilled to have finally won his beloved, Dick drove with Pat straight to Whittier, where he woke up his parents. Frank was out of sorts and Hannah said little. This did not make Pat feel welcomed into the family. The next day, she told her own family members of her decision to marry the young lawyer. Bill and Tom were happy for their sister, but it was bittersweet news. They were a close trio, and the two brothers adored Pat. In contrast, Pat's half-sister, Neva, blurted out, "What are you marrying him for? He's too quiet."

Pat's engagement ring was yet to be chosen, so she and Dick went to a jeweler on Spring Street in Los Angeles together to pick one out. Pat had simple but elegant tastes and eyed a wide gold band. But Dick wanted more for her and made her try a pretty diamond set off by two smaller stones. The ring had a matching diamond chip band. The set cost a whopping $324. Adjusted for inflation, this is equivalent to $7,099 in 2024. This sum would have been a princely one for Dick at the time, as he made just $50 a week. Pat chipped in to help defray the cost.

In contrast to Dick's dramatic moonlit proposal, putting the engagement ring on Pat's finger was much less romantic, as related by Julie Eisenhower in a book about her mother and corroborated by Pat's good friend Alyce Koch.

ENGAGEMENT STORY TAKE ONE:

The best-known account of how Pat received her engagement ring:

> On May 1, the ring arrived at the jeweler's. Dick sent word for Pat to meet him at his parents' house at noon, when they would be at work. Alas, Pat waited her entire lunch hour for Dick and the ring, but her fiancé was a no-show. She returned to school and was grading papers at the end of the day when an envoy from Dick arrived. Tom Seulke, a Nixon cousin who worked at the Nixon market, placed a May Day basket in front of Pat, and there, glistening on a bed of straw, was her ring. Pat, by now perplexed and perhaps upset, wasn't quite sure how to react and pushed the basket away.
>
> Shortly thereafter, Pat's friend and fellow teacher Alyce arrived and saved the day by slipping the ring on Pat's finger. Soon all the other teachers spilled into the room to congratulate the still stunned Pat. Richard Nixon himself writes in his memoirs about sending Pat the ring in a May Day basket.

ENGAGEMENT STORY TAKE TWO:

Nixon cousin Tom Seulke, who delivered the ring to Pat, related the tale with a different twist:

> He [Dick] asked if I could go to Malin's Flower Shop right here in town and pick up some flowers and take them down to Whittier High School where Pat was a teacher. He told me her room number just to deliver these flowers from him. . . . When I got to Whittier, I picked up the flowers wrapped in green paper at the flower shop, took them to the high school, found the room and of course, as a young boy I was kind of embarrassed to be walking on schoolgrounds with a bunch of flowers. I took them to Pat. . . . When I came back to the store, Dick's mother asked if I'd taken the flowers to Pat and I said "Yes." She said Dick had called and wondered if I had. Then I found out later

that Dick had purchased an engagement ring, put it in the bouquet of flowers before I picked them up and that's how the ring was delivered. But Pat didn't know it either. She took the wrapping off the flowers, put them in a vase, threw the paper in a waste basket. Dick found this out, went down to the high school and got there just when the janitor was dumping out the trash and they went through it and found the ring box.

Regardless of which story is correct, no record exists of how Pat felt about receiving the ring from a third party, nor if she and Dick quarreled about it. As Whittier College archivist and historian Joe Dmohowski notes: "The big question is, why did Dick send an engagement ring to his sweetheart in a bouquet, rather than presenting it to her directly?"

A few weeks later, Dick wrote her a letter that seems to have smoothed things over. Calling Pat his "Dearest Heart," Dick wrote, "You have always had that extra something which takes people out of the mediocre class. . . . It is our job to go forth together and accomplish great ends and we shall do it too."

Shades, perhaps, of what was to come. Pat wanted a bigger, broader life, and this she would accomplish with her marriage. But she also wanted love and affection, something her smitten fiancé also assured her she would have forever: "Through the years, I shall always be with you—loving you more every hour and attempting to let you feel that love in your heart and in your life."

———

On May 1, Frank and Hannah held an engagement party at their new, imposing home at 6799 Worsham Drive. On June 9, Hannah and Pat's friends Marian Wilson, Edith Holt, Dorothy Brown, Margaret O'Grady, and Alyce Koch gave a girls' wedding shower with Hannah at the Green Arbor restaurant in Whittier. A tea and wedding shower and a dinner dance at the Town House in Los Angeles led up to the wedding itself, which took place just three months after the engagement. Only when Dick and Pat went to the Riverside County courthouse to apply for their marriage license did Dick belatedly learn that Pat's given name was Thelma.

On June 21, 1940, Pat and Dick found themselves at one of the most sought-after wedding venues in California: the Mission Inn in Riverside, California. Though the bride usually chooses the wedding location, this was a spot Dick had suggested that appealed to them both. The couple had previously spent many happy evenings dining together outside in the hotel's charming courtyard. What began as an adobe boardinghouse in 1876 had evolved by 1940 into a Mission Revival–style fantasy with wings added on as demand grew. The hotel was filled with artifacts, artwork, and objects from the owner's global travels. There could not have been a more appropriate place for this couple to be married given their world-wandering natures.

Adding to the luster of the inn were the Hollywood productions that had been filmed there, such as *The Vampire* in 1915 and *Idiot's Delight* in 1938. American luminaries such as Presidents Theodore Roosevelt, William Taft, and Herbert Hoover, movie stars Clark Gable and Bette Davis, and pioneering American women Amelia Earhart and Susan B. Anthony had all stayed there, imbuing the location with a touch of glamour and history that appealed to both Pat and Dick.

Other than selection of the wedding locale, Pat took charge of the planning and arrangements. Because Pat had never been affiliated with a particular church or religion, and to please her in-laws-to-be, Pat became a Quaker, but she declined to have a church wedding. She and Dick engaged the president of Whittier College, Dr. W. O. Mendenhall, a Quaker chaplain, to perform the ceremony. Never one for grand, large occasions, Pat wanted a small, intimate wedding with just close family and good friends in attendance.

Money was also a consideration, and Pat did not want to burden her brothers Tom and Bill with any extra expenses. She would not allow her soon-to-be Nixon relatives to foot the bill she clearly saw as her duty to pay. In addition, this allowed Dick to avoid having to invite all his business acquaintances to the event.

The couple rented the presidential suite for the wedding, not because it was grand (or because they could see into the future) but because it was the least costly option. As Pat's good friend and bridesmaid Margaret O'Grady remembered, the wedding itself took place "in one of the reception rooms. . . .

It wasn't in the large chapel there at the time in the Mission Inn. There were not too many people there as I recall. . . . And it was a very simple ceremony."

Pat had a total of five bridesmaids, Virginia Shugart and Virginia Hudson among them. Alyce recalled that almost the entire wedding party was made up of Pat's friends, with very few of Dick's in attendance. "This group was essentially made up of Pat's friends. The only exception would be Don, Dick's brother. Don came along and his wife Clara Jane." Of course, Dick's parents, brothers, and beloved Grandmother Milhous also attended. Pat's brothers Bill and Tom were there as well as their half sister, Neva, and her husband, Mark Renter. In all, Ed Nixon estimated, there were only about fifty guests.

The wedding was a relatively casual affair. Don Nixon picked up Pat at her apartment and drove her to the ceremony in her chic blue lace full-skirted suit with her "ashes of roses" close-fitting hat. Dick had given her a white orchid, which she pinned onto her suit. Sparkling crystal buttons adorned the fitted bodice of the jacket, highlighting her slim figure.

At 3:30 p.m. Pat walked into their rented reception room at the Mission Inn alone, as she had no father to give her away. (Strangely, neither Tom nor Bill Ryan took on that role.) If anyone had the confidence to walk to meet her groom alone, though, it was Pat Ryan. Dick joined her, clad in a dark business suit.

A brief reception with punch and cake (no alcohol, of course) took place in the Spanish Art Gallery of the inn. Hannah had put her locally renowned culinary talents to good use and baked "a many-tiered wedding cake, its top layer crowned by a sprig of lily of the valley and a formally clad white-tailed groom and veiled bride." Pat's brothers Tom and Bill surprised the couple by going in together to buy Pat and Dick a full set of Wallace Rose Point silver flatware. Dick's parents bought a full set of china in Pat's favorite "bracelet" pattern. (In 1975 Dick would note, "Pat is proud of the fact that not one piece of the set, which serves 12 people, has been broken in all the years we have been married.")

Before the newlyweds left that evening for a Mexican honeymoon, their friends decided to have a little fun with them. As there was not a plethora of places to eat along the way in those days, the newlyweds had packed a huge box of canned food to take with them. Alyce admitted: "We did the horrible trick of tearing off all the labels on the canned food, so they never knew on that trip what they were going to open. I felt guilty for weeks!" The happy couple departed early that evening for Mexico with $200 to finance the two-week trip. The two entered their marriage as full and equal partners: the car in which they drove to Mexico was Pat's, and half of their $200 was provided by her.

6

THE WINDS OF WAR

Instead of the faux Spanish town of San Clemente, the newly married Nixons were honeymooning in a foreign land, enjoying its exotic sounds, sights, and smells. Though they often ate breakfast and lunch from their potluck canned stash, at night they dined in local restaurants, enjoying the food, the music, and the colorful surroundings. The couple's big splurge was a one-night stay at the famous Mexico City hotel La Reforma.

From the luxurious La Reforma the newlyweds moved on to cheaper digs, the Los Angeles Motel, which became their home base for day trips to other cities nearby. "We didn't have the honeymoon trip outlined," Pat recalled, "We just went." Their mutual love of travel and exploration and their frugality along the way allowed the couple to do exactly what they wanted when they wanted, even if it meant one of them driving all night while the other slept. It was their first big adventure together, and it deepened their lifelong love for Mexican culture. As Dick recalled many years later, "We got to know Mexico and to love and respect our neighbors to the south, even more than we had before." The couple finally returned to Whittier on July 4, with fireworks exploding as they pulled into town. Their $200 honeymoon fund had dwindled to just $2, but there were no regrets.

They rented in Long Beach for the rest of the summer, then moved to an apartment in La Habra Heights, closer to Whittier. This was also a short-term situation. They finally settled on East Beverly Boulevard in Whittier, within a few miles of Pat's school and Dick's law practice. They lived in the rear apartment of a small newly built bungalow with a living room, bedroom, kitchen, and bath. The Nixons' beloved Irish setter, King, who had accompanied the couple on many early dates, died, and Pat was devastated. Eventually they would move to one of Frank Nixon's rental homes on Whittier Boulevard. Life would finally settle down into a regular routine as Pat continued to teach at Whittier High.

This school year, Pat met the woman who would become her closest friend, UCLA graduate Helene Drown. Helene remembered Pat's "beauty and fine sense of humor. We hit it off at once. She was chairman of the school's pep committee. . . . She asked me to be her helper, and I accepted." Intelligent, blond, blue-eyed Helene proved to be the perfect match for the more reserved Pat. Helene had no problem getting Pat to relax and have fun with her. Their shared sense of humor and fun drew the two women together. Pat and Helene would form a lifetime friendship at Whittier High that would endure during good times and bad.

———

Pat and Dick both wanted a more cosmopolitan life than Whittier had to offer, and they may have felt constrained by the small town's provincial atmosphere. In Whittier, "there were too many people who would be forever concerned with their lives and too few opportunities for advancement."

One item that had tied them down to Whitter was cut loose by December 1941. Dick's frozen orange juice company, Citri-Frost, was a disappointing failure. Though Dick was a partner now at Wingert, Bewley & Nixon and was acting as deputy city attorney, he knew he could only rise so far in his hometown. He and Pat were both itching for a change of venue. Pat soon gave her notice at school, and the couple began to think seriously about a new future outside of the Quaker town.

In later years, Pat would downplay Dick's early interest in politics, but as has been noted earlier, this interest was clearly present within him from the beginning of their marriage. Indeed, the young Dick had written about his desire to enter the political arena in eighth grade. As early as 1941, Pat recalled that Dick had mentioned running for California's State Assembly. Dick also told his new wife that he had attended law school in part so he could return to Whittier and get into politics. In 1942 he again considered a run for California's State Assembly, though he ultimately decided against it.

Dick thought his home state was too far removed from the national scene.

Washington, he felt, was the true stage. The center of American politics and power was where he needed to be. In these early days, Pat was happy to support her husband and his ambitions. Her half brother, Matthew Bender, supported this point of view: "Pat has always said that whatever her husband wanted to do she would support him to the utmost."

In November 1941, the opportunity both Dick and Pat had been waiting for finally materialized. Through the son of a Duke Law School dean, Dick was invited to interview for a position at the government's new Office of Price Administration (OPA) in Washington, D.C. The agency had been established just a few months earlier as a way of stabilizing prices after the outbreak of war in Europe. This could be their ticket out of California to the East Coast and their entry into what they viewed as a broader, more consequential existence.

Dick interviewed for the job at the Biltmore Hotel in Los Angeles and was hopeful it would result in an offer. Weeks went by with no word on the position, and the Nixons set off on a journey to frozen Michigan to purchase a new car. While on the trip, Dick received a telegram requesting another interview with him for the OPA job. The couple headed to San Francisco for the appointment; Dick aced the interview and got the job.

The Nixons had just come out of a movie matinee in Hollywood when they saw newspaper headlines announcing the Japanese bombing of Pearl Harbor. The young couple, shocked and horrified by the attack, were now determined to serve their country.

Both Nixons wanted to contribute to winning the war, and Dick's job offer at the OPA fit the bill, and it also served to take them out of the limiting atmosphere of Whittier. The young couple packed up their minimal belongings in January 1942 and drove cross-country in terrible icy weather to D.C.

It was nearly impossible to find housing in those early war days in Washington, but by sheer luck, Pat and Dick located an apartment in Alexandria owned by a California landlord. The California connection vaulted the couple off the waiting list and into a new home that very evening. Dick began work the next Monday, and Pat soon found a volunteer secretarial job with Red Cross national headquarters on Connecticut Avenue.

By summer, Pat acquired a full-time paid job at the OPA handling "hardship cases" for those businesses that feared collapse due to wartime price freezes. She became a government-agency Rosie the Riveter, taking over a traditionally male office job in service to the war effort. Years later, she would reference her OPA position in support of the proposed Equal Rights Amendment: "I am for women. I am for equal rights and equal pay for equal work. I competed against and worked with men."

Though Pat was now happily ensconced in her office at the OPA, Dick quickly became frustrated by the red tape involved in working for a government agency: "As a junior lawyer in the tire rationing division, I cannot say that I had much effect on OPA. But the experience had an enormous effect on the policies I later developed during my political career." Dick found the bureaucracy and petty power struggles at the agency demoralizing.

Dick decided he could not sit on the sidelines of conflict anymore. With Pat's approval, he applied for active duty as a naval officer that summer. Pat's support was critical to his decision, as his Quaker parents had hoped he could serve the war effort with a desk job stateside. They did not try to change Dick's mind, however, once his decision was firm.

Though Dick was a Quaker and could have declined to fight, his parents didn't object, and neither did Pat. Years later she revealed, "I would have felt mighty uncomfortable if Dick hadn't done his part. Sure, I was unhappy, but so were thousands of other young wives. Because of Richard's upbringing he did much soul-searching before he made his decision. But once it was made, it was all for the best."

It is also relevant that war service was not only encouraged but expected for any viable American political candidate of this era. This may have been part of the calculation on Dick's part. Historian Joe Dmohowski notes, "As a birthright Quaker, Richard Nixon could have opted for 'conscientious objector' status during World War II. This designation would have almost certainly blocked any future political aspirations. Instead, Dick enlisted in the United States Navy in 1942. He completed his pre-political progression when he achieved the status of WWII veteran. Each pre-political 'ingredient' contributed to Richard Nixon's ascent as a perfect post-war campaigner."

In August, Dick entered a two-month officer training program in Quonset Point, Rhode Island. Pat clearly missed her husband, writing him at 2 a.m. one Sunday, "Just had to write you to say how very much I love you! It was so clear all over again when talking to you on the phone." She also reassured

Dick, telling him not to worry about her: "I hope I said nothing to worry you—when you are working so hard, etc. It would be awful to add to the load." This was to be a recurring theme throughout their marriage. Pat never wanted to be a burden to Dick or to distract him from his important work. One of her jobs (but not her only one) at this time was to be his helpmeet, cheerleader, and confidence builder.

Halfway through the training program, Pat and Dick were allowed a weekend away in New York. Dick wrote Pat a gushing letter after the visit, already missing her presence: "Sweetie this trip was the best I've ever had. It was such a thrill to see you; you were *beautiful*—and every minute was like heaven. Our New York sightseeing trip was swell, the Rainbow Room—and the two dinner places—with you were wonderful. . . . I love you *so much* and I live for the day when we can be together again."

———

After officer training school was over, Dick hoped he would be sent to a battle fleet in the North Atlantic or the South Pacific, as he had requested. Instead, the newly minted officer was sent to the Naval Air Station in Ottumwa, Iowa. Both he and Pat were disappointed, but Pat gamely moved to the Midwest to be with him. There, Dick worked as the naval aide to the commander of the Naval Air Station. The young lawyer went about town in a brisk, businesslike way, but he was remembered by locals as reserved. Thelma Metcalf, a nurse on base, reported: "I never did see him in the Officer's Club. . . . He wasn't the party type."

Pat was more outgoing and more outspoken than her spouse, Metcalf observed: "Pat Nixon made strong impressions—ambitious, warm, wearing colorful clothes (some she made herself), tinting her hair and confiding dissatisfaction with her 'scandalously low' salary over lunch with Geneva Johnson, the bank president's secretary." Due to her past work with the OPA, Pat was hired to implement the bookkeeping for a stamp rationing program.

After months of boring desk work, Dick noticed that applications for sea duty were being taken, and he jumped at the chance for more exciting war experiences. He soon received orders to go overseas to New Caledonia, a small South Pacific island about 750 miles east of Australia. He and Pat packed up yet again, first heading to Whittier for a last goodbye to his parents and other family members before heading off to San Francisco for his deployment. Brother Ed Nixon remembered a solemn send-off as the family gathered at Union Station in Los Angeles to wave goodbye to the couple as they left for San Francisco: "We tried to keep the conversation upbeat during breakfast at Union Station's Fred Harvey House, but there was no denying the sadness of the occasion." Hannah held herself together, but the more emotional Frank Nixon cried openly at Dick's departure.

Just two days later, on May 31, 1943, Dick set sail on the SS *Monroe*, a former luxury liner repurposed for the war effort. He and thousands of other new recruits soon arrived in New Caledonia. Dick was then transferred to the South Pacific Combat Air Transport Command (SCAT). He and his comrades helped prepare flight plans and manifests for cargo and transport planes.

Back in the States, Pat was excited by the prospect of living in San Francisco on her own. Though she missed her husband, she saw living in the bustling big city as another exciting experience set against the dramatic backdrop of the war itself. Staying alone in Whittier waiting for Dick to return home held little appeal for her. The anonymity and cosmopolitan lifestyle of the Golden City offered the young woman a welcome alternative to gossipy, small-town Whittier (not to mention some welcome distance between herself and her in-laws).

Pat quickly found a small garage apartment at 2829 Divisadero Street. Thanks to the young woman's stellar resume and previous job at the OPA in D.C., she quickly found a job at the OPA's San Francisco headquarters, at Tenth and Market Streets. She made good money and focused on saving every dime she could from her salary, methodically putting away a nest egg for her postwar future with Dick.

After Pearl Harbor, the San Francisco Bay Area became a beehive of war-related activity. Military personnel who had been off duty were recalled, and harbor defenses were quickly shored up. Shipbuilding soon began at a furious pace. Tanks and munitions were shipped out constantly from the port of San Francisco. The Bay Area soon dubbed itself an American "Arsenal of Democracy."

There was a darker side to all this patriotic wartime activity. On February 19, 1942, just months before Pat arrived in San Francisco, President Franklin D. Roosevelt had issued Executive Order 9066. This order established military zones from which civilians could be excluded, and on March 2, the Army's Western Defense Command issued Public Proclamation No. 1, which directed "aliens" to specific areas. "Restrictions began with curfews and proceeded to relocation orders. Eventually, some 112,000 Japanese, a number that included 79,000 U.S. citizens, were ordered from their homes and imprisoned in camps in Arizona, California, Oregon and Washington."

Pat had grown up attending school with the children of Japanese American families who worked in the farming industry in Artesia. Some of these children were her friends and playmates. But now the government considered Japanese Americans living in coastal areas a security risk. To Pat, a young woman who grew up in an ethnically diverse community, internment and related government directives must have seemed brutal and inhumane. Throughout her life, Pat hated artificial barriers (she would famously go around a border wall years later in Mexico to hug children). The idea of internment camps would have been repugnant to her.

Pat and Dick were seeing the war from two different fronts. Both were patriotic, civic-minded people who had joined the war effort to support their country. What Pat would see in San Francisco on the home front and what Dick would see while living through wartime in the South Pacific theater would make both begin to question government rules and regulations and would shape their worldview in ways they couldn't yet comprehend.

7

NEVER JUST A WIFE

When Dick left San Francisco and Pat for the South Pacific on May 31, 1943, he left behind a will. By the end of World War II, an estimated 418,500 Americans would be dead from the conflict, and many of the young men who died left no will, perhaps thinking that they could not possibly be killed. But Dick had a fatalistic streak, having lost two brothers while they were young. He was also a lawyer and liked to spell things out, leaving nothing to chance.

Dick's will is a testament to his love for Pat and his concern for her well-being should he be lost in the conflict. This document also illustrates his complete faith in Pat not only as his wife, but also as a competent and trusted equal in the administration of their estate. Dick drew up this will on May 31, the same day he left for New Caledonia:

WILL

I hereby make my will as follows:

All my property and all property in which I have or may subsequently obtain an interest I devise and bequeath to my wife Patricia Nixon. This shall include any interest I may have in the estate of my parents or any other estate.

I direct that my funeral be as simple and inexpensive as possible.

I appoint my wife as executive without bond. She is to have absolute discretion in settling my estate.

The remarriage of my wife after my decease shall have no effect whatsoever on her rights under my will. I believe that such an action by her would be for the best.

Richard Milhous Nixon
May 31, 1943

While Dick sweated it out in the South Pacific, Pat was alone in foggy San Francisco. She arrived knowing no one at all, but this didn't seem to trouble her. She certainly wasn't the only new kid in town. Pat was part of the tidal wave of working women entering the job space at the lower to middle tiers while the men were away at war. Close to six million women took jobs during World War II. By the time the war ended, women had become more than a third of the working population.

Some of the old prejudices regarding married women working were rapidly dissipating, not out of any sense of political progressivism but out of sheer necessity. A 1936 Gallup poll found that 82 percent of Americans were against married women having paid jobs. Many states even prohibited the employment of this group outside the home. However, by the time the United States entered World War II, another Gallup poll found that only 13 percent of Americans opposed women working outside the home. Thanks to the wartime economy, women like Pat became the backbone of the workforce.

A sisterhood developed between the many women, both married and unmarried, who flooded cities like San Francisco in support of the war effort. "The forties was a time when women rediscovered the community of other women." Women would go to movies together, go to dances together, and eat meals together. Whether they were married or engaged, dating or single, it seemed like everyone was waiting for a loved one to return home, be it husband, boyfriend, brother, or son. Women of all ages and backgrounds drew closer together in wartime sorority.

The wartime workplace was a fertile ground for developing strong female friendships. Not only was Pat's job at the OPA necessary for the Nixons' financial well-being, but her occupation also provided her with a daily routine and relationships that enhanced her social life.

While working at the OPA, Pat met Gretchen King, a North Carolinian who had also worked in Washington for the Works Progress Administration

(WPA). She and her husband, Robert, had transferred to San Francisco in 1940 for his FBI job. The two co-workers clicked instantly. Gretchen remembered, "As one seems drawn to some people more than others, I immediately liked Pat and we became friends. More often than not, we lunched together." She liked Pat's poise and ability to handle most any situation that came her way. Pat wasn't easily thrown, keeping her cool in challenging situations, and Gretchen liked that too.

———

During their wartime separation, Dick and Pat wrote each other daily on a wide variety of topics. Hundreds of these letters were packed up in boxes and left in Hannah Nixon's garage for years. Sadly for future historians, mice got into the letters, destroying about a hundred of Dick's letters and almost all of Pat's. The letters that did survive (some revealed here for the first time) show a tender side of Richard Nixon that few knew. These are evidence of a strong, passionate, and selfless early marriage: a counternarrative to some long-standing notions about the couple's relationship.

Dick was proud of Pat for many reasons, not the least of which was her intelligence and career savvy. He never expressed any qualms about her working; indeed, since their honeymoon they had relied upon her salary to help support their household. Dick also had no problems admitting that Pat had risen above him in her job at the OPA. "Your job is far more important than mine was with O.P.A. I'm really *very* proud—as I always have been. I like to tell the gang how smart you are as well as being the most attractive person they'll ever see!"

In another letter around the same time, Dick reiterated his pride in her career: "I'm proud Pat, that you're smart enough to hold down a top-notch job and that you're so attractive that everyone always turns around when I go by with you." His wife's combination of brains and beauty was something he admired and enjoyed showing off to others.

Dick urged his wife to treat herself and not to be too austere with their finances. "Dear One, I have nothing to spend money on here . . . I want you to make up for me there. Get good dinners, see lots of shows, buy nice clothes, have your hair fixed—and anything else you want or need."

But Pat's thriftiness was part of her DNA. She just couldn't bring herself to spend money on things she could do or make herself. As a child of the Depression, she could not bear waste. She fit the wartime ideal of women promoted in magazines like *Ladies' Home Journal, Woman's Home Companion, McCall's,* and *Redbook* in this regard. "Virtually all aspects of magazine content . . . instructed readers on ways to assist in the war effort: planting 'victory gardens' to counteract food shortages, writing encouraging letters to absent husbands, and coping efficiently and cheerfully with product rationing and shortages."

Pat wasn't a mother yet, so the traditional rules of staying at home and not working unless necessary—even during wartime—didn't apply to her. Young, with her husband overseas, and in need of a paycheck, she suffered none of the guilt that working mothers were told they should feel for leaving their children at home to pursue a job.

"Although the magazines seldom overtly encouraged women to look for *paid* employment outside the home during the war, they contained ample evidence that women were replacing men in factories and businesses." Pat was certainly living proof of this wartime workplace.

———

In a letter dated August 31, 1943, exactly three months after his departure, Dick wrote his "Dear Heart" recalling the difficult day when he set sail for the South Pacific, leaving Pat in San Francisco: "I remember now the heavy feelings I had in my heart as I walked up that little passageway outside your room—stopped by to speak through the screen—and then on to the street. All the way to the dock. And for days afterward it was the same." Dick exclaimed that when he finally did return, "let's always go everywhere together—as we used to. I'll even take you to your Woman's Club meetings!" (A major sacrifice, clearly, on any man's part.)

In another one of these letters early in their wartime separation, Dick wrote longingly of their more intimate moments together, ones that "outsiders" knew nothing of. "I love you most for the traits I know so intimately—and which outsiders do not have the opportunity to see—the way you get up in the morning, full of cheer—your sweet modesty—the soft caress of your hand in the movie. The delicate fragrance of your hair as you sleep with your head rested on my shoulder." Dick was a romantic, sentimental and even poetic at times.

The few letters from Pat that survive are like the ones from when they were courting: her notes are snappy, full of news and activity. But now Pat openly professed her love for Dick, calling him "Dear Heart" or her nickname for him, "Plum." In one letter, she wrote of her delight in receiving several letters from him at once: "Here's to say it is wonderful to love anyone or thing as much as I love you!"

In one letter, he assuaged any jealous feelings Pat might have had, noting that there were very few women around at all. "The only women here are a few Red Cross workers and Army nurses. They are certainly the most horrible looking specimens I ever hope to see—but you should see the play the doctors and pilots give them—NOT for me! I love you—only—and always."

The holidays finally rolled around, and like many young married couples during the war, the two remained thousands of miles apart. Dick's letter to his beloved written that Thanksgiving Day of 1943 extolled Pat's virtues. Above all, he praised her thoughtfulness, her intelligence, her beauty, her creative ability, and her willingness to do without for his sake.

On Christmas Day, Dick recalled their Christmas together in Ottumwa: "Our first together in snow country. The beautiful tree, our newly furnished rooms, our new coffee maker purring away in the morning." It must have seemed surreal to them both to think back on that frosty Iowa Christmas considering their present circumstances.

Though Dick had begun his South Pacific career in Nouméa, on the island of New Caledonia, he spent most of his deployment trying to get closer to the action with a battle station assignment. Finally, in January 1944, his wish was granted when he was assigned to Bougainville. The Japanese frequently bombed the area. Shortly after Dick arrived, his tent was destroyed and the area close to his air raid shelter pockmarked with shell holes. He would later serve on Green Island as well, supporting an invasion operation there.

Despite the omnipresent danger and the fact that his Quaker background forbade gambling, Dick became quite a good poker player, piling up winnings that he squirreled away for use once he returned home. He also ran "Nick's Hamburger Stand," serving free Australian beer and hamburgers to the grateful fighter pilots who passed through. And the young lawyer perfected his swearing—something else his Quaker parents would not have approved of, but it helped him to fit in with his unit.

By February, things were calmer, and Dick had more time for letter writing. He missed Pat intensely and spent hours recalling their happy prewar days together. His war service had thrown him together with all different kinds of men from varying backgrounds. Some of their attitudes toward women rankled him. He found some of the commentary about women within his unit to be both offensive and outdated. "So many of the men out here look upon their wives as a possession—something owned but not much more. You are so much more to me. I want you to be happy and I am selfish to the extent that I want to share your happiness."

On Valentine's Day, Dick assured Pat of his love and fidelity, writing: "On this day, I want to tell you again that you will always be a sweetheart, never just a wife." He was clearly thinking about the comments he had heard from some of his fellow sailors that a wife was just a possession. A sweetheart—well, that was something far more precious, something that had to be fought for, won, and maintained. "I shall ask you for dates and you will never be taken for granted," he wrote. Dick remained dazzled by his good fortune in marrying Pat and went to great lengths in his letters to emphasize she was the only woman for him. "Dear one, you will always be someone special, someone new. That's why I could not be interested in anyone else."

Though Dick was clearly smitten and still in awe of his bride, at times he fell back on familiar female stereotypes of the era to express his concerns about her. When Pat confessed to occasional jitters about living alone in San Francisco, he consoled her by writing: "I'm awfully glad you haven't felt that nervousness again. I worry a lot about you—dear one. . . . Just wait until I get back. You'll be taken care of like a China doll!!" Pat was no China doll; she was a warm but tough young woman whose hard childhood and adolescence had made her self-sufficient and self-reliant. Dick needn't have worried about her being able to take care of herself in San Francisco.

Dick made frequent reference in his letters to how beautiful Pat was, and how he loved to show her off: "You know I always get a kick out of taking you places because people thought you were so beautiful." He pestered her for many months to get a professional photo of herself taken. This way he could show her off to his buddies like a glamorous pin-up.

When the long-awaited photo finally did arrive (it took nine months; Pat probably wasn't too keen on having the photo taken to begin with), he exulted: "Today was the most wonderful day of all because the picture finally came. It's a swell shot—even though no picture can do you justice as I tell everybody that sees it. You'll never know how proud I was to show it to all the fellows. Everybody raved—wondered how I happened to rate! (I do too!)" Dick continued, "Jimmie Stuart said you were like a much younger and prettier Greer Garson and he's a real judge too." Even smart, working women like Pat were still critiqued primarily by their looks. While Dick meant this all as a compliment to his wife, his comments showed that looks were still a valuable commodity a desirable wife had to offer.

By July, Dick had his orders to go home. A flurry of letters between the couple that spring cheerfully discussed their future. They could go anywhere at this point, do anything they wished. At this juncture, their union operated through mutual agreement: any move they made would be a joint decision. Dick queried: "Do you still like San Francisco? As well as or better than L.A. or D.C.? Should we live there afterwards? Let me know how you feel—because it will be fun to talk about it and it will do no harm to plan ahead."

Pat had enjoyed her time on her own in San Francisco immensely. She had money, friends, and a sophisticated big city as her home. She could do whatever she liked when she liked, with no one to answer to. There were no suits to press except her own, no meals she had to cook, no children to tend. Other than the fact that Dick was not with her, it was just about a perfect situation for the independent, confident young woman she was.

She may have begun to mourn the loss of this precious time alone shortly before Dick returned to her. As much as she missed him, she had thoroughly enjoyed her freedom and privacy. In one of the last letters that Pat wrote to Dick, she subtly reminded him not to take her for granted:

Being with you, sweet, is all that matters, and the thought of building a life without you seems so dull. However, I will have to admit that I am self-reliant and that if I didn't love you, I would feel very differently. In fact, these many months away have been full of interest, and had I not missed you so much and had I been foot loose, could have been extremely happy. So, sweet, you'll have to love me lots and never let me change my feelings for you which has been so beautiful all these years.

In historian Roger Morris's analysis, the letter was "a kind of epitaph on the old independence she had regained and clearly enjoyed in his absence. It was in its way a warning and a foreboding." Both Pat and Dick had been living in a kind of romantic haze, a suspended animation where time stood still. Absence is always apt to make the heart grow fonder and more forgiving. But even at that time, Pat was wary. She had opened her heart up to the man she loved, but the letter indicates she wasn't wholly trusting. She felt a need to (sweetly) remind her husband of his obligation to her. Their marriage, and their relationship with each other, should always come first.

Dick had long fantasized about his return home. In February 1944, months before he would be discharged, he wrote Pat about the day they would finally be together again. "Hundreds of times I have pictured our first meeting again, wondered about where it would be, what you would be wearing. Whether it's in the lobby of the Grand Central or the St. Francis Bar—I'm going to walk right up to you and kiss you—but good! Will you mind such a public demonstration?"

Ultimately the couple would meet again not in New York, as Dick had dreamed, but in San Diego, on July 17, 1944. Dick's ship home sailed from Hawaii and docked at the Southern California port. Pat flew from San Francisco to meet him there. In his memoirs, Dick recalled the reunion in vivid detail: "I was at the airport gate waiting for her. She wore a bright red dress, and when she saw me standing there, her eyes lighted up, and she ran to the barrier and threw her arms around me."

The reunion would have mirrored a scene from one of those Hollywood movies they both loved—perhaps *Since You Went Away*, the 1944 box office smash. Instead of Claudette Colbert and Joseph Cotton in the starring roles, it was Dick and Pat who got their happy ending. But the end of the war and Dick's safe return home were just early chapters of the Nixons' dramatic story. Hollywood's tidily packaged tales would never be able to compare with the couple's real-life dramas, only just now beginning to take shape.

8

THE PAT AND DICK TEAM

When wars are over, people rejoice. They return home to sweethearts they have dreamed about for months or even years. For a short period of time, couples may live in a blissful suspended state. However, once the novelty of having a partner home wears off and the daily routine returns, major adjustments must be made.

Though Pat was thrilled to welcome her husband home, she must have somewhat regretted the end of this wartime idyll, knowing she might never again have such a free, unfettered existence. Pat was part of the mass exodus of women leaving the workforce almost as quickly as they had entered it. "Within two years after the war ended, two million women had been displaced from their jobs by returning veterans."

A postwar economic boom would soon begin to sweep the United States. With war rationing suddenly over, abundance replaced scarcity, and consumers once again began consuming—anything and everything. Clothing styles, long a bellwether of the world economy, were among the first items to show the uptick in prosperity. In 1947, French fashion designer Christian Dior's "New Look" was an international sensation. "The collection was all about creating a curvaceous silhouette—prominent shoulder pads, moulded busts and voluminous bouffant skirts, all anchored by a shapely cinched waist."

After his homecoming, Dick became part of the noncombatant Navy at Alameda Naval Air Station near San Francisco, processing contracts. In January, Dick was transferred to Philadelphia; after that, he was transferred first to New York and then to Baltimore. While living in New York, the young couple learned Pat was pregnant with their first child.

Though they had seriously considered settling in a large city far away from Whittier, fate had other plans for them. Near the end of his enlistment, an unexpected airmail letter arrived for Dick from Herman Perry, an old family friend from Whittier, inquiring as to his interest in running for Congress to serve as a representative for California's 12th Congressional District. Dick's opponent would be formidable: Jerry Voorhis, a five-term incumbent liberal Democrat. In the summer of 1945, local Republicans had formed a "Committee of 100" to find a suitable candidate to face off against Voorhis. Perry knew Dick well, having worked with Frank and Hannah as their banker for many years. Dick jumped at the chance, and soon he and Pat were on their way back to Whittier, the very place they had planned to escape.

He won over the Committee of 100 with ease. "I will be prepared to put on an aggressive and vigorous campaign on a platform of practical liberalism and with your help I feel very strongly that the present incumbent can be defeated."

Dick returned to Baltimore, where he and Pat awaited news. At 2 a.m. on November 29, Dick received a call from committee member Roy Day that he had won the nomination. Pat remembered that after that call they were both too excited to sleep and stayed up talking until the early morning, barely believing this new turn their lives were about to take.

While Pat was excited for this new chapter with Dick, she was practical and careful with their money. Her work at the OPA as a price administrator had stuck with her, and now she oversaw economies at home instead of in the office. She worried about the cost of the campaign. How would they be able to pay for the race? They only had $10,000 and wanted to use that nest egg to buy their first house. Like so many young postwar couples, they had a baby on the way and needed more space.

Pat's good friend from Whittier High School Edith Holt, a Spanish teacher there, later recalled Pat's comments to her about Dick's run for Congress. "Pat said to me at the time, 'Dick has been interested in politics for so long. We saved every dime we could to have a home. But now we're going to spend it all on this politics thing. I'm willing to do whatever he wants to do. . . . He has always been interested in it.'"

In addition to budgetary concerns, Pat also worried about how politics would affect her growing family. How could she keep those two spheres separate? Hoping to keep their home life peaceful, she asked Dick for two concessions. First, she would never be required to give any political speeches. She was not the candidate. And second, she wanted home to be their oasis, their shelter from political turmoil.

There is further evidence that early on Pat had reservations about entering the political realm. The Nixons' mutual friend Hortense Behrens had acted with Pat and Dick in the Whittier Community Players production *The Dark Tower*, where they first met. When asked if she thought her friend Pat enjoyed campaigning, she replied: "I really honestly feel she didn't like it at all. I think she's very, very proud of him. But I'm sure she would have much rather been a lawyer's wife. . . . She wasn't pleased with running for office, let's say."

Now that the war was over, the former career woman was moving on to the next expected stage: that of wife and mother. However, in Pat's case she would have to balance her domestic role, one she would always consider the most important, with that of a political wife. She would find that maintaining her equilibrium in this fishbowl could be thrilling, but her natural wariness of public life would prove to be well-founded.

———

In January 1946, Pat and Dick returned home to Whittier, moving in temporarily with Hannah and Frank Nixon. Dick's brother Ed was still living at home with his parents as well. It must have been difficult for Pat to give up her dream of life in a large, cosmopolitan city to move in with her in-laws. She and Hannah were not close, and now they had to deal with each other daily while she was heavily pregnant.

Dick's very first political speech was made on February 5 to the Alhambra–San Gabriel Women's Republican Study Club, followed by his campaign debut dinner in Santa Anita. How intriguing that Dick's maiden speech was given to female voters. He seemed to know instinctively how important this voting bloc was—perhaps thanks to his Quaker background and his marriage to a strong career woman.

Republican clubwomen became an important organizing force after the war, as well as a source of volunteer labor for Republican candidates. "Local Republican organizing and fundraising in the 1950s (and earlier) became clearly identified as women's work . . . the party relegated the work of local party organizing to clubwomen, while not treating them as an interest group with legitimate claims on patronage or power." Historian Catherine Rymph calls these efforts "the housework of government." These conservative club-women were the Cinderellas of postwar Republican politics, taking charge of grassroots organizing and grunt work behind the scenes. All too often, their contributions escaped mention at victory balls.

However, Dick himself acknowledged the critical importance of these women in his memoirs, citing "'house meetings' in which Republican sup-porters would open up their houses to as many—or as few—of their friends and neighbors as were interested in coming to meet me. . . . These house meetings permitted me to meet hundreds of voters and helped me to enlist the women volunteers whose dedicated work is so important to any campaign. They also let me know what was really on the minds of the voters."

The Nixons' entire nest egg was going toward campaign expenses. The state Republican committee was not yet ready to invest much in Dick Nixon. Many dismissed his campaign against the well-known and popular Voorhis as futile. No staff were paid except for campaign strategist Murray Chotiner, a lawyer from Los Angeles. It was only with the help of friends and family, Dick's small law firm salary, and all the Nixons' savings that the campaign was mounted at all.

On February 21, Pat went into labor with the Nixons' first child. Be-cause Pat was at the "advanced age" of thirty-four, her doctor had predicted a lengthy labor before the baby arrived. Dick went to a campaign-related lunch in L.A. on this assumption. However, the doctor's prediction proved incor-rect, and Pat's labor progressed quickly. Her dear friends Helene Drown and her husband Jack accompanied her to the hospital in her husband's absence.

A seven-pound baby girl was born at 1:26 p.m. The infant's shoulder was broken during the short labor, because she arrived feet first. Dick drove well over the speed limit to get to Pat and his new daughter at Murphy Memorial Hospital. Because Pat had been convinced she was having a boy, and had planned to name him Richard but call him "Nic," the new baby girl's name was undecided for days until Dick finally suggested Patricia, whom they would call Tricia. In a speech not long after Tricia's arrival, Dick gave his new daughter a shout-out as "the only boss I recognize. . . . She will grow up in the finest state in the union, in the greatest country on earth, and when the time comes, she will register and vote Republican."

The Nixons rented a one-bedroom Spanish-style bungalow from family friends that was located at 320 East Walnut Street. However, the tiny home had a major drawback: the next-door neighbors were three hundred minks—part of a mink farm operation. Years later the landlord's son William remembered: "It used to bother Richard quite a bit because the mink would chirp quite a bit in the mornings and half the night." The smelly, furry creatures lived in small cages fifty feet away from the Nixons' rented home. This could not have been a restful place for an aspiring politician, a new mother, and an infant to live.

Despite these noisy next-door neighbors (or maybe because of them?), a short three weeks later Pat was back at work at the campaign office. Each morning she would drop Tricia off with Hannah so she could continue to support her husband's campaign. The problem was that Hannah allowed Tricia to sleep most of the day. When Pat got home at night, baby Tricia was full of energy and ready to play.

Pat worked day and night in the small storefront on the corner of Philadelphia Street and Bright Avenue in Whittier that she and Dick had rented as their campaign headquarters. The young mother, along with a few family friends, set up shop. Acting as volunteers, without pay or the benefits of patronage, these women did much of the menial but crucial tasks of organizing for Dick's campaign.

Taking Rymph's "housework of government" concept a step further, Pat Nixon symbolized the ultimate "housewife of government" at the beginning of her campaign career. She worked in the campaign office, typing, copying, writing letters, and keeping the office machinery and staff in working order so that her husband could achieve his political goals.

This infrastructure was the platform upon which many Republican campaigns were based. Without the grassroots support of women like Pat, a run for office could very well have collapsed. Men of the era saw these organizing tasks as beneath their pay grade. This male attitude of taking GOP female volunteers and their hard work for granted would continue for decades to come. Pat's role, however, would grow as her husband's political stature grew, and as she gained experience and confidence.

During this first campaign, Pat began to see the seedy side of politics. Her first brush with opposition dirty tricks occurred when a labor leader came into the Nixon office asking for a large number of their expensive four-page color brochures, which she eagerly gave them. She later was "furious and embarrassed when advisers warned [Dick] Nixon—and her husband in turn reproached her—that the opposition was probably taking the material to destroy it." This was followed in the same week by a break-in at their headquarters in which even more campaign literature was stolen.

Pat took all this to heart. It was for her personally "a bitter blow. She had sold her share of the Artesia property to her brother Tom for three thousand dollars, her entire inheritance, and had invested most of it in the printing of the pamphlets." This divested Pat early on of any illusions she might have had about fair play in political campaigns.

The slings and arrows, which Pat first assumed were thrown only at the candidate, were soon flung at her as well. Roy Day, Nixon's campaign manager, recalled one of Pat's first forays into the political arena of the 12th District—a tea party in San Marino, a wealthy enclave that Day called "the silk-stocking district." The only feedback he received later about Pat from her hostesses was that "she was a lovely lady, but she wore the wrong nail polish." These kinds of catty observations would have stung the young wife who wanted so badly to make a good impression for her husband's campaign.

Day also recalled that at first Pat "was nervous, uptight, and tense. It was all so new to her." However, Pat quickly learned the ropes, and her warm, sincere manner won over many voters. Day noted that she turned out to be her husband's secret campaign weapon: "She was a hell of an asset. . . . She won a lot of brownie points for Dick with those appearances."

Day also remarked upon the critical importance of "house meetings" and of Pat's presence at them. He noted that Dick's "'strongest point' often came in the coffee hours, small gatherings set up in the district where he and Pat together and sometimes separately met the voters." These local coffee hours were a joint effort and where the Nixons had their greatest success as a team. "At each event, Pat listened as Dick made his remarks and answered questions before departing for the next appearance, while Pat remained to socialize and thank female volunteers for their efforts before moving on to the next appearance to join him." This strategy marked the beginning of the famous "Pat and Dick Team," a collaboration that would prove to be the Nixon campaign's secret sauce for years to come.

Pat was Dick's staunchest supporter and co-campaigner in this first, most important race. However, even as he acknowledges her critical role, he writes about her as "my best helper," not as a co-campaigner. Dick was still of his era, considering Pat more of a junior partner at this point in his career efforts.

Still, she didn't coddle his ego. When she thought his speeches were not on point, she did not hesitate to let him know. According to Adela Rogers St. Johns, a journalist and writer who covered the race, Pat could be brutally honest with her husband if she felt his campaign speeches were lacking.

Finally, the donations began to roll in. Dick's friend Donald Fantz, who volunteered for his campaign, vividly remembered Pat working side by side with her husband in the campaign office. "I was in his office in the Bank of America Building and Pat was right there working and taking contributions as she recorded them, along with three other girls. Pat said, 'Huh, boy! These people must really believe we're going to win the way the donations are coming in!'"

The big day finally arrived and, as in most elections, emotions ran high. William Garrett, who was at the Nixons' home the day of the election, recalled how shredded Pat's nerves were from the intense campaign. "One of the most dramatic sights I remember about the Nixons, when Dick ran for Congress and voting was taking place, she was crying just like a baby. I said, 'What's the matter?' She said, 'He's losing!' And it wasn't more than an hour after that till he was winning. That's the way the election was going, and I sure felt sorry for her."

During this first campaign, Pat wore her heart on her sleeve. She had not yet learned to conceal her emotions. The couple had invested everything they had in the race: they couldn't afford to lose. Thankfully, on November 6, 1946, Dick won the election. It was a prolonged race, and the Nixons didn't know the outcome until 4 a.m., as the ballots had to be hand-counted. But Dick unexpectedly swept the race, garnering 57 percent of the vote.

Dick and Pat were jubilant, ecstatic, and perhaps a bit dazed. In his memoirs, Dick would cite this victory as the sweetest one, declaring, "Nothing could equal the excitement and jubilation of winning the first campaign. Pat and I were happier on November 6, 1946, than we were ever to be again in my political career."

Years later, when Dick ran for president, his former campaign manager Day was asked what kind of First Lady Pat would be. His comments would prove to be spot-on. Describing what would be her style throughout all the many campaigns that would come before the presidential runs, he remarked, "Well, she'll never be traipsing along behind the President, she'll never be running around in front of him—she'll always be at his side."

PART II

WASHINGTON WIFE

9

THE GREEN BOOK

In December 1946, Pat and Dick moved to Washington, D.C. Baby Tricia stayed in Whittier with her Nixon grandparents and uncle Ed while her parents searched for a low-cost rental home. This was no easy task given the severe postwar housing shortage. The young couple eventually located a suitable townhouse in the Park Fairfax neighborhood of Alexandria, Virginia. Hannah, Frank, and Ed Nixon drove to D.C. with Tricia in time for the new congressman's swearing-in ceremony on January 3, 1947. Hannah and Frank would soon buy a dairy farm in York County, Pennsylvania, only ninety miles from D.C., so that they would be nearby and available to help with Tricia as well.

In 1947, the Nixons' home state of California was regarded as the ends of the earth by the eastern establishment. Washington was considered by the eastern elite to be the center of the civilized universe; to this group, California still seemed like the Wild West. The new couple were initially perceived as naive and perhaps a bit provincial by some upper-crust Washingtonians. Old established D.C. families tended to be clannish and disinclined to letting in outsiders like the Nixons, who might come and go with the political seasons.

The "Antiques," as Mark Twain first called them, soon became more popularly known as "Cave Dwellers" due to their exclusivity. "Mainly from landed, slave-owning southern Democrat families, the early Cave Dwellers could trace their heritage in Washington back to the first political administrations in the capital."

By 1932 these pedigreed socialites populated the pages of *The Green Book* (so called because of its iconic green cover), a social register compiled and distributed by Helen Ray Hagner, whose aunt Belle Hagner had served as the first White House social secretary under First Lady Edith Roosevelt. Washingtonians who were "in the know" eagerly awaited the guide's annual publication.

However, it soon became apparent to Hagner that with each new election came new government officials and diplomats. She consequently added a section to cover these newcomers as well as the Cave Dwellers who remained. After Hagner's death in 1943, her daughter Carolyn "Callie" Hagner Shaw took over from her mother, running *The Green Book* until her death in 1977. Though it was promoted as simply a reference guide, it was much more than that. From the start the iconic green cover was a signifier of power, money, and class in D.C. It became *the* list of who was "in" and who was "out." Upon the Nixons' arrival Pat would have studied *The Green Book* assiduously, trying to acclimate to D.C. society. It would tell her who was who and provide the correct diplomatic protocols to follow.

Being a devoted wife and mother came naturally to Pat, but now she was also expected to be a flawless hostess and the ideal congressman's wife among the sharp-eyed Cave Dwellers. Pat had grown up in the nonhierarchical, diverse communities of Southern California, and so the D.C. of the late 1940s and early 1950s must have been a cultural shock to her. It was probably also a source of anxiety—would she do or say something wrong? Something that might embarrass Dick and be bad for his career? In California, a misstep might result in gossip among town matrons, but here in the nation's capital, the wrong move on a political wife's part might harm a husband's promising career beyond repair.

Daughter Julie noticed years after the fact that her mother had Scotch-taped a newspaper clipping to the front of her congressional wives' handbook. The clipping, entitled "Table of Precedence," provided rankings for those holding office in various parts of the government—the cabinet, the Supreme Court, and Congress. However, "it was difficult to know what was expected, so haphazard and informal was the introduction to official Washington. There were no briefings offered wives of freshman congressmen, no 'welcome to the nation's capital' kits."

There were also no written guides for the peculiar Cave Dweller dress code, though Pat looked high and low for one. Pat's sartorial fears were realized when she and Dick were invited to the elegant home of aristocratic congressman Christian Herter for an "informal" dinner party. Dick was dressed smartly in a conservative blue suit, Pat in a teal silk cocktail dress. It must have been horrifying for the couple to walk into the foyer into a sea of tuxedos and long gowns. "In Washington, 'informal' meant black tie; 'formal,' white tie." But how was a young couple new to Washington to know this?

Many politicians of the era were born with silver spoons in their mouths, accompanied by the requisite East Coast accoutrements. For example, after their marriage in 1953, John F. Kennedy and his stunning wife, Jacqueline, would have found the D.C. social code as easy to follow as Pierre L'Enfant's grid of Washington's streets. "While the John F. Kennedys, who lived in elite Georgetown with a housekeeper and a valet, had entrée to the city's prominent social circles, the Nixons were adrift."

Dick and Jack had become friends when they served together on the House Education and Labor Committee, sitting at opposite ends of the committee dais. "We were like a pair of unmatched bookends," Dick would later note. The two young men had much in common. Both hated the loud, backslapping forms of politics popular at the time. Both were shy but highly intelligent. Dick already had and Jack would later acquire a beautiful, elegant wife who would be a notable asset for her husband's political career.

During their first year in national politics, Pat did her best to paddle through the murky social waters of the D.C. swamp, while Dick navigated the halls of Congress. When he arrived in D.C., Joe Martin was Speaker, and Republicans controlled the House. After his experiences in the Navy during World War II, Dick had developed strong pro-trade, anti-isolationist feelings, and, noting his interest in this area, Martin appointed Dick in the summer of 1947 to the Herter Committee, a small congressional delegation of nineteen led by Massachusetts representative (and later Dick and Pat's dinner party host) Christian Herter. The charge of the group was to travel to Europe to survey the damage from the war, keeping in mind the suggestions of what would become Secretary of State George Marshall's plan for European economic recovery.

Dick wrote Pat almost every day he was away from her on his European fact-finding mission with the Herter Committee. Seeing the Europe he had dreamed about for so long in ruins was formative for Dick. Scars of violence were evident not only in the landscape but also on the everyday people Dick encountered during his travels.

In Greece, he was introduced to a young woman whose left breast had been cut off by communists when she refused to betray her loyalist brother. In Trieste, Dick "witnessed firsthand the violence that sometimes accompanied the Communist threat." Right outside his hotel and across from the local communist headquarters, he saw the body of a young man whose head had been blown off by communist leaders.

The Herter Committee members met with scores of local leaders, and here Dick found yet more evidence of the postwar communist threat. In one of his daily letters to Pat, he wrote, "The Italian industrialists . . . are all afraid of the Communists who they say are armed and well-financed and they have little faith in the current government."

Dick clearly missed Pat on the trip and wished she could have gone with him, as they had always planned to visit Europe first together. He wrote his wife longingly from Venice, "This may sound like a junket, but it has been a tough trip. . . . The pleasure will have to wait until we can come together. All my love, I miss you every moment."

———

While Dick was working day and night within his government role, he was fully engaged with politics both at home and abroad. He might come home worn out at night, but his work was satisfying. In contrast, at the end of her first year in Washington, Pat found herself exhausted by the dual demands of caring for a young child while simultaneously dealing with her aging in-laws. Hannah and Frank meant well, but Pat all too often ended up caring for them and her young daughter simultaneously.

In addition to child and in-law care, Pat cooked, ironed, scrubbed, baked, and pressed. (This period must have felt like an unwelcome return to her teenage years after her mother died and she had to oversee the Ryan household.) Dick was not at all mechanically inclined, so Pat became a household Mrs. Fix-It. "She stopped faucets from leaking, hung pictures, unstuck doors, put up shelves, and performed any other handywoman chores that came up." Pat was taking care of not only the traditionally feminine tasks but also some of the traditionally male ones as well.

The Nixons could not afford a maid or outside childcare to give Pat a break at this point. The pair scrimped and saved as much as they could while still trying to project the image of an up-and-coming political power couple. This image was easy to project if you had money and servants, as many of their other contemporaries did. But this keeping-up-with-the-Joneses model was a huge strain for a young couple on a strict budget.

Pat's exhaustion was also compounded due to her second pregnancy, with the child due in July 1948. Dick was so busy in Congress he seemed to barely notice her distress. She finally did talk to Dick about her dissatisfaction with the status quo. He was apparently "stunned when she finally told him how deep her discontent was." He did not talk things out with Pat in person, preferring to put his feelings on paper instead. This is a tactic Dick would often fall back on, as he hated any sort of personal confrontation—perhaps due to his father's loud, aggressive nature. Dick seemed much more comfortable pouring out his feelings on paper. His letter to his overworked wife emphasized his deep love for her. He also agreed that he would spend more time with her at home.

Daughter Julie was born just after Independence Day, in the early hours of July 5. Pat stayed in the hospital to recover for five days, a rest she sorely needed. However, when she came home, she faced several immediate challenges. The first was the predictable reaction of two-year-old Tricia, who eyed the new bundle of joy with suspicion, pointing her finger at baby Julie and asking her parents, "What's that thing?" The second, more unexpected issue was Hannah Nixon, who had come to the Nixon household to babysit Tricia but had become ill. Pat once again had to take charge of the household while she was recovering from giving birth just a few days before.

Dick did not make good on his promise to help Pat. Once again, the siren song of politics drew him away from family life. Scarcely a month after Julie's birth, the Alger Hiss case hit the press. Dick Nixon would soon be thrust into the spotlight, becoming a well-known figure at the center of a lurid tale of communist spies infiltrating the federal government.

In his book *Six Crises*, Dick recalled the seemingly mundane testimony from Whittaker Chambers, a senior editor at *Time* magazine who admitted to having been a communist functionary in the 1930s. He had renounced communism and was trying to make amends for his past affiliation with the

Communist Party. The House Committee on Un-American Activities (HUAC) had subpoenaed Chambers after July testimony from Elizabeth Bentley, a former communist spy who had worked as a courier for a Washington-based spy cell during World War II.

Chambers accused certain high-level government employees of having communist ties, including the distinguished and popular Alger Hiss. Hiss was a diplomat who had worked under the assistant secretary of state in FDR's administration and as an advisor to Roosevelt at the Yalta Conference. Hiss demanded an audience with HUAC and appeared before the committee on August 5, just a few days after Chambers made his accusations.

The suave diplomat managed to put on a convincing performance, defending his innocence with outrage. But Dick's radar was up, perhaps due to his trial lawyer training, and he felt uneasy with Hiss's protestations. Hiss seemed too smooth, too assured in his replies. A phony.

Around this time, Dick made the acquaintance of Father John F. Cronin, a Jesuit priest of the Sulpician order. Cronin had taught economics at St. Mary's Seminary and University in Baltimore, and he was also active in labor organizations in the city.

Soon after meeting Dick in 1947, Cronin shared with him his 1945 report entitled *The Problem of American Communism in 1945: Facts and Recommendations*. In the report, Cronin claimed that communists operating within American government had a strong "tendency to enter the State Department and other groups which might have the power to influence foreign policy." Within the report, he mentioned Alger Hiss several times and declared that inside the State Department, "the most influential communist is Alger Hiss." In a 1976 oral history Cronin claimed: "I was able through my FBI contacts to get Nixon information that was critical in convicting Hiss" for perjury in 1950. However, Nixon historian Irwin Gellman suspects Cronin was overstating his role in the Hiss conviction.

Still, it is undeniable that the two men formed a bond over the subject of communism in American government. Both feared that communism was spreading within American government and the public at large. They would connect over their shared theories, and a few years later Cronin would work for Nixon as an unpaid speechwriter and become a cherished family friend and confidant. Tricia recalled: "Father John Cronin was a tremendous supporter of my father and his policies. Both my father and John Cronin were men of faith to whom communism was anathema."

When Alger Hiss was finally convicted in 1950, he not only went to jail for almost four years but also suffered a blow one could never recover from in Washington society: his name was forever dropped from *The Green Book*. This was a social death from which no one's reputation could be resuscitated.

Dick Nixon, a social upstart, had brought low one of Washington's own. For this "crime" some would never forgive Nixon. While Dick was lauded by many conservatives, he was equally despised by many on the more liberal establishment side who thought Hiss was an innocent victim of communist hysteria. Hiss would continue to fight the espionage charges the rest of his life. Only in 1996 with the publication of the Venona decrypts was indisputable evidence shown that he had indeed been an important communist operative.

In the meantime, the Hiss trial and its outcome established Nixon's career, and he was now firmly on Washington's political radar. But at what price? Dick was now viewed with suspicion and outright contempt by many in Washington—and so was Pat, since a political wife of this era, much like a military wife of the time, was considered an extension of her husband. Frank Gannon, a Nixon White House aide and friend who later worked with Dick on his memoirs, "believed that the Nixons had enjoyed Washington in their early years—Pat even got Dick out on the dance floor at the Shoreham Hotel—but that 'Hiss queered it all. Doors closed on them. Invitations were withdrawn. She discovered that politicians were weasels.'"

Daughter Julie recalled that in 1978, Pat had a short, strained conversation with her regarding the Hiss case. Her mother's deep hurt was still starkly apparent thirty years after the event. Pat stated: "The reason people have gone after Daddy is that no one could control him—not the press, not the lobbyists, not the politicians. He did what he felt was right, and from the time this became apparent in the Hiss case, he was a target."

Dick too was aware of the fallout from the Hiss trial and how it affected his career from 1948 forward. In *Six Crises*, he claimed: "I was to be subjected to an utterly unprincipled and vicious smear campaign. Bigamy, forgery, drunkenness, insanity, thievery, anti-Semitism, perjury, the whole gamut of misconduct in public office, ranging from unethical to downright criminal activities—all these were among the charges hurled at me, some publicly and others through whispering campaigns."

Dick was the primary target of such political ire, but Pat too suffered the consequences of his rejection from D.C.'s political establishment. She also had seen all her time with Dick alone disappear—two vacations scheduled in 1948 were canceled due to his pressing work on the Hiss trial. Pat's deepening disenchantment with politics would begin to affect her marriage and her relationship with her husband as the 1950s dawned.

10

HAPPY DAYS ARE HERE AGAIN

The evening of November 2, 1948, found Pat and Dick with their best friends, Jack and Helene Drown, in a most unlikely place. With Dick's reelection to Congress assured (having won both the GOP and Democratic primaries, he had no Democratic opponent), the couples decided to celebrate his successful run for office together at the Coconut Grove nightclub at the Ambassador Hotel in Los Angeles. Jack had planned a mischievous surprise for his old friend Dick. He had arranged for the famous cabaret singer Hildegarde to introduce him that evening to the crowd: mostly Democrats celebrating Truman's presidential win.

Despite her fame and sophistication, the sultry chanteuse was upstaged by the young congressman's deadpan humor. After her introduction and a blast of trumpets, Dick stood up and thanked her, saying: "I realize there are mostly Democrats here having fun, I almost wish I were one of you! But don't jump to conclusions, I'm not going to switch parties. But it just so happens that I love Democrats, I even married one!" With Pat surely blushing at their table, Dick continued, "I would like to introduce my beautiful wife who was a Democrat when I married her. Patricia Ryan, born on St. Patrick's Day—and if they come any more Irish or Democrat than that, I don't know what it could be." The crowd instantly erupted in rowdy cheers.

However, after his victorious evening out, Dick knew he had to take a new tack politically to stay on top. "Dewey's defeat and our loss of both houses of Congress turned me overnight into a junior member of the minority party, a 'comer' with no place to go. For the first time, I began to consider the possibility of trying to move up on my own instead of patiently waiting for seniority or party preferment in the House of Representatives."

Dick began to consider and then implement a new strategy. He began laying the groundwork for a Senate run. Sheridan Downey, California's Democratic senator, had a term set to expire in 1950. He was a popular incumbent and would be hard to beat. Dick's advisors and friends discouraged him, with many telling him that "running for the Senate would be tantamount to political suicide." But Dick instinctively knew that the run would be worth the risk due to the "nationwide publicity that the Hiss case had given me—publicity on a scale that most congressmen only dream of achieving."

Pat agreed with Dick's strategy and dutifully threw herself into the race. Pat, "'the strongest supporter of Nixon's own urge to advance,' was in favor of a Senate run."

In April 1949, the Nixons closed on their new home in Whittier at 14033 Honeysuckle Lane. They were the first owners of the property, which was located near the Candlewood Country Club golf course. Their next-door neighbors, the Daniels family, also had two young girls, Dottie and Barbara, who would become frequent playmates of the Nixon daughters. Due to Dick and Pat's constant campaigning, the Danielses often included Tricia and Julie in activities with their own children: "Wherever we took our girls we took theirs. The girls missed their parents a lot while they were away campaigning."

Helen Daniels recalled that the two husbands would speak to each other while getting the morning papers, and that she and Pat would often chat while their girls played together. "I thought Pat was very nice and I liked her a lot. She was very reserved and kept everything to herself." However, Pat projected a strong belief in her husband's abilities in these early days. "She did say about Dick, 'Somebody has to do something for our country.'"

On November 3, 1949, Dick announced his candidacy for the Senate. What followed, according to Dick himself, was "one of the most hectic and heated campaigns of my career."

Dick had expected to be running against Democratic incumbent Sheridan Downey. But Downey ultimately withdrew from the Democratic primary in May due to poor health, leaving the fight for the nomination between Manchester Boddy, publisher of the *Los Angeles Daily News*, and Helen Gahagan Douglas, an actress and three-term congresswoman. "A rarity as a woman in politics, Douglas, wife of the famous actor Melvyn Douglas, was a high-cheekbone dish, a former actress and light opera star who attracted the wandering eye of Congressman Lyndon Johnson of Texas, among others. She was a bleeding heart liberal, an early model of radical chic."

Before Downey withdrew from the race, however, he gave Dick something opposition candidates can only dream about: a declaration that Douglas was unfit for office. His public comments on his rival were devastating: "She has shown no inclination, in fact, no ability to dig in and do the hard and tedious work required to prepare legislation and push it through Congress." He also stated that she had supported the Soviet government by vetoing aid to Greece and Turkey.

Further aiding the Republican campaign were accusations from Douglas's opponent, Boddy, who pointed out the similarities between her voting re-cord and the voting record of Vito Marcantonio, the sole pro-communist congressman. The claims during the Democratic primary that Douglas was a communist, a "red queen," were arrows aimed at her by her own party. As the Republican challenger, Dick couldn't have had a more promising start.

Dick and Murray Chotiner, his hard-charging campaign manager, de-cided to build on Boddy's own work. They reprinted his comparison of the Douglas and Marcantonio voting records, but with a twist. While Chotiner and Dick were finalizing the print job for the voting record comparison, Chotiner recalled: "In the stock we found a piece of paper with a pinkish tinge to it." One can just imagine Chotiner winking while making this next statement: "And for some reason or other it just seemed to appeal to us at that moment." The leaflet almost instantly became known as the "Pink Sheet" and was soon the talk of the California Senate race.

Now enraged, Douglas struck back, calling Dick all manner of uncom-plimentary names. The mudslinging began in earnest and would do last-ing damage to Dick's reputation. Her campaign insisted the Pink Sheet was a "smear." Julie wrote later about the bitterness of the campaign and Pat's horrified reaction: "My mother in particular recoiled from the shrillness of Helen Gahagan Douglas's personal characterizations of my father. She fre-quently referred to him as a 'pip-squeak' and also called him a 'peewee' and 'tricky Dick,' a label that would be resurrected time and again after the Sen-ate race was history."

The campaign would prove grueling as Dick and Pat drove all over their massive home state in their station wagon, which sported "Nixon for Senator" plaques on each side and portable sound equipment to blast impromptu speeches and songs to the crowds.

Though Pat loved clothes and looking stylish, she didn't have the money to go out and buy an extensive campaign wardrobe. A group of Whittier matrons, Helen Bewley Hathaway, Beulah Redman, Vera Riley, and Kathryn Bewley, knew this and wanted to make sure Pat was suitably dressed for her travels. These resourceful women took on Pat's skimpy wardrobe as their personal contribution to the Nixon campaign and knitted her a campaign trousseau of dresses and suits. The outfits served another purpose too, as a walking advertisement for the Nixons' thriftiness and hometown support. (Indeed, one of these dresses would later have a starring role on television when Pat wore it for the famous "Checkers" speech.)

The Whittier knitting gang adored Pat and had spent enough time with her to understand her personality and the issues she would face as a political candidate's wife. Kathryn observed: "This political bit might have been hard for her because I don't think it was natural for her. She was sincere and I think the insincere, indiscriminate way of reaching out was not her way."

Pat, owing to her reserved nature, must have balked at the thought of being constantly on display during these long, dusty interstate car trips during the campaign season. Always a team player, Pat smiled, said little, and did not complain. "Driving the dented, yellow, wood-paneled Mercury station wagon, Nixon and Pat traveled ten thousand miles around the state of California, stopping wherever they could to attract a crowd. Pat handed out sewing thimbles printed with the words SAFEGUARD THE AMERICAN FAMILY" while Dick gave speeches, shook hands, and answered questions. Fittingly, since she was billed in the Nixon literature as a domestic goddess, Pat would give away over sixty-five thousand thimbles during the campaign.

Pat was often totally wiped out after long days on the road, while Dick was energized by the speeches and interactions with the crowds. Dorothy Cox, Nixon's personal secretary, came from Nixon's Washington office to help with the Senate campaign, and years later she told Nixon daughter Julie:

Sometimes your mother's face would look so tired in repose. And I knew that she was probably more tired than she even looked. I don't know how they stood the pace day after day. If there was enough time, she would roll her hair in the car and when we arrived at the next stop, she would get out, looking just lovely. I noticed that she kept a record of the clothes she wore and at what functions so she would not duplicate. She was meticulous.

Dorothy would also be witness to one of the most unusual campaign donations in political history. One afternoon while Dick and Dorothy were working in their Washington office, Dorothy announced an unexpected visitor had arrived. Jack Kennedy strode in and proffered an envelope. "Dick, I know you're in for a pretty rough campaign . . . and my father wanted to help out." The two old friends discussed the campaign, and Kennedy concluded: "I obviously can't endorse you, but it isn't going to break my heart if you can turn the Senate's loss into Hollywood's gain." The envelope contained $1,000.

———

While out on the campaign circuit with her husband, Pat worried constantly about the welfare of her girls at home. Both children missed their parents, especially Tricia, as she was the older child and more aware of Pat and Dick's constant comings and goings. Evelyn Dorn, Dick's longtime secretary from both the law firm and his previous campaigns, recalled Tricia's distress when her parents would be gone for three or four days at a time campaigning for the Senate seat. "A young girl was taking care of both Julie and Tricia during the day, but at night grandparents Frank and Hannah Nixon would come to the house on Honeysuckle Lane to spend the night with the girls after they worked all day at their grocery store." Evelyn remembered Frank Nixon telling her that "it worried Tricia more than it did Julie that the parents were gone. Tricia, of course, was an older little girl. And he told me on many occasions he and Mrs. Hannah Nixon would be asleep, and he would feel this little hand on his face, and it would be Tricia—she was just a little tot—finding out whether or not her parents were home yet. And he said, 'I'd just lift her up into our bed and put her down between us and she'd go to sleep, and she'd be all right.'"

Tricia often sought comfort in the same way from her parents when they returned home from their trips. According to biographer Lester David, Tricia would come into Pat and Dick's bedroom at night, where Pat did the same thing Frank Nixon did to ease her child's anxiety. When the Nixons began packing in preparation for yet another campaign trip, frequently both girls would cry even as their parents had to shut the door and leave them at home.

In the media coverage of the Senate race, Pat's conflict was clear. In one interview after another she mentioned how hard it was to be separated from Julie and Tricia, as well as the repercussions of misbehavior when she was not around to enforce the rules. "I miss the little girls . . . and no one disciplines them but me!" Dick was certainly not home enough to discipline the children, nor was he inclined to do so with either of his daughters. He adored them and enjoyed being with them when he was home, but the important parental duty of keeping the girls in line always fell to Pat.

When one radio show commentator accompanied Pat to one of Dick's speaking engagements at La Sierra College, she was able to watch Pat's reactions closely. The commentator's observations were telling: "As she listened to her husband speak—expounding on the five-point post Korean War plan, I couldn't help but watch her face—it was absorbedly interested . . . and she seemed happiest when someone said something nice about Mr. Nixon." When asked if she was proud of her husband, Pat replied, "Prouder than anything in the world." Historian Mary Brennan notes that this may have been the beginning of the media set-up for "Plastic Pat": the image of Pat as an adoring political wife who robotically paid attention to her husband's every word. At this point, however, politics was still relatively fresh and exciting for Pat, so her enthusiasm seemed genuine to observers.

There is no doubt, however, that the long, often tedious days shared in the small space of the car grated on both husband and wife. Naturally, tempers frayed on both sides in this high-pressure environment. Pat and Dick snapped at each other from time to time. Both were surely exhausted from the unrelenting pace as well as the separation from their children and the daily routines of home.

Writer, reporter, and Nixon supporter Adela Rogers St. Johns, who traveled with the Nixons on the Senate campaign trail, claimed that Pat could be demanding and perfectionistic with Dick. She told biographer Fawn Brodie, "God, she made it rough for him. She would say, 'That was certainly a disaster,' or 'Well, I've heard you make lousy speeches, but that was the worst.'"

It should be noted that Adela was highly opinionated in her recollections about both Nixons. She often tossed off double-edged commentary regarding Pat in particular. In a 1971 oral history, Adela remarked: "I don't know anybody that my heart breaks more for than Mrs. Richard Nixon, who is a gal who—publicity and public things and appearing in public and everything are just agony. Always have been. She was a quiet, charming, gay, young, red-headed schoolteacher, and I think it's her temperament—I think she's done a magnificent job, all things considered, but her temperament is against it."

Tom Dixon, a Los Angeles radio announcer who was hired to work with Dick on the Senate campaign, claimed to have observed a clash between the Nixons that fall, toward the end of the campaign. Dixon recalled that Dick was rehearsing a speech for a radio show when he unceremoniously waved his wife out of the studio. "You know I don't ever want to be interrupted while I'm working," he supposedly snapped at her.

Still, Dick and his early campaign advisors seemed to understand what an asset Pat was, despite these occasional minor dust-ups. While she said little, leaving the issues to her husband to expound upon, she was clearly his bulwark during the fierce campaign. She was always there with him for all the voters to see. Her constant, supportive presence was crucial for the Nixon campaign's optics, for it telegraphed stability, family, and an all-American look.

Pat also had a strong appeal to female voters, who in 1950 were becoming more and more important to candidates. "Pat exemplified to many American women—especially to Middle American women, where the Nixons pulled strongest—the type of wife and mother they still believed was the best kind to be: a woman with all her chores done, perfectly of course, yet still looking fresh, poised, and squeaky clean."

But underneath Pat's apple-pie perfection was a core of steel. Pat was the engine that pulled her husband along when he was tired, and behind the scenes she urged him toward excellence. She carried more weight with Dick than Chotiner, his campaign manager, probably wanted to admit. Despite that, Chotiner often treated her "as an ornament, a theatrical prop." This was the beginning of attempted minimizations of Pat by some of Nixon's campaign advisors, against which she would push back in various ways over the years.

Perhaps the toughest moment of the campaign for Pat involved her struggle to keep her two little girls quiet on an election eve television broadcast purchased by the Nixon campaign. This was her first time ever on television and a true baptism by fire. While Dick gave his last-ditch speech, Pat minded two-year-old Julie and four-year-old Tricia, surely praying they would both behave. Perhaps female voters who watched her that night sympathized with her plight, relating to the young mother's predicament. It would be another twelve years before the Nixon girls were included in another television appeal.

By the end of the campaign, both Pat and Dick were bone-tired. Even though his prospects looked bright, with a solid lead going into the campaign, Dick was gloomy and anxious on Election Day. He and Pat voted in Whittier and then tried to head to the beach for a picnic, but the weather was chilly. They opted instead to see a movie in Long Beach to distract them and calm their nerves. That evening they retreated to their campaign HQ in the Garland Building to await the final tally. Dick won the election by 680,000 votes, the widest margin of victory by any Republican candidate that year and the largest margin of victory for any Senate race nationally.

The couple celebrated with gusto, going from one victory party to another. Dick played "Happy Days Are Here Again" on multiple pianos. Pat remembered vividly how exhilarated her husband was at the victory. But she would not forget how hard-won the battle had been or the many slights against her husband, which stung her far more than they did him. "No one crossed Pat Nixon lightly, nor did she forget a slight upon her husband—in her mind, an attack upon him was an attack upon her." However, Dick's success was also her success, and she would work just as hard as her husband to ensure he achieved his goals.

———

With the combative Senate race won, the Nixons prepared for a cross-country move. They sold their house on Honeysuckle Lane at a nice profit and applied the proceeds to a new two-story white brick home in a new residential section in Northwest D.C. called Spring Valley. Even with the proceeds from the Whittier house and Dick's honorariums from his many speeches, the seven-room home in D.C. was a stretch for the young family at $41,000. But the Nixons needed an appropriate house reflective of their new status as a senator and a senator's wife. Pat would be expected to do more entertaining, both for Dick's colleagues and for her own friends among the House and Senate wives.

The new home being constructed for the Nixons at 4801 Tilden Street promised to be roomy and luxurious. The plans for the house boasted three upstairs bedrooms: one for Dick and Pat, one for the girls, and one for Hannah and Frank Nixon, who would be frequent visitors and babysitters. There were also two full baths upstairs. The downstairs featured a living room, dining room, den with a fireplace, and a half bath, and a recreation room and half bath were located in the basement. Best of all, Pat told Helene in a letter, was the "electric kitchen with dishwasher & disposal." Tilden Street was a postwar housewife's *Good Housekeeping* dream.

Though the home was purchased in February 1951, it would be several months before it was finished and the Nixons could move in. In the meantime, they were all squashed into a rental apartment. However, Pat seemed delighted to be back in Washington, writing Helene excitedly about the many movers and shakers she met when she was out socially that winter and spring. One highlight: a British embassy reception where Pat met Princess Elizabeth, whom she characterized as "very pretty and most gracious," and she summed up Elizabeth's dashing husband, Philip, with one word: "smooth."

Pat's enthusiasm took a momentary dip, however, when the house move-in was delayed until July. Pat was by now immersed in the drudgery of packing up and organizing their belongings for the impending move. By this point she was well practiced at this chore, but she was resentful that she had to go at this project all alone. "I have moved so many times and the actual process has always been gruesome. Dick is always too busy, at least his story, so I do all the lugging, worrying, and cussing."

By September, though, things were looking up. Despite bad weather, which left them with a flooded basement, and a garage that would have to be rebuilt, the young family finally moved into 4801 Tilden Street. "With it all, we are pleased with the house, the decorating, and the neighbors. What a luxury to have S-P-A-C-E. The children have nice playmates. They have never been as happy as here with the space to dig, their Sears Roebuck swimming pool, their gym set with swings, etc." Pat also finally had some help: a woman named Mary, who, though not always reliable in terms of showing up, did provide her with some respite from childcare.

Pat delighted in decorating, and for the first time, she was able to hire a local designer to help her. To save money, she made most of her old California furniture fit into the new home. She splurged the most on the decor for the primary bedroom and for the living room, where she would be entertaining. She wrote to Helene, "I had a little help from a decorator who dreamed up dramatic touches such as silver tea paper on one wall of our bedroom with a mural by a local starving artist. You would like the living room. One wall is mirrored, the others are aqua . . . and the draperies. And two fireside chairs are peacock blue."

Pat was beginning to worry, however, about Dick, who had developed severe neck and shoulder pain. She wrote Helene that she hoped they could work in a holiday together soon, as "Dick is more tired mentally than I have ever seen him. The doctor told him he would have to get away and take it easier." His long hours of work and constant travel were beginning to catch up with him. In November she reported she and Dick had finally gotten a ten-day vacation in Sea Island, Georgia. They biked, swam, and played golf together, happy not to be recognized or bothered.

In December, at the urging of his new friend Florida senator George Smathers, Dick took another restorative vacation alone in Florida. Smathers connected Dick with a former high school classmate, Cuban American businessman Charles "Bebe" Rebozo. Rebozo and Dick would eventually become fast friends, and Rebozo would become an honorary member of the Nixon family. The charming and urbane Rebozo was nonjudgmental, fun, and easy to be with. He didn't talk much but soaked up Dick's commentary with interest and discretion. Just what the doctor ordered to help relax an anxious young senator.

The best news of all, however, concerned Tricia. Now that Pat was home with her and not gone for days on the campaign trail, the little girl was happy and well adjusted. She was not old enough for first grade in D.C., so she instead began attending kindergarten at a community nursery school. The school was newly started, so Pat and the other mothers took turns hosting the children in their homes until a paid teacher took over.

Thereafter Pat would continue helping at the new school every ten days. The result was rewarding. Pat wrote Helene that Tricia "loves kindergarten and comes home bubbling over with all the news. She is not the shy, clinging type as you knew her—a victim of the campaign." With their mother close at hand, the girls had a pleasant, more stable environment. Pat had a new house with help, as well as exciting parties and events to attend. She and Dick had come a long way from their lower-middle-class, small-town origins. Now they were an up-and-coming power couple operating at the center of national politics. At only thirty-seven, Dick already possessed a prestigious Senate seat. There was nowhere to go now but up.

11

TAKING THE VEIL

The Nixons' new home in Spring Valley exemplified a postwar lifestyle explosion. This neighborhood was modeled along the same lines as the famous Levittown on Long Island, New York, begun in 1947 as "America's prototypical postwar planned community."

However, hiding behind these white-picket-fenced dream homes were purchase agreements containing racially restrictive covenants. These clauses prohibited African American, Jewish, and other minority-group members from owning homes in the area. Like all the other homes in Spring Valley, the Nixons' home was subject to such a covenant, which was based on the Levittown model.

Both Pat and Dick had grown up in racially diverse areas of California and found the covenant offensive. Unfortunately, this practice was common in postwar suburban communities and continued for decades. Such covenants would not be struck down by the federal courts until 1972.

While there was a total lack of diversity within Spring Valley and neighborhoods like it nationally, there were many positives for the women who resided in such developments. These suburbs often produced tight-knit communities of housewives who formed their own cooperatives to help raise the community's children.

Pat's Tilden Street neighbor and good friend Margaret Fuller wrote to Julie Eisenhower years later about this picture-perfect suburb:

> It was such a quiet simple neighborhood then, like a small village. The 4800 block [where the Nixons and the Fullers both lived] was just being built, and the street and utilities being installed, so it was like pioneering in

many ways. We all helped each other, sharing, doing errands, digging out stuck cars, using phones, etc. This made for a close neighborhood feeling and having so many young children also added to the interrelationships.

Margaret also mentioned how safe the area was. Milkmen, cleaners, and laundry services were welcome to come inside the houses to drop off items unsupervised. Older children played outside without fear and got on and off the school bus a block away unaccompanied by adults.

Margaret recalled how Pat fit in seamlessly with the neighborhood women, despite being a bit of a celebrity as a senator's wife. "She was always a lady, yet so warm and friendly with those close to her. She had a wonderful sense of humor, and I loved her deep throaty laugh. She was ever so intelligent and alert to everything going on around her, with a quick wit and comeback to any barb. Always fun to be with."

Margaret also remembered that the senator's wife put time into the local group activities just like any other neighborhood mom would have, with no excuses and no airs. "She always took her share of days at the cooperative Nursery School and Kindergarten, as well as the Brownies." If Pat or Dick could not attend a party, ceremony, or school activity for their daughters, Pat would always make sure a neighborhood friend—someone the girls knew well—accompanied them. The girls would attend Horace Mann Elementary School, an integrated public school, until 1958, when Tricia graduated.

As busy as Pat was, she was also sensitive to the personality differences between Tricia and Julie and worked to harmonize their sisterly relationship. Pat showed her flair for diplomacy first at home with her own children. Writing again to Julie, Margaret revealed: "One day Tricia was setting the table with a lace cloth for tea, while you were organizing the children on the block for some parade. You wanted her to stop and be in the procession, but your mother persuaded you to let Tricia do her tea and you and the 'gang' come to it."

Daily life for the Nixons in Spring Valley was pleasant and idyllic in many ways, and far more stable than it had been in Whittier during the brutal Senate race. Pat had an active social life with the Ladies of the Senate Club and rolled bandages with the group every Tuesday for the Red Cross. She was not eager, however, to spend all her time socializing with the Senate wives, preferring to spend as much time with her daughters as possible.

Then there was the current First Lady, Bess Truman. Harry Truman had been a senator himself from 1934 to 1952. And so Bess, "as a senator's wife, . . . believed that 'a woman's place in public is to sit beside her husband, be silent, and be sure her hat is on straight.'" The unsociable Bess also seemed to believe that this was how Senate wives should behave around the First Lady. Engendering further dislike between Bess and Pat was the frosty relationship that had developed between their husbands over the Alger Hiss case. As president during that time, Truman enacted "executive orders and executive privilege to limit Congressman Nixon's investigation and dismissed the case as nothing more than political theater and a 'red herring.'"

Perhaps partly for this reason, Pat put off going to the Senate wives' luncheons for months, writing Helene Drown that she had decided she finally must go. "Since I have never been there to 'eat' I thought I'd break down and go. I'll probably be cold-shouldered by Bess but . . ."

Bess's cold shoulder didn't trouble Pat unduly. The frequent press attacks on her husband worried her far more. Pat was vigilant about shielding her children from these unflattering portrayals of their father, but she still couldn't isolate them completely from the problem. At only four years old, Julie heard a woman use a curse word in relation to her father. Political cartoons in the *Washington Post* depicted Dick as an evil character and a villain, upsetting both Tricia and Julie. Schoolmates called their dad a "monkey father" because of those scary, dark depictions.

Pat began to catch some of the runoff of vitriol directed primarily at her husband; slurs about Pat were often thinly veiled jabs at Dick himself. Model-thin, the young Senate wife was mocked by popular *Washington Post* columnist Drew Pearson for being so bony she had to have expensive gowns custom-made to fit her. This offended not only Pat's vanity but also her sense of thrift. She couldn't afford to have couture dresses, as Pearson suggested: she had to constantly economize to look the part of a senator's wife.

No one was more offended than Dick, who was furious at Pearson's cruel attack. Dick complained to writer Eleanor Harris, "It was the meanest, lowest thing a guy could say about a woman . . . the air around me was blue for some time after I read that." Pat also didn't forgive or forget. She wrote to Helene sometime after the incident, incredulous that Pearson had invited her and Dick to a party—an event the couple made sure not to attend.

In 1951 a new woman entered the Nixons' orbit, someone who would become critical to Dick's career as well as a beloved family friend. Rose Mary Woods, whom Dick had met a few years before through his work for the Herter Committee, became Dick's primary secretary and quickly gained the trust and confidence of both Dick and Pat. Indeed, Hannah Nixon recognized a kindred spirit in Woods right away, telling her son that Woods was "our kind of people." For many years Woods would act as Dick's de facto chief of staff. And woe to anyone who tried to get to "The Boss" or "El Boss," as she called him, without her approval.

Today we would call Woods Nixon's "work wife." In many ways she was like Pat. They were both slim redheads with pale skin, and both women were of Irish extraction. Both had their own opinions on things and tempers that simmered under the surface. While Pat had long ago learned to keep her temper under wraps, Rose Mary occasionally let hers fly. In other ways she was Pat's alter ego: she was able to say things to Dick in a professional mode that Pat, as his wife at home, probably could not voice. The two women soon became fast friends, and over the years to come they would form a deep bond.

Though Dick was often gone fundraising for the Republican Party, the Nixons did finally manage a trip to Hawaii with Helene and Jack Drown in April 1952. Dick had been invited to the swanky Royal Hawaiian Hotel in Honolulu to give a series of speeches. This was the excuse they both needed to escape. Pat told daughter Julie years later, "It was the last carefree vacation I ever had."

Dick's Senate tenure would represent just another rung on the ladder of politics. A 1952 Republican Women's Club newsletter reinforced this idea as well as Pat's place in political life, proclaiming that "the duty of a wife of a man in public life is to hold the ladder for her husband to climb." That was certainly Pat's designated role at this moment, and the ladder she held looked as if it could lead soon to bigger things.

———

The young California senator "quickly became his party's most sought-after speaker and soon blossomed into a Republican meld of Paul Revere and Billy Sunday. Across the land he trumpeted Republican gospel and warned the countryside to stop the Democratic hordes or face disaster." Nixon had name recognition from the Alger Hiss case and was a hot ticket at Republican fundraising dinners across the country.

By the spring of 1952, battle lines were being drawn between two strong candidates for the Republican presidential nomination. The two top contenders were Senator Robert Taft of Ohio, known as "Mr. Republican," and General Dwight D. Eisenhower, nicknamed "Ike," whom some in the GOP considered an "interloper." Dick had met Eisenhower twice in Europe in 1948 and then again in 1951. The two men also encountered each other in 1950, at the summer meeting of the Bohemian Grove, the exclusive men's club near San Francisco. Eisenhower had been impressed by Dick's work on the Alger Hiss case and told him so, which may have biased Nixon to support his candidacy.

Alice Roosevelt Longworth, the waspish daughter of President Teddy Roosevelt, had become good friends with Dick and Pat upon their arrival in Washington. Despite her Washington insider status, she had a soft spot for outsiders and mavericks, and she soon took the young couple under her influential wing. Alice warned Dick about the perils of a vice presidential nomination—she felt the VP job was a worthless proposition that could likely sideline his political career. Her own father had referred to the VP position as "taking the veil."

However, according to Dick's memoirs, Alice felt he and Pat should be prepared just in case he was nominated: "You should talk to Pat about it so that just in case it does happen you aren't caught with your drawers down!" Dick might have to take one for the team if the VP slot was offered to him, "for the good of the party," Alice told him.

When Pat and Dick attended the Republican convention that July in Chicago, Dick's name was in the air as a potential VP pick. Pat had listened carefully to Alice's counsel on the VP matter and was concerned about the long-term consequences of being vice president. While she found the convention politics exciting, she did not want to go through the grinder she had experienced in the 1950 Senate race again so soon.

Helene Drown had come along with Pat to the convention, and the two women had gone out for a late dinner. When she returned to her hotel room Dick was waiting for her, electrified by the prospect that he could be Eisenhower's pick for vice president. The two men formed a perfect political whole for the moment: "Eisenhower was tied to the East Coast foreign policy establishment. Nixon was an internationalist too, but he was close to the grassroots. He could bash communists and political opponents with equal fervor—letting Ike float above the fray. And he could deliver California."

Pat and Dick talked through the night about Dick agreeing to the vice president's role if it was offered to him. Pat still wasn't sure she wanted to face another campaign season, leaving her girls at home for weeks at a time yet again. At 4 a.m. the couple finally called in Chotiner to weigh in on the decision. When he arrived, he could instantly tell Pat was against the idea.

However, daughter Julie later wrote that Chotiner bluntly advised her parents: "There comes a time when you have to go up or get out." The Nixons' campaign advisor did not subscribe to Alice Roosevelt's school of thought on the lame-duck role of the VP. He left, and Pat and Dick continued their discussion, which ended up with Pat reluctantly agreeing to support her husband's candidacy if it came up. "I guess I can make it through another campaign," she conceded. She clearly wasn't excited about the idea, and though Dick certainly was, neither of them seemed to think his nomination was all that likely.

The very next day, on July 11, the situation began to pick up steam. Eisenhower received his party's nomination that afternoon. Only a few hours later, at 4 p.m., the news was announced in the press that Richard Nixon was Eisenhower's choice for VP.

At that time, Pat was eating a late lunch with Helene and Chotiner's wife at the Stock Yard Inn. Suddenly the television in the restaurant blared out the news—Richard Nixon was Eisenhower's choice for vice president. As daughter Julie tells the story: "My mother opened her mouth in astonishment and her bite of ham sandwich fell out. Helene exclaimed, 'Oh Pat, you're going to be in the history books!' Suddenly, Mother felt a tremendous sense of elation. She and Helene, though in high heels, literally ran back to the Convention Hall."

The speed of Dick's nomination by acclamation (and the lack of cellphones, texts, and social media apps) gave Dick little time to communicate with his wife before the announcement. But once Pat heard the news, the plan she had agreed upon with Dick clicked into place. Her careful attention to her outfit that morning suggests she knew the day might very well be a momentous one. Instead of picking one of her modest plain voile shirt-waists, she selected a bold, busy print outfit. Helene, Pat's unofficial stylist, had advised her to choose this ensemble, "a pretty, full-skirted dress dotted with black and white coins and trimmed with black-velvet cuffs and collar," as it would come across particularly well in the black-and-white newspaper photos.

After Dick's acceptance speech, which Pat watched from the convention hall's visitor's gallery, she threaded her way through the dense crowd, trying to get to her husband. She modestly told reporters following her: "I am amazed, flabbergasted, weak and speechless. We heard rumors, but we heard rumors from a lot of people." She did not hesitate when asked about the upcoming campaign and if she would accompany her husband: "We work as a team." Despite her initial hesitation, there was now no doubt she would be by her husband's side for the duration of the race.

Swept up in the pageantry of the occasion and the exhilarating feeling of party acceptance, Pat and Dick did something that was extraordinary both for them personally and for the era: they kissed twice—once for each other and once for the cameras and reporters—in full view of the convention. Pat must have found it hard to believe that her husband would now be campaigning with General Dwight Eisenhower, revered World War II hero. It all must have seemed surreal, like an impossible dream come true. A real fairy tale—or at least so it seemed on the convention platform that day.

However, this bubble of elation soon burst for Pat. That evening, a frantic phone call from Hannah Nixon, who was in Washington babysitting Tricia and Julie, brought her back down to earth. Reporters huddled outside the Nixons' Tilden Street home had burst into the house that night, waking up the little girls and scaring them by taking flash photos. A frightened Julie cried, "I want my mommy!"

The *Washington Times-Herald*'s "Inquiring Camera Girl," Jacqueline Bouvier (not yet married to Jack Kennedy), also visited the Nixons' block of Tilden Street soon after the Republican convention. She asked various Nixon neighbors the same question: "What do you think of Senator Nixon now?" One of the respondents was six-year-old Tricia, who gave her unfiltered response: "He's always away. If he's famous, why can't he stay home? See this picture? That's a coming home present I made for Daddy. Julie did one too, but she can't color as well as me. All my class was voting for Eisenhower, but I told them I was just voting for Daddy."

Any mother would have been worried and upset at the media's frequent invasions of her daughters' privacy and the trauma it caused them. Like the children of celebrities or royalty, Tricia and Julie were beginning to learn what it meant to be constantly in the limelight. Pat wanted badly to shield them from this experience, but she was often powerless to do so in the face of Dick's ambitions. The whole family had to be part of the picture presented both to the media and to the public to capture the vote. Pat and the girls became valuable symbols of the wholesome American family and the middle American way of life.

Soon the campaign began, and there was little time to worry about invasion of privacy. Every detail about Pat became fodder for newspaper feature stories. Her campaign bio revealed intimate details that she surely wouldn't have provided without prodding from the GOP campaign office. Pat's personal description reads: "5 feet 5″ in height—weighs 110 pounds—has reddish blonde hair." Her hobbies? "No time for a hobby at present—devote all time to taking care of our young children and to helping my husband." This all fit the mold of the perfect housewife/helpmeet, an image meant to appeal to the average GOP voter.

However, another layer was spun regarding Pat's image, that of the Republican campaign wife as teammate. She gazed up at him adoringly throughout his many speeches no matter how tired or bored she might be. When asked about campaigning, Pat struck a familiar refrain: "I've campaigned with my husband three times, twice for the House of Representatives, once for the Senate. We work as a team."

Her husband's comments, laid out next to Pat's in her bio, reinforced her statements: "For the campaign, where I go, my wife goes too. She's my campaign partner." Her role was to look pretty and to meet and greet but never make political statements. She was his partner in image-making, and the optics of them together were often as important as (and, when appealing to certain voters, perhaps more important than) the content of Dick's speeches.

As the duo prepared to begin stumping in earnest, thousands of letters poured into the Washington office congratulating Dick as a fast-rising political star. A note from one of his senatorial counterparts was saved and treasured by the young California senator.

Dear Dick:

I was tremendously pleased that the convention selected you for V.P. I was always convinced you would move ahead to the top—but I never thought it would come this quickly. You were an ideal selection and will bring the ticket a great deal of strength.

Please give my best to your wife and all kinds of good luck to you.

Cordially,

Jack Kennedy

12

THE FINANCIAL STRIPTEASE

What happened next reads like a political fairy tale, albeit one with a dark bent. Dick would soon be required to spin political straw into gold on television. Pat would be paraded financially naked through the streets like Lady Godiva. And, as in all good fairy tales, a loyal beast would help save the day.

Chotiner again signed on as Dick's campaign manager. The two men quickly plunged into strategy sessions with Eisenhower's team. They decided to have a four-day trial run of Dick's campaign speeches in solidly Republican Maine before hitting the "real" campaign trail in California in mid-September. Biographer Earl Mazo compared this Maine preliminary tour to "shows that try out in New Haven before opening on Broadway." The experience allowed Dick to test out speeches and get his campaign team (advance men, publicity staff, and Pat) in order before the more important fall events.

The West Coast whistle-stop train tour began on September 17 in Pomona, California, aboard a train known as the *Nixon Special*. Eisenhower was simultaneously campaigning in the Midwest on his own train, the *Look Ahead, Neighbor! Special*. The Nixons had begun their campaigns for both the House and Senate the same way, by using train stops as campaign platforms.

According to the *Los Angeles Times*, the *Nixon Special* boasted "a lavish car with large, beautiful beds for the candidate and his wife . . . two lounge cars, a work car for the press with typewriters on long tables, and even a special crew of Southern Pacific agents and Western Union 'experts' to handle the expected flow of copy for newsmen."

Daughter Julie recreated the scene of her parents' departure from Pomona on the Nixon Special in her biography of her mother: "My mother's red-gold hair glistened in the sunlight, a vivid contrast to the coal black of my father's. They were young, attractive, full of fight, and, in the opinion of those watching the scene, headed for victory. But within twenty-four hours their world came apart."

Earlier in September, just after a taping of the D.C.-based television show *Meet the Press*, syndicated columnist Peter Edson had drawn Dick aside. Though Edson didn't question him on the air, he asked for more details about a "secret fund" he had heard whispers of over the summer. Edson noted that Dick answered him forthrightly, giving him the telephone number of Dana C. Smith, a California lawyer who acted as trustee of the fund. After Dick became a senator, a group of California businessmen had set up this fund to help him with travel and campaign expenses. The fund, totaling $18,235, was no secret, and it was used only for the specific purpose stated. Many other politicians at this time kept similar funds to support their political activities—among them Democratic presidential candidate Adlai Stevenson.

Edson wrote a long article explaining the fund and its exact purpose. However, due perhaps to the Eisenhower campaign theme of rooting out corruption and scandal in Washington, the press corps jumped on the fund story. Soon both the *Washington Post* and the *New York Herald Tribune* were calling for Dick's resignation. Eisenhower, far from being reachable, was distancing himself from his VP pick while not yet outright dumping him. Reporters covering Eisenhower's *Look Ahead, Neighbor! Special* took an informal poll among themselves about whether to keep Nixon on the ticket; the vote was 40–2 against. Eisenhower heard of this polling and called the reporters together for an off-the-record chat (with a beer) on Saturday, September 20. The general's comments were promptly leaked: "I don't care if you fellows are 40 to 2. I am taking my time on this. Nothing's decided, contrary to your idea that this is a setup for a whitewash of Nixon. Of what avail is it for us to carry on this crusade against this business of what's been going on in Washington if we, ourselves, aren't as clean as a hound's tooth?"

That same day found Nixon's mother, Hannah, incredulous at the accusations against her son. She was babysitting Julie and Tricia at 4801 Tilden Street while their parents were on the *Nixon Special*. She told biographer

Bela Kornitzer, "I was completely shaken" by headlines on September 18 intimating "a New Teapot Dome" scandal. "There was just no foundation. As a Quaker, I can't say I got angry, but I was terribly put out. I watched every moment on television, and I felt I could hardly carry on."

The telegram she sent Dick that Saturday read:

GIRLS ARE OK. THIS IS TO TELL YOU WE ARE
THINKING OF YOU AND KNOW EVERYTHING WILL BE
FINE. LOVE ALWAYS, MOTHER.

In his memoirs, Dick himself translated the message, which had a double meaning in his Quaker faith. "In our family . . . the phrase 'we are thinking of you' meant 'we are praying for you.'" While he was touched, the message reminded Dick that the eyes of the nation were upon him.

If Hannah was "terribly put out," Pat was wounded and furious. She was not about to stand by and let her husband's career and reputation—which, by extension, were her career and reputation—go down the drain. Hearing Eisenhower's "hound's tooth" comments probably made her want to scream. She had been holding back her feelings since the eighteenth, and now she vented to Helene, "Why should we keep taking this?"

Eisenhower's grandson David Eisenhower contends that even though the situation looked bleak for Dick, he well knew that "Nixon could not be dropped from the ticket without losing the election. So, Nixon was going to be kept on the ticket. It was a question of form. How many spears do you have to fall on to give Eisenhower the opportunity to look as if he's judging the case?" However, Dick and Pat clearly felt a lack of support from Eisenhower at this point.

A campaign rally in Eugene, Oregon, on September 21 featured picketers bearing accusatory signs. One sign was directed at Pat's wardrobe: "No mink coats for Nixon, just cold cash." Nixon refused to comment on other signs, but this one he angrily pounced upon—he would not tolerate an attack on his wife before his eyes. "That's absolutely right," he sputtered furiously, "there are no mink coats for the Nixons. I'm proud to say my wife, Pat, wears a good Republican cloth coat." As the train pulled away, a scuffle ensued, and the offending sign was torn to bits. The "Republican cloth coat" soon became iconic, serving as a bit of armor for Pat against the accusations of a scandal-hungry press.

The *Nixon Special* chugged into Portland, Oregon, that afternoon, and Pat and Dick disembarked, taking a car to their lodgings. When they stepped out to enter the Benson Hotel, they had another gauntlet to run, this time a gaggle of demonstrators from Portland's Democratic headquarters, who shoved them, "threw pennies and shook tin cups labeled 'Nickels for poor Nixon.'" Pat was shocked by the "suddenness and ferocity of the attack." To the Drowns, who were traveling with the Nixons for the campaign, Pat repeatedly exclaimed, "It can't be happening. How can they do this? It is so unfair. They know the accusations are untrue."

In the evening of that exhausting day, Dick debated resigning from the campaign. He had yet to hear from Eisenhower directly, and he was losing ground with the press each minute. Other staff also discussed this as a real possibility, until campaign manager Murray Chotiner interjected: "You can't quit, Dick. Too many people believe in you. You can't let them down. And you have a wife across the hall who believes in you."

While Chotiner and Pat often didn't agree, this was one instance where they joined forces to support Dick. Dick wrote later of the conversation he had next with his wife—one that would be a game-changer for his slumping attitude:

> "You can't think of resigning," she said emphatically. With a typically incisive analysis she said flatly that if Eisenhower forced me off the ticket he would lose the election. She also argued strongly that unless I fought for my honor in the face of such an attack, I would mar not only my life but the lives of our family and particularly the girls.

Historian Fawn Brodie adds that Pat was "thinking always of her daughters" and "reacted with a steeliness of resolution that could only have astonished him." There was little doubt where her loyalties lay—with her husband, yes, but she was always thinking simultaneously about how events could affect her two girls.

Tom Dewey, New York's governor and an Eisenhower supporter, called to say that Dick must go on television to defend his honor and explain the purpose of the fund. Not until 10 p.m. that evening did Eisenhower finally call to endorse Dewey's suggestion. Even then, he didn't give Dick his unequivocal support. It was obvious he was still wavering and wanted to see which way the political winds might blow. Frustrated, Dick told the general to "shit or get off the pot." (The first edition of Dick's memoirs uses this verbiage; later editions would use "fish or cut bait." Clearly, though, the first edition expressed his exact feelings best.) Still, Eisenhower didn't budge. He told Dick he would have to wait for several days after Dick's televised speech to decide whether he would keep him on the ticket. Historian Irwin Gellman noted Eisenhower's characteristic tendency to "stay above the fray until the fray turned exactly as he wanted it to."

The VP candidate now knew his political neck was on the chopping block. Would this "fund crisis" prove to be Dick's Waterloo or his salvation? Eisenhower's cavalry was not coming to rescue him. But Pat believed in him, and she didn't hesitate to give him the support he so desperately needed. Bolstered by his wife's courage and faith in him, Dick began to stage his own intervention. "From that time on," he told his daughter Julie years later, "I never had any doubt that I would fight the thing through to the finish, win or lose."

The couple flew to Los Angeles the next morning. While on the plane Dick began working on notes for what would soon become an iconic speech. To save his candidacy, he would have to lay bare the couple's meager finances. Pat read some of his notes and flinched. "Why do we have to tell people how little we have and how much we owe?" she asked her husband. She had been further incensed at the rumors she had spent $10,000 of her husband's fund money on decorating her 4801 Tilden Street residence. Pat knew exactly what she had spent, and she had done much of the decorating work herself: not a cent had come from the fund.

For someone who had little growing up and who was a self-supporting career woman before her marriage, the idea of exposing her personal financial situation on national television was a nightmare. It was quite possibly the most embarrassing thing imaginable for someone as private and as hardworking as Pat. She might as well be paraded naked on television, the subject felt that intrusive to her.

At 5:30 p.m. that fateful Tuesday evening, Pat and her husband rode together silently to the El Capitan theater in Hollywood for Dick's broadcast. Though she didn't know it at the time, Dick had received a phone call from Tom Dewey an hour before in which he suggested that Dick resign at the end of the speech. He claimed the idea came from Eisenhower's top advisors. Dick was furious but didn't lose his cool. He also didn't agree to the request. Pat sensed she needed to stay quiet and let her husband have some peace during the car ride.

When the couple arrived at the El Capitan, the theater was empty save for the staff working on the broadcast. Dick didn't have a script, just his five pages of notes. The set, described by Dick's television advisor Ted Rogers as "GI bedroom den," was kept spartan and simple on purpose to appeal to middle-class audiences across the country. The lighting at El Capitan was powerful and the theater was chosen for that reason, as opposed to NBC's main television studios close by. Dick did not want to run through his remarks or practice at all beforehand. He wanted it to come across as spontaneous and fresh, not a canned speech.

Just minutes before airtime, Dick began to lose his nerve. He turned to his wife and said, "I just don't think I can go through with this one." Pat looked at him steadily, took his hand, and said, "Of course you can." A studio executive then appeared to escort them to the stage. Pat was going to sit next to him onstage, on camera, providing the ultimate show of wifely support. Rogers had questioned having Pat on set with the candidate, but Dick would have it no other way: "I want to feel she is here," he said.

Dick was placed behind a desk for his speech, while Pat was seated in an armchair next to him. What Pat provided that Chotiner and all the campaign aides in the world could not was the silent shoring up that Dick needed. It emboldened him to always do his best. When the red camera light turned on, he was ready.

Wearing a light brown dress made for her by the Whittier knitting ladies and a leopard-print scarf, Pat was unaware that a camera was trained on her throughout the broadcast. This image of her gazing intently at her husband during the speech would make an important impression on viewers.

What followed next has been described as Dick and Pat's "financial striptease." These words perfectly capture the humiliation of the whole exercise for both halves of this proud couple. Dick first explained the purpose of the so-called secret fund, with all of it dispensed for political expenses and not a dime going toward his or Pat's personal use. He also noted that an independent review of the fund had just been conducted and no wrongdoing was found.

Next came a meticulous and painful reveal of the couple's meager assets and their liabilities. Dick concluded with these words: "Well, that's about it. That's what we have. And that's what we owe. It isn't very much. But Pat and I have the satisfaction that every dime that we have got is honestly ours. I should say this, that Pat doesn't have a mink coat. But she does have a respectable Republican cloth coat, and I always tell her that she would look good in anything."

The one campaign gift that the Nixons were going to keep, whether anyone liked it or not, was a dog. "We did get something, a gift, after the nomination. . . . It was a little cocker spaniel dog . . . black and white, spotted, and our little girl Tricia, the six-year-old, named it Checkers. And you know, the kids, like all kids, loved the dog, and I just want to say this, right now, that regardless of what they say about it, we are going to keep it."

And finally, in a nod to the Pat and Dick Team spirit, Dick concluded: "I don't believe I ought to quit, because I am not a quitter. And incidentally, Pat is not a quitter."

After the speech Dick worried it was a disaster. He melted down, telling his wife in the dressing room, "Pat, I was a failure." She assured him he was not. Soon they would both know not only that he was not a failure but also that his speech was a phenomenal success. When the couple returned to their hotel suite, they were inundated by well-wishers and swamped with telegrams and phone calls. Dick would always remember a call from legendary Hollywood studio head Darryl Zanuck, who gushed that his speech was "the greatest production I have ever seen."

Nine million people had watched Dick's speech on television, many of them skeptical about him beforehand. After the speech, Dick accomplished his objective and won the hearts of many of these former cynics. "His tabulation of accomplishment and debt had struck a chord with millions of postwar families, gathered in their suburban dens and living rooms."

The relatively new medium of television allowed voters to see into the lives of their candidates in a way never done before. And it was not only these candidates who were expected to be onstage—or "in a fishbowl," as Dick himself had said. "Candidates' families—not to mention their pets—had been only occasionally visible in American politics; Pat Nixon's presence on the 'Checkers' set was jarring and inexplicable to many. After 'Checkers,' families would become central participants in a new political dramaturgy." It was a Faustian deal for someone as private as Pat—a deal she may not have realized she was making at the time. But as a rising star in politics, Dick recognized that in such "family struggles . . . [there was] a new way to build public rapport."

The fact that Pat, Dick, Hannah, Frank, Tricia, and Julie were relatable folks "just like us" played well in Peoria and across the United States. Middle America related to this middle-class family in a way they couldn't to the elitist Jack and Jackie Kennedys of the political world. Dick's Whittier friend and former neighbor Vivian Brashamp wrote to both Pat and Dick, "We all admire the way you two campaign together as such a perfect team—somehow it keeps you from becoming a pure 'politician' and holds you in that group of 'down to earth' Americans who would like to feel they have one of their own in high office."

Seeing her as "one of them," viewers of the Checkers speech—both female and male—were outraged by what Pat had to suffer for the campaign. A concerned viewer, James du Pont, sent a telegram directly to Eisenhower a few days after the Checkers speech to express his indignation for Pat and what she had suffered for his campaign. "I know a guy with a heart like yours realizes why I include Mrs. Nixon in this telegram. But I wonder how many other men realize what sheer courage Pat Ryan Nixon showed last night? To have to just sit still, in a ringside seat, and watch as your husband battled for his life, to *not* be allowed to stand up for him, and finally *not* to cry in righteous rage,—well,—if that isn't the kind of good taste and great guts we need in politics today—I'm crazy." As a postscript, du Pont added: "I hope Pat was allowed to tear up ten telephone books, and then go home and have a good, long cry last night."

When daughter Julie interviewed Pat many years later for her biography of her mother, Pat still found this particular episode too painful to discuss. The fund crisis wounded both Nixons deeply, but while Dick drew strength from the triumph of the event, remembering its anniversary every year, Pat preferred to put the unpleasant experience aside and never speak of it again. She was not a politician who could put it into a career perspective. Attacks on her husband and their personal integrity inflicted deep scars upon her spirit that would never fully heal. Nixon historian Bob Bostock concurs: "The Fund Crisis really soured Pat Nixon on politics. It was a very rude awakening to just how bad it can get."

In late September 1952, though, there was no time for tearing up telephone books or having a good long cry. Pat may have wanted to cry even more after a disappointing meeting with Eisenhower. Summoned to Wheeling, West Virginia, to receive the general's benediction, Pat and Dick were both angry and resentful. Though perhaps it was not visible to the public at large, there was now an undercurrent of mistrust between Eisenhower and the Nixons; how could there not be, given Eisenhower's treatment of his running mate? Pat also took exception to Eisenhower's questions based on false claims that the Nixons' decorating expenses had been paid out of the fund.

Pat seethed as Dick explained again to Eisenhower that these were unfounded rumors. "Mrs. Nixon was quietly infuriated—her home and her integrity were sacrosanct territory. . . . That Ike even raised this question with them was a disloyalty Pat Nixon did not easily forget. It probably took her a while to forgive Eisenhower, if she ever did." Since childhood, Pat's friends had noted her tendency to forgive but not to forget.

This would be true in her ongoing relationship with both Eisenhower and his wife, Mamie. When Mamie shared her fur coat with Pat against the cold night air of Wheeling, Pat remained silent. Mamie, used to being deferred to as the wife of the famous general, was clearly uncomfortable, as well as clueless about Pat's feelings. "I don't know why all this happened when we were all getting along so well," Mamie blurted out. "Pat could not contain herself. 'But you just don't realize what we've been through,' she said. That ended the conversation."

The soon-to-be First Couple's second-class treatment of the Nixons during the campaign, and their seeming obliviousness to the trauma it caused, seemed unbelievable to Pat after what she and Dick had endured on live television for all the world to see. They had laid themselves wide open for the campaign and now were still being treated with little respect. Dick found it easier to move on, but his wife kept silent score.

On the way back to the hotel, Dick made an astute observation about his wife and her relation to politics after the crisis. As she held his hand tightly in the car, he knew how proud she was that they had won this battle against heavy odds. However, he also knew that any illusions his wife had held before about politics were now completely shattered. He understood "how much it had hurt her, how deeply it had wounded her sense of pride and privacy. I knew that from that time on, although she would do everything she could to help me and help my career, she would hate politics and dream of the day when I would leave it behind and we could have a happy and normal life for ourselves and our family." At this point Dick was fully aware of his wife's unhappiness, but they were both caught up in the political machine. There was no turning back: the steel wheels of the *Nixon Special* would soon be carrying them through the final weeks of a grueling campaign.

13

THE CINDERELLA GIRL OF THE GOP

Soon after the West Virginia meeting with the Eisenhowers, the Nixons were back on board the Nixon Special. Still wearing her Whittier-made outfits, Pat continued to smile for and wave to the crowds by Dick's side. Her cheerful demeanor belied the deep hurt she carried internally after the fund crisis ordeal.

The Drowns remained on the trail with the Nixons for the remainder of the season, with Helene offering astute campaign advice along the way. Helene understood the power of Pat in relation to female voters in a way the mostly male campaign team did not. Her status as family friend also gave her the power to cut though Dick's campaign minions and go straight to The Boss and his right-hand woman, Rose Mary Woods.

From one campaign stop, Helene wrote Dick a note on Hotel Washington stationery, noting the power of mentioning Pat's roots as a Democrat in his recent speech: "Even your most used stories . . . about Pat being a Democrat still draw the biggest hand." Helene's primary focus, however, was on Pat's appeal to female voters and how she should be used even more. "Women like to be mentioned in a speech, i.e. your wives and mothers know how much the dollar buys at the grocery store—or have loved ones in the service, etc." Finally, she encouraged Dick to include Pat more as a physical presence in his talks, noting the audience points he could score simply by presenting his beautiful spouse to the crowd. "Women love it when you bring Pat up to share your ovation at the end of the speech (the men enjoy looking at her too!)."

Both Helene and Jack were named charter members of the "Order of the Hound's Tooth," a "club" founded by Dick that included around fifty or so campaign aides and press on the train with the candidate during and after the fund crisis. The group's name was a reference to Eisenhower's "clean as a hound's tooth" comment before the candidate's fund crisis comeback speech. "The Senator said the organization's only function was social; that the members would be given symbolic hound's teeth" and would meet after the election, "win, lose or draw." (Hopefully Checkers was not required to donate to the hound's tooth fund.)

Canine motifs continued to dominate the campaign. At a GOP rally in Somerville, New Jersey, an enthusiastic crowd presented the Nixons with a "tax free doghouse from the Republicans of Union County" for the now famous Checkers.

Pat was still too traumatized by Dick's televised financial striptease to find much humor in the Order of the Hound's Tooth or even the "tax free doghouse." However, after the fund crisis, Pat's personal star was rising. She was suddenly being described in the media as "the Cinderella Girl of the G.O.P." A reporter wrote breathlessly that Pat "makes her own hats, does all her own housework, has never had a maid, worked every cent on her way thru college, and saved most of the $10,000 nest egg they had when he [Dick] got out of the service." With a wave of the postwar media wand, this thrifty, hardworking housewife was transformed into an idol others could look up to.

"Organizers of Republican women in the fifties drew superficially on the main metaphor of 'social housekeeping'—that women's political activism might help clean up government and society's ills. In the [1952] election, for example, women voters were encouraged to clean up the mess in Washington by voting Republican; they were given 'Ike and Dick' brooms to drive the point home." Pat's image as the perfect housewife fit this campaign aesthetic. But she also had the glamorous good looks and movie-star poise that allowed her to morph into Cinderella at public events as needed.

In the weeks that followed, Pat became more publicly integrated into the Nixon campaign team. Now the "We Like Nixon" banners that waved at campaign rallies became "We Like the Nixons." The young couple were portrayed in the media using additional tropes that fit their new image. The public now seemed "to like a Vice-Presidential nominee that acts more like a fighting football player than a politician, and a senator's wife who is as natural and unsophisticated as a farmer's daughter which she is."

Pat won many hearts and minds with her personal appearances on the campaign trail, and not just those of adults. A natural with children, Pat received numerous letters from this demographic, including one from six-year-old John H. Van Hart, who had designed a special campaign button for her emblazoned with "I Like Mrs. Nixon." He wrote:

Dear Mrs. Nixon:
I saw you in Princeton today and you shook hands with me. Everybody is kidding me because you called me sweetheart. But I don't mind. I just told them I was going to make up my own buttons. I am sending you one.

P.S. I wish I could vote for your husband, but I am only six.

Pat's popularity after the fund speech soared, and the massive public interest helped boost the last stages of the Eisenhower-Nixon campaign. Pat had become Dick's most valuable campaign asset. Pat reminded voters of the neighbor who cheerfully picked up your kids from school, helped you make slipcovers for your furniture (as she had once done for Helene), and still managed to cook a nice meal for her family before she went off to a cocktail party. Soon this "Cinderella Girl of the GOP" might just be trading her cocktail dress for a gown to wear at the inaugural ball.

———

After an exhausting journey of 46,000 miles, 92 speeches, 143 whistle-stop appearances, and 214 cities, both Pat and Dick were wiped out. They felt like zombies, but they had no choice but to keep going. The couple's press nemesis, columnist Drew Pearson, threw out an eleventh-hour accusation just five days before the election claiming that the Nixons had lied about the value of their property to qualify for a tax exemption. It was not until weeks after the election that the accusation was proven false: another couple with the names Patricia and Richard Nixon were the ones involved. Pat would always regret not suing Pearson for these unfounded charges.

Still, Pat and Dick managed to look fresh-faced in a photograph that ran in the *Washington Evening Star* on Election Day. The accompanying article, entitled "Mrs. Nixon's Cinderella Story Reaches Climax," gushed: "The next 'Mrs. Veep' is a modern age Cinderella—Mrs. Richard Nixon, a small-town girl who worked her way through college and married a poor but ambitious hometown boy who made good." The Eisenhower-Nixon ticket's victory was resounding—they won by over 6.5 million votes, and the Republicans picked up twenty-two seats in the House and one seat in the Senate, giving the new administration a Republican majority in both houses.

The new Mr. and Mrs. Veep had finally earned a respite, and they took Julie and Tricia to Florida for some downtime before the holidays. But the whirlwind of congratulations continued, and Pat found it hard to even make time to shop for clothes suitable for her new role as Second Lady. In December 1952, she wrote Helene saying, "I haven't done a thing about inaugural ball dress, etc. I'm really going to have to concentrate soon." But she was much more interested in telling her best friend about Julie and Tricia's upcoming appearance on a television Christmas program and making sure the Drown children got their Christmas gifts on time.

January 20, 1953, was warmer than usual for the dead of winter in Washington, D.C. The day was cloudy, but by noon the temperature registered at 49 degrees. Julie and Tricia provided good copy for reporters during the event. Four-year-old Julie and six-year-old Tricia arrived separately from their parents to the ceremony. After Truman's term officially ended at noon and "Ruffles and Flourishes" sounded, the two little girls were nowhere to be found. "At that moment, it was discovered that Julie and Tricia Nixon were not yet in their seats! Somewhere they and their escort had been delayed." Uncles Tom Ryan and Don Nixon, who had been tasked with watching the little girls, finally appeared with their small charges. The family proudly watched Dick sworn in as the vice president of the United States.

As the new VP's wife, Pat was still wearing her Republican cloth coat. Even now, there was no fur coat for her. Mamie, however, had no such qualms. Helene was at home watching the inauguration on television with her children. She typed up her sharp commentary for Pat as she watched the event unfold, and she didn't spare the new First Lady. "Mamie looks as if she would like a cigarette and has her mink coat spread apart showing well-sprawled legs! As usual you look like a model with your good Republican cloth coat neatly around you. Wish you could have a cup of coffee and a Parliament with us now."

However, that evening at the inaugural ball Pat stepped out in a stunning new emerald-green evening gown. She outshone the older First Lady by a mile. Helene opined privately to Pat: "Everyone agreed that Nettie [Rosenstein, the dress designer] didn't do well by Mamie in her ballgown—maybe the color is beautiful, but it makes her figure look horrible!" Mollie Parnis, who designed many of Mamie's outfits, explained that the First Lady had very little fashion sense but relied on others to 'bring all the accessories she would need . . . to make sure Mamie would be put together correctly.'"

Despite the younger woman's youth, beauty, and innate style, there seemed to be little jealousy between the two women. The new First Lady rapidly took the young Second Lady under her wing. Only a few days after the inauguration, Pat reported to Helene, "Mrs. E. invited me to receive with her at the White House. . . . She was most friendly—took me up to her living quarters afterwards and showed me all the rooms. They [she and the president] then invited Dick and I to receive with them at the reception for the diplomats. The usual procedure is to entertain separately, so they have been extremely friendly."

Unlike Eisenhower, who maintained a professional distance from his VP, Mamie would invite Pat over several times in the first half of 1953. Pat's initial wariness wore off, and the two women became real friends. Pat would follow the First Lady's example in many ways as she developed her own Second Lady stamp. As biographer Mary Brennan notes, the two women had much in common: "Both were frugal housekeepers who pinched pennies. Both understood the importance of dressing appropriately for the occasion. Both doted on the children in their lives and responded warmly to the youngsters they met in public. Both attempted to keep their private lives separate from their husbands' work." Both women disliked obvious social climbers and snobs. Mamie was "intolerant of those who 'put on airs.' Perhaps it is her Army background that makes her wary of social climbing and of those who pull rank."

Pat also followed Mamie's example with her correspondence, endeavoring to keep up with the massive amounts of mail she received from the public. Pat learned from Mamie how much a personal reply meant to those who wrote to the White House. Pat would write the First Lady admiringly after

Eisenhower's 1955 heart attack, relating how much Mamie's reply to a get-well card meant to the sender: "People are marveling that you have personally signed so much mail, and they are filled with admiration and appreciation."

Another area where Mamie excelled was in household management. She applied her thrifty military-wife ways to White House operations. "The staff swiftly found out they were dealing with a general's lady. The chief usher, J. B. West, discovered that she gave orders that were 'staccato, crisp, detailed, and final.'" "She checked for cleanliness by running a white glove over windowsills as she passed through rooms . . . and she insisted that vacuum cleaners be run frequently to erase evidence anyone had walked on the plush carpets."

Mamie and her husband had their very separate spheres, which they inhabited and ran unopposed. Eisenhower, first as Supreme Allied Commander and then as president, was fully in charge within this arena, with no input from his wife. Mamie, however, was the chief domestic advisor, running their household without question, just as her husband ran his military operations. This division of labor worked well as it applied to the White House. Mamie ran the East Wing with no interference from the president. "Ike trusted her to make decisions and did not challenge her authority over East Wing matters." The West Wing staff all quickly learned that Mamie had the final say on event scheduling for all groups that visited the White House.

The Second Lady's only prescribed duties were to be head of the Ladies of the Senate Club and to stand in for the First Lady as needed. Pat wrote Helene that the women of the Senate Club "are very sweet to me and are complimentary." Each Tuesday the women of that group gathered to volunteer for the Red Cross. Pat would often see Jackie Kennedy there as they rolled bandages together.

Lady Bird Johnson, also then a member of the Ladies of the Senate Club, remembered that Pat "was probably the most faithful presiding officer . . . [she] never missed a meeting, unless she was helping her husband on some trip." Lady Bird, who had a journalism background and a keen eye, also noted Pat's detailed reports on foreign countries, which had a "'new' aspect." Pat's abiding interest in other cultures and countries, which later would serve her unique brand of person-to-person diplomacy, was beginning to reveal itself.

First and foremost, though, Pat was a mother. She wrote Helene excitedly about Tricia's seventh birthday party: "A party for fourteen—movies, etc. A wonderful day! Even Daddy was home!" She also mentioned a competition that had developed between the sisters over their teeth. "Tricia lost a front tooth Sunday—she is growing up! Julie is very jealous because she hasn't lost any so is working madly at the front ones!"

Pat finally had to hire a full-time Swedish housekeeper as well as a man who came weekly to clean the windows and floors. "She needed the help because with the demands on her time, she was unable to do it all. She would rush home from official receptions, change, and go directly to the local supermarket. And most of the time, she'd prepare the meals." She was burning the candle at both ends, trying to be the perfect wife, mother, and now vice presidential spouse.

The orderly daily life that Pat hoped for after the inauguration didn't last long. On June 3, she wrote to Helene with excitement as well as some trepidation about their summer plans. "The President asked Dick what his plans were for the summer . . . he was told, 'I want you to go on a good will trip and take Pat with you.'" Clearly, even in these early days, the new president recognized Pat's powerful appeal in the media. It wasn't just Dick whom he wanted to represent the country abroad; it was the Pat and Dick Team.

The trip which would eventually take the Nixons to the Far East didn't take place that summer, however, and was instead pushed out to October. In the meantime, the Nixons were invited to the wedding of the season—and perhaps of the decade: the marriage of Dick's old friend Jack Kennedy and Jacqueline Bouvier, the "Inquiring Camera Girl" from the *Washington Times-Herald* who had interviewed Tricia about her father's nomination for vice president back in the summer of 1952. The Nixons had to send regrets to the September wedding due to Dick's previous plans to golf with Eisenhower in Denver.

Soon enough, social events were far from the Nixons' minds. With their goodwill tour rapidly approaching, both the Nixons had to study up on the countries they would be touring. One State Department official who accompanied the Nixons on their tour said of the pre-trip briefings, "Pat being Pat took it very seriously. She has a naturally phenomenal memory and she studied hard. When we got out of the country, we suddenly discovered that she was our walking encyclopedia. Whenever we needed to know statistics or facts, we'd ask Pat."

Even though both of the Nixons loved to travel, Pat was clear that this would be no pleasure trip—it would be hard work and even more time away from her girls. Dick himself noted in his memoirs how wrenching this good-bye was: "It was a painful farewell, especially for Pat, who had never been away from the girls for more than two weeks: now we would be away from them for more than two months." Frank and Hannah would again act as babysitters for the girls while their parents were away.

Pat had recently started a diary (one that would be short-lived due to so many demands on her time and energy). On October 5, the first day of the Far Eastern goodwill trip, she wrote: "Today the excitement was high—the anticipation great but the thought of leaving Julie and Tricia dominated and saddened the day." After reading bedtime stories to the girls and listening to Tricia read her first book out loud, Pat kissed both girls goodnight and tucked them into bed, "knowing that it would be the last time for months I would see them. The hour was black with sad thoughts because the love for them made any thoughts of the thrill of travelling seem as a mere nothing. But a job had to be done—so full force ahead." This was an internal battle she would fight constantly in the years to come.

In his memoirs, Dick wrote that Eisenhower felt he did not yet have enough knowledge of the Far East to make important decisions there. The new president also felt Truman had neglected both Asia and the Middle East. So Dick and Pat would be his eyes and ears on the ground as well as emissaries of diplomacy and goodwill from the States. It would also give Dick the perfect vantage point from which to judge relations between communist China and the rest of Asia.

Pat and Dick "each took one small suitcase full of winter clothes, one of summer, and one small bag for shoes, accessories, and underthings." Pat also saved time by packing and unpacking herself and doing her personal laundry, to the consternation of the servants in the many palaces the couple visited during their trip. Pat's DIY ways would persist all her life, winning hearts but sometimes puzzling those who thought such economies beneath her station.

The Nixons departed on October 5 from Washington, flying from there to San Francisco and then on to Hawaii. From there the vice presidential entourage headed on to the Far East. Stops included New Zealand, Australia, Indonesia, Malaya, Cambodia, Laos, Vietnam, South Korea, Japan, the Philippines, Hong Kong, Burma, India, Pakistan, Iran, and Libya. In 1953, this would be the longest trip ever undertaken by an elected American official. And no wife of an elected official had ever been included in such a journey. Dick would meet with leaders such as Shah Reza Pahlavi of Iran, the Republic of China's Chiang Kai-shek, Indian prime minister Jawaharlal Nehru, and President Sukarno of Indonesia, among many others. Pat would also meet many of these world leaders. To prepare herself to meet Nehru, "she calmed her nerves by telling herself, 'You are just Pat Nixon from Artesia.'"

In addition to her diary, Pat took shorthand notes on destinations she found particularly fascinating. In Bangkok she commented on the gorgeous flowers and dinner table settings as well as the floating markets they visited. She spent time with the youthful queen, who already had two children. Pat wrote, "Queen beautiful, 21 years old. Interested in American fashions . . . [her husband] didn't expect to be king but former king assassinated. Has two children—girl 3 years old and boy 1-1/2 years."

While in Taiwan, Pat wrote Helene about her stay with President and Madame Chiang Kai-shek. Pat and Madame Chiang would develop a warm friendship during this visit that would continue over the years.

The Second Lady broke precedent on this trip, deliberately asking to "visit schools and institutions rather than fill her time with the customary teas and shopping expeditions. Her activities were all the more remarkable because in many of the countries, especially the Muslim nations, wives rarely accompanied their husbands in public." The fact that Pat was seen in public with her husband in these countries was striking: the images of the couple in the international media sent a powerful message about women and their importance in American society.

Dick's Secret Service agent Jack Sherwood would later explain Pat's approach to meeting the public in her dual roles as campaigner and the wife of a public official: "In many ways, Mrs. Nixon applied and learned to improve her application of techniques through years of meeting people through all walks of life as a political campaigner and as a diplomat, the two professions overlapping and interweaving for subtle and effective results." Though this assessment is accurate, Pat's approach to people was not calculated. Her instincts were simple and genuine; as she wrote, "People can sense when another is friendly and genuinely interested. *Smile* is the universal language."

The visits to schools and orphanages connected Pat to Tricia and Julie as she traveled. One only needs to see a photo of Pat hugging a child to understand how much she missed her own daughters. She wrote to them from almost every stop on the Far Eastern trip, buying them numerous souvenirs along the way. Pat collected dolls from many of the countries she was visiting, including a Māori one for her girls.

Pat ignored State Department pressure to fade into the background of the tour. The way she presented herself instead was as the vice president's partner in diplomacy, a role sanctioned by Eisenhower himself. Pat's visibility on the 1953 goodwill tour was groundbreaking and empowering for women across the globe. When Pat returned home, she told reporters, "Everywhere I went it helped women."

On December 14, 1953, the Nixons at last returned to Washington, D.C., to much fanfare and two deliriously happy daughters. Pat was first to emerge from the Lockheed Constellation plane, followed by her husband. Dick spoke to the press, saying, "We are happy to be home, to see our children and friends, to look forward to a milkshake and a hamburger, and to enjoy the Christmas season." The trip was declared a huge success by both Eisenhower and the press.

Pat was immediately brought back down to earth, however, by her domestic responsibilities. Tricia had been ill much of the two months her parents were abroad, and both little girls were running temperatures when their parents arrived home. The Second Lady was back on mom duty immediately. Christmas Eve was only ten days away, and the holiday season was in full swing. All Pat wanted for Christmas was a long winter's nap and time at home with her girls. Despite the glamour and the thrill of international travel and diplomacy as Second Lady, as 1953 ended, she was beginning to consider a life outside of politics more seriously than before.

14

LADY OF FASHION

As president and First Lady of the land, President Eisenhower and Mamie symbolized the decade of the 1950s for many. To Julie Nixon, "Mamie and Ike were plain folks, as common as cherry pie. Mamie mirrored to an incredible degree the moods and mores of the Fifties. Happily, the emphasis on the old-fashioned virtues of wife and homemaker fit Mamie's natural lifestyle." As Nixon historian Bob Bostock points out, the couple were the last president and First Lady to be born in the nineteenth century; that helps explain why their attitudes—especially Mamie's—today seem old-fashioned.

Although the political, social, and cultural landscape of the mid-fifties was beginning to experience dramatic changes, the image of the perfect American woman, wife, and mother, à la Mamie, was still standard-issue. The accolades Pat received in the press in the early 1950s remained in line with these feminine ideals. In April, Pat received a telegram informing her that she had been selected as one of "America's Ten Best Dressed Republican Women." Articles lauded her as a "Lady of Fashion" who was able to balance her family duties, political events, and international goodwill tours with ease.

One reporter described Pat with about as much saccharin as possible: "Grace and charm are equally hers when, in a dainty apron, she prepares coffee for guests in her immaculate white kitchen, handsomely arranged for time-saving efficiency, or in her homey, tastefully decorated living room as she serves a cup of tea." Advertising executives of the era couldn't have come up with a more perfect vehicle to sell the Eisenhower administration than Pat. The Second Lady was made to sound more like a cleaning product or an automatic coffeemaker than a person. Beneath this hackneyed *Mad Men*–era portrait, Pat possessed depth and intelligence that often went unremarked upon by the press, especially in her early years in the public eye.

These descriptions focusing solely on Pat's looks and perfect housewife image ultimately backfired, contributing to later, more negative characterizations. As Second Lady, Pat was portrayed as so perfect that her own press image would be used against her. Some women may have felt they couldn't live up to the impossibly high standards that Pat represented—aspirational fantasies created by women's magazines (most often run by male publishers), not by Pat herself.

———

One day, Pat wrote proudly to Helene about a dinner she and Dick had just attended at the White House. "The President and Mrs. E. entertained in our honor. It was truly a brilliant party as only White House ones can be.... I was thrilled with all the splendor—the beauty of the rooms, the striking gowns of the guests, the music by red-coated Marines, the beautifully decorated tables." In the receiving line, Mamie had even introduced the young couple "as two of their best friends," much to Pat and Dick's surprise and delight.

The Eisenhower-Nixon relationship was much improved after a year in office, in large part thanks to the friendship that had developed between Mamie and Pat. Fond letters went between the two women in 1954, with both Tricia and Julie making birthday cards for the First Lady. Mamie sent warm replies to both girls.

The president also admired Pat, which in turn helped his relationship with his VP. Eisenhower understood Pat's appeal from a public relations standpoint in a way some of Dick's later administrative staff would not. Like the women he had encountered during his wartime service, Pat was tough and competent at her "job" selling the Eisenhower operation. She gained his respect by displaying these prized attributes—ones shared by many of the women in his administration, such as Oveta Culp Hobby, who as secretary of the Department of Health, Education, and Welfare was part of his cabinet. The president's grandson, David Eisenhower, agreed that the president appreciated Pat's competent can-do nature: "They had good chemistry and they liked each other."

Kate Halberstadt Bender, Pat's mother, circa 1900, prior to her marriage to Will Ryan. *(Courtesy of Julie Nixon Eisenhower Personal Collection)*

Photo of Pat, age four, at her home in Artesia (now Cerritos), California. When she was a child and teenager, her friends called her "Buddy." Her father called her "Babe" while her mother preferred "Thelma." She did not go by "Patricia" or "Pat" until she enrolled in college in 1931. *(Courtesy of the Richard Nixon Foundation, Julie Nixon Eisenhower Collection)*

The adventurous young Pat next to her roadster in the 1930s. She would always love exploring new places and the open road. *(Courtesy of the Richard Nixon Foundation, Julie Nixon Eisenhower Collection)*

(Above) Pat and Dick Nixon at a wedding shower on the eve of their marriage. They could not afford a professional photographer for the wedding itself, which took place on June 21, 1940, at the Mission Inn in Riverside, California. *(Courtesy of the Richard Nixon Foundation, Julie Nixon Eisenhower Collection)*

Pat's photo taken in San Francisco in 1944 at her husband's request. Dick kept this photo with him while he served in the Pacific as a naval officer during World War II. *(Courtesy of Whittier College Special Collections and Archives, Wardman Library)*

The Nixons with General Dwight "Ike" Eisenhower and his wife Mamie. Pat was initially wary of Ike after he considered dumping her husband as the vice-presidential nominee during the 1952 presidential campaign. Ultimately Dick and Pat would serve as Vice President and Second Lady under President Eisenhower for eight years and enjoy a good relationship. *(Courtesy of the Richard Nixon Foundation)*

Helene Drown and Pat playing golf together on January 24, 1955. Helene was the only friend that Pat could completely relax and be herself with. The fun-loving Helene would see Pat through the many ups and downs of political life. *(Courtesy of Maureen Drown Nunn Personal Collection)*

(Below) Pat with a cadre of her husband's loyal secretaries in April of 1956: Pat stands next to Rose Mary Woods (on Pat's immediate right), Dorothy Cox, Priscilla Everts, Margaret Brack, and Louise "Loie" Gaunt. Rose Mary or "Rose," Dick's head secretary, was often known as "The Fifth Nixon" due to her close relationship with the Nixon family and her fierce devotion to "El Boss." *(Courtesy of the Richard Nixon Foundation)*

The first meeting of Vice President Richard Nixon and Martin Luther King Jr., flanked by Second Lady Patricia Nixon and Coretta Scott King, at the first Independence Day celebration of newly independent Ghana and the inauguration of Ghana's Prime Minister Kwame Nkrumah in Accra, Ghana, on March 6, 1957. *(Courtesy of Dorothy Davis and the Griffith J. Davis Photographs and Archives)*

Vice President Nixon's shattered car windows in the aftermath of an attack by communist protestors in Caracas, Venezuela, on May 13, 1958. The VP and Second Lady were on a goodwill tour of South America when they came dangerously close to assassination in Caracas. Pat's calm in the face of the violence was much noted, and the couple were celebrated as heroes upon their return to the U.S. *(Courtesy of the Richard Nixon Foundation/NARA)*

Mr. and Mrs. Walter H. Annenberg at a party given for the Nixons in May of 1958. Walter and his wife Leonore ("Lee") were lifelong friends of the Nixons in both good times and bad. President Nixon would name Walter Ambassador to the Court of St. James in 1969. *(Courtesy of the Sunnylands Archive)*

Jewel Stradford Rogers Lafontant-Mankarious was a young lawyer and civil rights leader who became the 1960 Nixon presidential campaign's civil rights advisor. She would second Nixon's nomination at the 1960 GOP convention. In 1969, then-President Nixon began to consider her for a Supreme Court position. He would appoint her deputy solicitor general in 1972. *(Courtesy of John Rogers Jr. Personal Collection)*

(Below) A glamorous dinner party at the Coconut Grove in Los Angeles on August 3, 1961, including Pat, Dick, daughter Tricia, and movie star Elizabeth Taylor. (Tricia is in the forefront of the picture, first seat on the left, Taylor sits two seats behind her, closer to Pat.) *(Courtesy of the Richard Nixon Foundation, Julie Nixon Eisenhower Collection)*

(Above) Members of the Nixon campaign team at a 1961 party for Bob Finch. Rose Mary Woods and advance man H.R. "Bob" Haldeman (sporting a terrifying tan) soon became rivals. *(Courtesy of Maureen Drown Nunn Personal Collection)*

The Nixon family in 1962 with daughters Julie (bottom left) and Tricia, and their famous black-and-white spaniel, Checkers. The reference to Checkers during the "Fund Crisis" speech helped save Dick's VP spot in the 1952 presidential election. *(Courtesy of the Richard Nixon Foundation/NARA)*

Pat (alias "Miss Ryan") working in her husband's New York law office in December of 1965. These years in New York in between political campaigns were among the happiest times in Pat's life. *(Courtesy of the Richard Nixon Foundation, Julie Nixon Eisenhower Collection)*

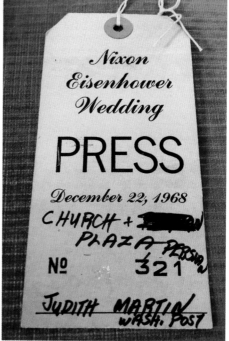

(Above) Julie Nixon and David Eisenhower were married on December 22, 1968, in New York. The couple declined a White House wedding, preferring a smaller, more intimate event instead. *(Courtesy of the Richard Nixon Foundation, Julie Nixon Eisenhower Collection)*

Washington Post reporter (and later etiquette columnist "Miss Manners") Judith Martin's press pass for Julie Nixon and David Eisenhower's wedding. Contrary to prevailing mythology, Martin did not crash Julie's wedding reception. She was in fact invited to report on the nuptial events. *(Courtesy of Judith Martin Personal Collection)*

(*Above*) Pat during her first term as First Lady, hosting a Christmas party for the diplomatic corps members' children at the White House on December 23, 1969. Pat adored children, and she would often scoop them up for spontaneous hugs. (*Courtesy of the Richard Nixon Presidential Library and Museum*)

After the Great Peruvian Earthquake hit on May 31, 1970, causing massive casualties, the First Lady led a humanitarian mission to Peru, traveling on an Air Force One jet loaded with relief supplies. On June 29, Pat and Peru's First Lady Consuelo Velasco climbed through rubble and inspected the damage near Lima for five hours (Pat wearing heels). Pat was later awarded Peru's highest honor, the Grand Cross of the Order of the Sun, for her outreach. (*Courtesy of the Richard Nixon Presidential Library and Museum*)

Still, the Nixons never became part of the Eisenhowers' inner circle during his administration. They primarily saw each other at official White House functions and related events. According to Dr. Michael Birkner, an Eisenhower biographer, "Ike socialized almost exclusively with an older cohort of friends. He probably saw Pat at various official functions, and no doubt liked her, but the Eisenhowers and the Nixons were never close, because they were not peers."

When administration officials pushed them to invite the Nixons to their Gettysburg, Pennsylvania, home, even Mamie resisted, saying of Pat, "What on earth would we talk about? We don't have anything in common!" Perhaps Pat's most damning fault in Mamie's eyes was that "she doesn't play bridge!" Former First Lady Bess Truman and Mamie had bonded over cards. But Pat had no use for games. Unlike these two First Ladies, she prioritized her official duties, putting them ahead of bridge, canasta, and mahjong, or other hobbies such as needlepoint.

Despite the clear respect and admiration between the First and Second Ladies, both women conformed without question to the rigid military hierarchy Mamie was so used to dominating. As wife of the commander in chief, Mamie expected to be the center of attention, while Pat's role was to be her handmaiden and the subservient junior spouse. As Julie Eisenhower notes, the First Lady was "an army wife whose husband rose to be the most sacred of all army gods. Mamie would have expected Pat to serve. It was one's duty." David Eisenhower agreed: "Mrs. Nixon was very deferential towards my grandmother."

Although Pat complied cheerfully with all Mamie's requests, she privately resented the fact that the extra duties were mostly social in nature and not what she considered useful or important work. As Pat confided in Helene Drown, "I would like to do part-time work rather than all the useless gadding I am expected to do."

Mamie's media image stood in vivid contrast to Pat's public persona as a Second Lady who worked tirelessly and visibly on behalf of her husband's administration and was consistently supportive of women conducting their careers and volunteering outside the home. Mamie's comments to *Today's Woman* magazine must have made the Second Lady cringe: "Let's face it. Our lives revolve around men and that's the way it should be. What real satisfaction is there without them? Being a wife is the best career life can offer a woman." Mamie made "clear by her every public utterance that she thought a wife's role entirely secondary and supportive."

Mamie's many years as a military wife had created a government-approved mindset. Midcentury military dictates found in protocol guides like *The Navy Wife* strongly encouraged wives of servicemen to be decorative, supportive, and silent regarding their husbands' careers, keeping their opinions to themselves. As the wife of the commander in chief, Mamie applied this prior indoctrination to her role as First Lady, opting for a limited approach to her First Lady duties.

Mamie's narrower view of her White House role was also due in part to her health issues. She had suffered for most of her adult life from insomnia, dizziness caused by Ménière's disease, and heart ailments. Her ill health often caused her to take vacations from the White House: she typically retreated to her mother's home in Denver or to the Eisenhower farm in Gettysburg. Rumors that she was an alcoholic were sometimes levied against her, but her grandson David categorically denies those rumors as "wholly false"; her family claims she was often unsteady due to her inner-ear issues.

At the White House, the First Lady spent much of her time in bed. "Mamie was also influenced by a skin specialist who told her if she spent one day a week in bed, she would never get a wrinkle. She spent so much time in her White House bed one of the maids nicknamed her 'Sleeping Beauty.'" And no one got between Mamie and her favorite soap opera: *As the World Turns*. "The staff learned not to schedule meetings with her in that time slot, because she invariably made them sit through the entire show—even commercials—before getting down to business."

As Julie herself noted, "If Mamie Eisenhower were First Lady today, she would be a fish out of water, subject to pressure—which she would have resisted—to be involved in First Lady projects, to project a prescribed image." She rarely gave interviews and only visited the Oval Office four times during her husband's presidency. "Everything Mamie undertook as First Lady was as Ike's wife." She did not regard herself as having a separate agenda as First Lady, or indeed any issues-based agenda at all. In contrast, Pat was individualistic, a product of her hardscrabble California upbringing, and possessor of an intelligent mind that needed meaningful occupation.

By the winter of 1954, not long after the Eisenhowers' dinner for the

Nixons took place at the White House, Pat and Dick had another serious discussion about their political future. Daughter Julie later wrote of her mother: "Although she still believed my father had much to give the country, she chafed at an existence in which they were not in control and in which their relationship with their boss, Dwight David Eisenhower, remained so delicate and tenuous."

On a piece of paper that Pat kept for years afterward, Dick listed out his concerns, both personal and political, regarding his vice presidential role. Chief among his personal reasons for getting out of the next presidential race was number three: "Wife—columns, *personal* stuff hurts." Pat was surely encouraged that Dick had begun to think about an exit strategy: perhaps she could finally live life as a lawyer's wife and stay-at-home mother, focusing on her family, and maybe later a part-time job that engaged her mind instead of official social duties, which she fulfilled flawlessly but often found to be devoid of real purpose.

———

By the beginning of the summer, Pat was looking forward to a vacation with her husband and the girls in Ogunquit, Maine. She wrote Helene excitedly about the rental she had located there. However, when vacation time arrived, Pat and the girls found themselves on their own, as Dick was stuck in Washington at work. She joked to her friend, "We are again enjoying a manless vacation. Perhaps not quite as the Governor has assigned us a *very handsome* state trooper to 'guard' us, drive us where we want to go, etc."

By October, Pat's enthusiasm for the political life seemed at a particularly low ebb. She confided again in her best friend, Helene: "Saturday night and all alone again! I am accustomed to it now." But in the next paragraph, she commented dryly that "the official schedule this year will be heavier than ever. One week there are four White House dinners. Oh joy, I can hardly wait."

Added to her evening commitments at the White House were scores of Washington luncheons, teas, fashion shows, and garden parties that she had committed to attend or endorse as Second Lady. Pat also reluctantly agreed to numerous press interviews—a chore she did not enjoy but felt compelled to participate in to support her husband, although she did her best to keep her girls out of the spotlight.

The year 1954 would see the congressional midterm election, and it was vital for the Republicans to campaign vigorously. Eisenhower kept his distance, conscripting Dick as his proxy in the campaign arena. The VP had to take slings and arrows meant for the general himself. While the president stayed at his in-laws' home in Denver for the first month of the campaign, playing golf in the afternoons after a few hours' work in the mornings, his vice president "traveled twenty-six thousand miles in six weeks, visiting ninety-five cities in thirty states and speaking on behalf of 186 GOP candidates. For the last three weeks he slept no more than five hours a night."

In the last weeks of the campaign, the personal attacks on the vice president were beginning to weigh more heavily. He later wrote that "the girls were reaching an impressionable age, and neither Pat nor I wanted their father to become the perennial bad guy of American politics." Dick wrote that the campaign had been so exhausting that "I had decided not to run again in 1956 unless exceptional circumstances intervened to change my mind." Due in large part to Dick's tireless campaigning, the defeat in an off-year election wasn't as damaging as it could have been. Still, the Democrats regained control of Congress, adding two seats in the Senate and twenty seats in the House.

Nixon's friend Father John Cronin had become one of his vice presidential speechwriters at this time. The two men had become fast friends during the Alger Hiss days and saw each other regularly. According to Cronin's oral history, he also acted as an intermediary or a conduit between the Nixons during this time. In the mid-fifties, Cronin claimed:

Once I'm quite sure he wanted me to intervene in a family dispute. I got a call from Rose [Woods] asking if I'd go to his house one evening which I did. Pat was quite surprised: she answered the door and hadn't expected me. I said, "I got this request, and I don't know what it's all about." So, it's around dinner time, so she gave me a cocktail. I stayed for a while, but he didn't come so I left. So, I talked to Rose the next morning, and she said, "Well they had a fight that morning, and I guess he wanted you to intervene, but he was too shy to tell you."

Cronin later gave an interview in which he said he felt "Nixon's marriage was strained . . . by the 1950s, it had become a marriage of convenience."

Pulitzer Prize–winning historian Gary Wills, who interviewed Father Cronin for his book *Nixon Agonistes*, claims that Cronin said he had "noticed that Nixon wasn't going home for a certain period but using the hotel he kept for presiding over the Senate or other duties. N[ixon] said there was no real problem but asked C[ronin] to go pick up some papers he needed from the house. Pat flew at him saying Oh no he can't use a priest to get back! The priest knew of other quarrels—e/g she made him swear to never run for office again."

The other intermediary employed by Dick when things got tense at home was his mother, Hannah. Though Pat and Hannah were never close, Pat had deep respect for and trust in her mother-in-law. When Dick was unable to handle Pat's temper, he "would telephone his mother in Whittier and ask her to talk to Pat. Hannah had her ways and, with her sympathy and understanding, would smooth things over." Biographer Lester David claimed that "on at least one occasion, a quarrel was so serious that Pat wouldn't talk to her husband for days and intervention by telephone did no good." Hannah got on a plane and came to Washington to "act as peacemaker. Her way was to ignore her son and concentrate on Pat and her grievances. She listened well and, before long, Pat's anger ebbed and she unfroze."

While there is little doubt there was tension between the Nixons due to their backbreaking schedules and the lack of family time together, Pat's letters to Helene, the vice presidential itineraries, and press reports show that Pat was fully engaged both at home and with her Second Lady duties. Tempers were often frayed by the constant work both partners were putting into Dick's career. And Pat clearly missed her husband's presence at home and on vacations. But neither partner had given up on the relationship.

———

As the calendar pages turned to 1955, the Pat and Dick Team was tasked with another goodwill mission: this time to Central America and the Caribbean. The couple set off again on February 6 and would be gone for a month to bolster the American image (and tamp down Communism) in the region. During this extended trip, the Second Couple would visit Cuba, Mexico, Guatemala, El Salvador, Honduras, Nicaragua, Costa Rica, Panama, the Virgin Islands, Puerto Rico, and Haiti. Pat won praise for her visits with children at orphanages and hospitals. In San Salvador she visited a child rehabilitation clinic, doling out candy and hugs to the children in equal measure.

Despite the U.S. State Department's reluctance, Pat insisted on visiting the inhabitants of a Panamanian leper colony. "Pat sought to influence public attitudes about leprosy by making an unprecedented visit to the Palo Seco Leprosarium. . . . When she shook hands with some of the lepers who had been almost cured, she was moved." By reaching out to those suffering from leprosy, a feared and sadly neglected population, Pat was decades ahead of Princess Diana's similar engagement with AIDS patients. Like the princess in the 1980s, Pat became a queen of the people's hearts in Panama in the 1950s: her visit to the leprosarium was much publicized in that country.

When Pat later gave a speech about this experience at the Ladies of the Senate Club, she was asked if she had hesitated to shake the hands of the patients of the leprosarium. She said simply, "No, because I honestly feel that when you do what you know is right, God will take care of you. I was not afraid."

1955 also brought a new and powerful couple into the Nixons' lives. While in California visiting the Nixon family and the Drowns, the Nixons began a unique friendship that would endure over many years. FBI director J. Edgar Hoover and his partner and FBI second-in-command Clyde Tolson hosted a dinner in honor of the Second Couple at the Hotel del Charro in La Jolla. This new boutique hotel built by Texas multimillionaires (and major Eisenhower donors) Sid Richardson and Clint Murchison had quickly become a hub for the rich, famous, and politically well connected—especially for stars of the Eisenhower administration. Sometime that summer of 1955, Dick "arrived poolside in suit and tie with his wife, Pat . . . the occasion cemented social ties between the two couples."

The Nixons and the two G-men soon became close friends, enjoying lunches, cocktails, and social gatherings together. "Over the course of the 1950s, Hoover and Tolson spent enough time with the Nixons to develop regular haunts, favorite foods, and inside jokes, the stuff of which long-term friendships are made." Pat and Dick sent invites to both Edgar and Clyde as a couple—just as Clyde and Edgar issued invitations to Pat and Dick. The foursome clearly enjoyed each other's personalities. Edgar particularly enjoyed relaxing at the Nixons' Washington home, which Pat always made warm and welcoming for both him and Clyde. This was an important friendship that would serve the vice president well politically as the years went by in Washington.

———

Tricia and Julie were back in school in September, and life settled into its familiar fall rhythms. The autumn social season had begun in full force. Around 5 p.m. on September 24, 1955, Pat and Dick had just returned home from the afternoon wedding of one of Nixon's secretaries, Drusilla Nelson, to Henry Dworshak, son of Idaho's senator. The phone rang while Pat was upstairs changing out of her wedding attire.

Dick picked up the call and found Jim Hagerty, the White House press secretary, on the line. "Dick, the President has had a coronary." The VP was so shocked he didn't reply for several seconds; Hagerty thought he might have been disconnected. "Are you sure?" Dick gasped. Hagerty replied, "We are absolutely sure." Dick's next call was to his good friend Bill Rogers asking him to come over. He then went upstairs to break the news to Pat, and next called Rose Mary Woods, who was still at the wedding reception, to come to the house to handle his calls.

In the weeks that followed, the Nixons had to carefully present themselves and their substitute status to a shaken public. The vice president and Second Lady "were on guard against any appearance of assuming President or First Lady roles." While Dick stepped in for the president, moderating important meetings and carrying out presidential duties at the White House, the couple together "took over the entertaining of foreign dignitaries, and their days lengthened to an average fourteen to sixteen hours."

Dick later described this presidential purgatory: "My problem, what I had to do, was to provide leadership without appearing to lead." His problem was also Pat's problem. She would have to walk the same tightrope as her husband: act as First Lady while not moving beyond the limits of her role as Second Lady.

While the vice president was lauded for his steady hand during the crisis, the Second Lady also received glowing reviews, especially from the State Department. "During the dark days following President Eisenhower's heart attack, she more than once rescued the department from a difficult dilemma of international protocol by quietly shifting her busy schedule to greet visiting dignitaries," including hosting the presidents of Italy, Brazil, Guatemala, and Uruguay.

Pat sent the absent First Lady an affectionate letter in October 1955, just after Dick had visited the president in Denver. She wrote "that our thoughts and prayers have been with you constantly. We join in the rejoicing of people everywhere that the President is improving." Pat also wished "there were some way I could lighten your burdens. At any rate, please know that you have my love and affection always."

Mamie replied on October 18 to Pat, thanking her for her "warm and encouraging letter. The President was as deeply touched as I was when I read him your kind sentiments and joins me in warm appreciation for this further example of the way that you have brightened our spirits during this time of anxiety."

After seven weeks of recuperation, the Eisenhowers finally returned to Washington in early November. But the "increase in social activity was to become permanent" for the Nixons. Pat continued to help Mamie by assuming many of the First Lady's entertaining duties so that Mamie could stay by her husband's side.

While Pat was drowning in White House social obligations, her husband was mentally recharting their course. "Fully engaged in leading while trying not to look like it, Nixon was no longer thinking of quitting politics, his promise to Pat notwithstanding." The "exceptional circumstances" he had mentioned in 1954 had presented themselves. A presidential heart attack had changed the game.

The day after Christmas, Dick was called into the president's office to talk about the future. After some casual chatting, Ike mentioned that the VP's poll ratings were low. Perhaps he should consider a cabinet post instead of the vice presidential slot in the 1956 election? "Eisenhower looked at Nixon the way a general does at an up-and-coming colonel. He believed that the young politician needed seasoning, maturity, and training in management and leadership . . . Nixon could only think of the political ignominy of demotion. He took it personally."

So did Pat.

After the fund crisis, the Nixons were about to experience a renomination crisis, with the president letting Dick dangle until he could see which way the political wind was blowing. By late February, what became known as the "Dump Nixon" movement had gained momentum. The effort, led by former governor of Minnesota and Eisenhower's cabinet-level advisor on disarmament Harold Stassen, was deeply upsetting to both Dick and Pat. "It was 1952, redux. Ike wanted Nixon gone—but was leaving it to him to cut his own throat, to minimize the political cost."

Even Dick's friend Jack Kennedy was aghast at the president's behavior toward his friend. JFK told historian Arthur Schlesinger, "He [Eisenhower] is terribly cold and terribly vain. In fact, he is a shit." David Eisenhower also claimed that "Nixon was a much nicer man, much easier to be around" than his grandfather had been. The president knew his VP was destined for more but was not about to let on that he thought this. He had a more impersonal military mindset in terms of his subordinates. Dick was a political animal, however, and he was subsequently baffled by his boss's behavior. "What [Ike] was actually dealing with was a young man who's running for President. He's not about to take a demotion. That's a political rule."

Pat was concerned and wary as she watched this behavior from the president. While she was looking for an eventual exit ramp from public life, she was not about to allow anyone to push her husband off the ticket. Pat told her daughter Julie that her father had been "more depressed than she ever remembered" in the weeks that followed. He was so worn down that he "checked in to Walter Reed Medical Center that winter suffering from exhaustion and various ailments, both real and imagined."

Still, Pat and Dick were good soldiers, representing the Eisenhower administration on a five-day trip to Brazil for the inauguration of the new president in Rio. As always, Pat was balancing her roles as the glamorous globe-trotting Second Lady with that of devoted mother to her two girls. She wrote Helene that "the trip to Brazil was the usual busy one" and complained of the "endless formal parties . . . However, on the sunny side, Rio was the most spectacularly beautiful city I have ever seen." In almost the next sentence, Pat changed roles, from Madam Diplomat back to

"Housekeeper Pat [who] must rush for the kitchen—children will be here for lunch in minutes."

In June the Nixons would be sent off again on a trip to Asia with stops in Hawaii, the Philippines, and Turkey. The Second Couple was indispensable to the administration as their eyes and ears on the ground and as sophisticated diplomats. Despite their hard work and devotion, Eisenhower still allowed Dick to think he might not be up to snuff for the 1956 VP slot.

The president's seeming disregard for her husband's talents and his waffling on the renomination were upsetting for Pat, but David Eisenhower noted that "Pat understood maybe better than Richard Nixon . . . the impersonality that has to govern professional relations at that level." Still, being placed in purgatory by the president along with her husband—not once but now *twice*—brought out her fighting spirit. When the Nixons saw the Drowns at Easter, Pat made her own position clear: "No one is going to push us off the ticket."

15

GRACE UNDER FIRE

By late April 1956, the question of Dick being back on the Eisenhower presidential ticket seemed to be on its way to resolution. On April 25, the president gave a press conference saying that his VP had not "'reported back' his decision yet, which made it clear that Nixon would have to be the one to come to him." The next day, the young man met the president in the Oval Office to formally tell him he would like to stay on the ticket. "With Jesuitical innocence, Eisenhower asked him why he had taken so long to say so."

Still, the controversy surrounding Dick as VP continued with Stassen's dogged quest to run him off the ticket. Daughter Julie later wrote, on July 23, Stassen "launched a formal campaign to replace my father with Christian Herter, the governor of Massachusetts." Once again, there was no lifeline thrown from the president to the VP. However, as historian Irwin Gellman writes, the whole Dump Nixon initiative was doomed to failure from the outset. "Stassen had little influence in the GOP, Herter had no interest in the vice presidency, and by the time the convention opened, Nixon already had enough committed delegates to win the nomination."

In August, the Republican convention was held in San Francisco. Pat had by now learned how to hold court with the women's press corps on her own terms. She reached out proactively to female reporters at the convention, inviting them to a 10 a.m. coffee hour on the eleventh floor of the Mark Hopkins Hotel. The invitation explicitly stated: "This is not a press conference, and no politics will be discussed."

That evening, the Second Lady was rewarded with cheers when chairman Leonard W. Hall pointed out Pat sitting in the mezzanine area. The slightly embarrassed Pat "got a roaring ovation, the loudest thus far at the convention.

Cheers rang out through the hall, signs were hoisted aloft and the band played 'California Here I Come.'"

Finally, on August 22, Dick's renomination for the vice presidency was announced and approved, with Stassen forced to second the nomination. Another crisis averted. But as fate would have it, the couple's triumph was tinged with tragedy. Frank Nixon had fallen gravely ill during the last days of the convention, and Pat and Dick hurriedly flew to Whittier. Frank temporarily rallied, and Dick was able to return to the convention to give his acceptance speech. The Nixons then returned to Whittier to be with Frank and Hannah as well as Julie and Tricia, who by now were staying with their grandparents. Though Frank improved for a time, heartened by his son's victory, he would die on September 4.

In the midst of all this sadness, the Nixons were receiving messages of congratulation, some from international quarters. Madame Chiang Kai-shek and her husband had remained friends with the Nixons after their 1953 visit to Taiwan. Madame Chiang wrote Pat on September 5, "I was so delighted that Mr. Nixon was renominated by the Republican Party, and I am sure that he and President Eisenhower will be successful in the November election." However, the real purpose of Madame Chiang's letter was to thank Pat for sending her a hair dryer as a gift. Pat's woman-to-woman approach to diplomacy was pure genius.

Soon enough, though, the parties and praise were over, and the Second Couple was back on the trail for Campaign Roadshow, Part Deux. This time they were upgraded from a campaign train to a campaign plane. Despite the more convenient method of travel, the schedule this time was even more brutal. The couple would visit thirty-two states by chartered plane in sixteen days. When Julie asked her mother years later how she coped with the hectic schedule, "she replied with a wry smile, 'We killed ourselves.'"

On November 6, 1956, all the Nixons' hard work paid off. Eisenhower defeated Adlai Stevenson a second time, this time with the Eisenhower-Nixon ticket pulling in 57 percent of the vote. Just like the 1952 election, the 1956 one was again powered by the female vote.

"The elections of 1952 and 1956 showcased the impact and importance of the women's vote. In an unprecedented turnout of the 1952 election, nearly 17.6 million women voted for Dwight D. Eisenhower out of the nearly 34 million votes cast in his favor. Never before had a political campaign gone so far to court the women's vote as did the Eisenhower campaign."

For her second inauguration, Pat worked in advance with beauty mogul Elizabeth Arden on her gown, visiting Arden's salon on Fifth Avenue for fittings. Even though the design was a secret, interest in Pat's outfit was so high that sketches were leaked. Julie remembered that for several weeks before the inauguration, she and Tricia would open "Mother's closet door at least two or three times daily to look at her ice-blue Elizabeth Arden gown with its dazzling bodice of pearls and crystal." But the two girls were seriously disappointed by their own attire, short age-appropriate party dresses instead of the "ballgowns" like their mother's that they had envisioned. Tricia recalled that her mother had in fact ordered long ballgowns to match hers for her daughters, but short ones had been sent by mistake. Pat clearly paid close attention to her little girls' requests despite her heavy official obligations.

Aside from conversation about Pat's gown, Arden also praised Dick as Pat's "courageous husband and the grave responsibilities of his errand abroad . . . to assume which I can think of no one better fitted or more able." The "errand" Arden was referring to was Dick's mission to visit Hungarian refugee camps in Vienna, Austria. The Hungarians in those camps were fleeing Soviet repression after a Hungarian revolt against Soviet control that October. Dick had traveled to Vienna to study the issue and make recommendations about bringing Hungarian refugees to the United States.

What Arden and the public would never know was that Dick had proposed that Pat lead the mission herself. The vice president suggested that "Mrs. Eisenhower or his own wife fly to Austria on Air Force One and pick up a plane load of refugees—as a 'mission of mercy.'"

Dick's confidence in his wife and her deepening diplomatic abilities is evident here. Though this particular trip didn't materialize, it would not be the last time her husband suggested Pat fly solo on a diplomatic, humanitarian mission. Even as early as 1956, the vice president was keenly aware of the popularity his wife possessed and how it could be leveraged on a global scale.

The new year brought little rest for the Second Couple. By late February they were back on the road with another goodwill trip, this time a three-week diplomatic mission to Morocco, Tunisia, Liberia, Uganda, Sudan, Libya, and Italy.

The most important stop on the agenda was Ghana's independence ceremony in Accra on March 7. The ceremony garnered much international publicity and ignited an important new friendship. At the celebrations, "Nixon unexpectedly met the Reverend Martin Luther King Jr., fresh off his leadership of the Montgomery, Alabama, bus boycott. The photograph of their encounter appeared in Black media throughout the U.S., sending the message that Nixon had his ear to the rising civil rights movement as well as to Africa."

A historic photo by Black photographer Griffith Davis shows MLK and his wife, Coretta Scott King, with Pat and Dick, both couples stylishly dressed to celebrate the historic conversion of Ghana from British rule to full independence. Dick and MLK would make plans here for another meeting once they returned home. Journalist and Nixon admirer Ethel Payne came to Ghana to cover the independence ceremonies and noted in her dispatches home the important meeting between the two young leaders. The relationship between the two men, which hadn't yet moved forward on the home front, was jump-started by their meeting in Accra.

Thanks to their fortuitous encounter in Ghana, the VP and MLK would have their official meeting in Washington that June. MLK and Ralph Abernathy arrived at Dick's office on June 13 expecting an hour-long appointment, but the meeting lasted almost three hours as the men discussed civil rights issues. Though not everyone in the Black press agreed, the Nixons' friend Ethel Payne, who covered this historic meeting, felt that the VP "was the hero of the day. Unlike the Democrats who pledged to support civil rights, this Republican was taking tangible action."

Dick had long supported civil rights causes. He was an honorary member of the NAACP due to his work in Congress. He was the first in the Eisenhower administration to publicly support the *Brown vs. Board of Education* Supreme Court decision in 1954, and he would soon back the Civil Rights Act of 1957.

Pat shared her husband's commitment to civil rights both at home and abroad. Her skillful exercise of "soft" diplomacy on the ground in Africa won her much praise. Soon after the trip the Capital Press Club, an organization of African American newspaper reporters, gave Pat its 1957 International Relations Award for her "good will activities among the people of eight African countries."

Pat's dry sense of humor also charmed staffers traveling with her in Africa. Air Force major James "Don" Hughes joined the Nixon VP detail in 1958 along with Marine colonel Robert "Bob" Cushman. The staffers' first journey with the Nixons was the trip to Ghana. No vice president had ever had military aides, and Hughes remembered, "Both Mrs. Nixon and Vice-President Nixon didn't want us!" But President Eisenhower insisted they take aides with them for protection.

As the Nixons were preparing for the evening's Independence Day events, Dick suddenly realized he was missing his trousers. Hughes and Cushman let loose with expletives, as they now would have to drive sixty miles back to the plane to retrieve the pants. The two aides were able to retrieve the misplaced item and get back just in time for the evening event.

When Hughes got in the car with Pat and Dick, she told Cushman quietly, "Colonel, I was happy to hear you got the old man's pants!" Hughes laughed as he recalled, "She just let that lay there while we turned purple." Hughes and Cushman realized instantly that Pat had overheard their expletive-laden commentary through the thin hotel walls and the open windows. "Mrs. Nixon got her share of Marine and Air Force language while we figured out what to do!" Their profanity-laced tirade and labeling of her husband as "the old man" didn't faze Pat; to the contrary, she was in on the joke.

When the Nixons finally touched down again in D.C. on March 21, they were welcomed back into a new home. Just before leaving Africa, the couple had purchased 4308 Forest Lane. Their new residence was in Wesley Heights, an affluent suburb just south of the Nixons' previous home in Spring Valley. The couple had learned their lesson from their previous home purchase. This time they scoured the fine print for racially restrictive covenants. One was also embedded in the Wesley Heights contract, and the couple took pains to strike the offensive covenant before closing. Journalist Ethel Payne and other members of the Black press took note.

Thankfully, three of Pat's good friends took care of the packing and unpacking for her, so when she and Dick returned from their trip, the furniture was placed exactly as Pat had wished. Pat must have been relieved to kick off her shoes and deal with smaller issues, like the new kittens that Tricia's cat Puff Ball had given birth to in Julie's toy baby carriage—"a step up, since her last litter had been born in a trash can."

The English Tudor–style house had once been owned by FDR's attorney general and was perfect for the privacy-seeking Pat. The home was located on a "dead-end street and had a large backyard surrounded by dense woods." The family now enjoyed more space in the eleven-room house than either Pat or Dick had ever had before.

The home became Pat's favorite of all her many residences, though it required a major decor overhaul to achieve the sunny light-filled look it eventually acquired. When reporter Bess Furman visited the home, she was impressed by the many treasures the Nixons had acquired on their international travels, which lent the home an exotic flair. "The chief conversation pieces in the room were matching copper butterfly candelabra from a Korean temple in Seoul. In close competition with the big copper butterflies was a small teakwood chest inlaid with mother of pearl." This last item had been given to Mrs. Nixon by Madame Chiang.

For the dining room, Pat selected a Karastan rug that her girls called "the cookie rug," as its busy patterns covered up any crumbs or debris that happened to fall upon it. The kitchen was a favorite spot for the Nixon girls: bright and cheery with a lemon and green vine design, it was their favored spot for their after-school snacks and tête-à-têtes with their mother. Pat's fudge was an eagerly anticipated after-school treat. The girls and Pat cherished these times together, alone and out of the political spotlight.

———

The late fall brought more health challenges for the president. On November 25, 1957, he suffered a stroke. This turned out to be relatively mild, but the illness led Eisenhower to work with his vice president; Bill Rogers, his attorney general; and Foster Dulles, his secretary of state to create a procedural plan should he become incapacitated and unable to continue his duties. Dick would act for the president if needed for the short term until he recovered, as he had done already during the heart attack episode, or for the balance of the Eisenhower term if the president was incapable of returning to his job.

After the stroke, the pressure on the Nixons to entertain as substitutes for the Eisenhowers increased. Once again, the couple worked overtime to keep up with their mounting official duties. That March, Pat badly strained her back lifting Julie up to see a bird's nest; so severe was her resulting pain that Helene had to come to Washington to help her with the family while Pat entered the hospital. Sonar heat treatments helped but didn't completely alleviate her pain.

1958 was an election year, and recession seemed to be taking hold of the country; Dick felt he should be in the nation's capital at this time and not abroad on another ceremonial trip. However, under pressure from the president, Dick reluctantly agreed to go to South America and take Pat with him. Dick was sure that the trip itself would prove "relatively unimportant and uninteresting." Though not fully healed from her back injury, Pat pulled herself together for yet another grueling goodwill trip with her husband that April.

The central objective of the trip was for the Nixons to represent the United States at the inauguration of the newly elected Argentine president, Arturo Frondizi, in May. Their presence would show American support for democracy abroad, tamping down communist sentiment and demonstrating the United States' firm rejection of dictatorships. What had been presented to the Nixons as a week away from home soon expanded into almost three weeks abroad. The Nixons would visit Argentina, Bolivia, Colombia, Ecuador, Uruguay, Paraguay, Peru, and Venezuela, with a short stop for refueling in Trinidad.

The initial stops, in Uruguay, Argentina, Paraguay, and Bolivia, went fairly smoothly except for the Nixons missing the Frondizi swearing-in ceremony due to traffic issues. However, Lima was where the real trouble began. On May 7, local police discouraged Nixon's trip to San Marcos University, scheduled for the next morning. After much internal debate and consultation with staff at the university, the VP decided to go, despite hearing chants of "Fuera Nixon, fuera Nixon, fuera Nixon!" (Throw Nixon out!) all evening outside his hotel. After a sleepless night, Dick asked Pat to stay put at the hotel, where she anxiously awaited his return.

Arriving at the university, Dick faced a mob of some two thousand rioters. After trying to address the crowd and enduring a pelting with rocks, the vice president and his small entourage were forced into a slow retreat. When the VP returned to the hotel, he encountered another angry mob. "Pat endured a nerve-racking vigil as she watched out the hotel window as a frenzied crowd threw things at her husband as he entered the hotel."

Back in Washington, Tricia and Julie heard the news from Peru even before the VP's office received word of trouble there. The two daughters were home from school as usual for lunch and saw a bulletin on television "announcing that Vice President and Mrs. Nixon had been attacked in Lima, Peru, by a mob. There were no further details. Almost hysterical, Tricia ran into our parents' bedroom and telephoned the office." By 3 p.m., office staffer Loie Gaunt had let the girls know through the school principal that their parents were safe.

From here, things deteriorated further. The last stop on the Nixons' itinerary was Caracas, the capital of Venezuela. Dick later wrote that "the State Department considered Venezuela potentially the most important stop of the entire South American tour." Marcos Perez Jimenez, the Venezuelan dictator, had recently been overthrown. The United States had granted Jimenez sanctuary, but the Nixons were there to show their support for the new democratic regime. "We were in a position of having to explain how we could grant sanctuary . . . and to demonstrate that we believed in democracy and preferred the new ruling junta."

Hughes had been on the phone with his wife, Betty, earlier that day. She told him that Washington intel "knew in advance it wouldn't be a friendly visit." Pat and Dick's courage would be tested almost immediately by unfriendly mobs intent on intimidating their American guests. The minute the group got off the plane at Maiquetia Airport on May 13, they knew they were in trouble.

Julie described the scene from her mother's point of view: "At first the spit looked like giant snowflakes, but it turned to foul, dark blotches when it hit my mother's red suit." Despite these indignities, Pat still "stopped to hug a child who had given her flowers." She also leaned "across the barricade to pat the shoulder of a young girl who had just cursed and spit on her. The girl turned away in shame."

The vice president cut the welcome ceremony short, and the entourage headed quickly to their cars. Before anyone could get into the vehicles, Pat spotted a gob of spit on the seat. "She beat me to it," related Hughes; "she wiped it off with her hankie and didn't say a word." Hughes got into the jump seat of the car, while the driver and Secret Service agent Dale Grubb were seated in front. Mrs. Nixon and the wife of Venezuela's foreign minister were in the backseat. The vice president was in the car ahead of them, accompanied by his Secret Service agent Jack Sherwood and the Venezuelan foreign minister.

As the group sped off toward the embassy, the situation worsened dramatically. When their cars approached the outskirts of the city, communist mobs surrounded them and began hurling bricks and rocks at the vice presidential motorcade. Hughes would never forget "my feeling we were going to be seriously hurt, if not killed, because the faces of the people outside were pure hate. . . . They were mouthing all the epithets they could think of, and they were throwing big rocks and projectiles." A brick shattered the window of Pat's car, and Grubb began preparing his gun to fire. A truck had blocked the motorcade and things looked grim.

While many people would have been legitimately hysterical under such dangerous circumstances, Pat displayed a preternatural sense of calm during the assault. Hughes had a bird's-eye view of her demeanor, and he was astounded. "Mrs. Nixon had her arms around this lady [the foreign minister's wife] and [was] trying to calm her down, she was weeping and speaking incoherently but Mrs. Nixon had her throughout the entire thing. . . . I tell you she showed me a lot of fortitude because I was really concerned that we weren't going to make it." Dick was constantly checking from his car as best he could to get eyes on Pat. From his viewpoint, "Pat appeared to be talking to the Foreign Minister's wife as calmly as though the trouble were no worse than an afternoon traffic jam on the Hollywood Freeway."

Next, one of the communist demonstrators whacked the vice president's car with an iron pipe, shattering the glass. Shards hit interpreter Vernon Walter's mouth. The foreign minister was cut in the eye and bleeding profusely. Sherwood was hit with a projectile and lost a tooth. Then the angry mob of more than five hundred got hold of the vice president's car and began to rock it with the intent to haul the VP out and set his car on fire.

Suddenly, the car was able to move forward through the blockade as a path became clear thanks to a press truck up ahead. Mrs. Nixon's car followed her husband's vehicle deliberately down the wrong side of the road. Rose Mary Woods, who had been stuck far behind in the last car of the motorcade, was finally able to get away from the mob thanks to a tear gas bomb that cleared a path. Woods recalled: "I was in the last car. . . . Two of our windows were broken. I received two cuts, one near my eye, and another on my wrist. I didn't realize how scared I was until it was over." At Dick's direction, instead of heading to their previously designated lodgings, the party went straight to the American embassy, where Hughes later remarked they found "American soil and a little bit of heaven."

President Eisenhower had ordered a precautionary American troop movement into Caribbean bases for the Nixons' protection. Despite the scary circumstances, Dick thought this was unnecessary and issued a press statement the next day saying diplomatically that there was no need for outside assistance, as the new government now had the situation under control. After a sleepless night spent at the securely guarded American embassy and an interminable luncheon the next day, the Nixon entourage gladly left Caracas for the safer haven of Puerto Rico. President Eisenhower had asked them to delay coming home by one day to give staff time to prepare for a celebratory welcome-home event.

The Nixons returned home on May 15 as American heroes. Government officials were given the day off and a "welcoming reception" was quickly arranged. Fifteen thousand people were present to cheer for the Pat and Dick Team, who had presented themselves so courageously under hazardous conditions. President Eisenhower himself came to the airport to greet the Second Couple with the cabinet, congressional leaders, and diplomats.

Both parents must have hugged their girls extra tight that day. Dick recalled, "Tricia and Julie were waiting for us at the bottom of the [airplane] stairs, and they could hardly contain their tears of joy." Julie remembered, "The next two hours were a blur of excitement as we were ushered into President Eisenhower's open-top car for a ceremonial ride with him and my parents to the White House." A hundred thousand people lined the streets. Julie noted that for many years afterward, she had no idea how close her parents had come to death in Caracas. Her mother characteristically didn't dwell on the incident.

Perhaps most telling was the abrupt about-face of some politicians regarding Richard Nixon. "Lyndon Johnson, then Democratic majority leader, was among the first to embrace the vice-president. When a reporter, who had earlier heard Johnson privately call Nixon 'chicken shit,' asked him about the embrace, it is said that Johnson replied, 'Son, in politics you've got to learn that overnight chicken shit can turn into chicken salad.'"

———————

In June 1958 Tricia graduated from Horace Mann Public Elementary School. "That September, the Nixons enrolled her [Tricia] and Julie in the private Sidwell Friends School to expose them to Quaker teaching in line with their faith. The school had been segregated until 1956, when it 'initiated a plan of progressive integration,' starting with kindergarten and integrating grade by grade each year."

Once Pat made sure the girls were settled into their new school, she turned her attention to yet another vice presidential trip. On November 24, she and Dick left Washington on a five-day visit to England, where they would meet with not only Prime Minister Harold Macmillan, Lord and Lady Mountbatten, and the Duchess of Devonshire, but also with Queen Elizabeth II. Pat had met then-Princess Elizabeth and Prince Philip in 1951, and the Nixons had both met the queen and Prince Philip on their October 1957 visit to Washington. But this time the Nixons were the honored guests acting as representatives of their country. Pat must have had to pinch herself: Pat Nixon from Artesia was also a diplomatic success story as Second Lady of the United States.

Pat's press from England was mostly complimentary. Even the cynical British women's press corps seemed to like Pat. One headline read, "Gals of Fleet Street Wowed by Pat Nixon." However, Pat's uncomplaining, cheerful nature read as too Mary Poppins perfect for some. The British periodical *The Spectator* wrote: "Mrs. Pat, face to face, is like a Republican Coppelia. She chatters, answers questions, smiles and smiles, all with a doll's terrifying poise. There is too little comprehension. Like a doll she would still be smiling while the world broke." The criticism that she was always "too perfect" would follow her back across the pond.

In July 1959, Pat and Dick were sent on an important goodwill mission to Russia. While there, they would represent the United States at the American National Exhibition in Moscow. As Dick described in his memoirs: "Russia was still shrouded in much of the sinister mystery of the Stalin era. The Iron Curtain was pulled tight across Europe, and Soviet missiles were feared in

Bonn, Paris, London—and in Washington." The vice president would be matching wits with Soviet premier Nikita Khrushchev, trying to pave the way for talks with Eisenhower.

While the VP's job was clear, Pat's role was much less defined. Daughter Julie later wrote, "Mother's role on the trip was especially vague since Mrs. Khrushchev and the wives of other Soviet officials did not accompany their husbands in public." Her female-focused diplomatic performance on this trip would help to thaw the Cold War tensions between the two men and their two countries to an important degree.

Pat assiduously studied the briefing materials prepared for her by the State Department. Of particular interest to her were two studies on American women, which she marked up in red ink. Pat put two exclamation marks next to this sentence: "Since the fundamental basis of a free society is the family structure, their most vital job is that of homemaker." She also underlined evidence of women's accomplishments in the work world: "women hold a third of the Nation's jobs" and now "hold important political posts and have won many elective offices." She wrote "Good!" next to this phrase: "Women in the United States usually withdraw from paid employment when their children are young; many later return as mature women with less demanding family responsibilities."

These notations show the balanced sense Pat had of both family and work life for women. Both spheres were important, and neither was exclusive. A woman could have a presence in both worlds depending on her stage of life and that of her children.

When the Nixons arrived in Moscow, they received a cool reception due to President Eisenhower's recent "captive nations" congressional joint resolution, which had upset their Soviet hosts. The vice president and the premier soon sparred over their political differences inside the American model kitchen at the exhibition, a discourse later known as the "Kitchen Debate." At a welcoming luncheon at the Kremlin, Pat toasted to peace between America and Russia, pointedly mentioning to the premier and his staff that she would like to meet their wives.

Later that afternoon, Pat toured a Russian market and a hospital and visited a Russian kindergarten, where she handed out cellophane-wrapped lollipops. Simple gestures like this endeared her to the Russian press and to her hosts. "Children are the same the world over," she observed. In a stunning turn of events that evening, Khrushchev and his deputies arrived at the American embassy dinner with their wives on their arms. Pat had achieved another female-focused diplomatic breakthrough.

The evening was so successful that the couple was invited to spend the night at the premier's dacha in Usovo. The next day at noon they found more unexpected guests: "The wives of Premier Khrushchev, Anastas Mikoyan, and Frol R. Kozlov arrived, bubbling over their unprecedented opportunity to attend a male luncheon." While the VP and the premier debated world politics, the women silently bonded without many words but many gestures of friendship and commonality.

One American reporter wrote that in retrospect, "the friendly, personable Pat probably did more to convince the Russians that Americans are nice people than could years of diplomatic exchanges." This person-to-person connectivity was a skill at which Pat excelled. Her ability to reach across borders, nationalities, and ideologies to the core humanity of a person was her superpower.

After the Russian trip, the Nixons wrapped up their journey with a stop in Poland, where the Second Lady was again in her element as an international diplomat, working through her female counterparts for world peace. Indeed Pat, Madame Khrushchev, and the two other Russian wives who met at the dacha on that historic visit may have made more progress toward peace than their husbands had. As Pat recalled: "Afterwards, the four of us agreed that if men would let women run the world, there would be eternal peace for our children and grandchildren. They kissed me on the cheek as I left."

16

1960 ELECTION: JEWELED JACKIE VS. DRIP-DRY PAT

When Helene Drown returned to California after visiting the Nixons in the spring of 1958, she knew she had to talk to Dick about Pat's feelings. She was aware that her friend at times had trouble expressing her needs to her husband, so she often acted as intermediary between them. Helene wrote Dick in the run-up to the 1960 election, "urging him to clear the air about looming political questions" with his wife. Helene listed their choices, which included the option to quit politics and return to a law career. The second choice? "Refuse to run in 1960 and leave the country in a mess, because who else is there? Not fair to you and Pat when you have put so much in and others have worked for you because they believe in you both." Or choice three: pursue the nomination.

Ultimately, Dick pursued choice three, and as always, his wife backed him up. After all the hard work they had put in and her refusal to let her husband be dumped from the Eisenhower ticket, this was the logical conclusion and one they had worked for years together to achieve. With his running mate, Henry Cabot Lodge, Nixon proposed "the most liberal platform on civil rights ever to be accepted by the Republican party." Delegate-at-large Jewel Stradford Lafontant, a Chicago lawyer who was the first Black woman to receive her J.D. from the University of Chicago, was asked to give the seconding speech.

As historian Dr. Luke Nichter explained, "Much of the equality struggle of the 1960s was waged according to skin color, not gender . . . and the major legislative achievements of the decade also focused on race. Women had not received comparable attention. Nixon planned to do something about that."

While gender equality was not center stage in the 1960 campaign, women's votes would continue to form a bedrock for the Republicans that had to be taken seriously. Dick corresponded regularly with Helene Drown on this issue, and he appreciated her advice regarding the women's vote. In the spring of 1959, Dick replied to a letter Helene had written him on this topic:

> I couldn't agree more with you on the power of women at the polls. One of the most encouraging features of the polls that have been run between the various candidates for 1960 is that I generally do better among women than men! What we have to do is get more women out there talking as you are in order to accentuate that trend.

Helene took Dick's advice to heart, and she often gave talks to women's groups on behalf of the Nixon campaign. When she talked about Pat's background, she took care to emphasize the Second Lady's humble origins and capacity for hard work: "IF PAT NIXON IS TO BE FIRST LADY, she will be the first in modern times whose early days were a constant struggle for pennies and dollars for survival. Certainly, no other candidate's wife is so TYPICALLY THE AMERICAN WORKING GIRL AS PAT NIXON."

Pat's relatability quotient for the average woman of the era was high, as she came from a hardscrabble background and had to work for everything she had. She also clearly adored her children and loved being a mother and homemaker. Due to her broad life experiences, she could connect both with housewives and with women in the workforce.

Pat would perhaps work harder on the 1960 campaign than she ever had before. "She traveled with and without him [Dick], her daily schedule crowded with the customary news conferences, chats with women's groups, receptions, visits to hospitals and homes." She may have been reluctant to run again, but once she was committed, there was no stopping the Second Lady. She was in it to win it.

Going into the 1960 election, the female vote continued its important reign, building on strong showings by women voters in 1952 and 1956. Indeed, during the Eisenhower administrations, clubwomen became critical GOP workers. "A survey conducted in the 1950s indicated that among core

Republican Party activists, 56 percent were women. This was noticeably higher than in the Democratic Party, where women were only 41 percent." As Dick himself would note later, "The best advice I can give to those planning to run for public office is simply this: get a corps of dedicated women committed to you and working for you—and you have it made!"

Political commentator Rachel Maddow gives these conservative women their due as the engine of an ideologically disparate Republican Party of the 1960s: "Inside the party, everybody knew who the real activists, the real soldiers, were: Republican women." Maddow's comparison of Democratic labor unions and grassroots Republican women's groups as the organizers of their respective parties is an apt one.

It was the Republican Party (not the Democratic Party) that had supported the ERA first, beginning in 1940. The Republican platform in 1960 continued its support for the Equal Rights Amendment, and Dick himself authored a statement as vice president supporting the ERA. He acknowledged: "The task of achieving Constitutional equality between the sexes still is not completed." In addition, Dick cited President Eisenhower's previous statement: "I believe that the Congress should make certain that women are not denied equal rights with men."

Republican clubwomen did much of the tedious daily work that was crucial to campaigns but not splashy: "ringing the doorbells, filling out registration cards, and generally doing the housework of government so that the principles of the Republican Party can be brought to every home." In this context, the candidate's wife was a critical component of his electability, becoming more important than she had been in past elections.

Previous First Ladies Bess Truman and Mamie Eisenhower were not nearly as visible on the campaign trail as Pat nor as hardworking once they entered the White House. During their eras, these expectations were not in place for First Ladies. Neither Bess nor Mamie had much interest in politics in general and even less interest in promoting the women's vote. In particular, their presence on the campaign trail was rare. "Bess Truman and Mamie Eisenhower avidly avoided the spotlight and professed, and certainly appeared, to have little if any interest in the potential of their East Wing platform."

In the 1950s these tendencies were not held against a First Lady, but as the new decade approached, the public expected First Ladies to up their game. Fashion and feminine image as well as campaign visibility connected directly to female votes. As one reporter noted, "This fall the question of style for a President's wife may be a Great Issue. Can too much chic—or too little—mean votes?" Lady Bird's biographer Julia Sweig noted: "Jackie Kennedy, pregnant and worried about more miscarriages, mostly stayed out of the 1960 campaign." Her absence in public was noted, and it did not help her husband's presidential chances.

The duel to become First Lady between Jackie Kennedy and Pat Nixon would fall along just such lines. It wasn't just about the Republican Party versus the Democratic Party, but it was also a contest over appearances on the campaign trail and style projection. Both candidates' wives were beautiful and chic, but who would be voted "in" and who would be voted "out"? American women would have a heavy hand in deciding the outcome.

The 1960 election was first and foremost between frenemies Dick Nixon and Jack Kennedy, but it also pitted their wives against each other as potential First Ladies. Each represented an image both supplementary and complementary to their husband's. Pat's role was that of the fresh-faced mom next door who campaigned with her husband, while Jackie's designated part was slinky, sexy sophisticate who avoided the campaign trail. These images were media constructs featuring a pinch of the truth leavened with a lot of spin.

The two candidates' wives had been friendly for many years. When Pat first met Jackie in 1953, she noted in her diary, "Met Senator Kennedy's fiancée, a darling girl." But now politics forced the two women to go toe to satin-shod toe in the media.

With her good-girl credentials well established, Pat wisely didn't try to outdo "glamour girl" Jackie, who was younger than her by seventeen years. (In 1959, Pat was forty-seven and Jackie was thirty.) When asked by reporters about Jackie and her sex appeal (an undignified question that surely horrified proper Pat), she replied graciously, "She's a very glamorous person and I couldn't hope to compete with her."

While Pat was seen as practical, thrifty, resourceful, and ever present at her husband's campaign events, Jackie was seen as a young, sexy clotheshorse who rarely showed up to stump for her husband's candidacy, perhaps because she was pregnant during the 1960 race. However, in contrast, Pat had campaigned with her husband in 1948 when she was pregnant with Julie.

Jack Kennedy was not pleased when his wife remarked in a campaign interview that "I simply don't like crowds." The young Kennedy wife also made clear by her remarks and her social choices that "she had never cared for political types, preferring the artsy set. She was more at home with talk of high fashion, modern art, the latest plays, and the Beautiful People gossip than analyses of which way the vote would go in the 14th ward."

Jackie unintentionally added fuel to the press fire about her wardrobe with her infamous "sable underwear" comments. "I'm sure I spend less than Mrs. Nixon on clothes," she claimed (unconvincingly). "A newspaper reported Sunday that I spend $30,000 a year buying Paris clothes and that women hate me for it. . . . I couldn't spend that much unless I wore sable underwear." Regardless of the truth, it was the sable underwear image that stuck in people's minds, not a helpful one for the Kennedy campaign. Even her husband, Jack, reportedly exclaimed, "Good Christ, that's the last interview that goddamned woman will give until after the election."

Pat laughed off Jackie's comments, "emphasizing that she only patronized American designers and stating that she bought many of her clothes off the rack." While Pat didn't take these clothing wars seriously, a candidate's wife's wardrobe and how she presented herself in it were important parts of the optics of any campaign. Jack Kennedy knew this and worried about his wife's presentation in the press. He was "concerned about the growing impression of her as a Newport snob with bouffant hair, French clothes, and a hatred for politics."

Contrasted with the all-American Pat, Jackie came across as elitist and unrelatable to many women. "The contrast between the two wives was sharp. Jackie gave an interview while lounging in purple Pucci slacks on the carpet of her Georgetown home. Pat gave interviews with her hands folded in her lap, wearing one of the five new dresses she had bought in one fast hour's shopping, guided only by whether they were conservative enough and how well they would pack."

Kandie Stroud, a well-known reporter for *Women's Wear Daily*, covered Pat on the campaign trail, and she remembers well the sartorial duels that took place between the candidates' wives: "When I first met her, I was covering some campaign. She was at a meet-and-greet . . . I think they even wore gloves like Mamie Eisenhower. She had injured herself; I can't remember, it might have been her ankle. She stood in that line for hours! Totally stoic, never complaining."

Stroud, who has been blamed (incorrectly) in the past for Pat's nickname "Plastic Pat," explained: "When I worked for *Women's Wear Daily*, John Fairchild [*WWD*'s publisher], I guess, didn't like her . . . with John it was all about 'Were you the next Jackie Kennedy?' She [Pat] wasn't the best dressed, she wasn't going to make the front cover of *WWD*. But he was the one who coined the phrase. He told me, 'I want you to call her Plastic Pat.' That was John Fairchild, not me."

Perhaps contributing to this attitude was that Pat didn't bow down to fashion arbiters like Fairchild. When the Nixon campaign turned down a request for Pat to be photographed for a Fairchild Publications magazine, the editor in charge wrote Bessie Newton, Pat's secretary, with this critique:

> I cannot urge your publicity office enough to make the most of the beautiful Mrs. Nixon in campaigning; because stacked against the unwashed Mrs. Kennedy, she will carry the country. When Mr. Klein [Dick's press secretary] failed to let us talk to or photograph Mrs. N. before leaving, we of the women's side of the press can do much to help the cause through cooperation from him in relation to Mrs. Nixon . . . Tell Mr. Klein to knock down that iron curtain he has flung around our future first lady.

This lack of press accessibility would only nominally affect the 1960 race, but it would become a major issue in future Nixon campaigns. The "Old Nixon" team that had handled Nixon's campaigns for years—staffers like Bob Finch, Herb Klein, Leonard Hall, and Rose Mary Woods—were being supplemented with newcomers. These young men most often came from worlds outside of politics.

The first of these "New Nixon" team members to join the old gang was Harry Robbins (H. R.) "Bob" Haldeman, a New York–based advertising executive. He had worked on the 1956 presidential campaign as an advance man, and he was now head of the nineteen-member Nixon campaign advance team.

In the fall of 1959, Haldeman recruited his college friend John Ehrlichman as his "key assistant" on the advance team. The two men and their wives, Jo and Jeanne, had known each other since their student days at UCLA. Bob and John were both settled into promising careers, but the lure of politics was tempting. The two college buddies planned and executed the 1960 campaign events with meticulous preparation and organization. They became skilled operators in this highly specialized arena.

Despite their well-tuned organizational skills, most of these young upstarts "had less political experience than older members of the team such as Leonard Hall and Robert Finch. They were less likely to stand up to Nixon, more fearful of telling him something was a bad idea, and more inclined to flatter him and follow his lead."

But why would any of these young men abandon their successful careers for months at a time to support a presidential campaign? Perhaps their daily lives and careers seemed drab and boring in comparison to the perceived glamour of political life. As Ehrlichman recalled years later, "Bob Haldeman was suggesting I run away to the circus for a little while, and it was irresistible."

———

Tricia and Julie were sent off to summer camp in Montecito, California, in July before the furor of the Republican nominating convention began. Dick's letter to Tricia at camp before the convention encouraged her to take the political temperature of her camp friends: "When we see you, I will be interested to get your report on what the girls at camp think of the political campaign. I am sure they have probably given you their views on Kennedy and Johnson, and the chances they may have in the election. Our convention should be very exciting, and I know you and Julie will have a 'blast' attending the various sessions." Dick not only valued his daughters' presence by his side at the convention but also solicited their thoughts and feedback. He took the female vote seriously and wanted to know what every age group thought.

The Nixon campaign even had teenage girls taking part in the campaign. The "Nixonettes," as they were popularly known, wore "pleated dresses, sashes, and Nixon boater hats." The young women were a prominent feature of the campaign rallies. Though many were not yet of voting age, they soon would be. Early cultivation and inclusion of potential female voters would be strategically important in all the Nixon campaigns.

When the Republican nominating convention began on July 25 in Chicago, Pat found she was a central figure in the proceedings. The Republican National Committee, in conjunction with the Nixon staff, created the "Pat for First Lady" campaign, which was launched at the convention. One reporter "evoked historical precedent when she pointed out that Pat Nixon was the first woman around whom a separate campaign was being built."

One notable event Pat turned down was the Hawaiian Hukilau Luncheon at the Palmer House in Chicago. Though this was one of the largest women's events at the Republican National Convention, Pat sent her regrets despite a personal invitation and request for her presence by none other than the uber-conservative Phyllis Schlafly—at that time acting in her capacity as president of the Illinois Federation of Republican Women. Schlafly would later dash the hopes of women everywhere who supported the Equal Rights Amendment with her successful campaign to shut down the amendment's ratification. Pat had supported the ERA her entire political life as part of the Republican platform and was herself very pro–women's rights. One has to wonder if she was turned off by Schlafly's ultra-conservatism early on.

A planning memo between Rose Mary Woods and Dick in early July indicates that Pat had preapproved the song, colors, and slogan for the campaign and knew there would be a "'Pat Precinct Plan,' having an all-out week of concentrated effort worked into the campaign aiming it at Pat." (Pat may have had to steel herself, as she did not like being the center of attention, but she knew what was coming.) "Complete with her own buttons, banners, and song, the Pat for First Lady operation led to numerous teas, socials, and women's club appearances and culminated in a Pat Nixon Week in October."

Pat would receive some criticism for being *too* active on her husband's behalf. The press noted no other "presidential campaign previously in which the wife has taken such an active part." Ironically, one of the main sources of this criticism came from Kennedy historian and campaign advisor Arthur M. Schlesinger Jr., who said it was "degrading" that Dick so frequently referred to "Pat and I" in his speeches.

Pat was a fighter, and she pushed back against Schlesinger's antiquated view of women as campaign partners. "I think that women all over America are taking a very active part not only in political life, but in all activities in our entire life." She went on to say that while women used to stay home, now "women not only take care of the families, but . . . they have the interest and the time for many other jobs which are very important to the progress of our country." This included stumping for her husband.

Both Nixons were progressive on women's issues, while the Kennedy camp seemed to promote the older view that women should be staying home with their children, not out in the political world. Perhaps this was a covering strategy since Jackie was doing so little campaigning for her own husband. Nevertheless, Schlesinger's view—and that of the Kennedy campaign—was far from enlightened as far as women were concerned.

Although she won points for her activism from many, Pat's "too perfect" image still haunted her. A *Time* cover story on Pat from this period painted her as a perfectionist workhorse. "Her critics . . . say that Pat Nixon is too serene, too tightly controlled, that she smothers her personality with a fixed smile and a mask of dignity." Pat's quotes in the story didn't help her case. When asked if she had a temper, she replied, "I never have tantrums . . . if anything makes me mad, I'm silent. If I'm not talking, leave me alone."

Pat claimed her silence did not mean she wasn't part of the Pat and Dick Team: "I've always been part of what's done . . . but a silent partner." She was clearly a mobilizing force for Republican women's organizations, who worked with her to consolidate the important women's vote.

In August, Pat flew solo to Meriden, Connecticut, to headline Pat Nixon Day. (Both her father and her grandfather had ties to the area.) "Pat told a crowd of twelve hundred that she and Dick had "'always campaigned as a team . . . I've always made the miles with him.'" She made another campaign appearance and spoke at the Alpha Phi Alpha Wives annual convention in D.C. in late August. Alpha Phi Alpha was the largest and oldest Black fraternity in the country. Like the women's vote, the Black vote was much valued by the Nixon campaign. Pat would consistently demonstrate her commitment to this constituency, as scores of admiring articles about her events in the Black community from the 1950s onward attest.

College women were another demographic of particular interest to Pat, as she and her husband's campaign team had noticed a strong College Republican presence. And of course, Pat was a college graduate herself, not so common in this era. "I am particularly interested in the work that is being done by our college women. It has often been said that the bulk of the work in any campaign is done by the women, and I know this to be true whether it is the senior women's organization or the college Republican women."

In yet another letter dated October 1960, Pat again addresses collegiate women, this time for the Monticello College alumnae magazine. "In this campaign year women will surely be the key to victory. Women of voting age today outnumber men by over three million and we are turning out a steadily growing proportion of our potential vote. If recent trends hold steady, more women than men actually will cast ballots into the box in 1960."

Though Pat might not have been out giving policy speeches for her husband, she was engaging with voters directly through campaign letters and with her constant, steady presence on the campaign trail both with and without her husband. Reaching these female voters of all races and socioeconomic levels was critical for the Nixon campaign's success. In this area, Pat led the charge.

———

Despite the careful planning and his popular wife's solid support, some critical things went wrong for Dick at the beginning of the campaign. First, "he functioned as his own campaign manager, a major mistake. (Murray Chotiner had been sidelined by an influence-peddling scandal.)" His second mistake was campaigning in all fifty states, an overwhelming task that would wear him out and make him ill. And pure bad luck caused the GOP candidate to bang his knee on a car door in August, resulting in a staph infection so bad that it "almost cost him his leg."

Dick's illness did not bode well going into the election against the seemingly vigorous, tanned, and relaxed Democratic nominee, his old friend JFK. A famous television debate would make this disparity more evident. During the first debate, Pat would not be onstage beside him. She flew home from Chicago to spend time with her daughters and watch the debate on television, leaving the candidate on his own.

September 26 would mark the first of four Nixon-Kennedy sparring matches leading up to the election in November. The debate garnered the biggest TV audience to date for a political program. "Nielsen Television Index reported that out of the total of 45 million United States homes with televisions, 66.4 percent viewed the debate for at least six minutes."

Nixon lent Kennedy gravitas by agreeing to debate him at all, a decision he later came to regret. It raised Kennedy's profile and credibility, a strategic mistake Dick later admitted.

Dick regained any perceived lost ground in the three subsequent debates, and by the end of campaign season the two men were locked in a dead heat. Meanwhile, the Nixons crisscrossed the country holding rallies. Dick later told daughter Julie that "the only way he and Mother could sustain the pace during the entire campaign was to live like Spartans—little food, tempers under control, no alcohol. Sometimes the entourage had to fly all night. The only way many could keep awake during the daytime was by taking mild pep pills."

In mid-October, Eisenhower decided to help shore up the Nixon-Lodge presidential ticket by launching a 6,500-mile "nonpolitical tour" from October 17 to 25. He extended the tour by several days, speaking in Virginia on the twenty-seventh. The next day, Eisenhower's physician wrote in his medical diary: "Mamie was plugging at me to tell the President he had to quit speaking and plugging for Nixon—that he might pop a cork."

With the nail-biting race concluding, it was critical that Eisenhower demonstrate his late-game support for Dick. The polls were showing such a close race that even the normally stoic Pat began to show concern. On October 30, she received an unexpected phone call from Mamie. "The First Lady sounded distraught. She reminded Pat that Ike was seventy years old . . . his blood pressure simply could not withstand the pressure of campaigning. She urged that my father must not ask Ike to undertake any additional campaigning—and not to let him know that she called." The next day Ike's doctor also called Dick, begging him not to allow Ike to do additional campaigning due to the strain it might cause to his heart. In his memoirs, Dick admitted, "I could make no other decision than to discourage him and limit his participation."

When the next day in a meeting the candidate refused the president's help without explanation, he became "angry—and confused, as were the political strategists, who were baffled by Nixon's abruptness." Due to Mamie's request,

Dick felt he could not explain his actions to the president. "It was not until years later that Mrs. Eisenhower told him the real reason for my sudden change of mind regarding his campaigning." By doing the noble thing, Dick had sacrificed potential votes and caused a rift with a supportive president.

As the last, debilitating days of the campaign wore on, both Pat and Dick's energy reserves were fast being depleted. The GOP candidate, with Pat in tow, had fulfilled his promise to campaign in every state, but at great physical and mental cost to them both. "Election Day came after almost seventy-two sleepless hours of campaigning, traveling, making appearances, and smiling." Pat and Dick, along with their daughters, flew from Chicago to Los Angeles. After a brief rest at the Ambassador Hotel, the Nixons cast their ballots on Election Day in their precinct in East Whittier. Dick then spent the day with several staffers in Tijuana, drinking German beer, eating Mexican food, and trying to escape the Election Day furor.

While Dick watched the early election returns that evening with his staff in the hotel's Royal Suite, Pat retreated to her room. Tricia and Julie spent the day with the Drowns at their home in Rolling Hills, returning with Helene to the hotel in the late afternoon. The votes were not going in their favor, and Pat "had been hearing the rumors of voting shenanigans in Illinois and considered Kennedy a fraud and a scoundrel." She suspected voting irregularities and refused to go downstairs to talk to supporters when Dick first asked her to accompany him to address the crowd. As Pat left to go back to her room, Helene stopped her, telling her she had no choice but to go downstairs with Dick. Pat agreed, knowing her friend was right, but she was visibly upset.

Bob Finch recalled that Dick had taken a "middle of the road" approach, not yet conceding the election, but indicating he would if the voting trend continued. Campaign press secretary Herb Klein recalled:

At about 11:00 he decided he probably had lost, and he called Pat and had her come down to where he was. He normally isolated himself on election nights. Had the family in one suite, and he would be by himself with some of us going in and out, and so he wanted to give up at that time, and Bob Finch and I convinced him that he should not, that there was still a chance that we could win; it was going to be close. And so he went down to the ballroom and told him [Finch] that he was going to wait until morning to decide what had happened. It was a very touching speech and Pat Nixon started to cry when he was making his speech, and it choked us all up. But he did it.

The film footage of Pat Nixon next to her husband as he conceded the election to Kennedy is heartbreaking. She had lost ten pounds from her already slim frame, and her face looked drawn, tired, and teary. Dick himself recorded in his book *Six Crises* that "as I was writing this book, she was to tell me, 'That was the saddest day of my life.'" He would dedicate the book to his wife: "To Pat: She also ran."

Soon after the election, Helene wrote Pat in a gloomy but reflective mood. Like the Nixons, the Drowns were crushed by the election results, and they also questioned their validity. "And it is not because the gold ring of the election was not snapped that causes the greatest concern, but the fact that it was stolen that bothers us. And we are so helpless. . . . All we can do is stare at a lot of broken ideals and wonder if it is worth it to try and mend all the pieces."

Helene praised Pat for the stoic courage she had shown in the face of a devastating outcome. Helene noted that Pat had showed "courage, and unselfishness and loyalty. . . . Perhaps a history book won't record your deeds of valor, but there is more immortality in the hearts of men."

Pat was devastated by her husband's presidential loss. She would always maintain that the election was stolen from them. Her daughter Julie shared, "I think the reason 1960 was a turning point for my mother is that she believed my father won the election and that chicanery took it away. They had exhausted themselves physically and emotionally. [In] all 50 states."

But now Pat was strangely free. Wasn't a private life what she had wanted all along?

17

PEOPLE ARE NOT CATTLE

The Nixon family returned to Washington in a late fall funk. The weather was gloomy, matching everyone's mood. Pat and the girls were crushed. They had a hard time accepting the defeat due to reports of widespread voting issues. "Kennedy had won the popular vote by an official count of 112,827 votes out of approximately 68.8 million cast, a paper-thin margin." Furthermore, "in Chicago, where a switch of just 4,500 ballots would have given the critical state to Nixon, there were rampant charges that Mayor Daley had turned out the graveyard vote."

Accusations of voting irregularities ultimately surfaced in eleven states: Delaware, Illinois, Michigan, Minnesota, Missouri, Nevada, New Mexico, New Jersey, Pennsylvania, South Carolina, and Texas. Republican National Committee chairman Thruston Morton had still not conceded the election to Kennedy on November 10. However, Nixon "discouraged any initiative from the RNC, telling reporters he knew nothing of a recount."

On November 11, Pat, Dick, and the girls arrived at Key Biscayne. Bebe Rebozo, Rose Woods, Don Hughes, Bob Finch, Herb Klein, and several spouses joined them there to recuperate. The second night the Nixons were in town, they went out to dinner at the Jamaica Inn. Suddenly the phone rang at the maître d' station. As Herb Klein recalled:

> They said it was for Mr. Nixon, and so I said, "Well, I'll take it." And I picked up the phone, and it was Herbert Hoover. Herbert Hoover had had a call from Joe Kennedy, who said, "Would the Vice President speak— meet with my son?" And so Hoover called to ask him whether he would meet with Kennedy and so I went in to the dining room table and told him

what the conversation had been, and he immediately got very excited and interested and just revived, and he decided that he should.

Dick also talked to Eisenhower to run the JFK meeting idea by him. Eisenhower approved.

One can only imagine how upset Pat must have been at the thought of her husband meeting with JFK after what she considered a fraudulent victory. There is no record of what she said that night at the Jamaica Inn, but she could not have taken kindly to the idea of her husband meeting with Kennedy so soon. Echoing their mother's sentiments, Julie and Tricia were also much opposed to the meeting. Dick wrote that when he told the girls the next day about his plans to meet the president-elect, "they both berated me roundly: 'How can you possibly talk to him after what he said about you during the campaign?' . . . Julie still protested, 'He didn't win. Haven't you heard about all the cheating in Illinois and Texas?'"

Still, Dick stuck to his decision. Herb Klein noted:

So on Monday, he [JFK] came to Key Biscayne, and they met, just the two of them, in one of the suites at the Key Biscayne Inn. And that was when Nixon told him he was not going to contest the election, and then Kennedy offered him a job in the Cabinet. . . . He said, "No, I should be the loyal opposition." That was his term. I think that was one of the most important decisions he made at the time.

Pat wrote Helene a frank letter when she returned to Washington: "The Florida trip was almost like a nightmare—tenseness everywhere, office hours for Dick, the girls hearing far too much ugly discussion, etc. Also, I was in a state of numbness with faith in the 'right' shaken to the point I could not discuss the situation anymore." Pat always found it easier to pour her heart out to her best friend than to talk to her husband directly about her feelings.

When Inauguration Day dawned on January 20, Washington was blanketed with eight inches of snow. "Since presidential inaugurations moved from March to January in 1937, none have stirred up as much weather drama as John F. Kennedy's in 1961, when a surprise snowstorm the day before brought Washington to a standstill."

The winter weather caused massive traffic jams and a whiteout at National Airport. Former president Herbert Hoover found himself unable to fly in for the ceremony. Cars were skidding and crashing on the icy roadways. However, by late morning, thanks to a huge effort from the U.S. Army Corps of Engineers, Pennsylvania Avenue was navigable, and the day's inaugural events proceeded.

Tricia later provided a concise summary of events in her diary with an indignant aside:

D Day 1961 January 20.

Dear Diary,

Mommy and Daddy left at ten thirty for the Inauguration. They had a police escort. First, they stopped at the White House for coffee. Then they drove down Pennsylvania Avenue to the Capitol where JFK was inaugurated President at 12:20. (Daddy should have been; he won the popular vote!) [Tricia was discounting the allegedly fraudulent votes for Kennedy in Texas, Illinois, and Missouri.] Next they went to a private luncheon at the F Street Club. Julie and I watched the ceremony on TV. Bad day.

The day after the inauguration, Pat and Dick left for a long-overdue vacation in the Bahamas, traveling by private plane and staying at the residences of friends in Nassau and Eleuthera. Their friends Roger and Louise Johnson accompanied them, as did Bebe Rebozo. The respite was to last a month, but after several weeks of downtime Dick was bored. The couple returned to Washington to pack up his office. Pat and the girls would stay and finish the school year in D.C.

In his memoirs, written years later, Dick wrote that he somehow knew his defeat in 1960 would not be the end of his political life. While driving through D.C. with Pat the night of the inauguration, looking upon the city where he had spent much of his life since 1947, he was "struck by the thought that this was not the end—that someday I would be back here." He admitted he was drawn "irresistibly" to public life. He had "drunk too deeply of the stuff which really makes life exciting and worth living to be satisfied with the froth."

Pat had drunk from this same cup, but instead of tasting "the stuff which really makes life exciting," she had tasted its bitter dregs. Going back to that political life would be a hard sell for a Second Lady who had campaigned her heart out in 1960 only to have her hopes for her husband dashed. She would never forgive Kennedy for what she considered a fraudulent election. She could hardly wait to put political life behind her—perhaps this time for good.

Dick decided to go ahead to Los Angeles to begin his new job at the law firm of Adams, Duque, & Hazeltine. He rented a home on North Bundy Drive in Brentwood from the movie producer Walter Lang until his family could join him in California. He enjoyed the satisfaction of Kennedy seeking his counsel early on in his new administration during the Bay of Pigs debacle. Tricia was the one who took the phone call from Kennedy's office on April 20. On a piece of yellow legal paper, Tricia wrote in her impeccable script:

JFK called Daddy.
I knew he'd come crawling sooner or later.

June finally arrived and the girls' school year ended. Pat and her daughters reached California with high hopes for a new beginning. Dick was still living in their rental home while their new house was being built in a development called the Trousdale Estates in Beverly Hills. They had numerous visitors, including old friend J. Edgar Hoover, who attended the performance of a "water ballet" performed by Julie in the pool. Hoover was deathly afraid of water and could not swim, so the visit showed his dedication to maintaining a friendship with the Nixon family.

The Nixons were celebrated with a huge welcome-home party early in their residency. Pat soon received an honorary degree from her alma mater, the University of Southern California. The girls were preparing for a new academic year at the private Marlborough School in Beverly Hills that fall. Pat, who was happily contemplating decorating her new Southern California dream house, gardened, saw old friends, and played hostess to the girls' friends throughout that summer and fall. Dick, however, was busier than ever. He worked on a book that would be titled *Six Crises*, wrote a syndicated column, maintained a vigorous speaking schedule, worked at the law firm, and campaigned for other Republican candidates.

Dick had not made a clean break with his political cronies: he brought the closest members of his campaign team to Southern California with him. Loyal "work wife" Rose Woods moved to Los Angeles, staying on as personal secretary to The Boss. Loie Gaunt, Don Hughes, Bob Finch, and Bob Haldeman were also on hand to help Dick transition from the East Coast back to West Coast life. Even if Pat had convinced herself their political life was over, many others surely knew The Boss wasn't about to give up this arena.

By the end of the year, the young family had moved into their completed home at 410 Martin Lane, "long, low, and ranch style, with seven baths and four bedrooms." The neighborhood boasted many Hollywood stars, including Groucho Marx. The Nixons also met a Spanish-born couple who would become trusted employees and a dependable, reassuring presence in the family's daily lives. Manolo and Fina Sanchez had only recently escaped from dictator Fidel Castro's Cuba when they were hired to help manage the Nixon home and help keep an eye on Tricia and Julie.

But Pat's respite from the political world was short-lived. She was soon sucked back into the vortex when Dick began to consider a run for governor of California. Dick admitted that "I dreaded bringing up the subject with Pat and Tricia and Julie, so I left it until the last possible moment." As expected, Pat came out strongly against the idea, saying that if he did run, she would not campaign with him as in the past.

In Dick's telling, Julie said she would approve whatever her father decided, while Tricia supported the idea. However, Julie claims her mother told her years later: "You voted for running, Tricia and I voted no." Later Tricia persuaded Pat to change their votes. Pat came up to the study where Dick was working late and gave him her reluctant blessing to enter the campaign. Still, she warned him that "if you run it will be a terrible mistake."

In November 1962, *Ladies' Home Journal* ran a telling article entitled "Crises of a Candidate's Wife" with Pat Nixon's byline. The article reads as slick campaign material, not as a piece that Pat would have authored. In the article, "Pat" apologizes for sitting next to Dick during the Checkers speech "like a wax figure, afraid if I made one move, I might show too much emotion, my control might give way." This unlikely quote traps Pat in the "silent doll" image she so hated, showing her as powerless against the wishes of her husband and his campaign advisors who had clearly written the script for her.

While "Pat" admits she was opposed to the gubernatorial run at first, her conclusion is that Dick's run is for the good of the country, and she is willing to sacrifice her family life once again for this purpose. It is likely that this magazine piece was ghostwritten for her by one of the men on Dick's campaign staff—perhaps Herb Klein, who had worked on Dick's previous campaigns, or new press staffer Ron Ziegler. It is not Pat's true voice that we hear in the article.

Pat's real feelings ran contrary to the *LHJ* piece, and she unwittingly revealed them early in the campaign. The night Dick's candidacy was announced, the Nixons were having dinner with their friends and campaign stalwarts Bob and Carol Finch along with Herb Klein and his wife and Rose Mary Woods. In a rare moment of candor, Pat blurted out, "Carol, I'm trapped. Which way can I go?" From here there was nowhere to go but back on the campaign trail, back into the fishbowl existence she dreaded.

———

Pat originally said she would not campaign with her husband. While she ultimately relented, she held her ground in her own way. "Pat campaigned as she had promised, but most of her appearances were to community teas as part of the Action Package Program."

In a politically savvy move, Pat "chose the title 'Community Receptions' herself" for these teas "because she realized that her constituency included Independents and Democrats as well as Republicans, and she did not want them to be scared away by the idea of attending a partisan event." In this manner, she delineated herself as a distinct part of her husband's campaign— one that was politically all-inclusive. Perhaps this was her way of declaring some independence from Dick's decision to run and from his team, who were beginning to hem her in and advise her in ways she did not appreciate.

After Dick announced his candidacy for governor against popular Democratic incumbent Pat Brown on September 27, the Nixons were off to their separate arenas, with Pat focusing again on gaining the women's vote. Pat's secretary Bessie Newton handled much of Pat's campaign scheduling. Bessie also ran interference with Nixon's staff, such as his campaign manager Bob Haldeman. Haldeman had stayed in constant touch with Nixon after the 1956 race. This time he was working behind the scenes with Murray Chotiner, Dick's former campaign manager.

Haldeman absorbed some rough-and-tumble campaign strategies from the old political hand. Pat hadn't liked Chotiner, and she would come to like Haldeman even less. He came from the same mold as his mentor, but in deeply tanned, slick Madison Avenue packaging.

Still, many of Dick's staffers would take note of Pat's star power. Future governor of California Pete Wilson was a young advance man in the 1962 campaign. He recalled: "Campaign strategists soon learned that Pat Nixon was a far bigger draw than the incumbent governor that they were running against."

Another young staffer Pat grew fond of during election season was Jack Carley, an idealistic twenty-one-year-old who had come to California from New Jersey to work on the Nixon campaign. He was quickly engaged as Mrs. Nixon's aide and driver. From this position he enjoyed a bird's-eye view of the race as well as proximity to Pat.

Carley's diary from this time describes Pat as a seasoned campaigner with superb political instincts and incredible stamina. She also had a detailed memory for names and a warm nature that allowed her to connect with individuals in a meaningful way. Spending hours in the car with her, he found out she loved Fred Astaire, her favorite street in L.A. was Roxbury Road, and she liked to smoke Parliament cigarettes when no one was watching. "We developed a rapport . . . she may have viewed me as a son or nephew."

Carley related that Pat had fallen and cracked three ribs early in the campaign. "The proper cure, of course, was bed rest for a few weeks, but she would not consider it. Despite her obvious discomfort, she continued the campaign with a full schedule and no excuses."

October 3 was a typical campaign day for Mrs. Nixon. This included a morning tea, two afternoon rallies, one in Encino and one in Los Angeles, and an 8 p.m. rally for her husband in Pasadena. She would not return home until 11:30 that night. The next day she would repeat the entire cycle of speaking, shaking hands, and listening to her husband's evening speeches again. Julie confirmed this breakneck pace: "In 1962, she was scheduled for more events than in any previous campaign."

Pat was warm and personable with each person she met at these gubernatorial rallies and programs. Social status or fame made no difference at all to her. As Carley recalled, "I saw her treat common, ordinary citizens to celebrities in exactly the same manner, which was unfailingly warm, gracious and courteous. Above all she seemed to act as if each individual and his or her feelings were paramount . . . she would make the necessary effort to establish personal contact with those who came to see her so that they might remember that moment as a special one."

Pat instinctively knew that shaking a person's hand—establishing a personal connection between politics and people—was cherished and valued. She treated these meetings with individuals in the same manner as she had always treated her correspondence as the wife of a high-level government official: as a sacred trust that deserved her undivided attention. Meeting her or receiving a letter from her might be a once-in-a-lifetime event for the average American. Carley learned about her views on this when he tried to move a reception line at a campaign event along a bit faster. "At some point, Mrs. Nixon leaned over to me and said, 'Please don't rush them, Jack, people are not cattle.'"

The only overtly political comment Pat made to the young man was about the Cuban missile crisis in mid-October 1962, which put the entire world on the brink of nuclear disaster for days. As Carley drove Mrs. Nixon to the airport, they happened to catch Kennedy's speech about the crisis. "I remember that Mrs. Nixon's only comment was to the effect that 'this wouldn't have happened if Dick were President.' Beyond that, there was no conversation on the effect it would have on the upcoming election or its importance."

Ultimately Dick would lose the California governor's race to Brown, fulfilling Pat's prediction. The Cuban missile crisis hadn't helped; it "had distracted the press and reversed some Nixon progress in the polls. From Washington, President Kennedy had sent an Air Force jet to pick up Governor Brown to 'consult' on the crisis, an outrageous ploy to boost the Democratic candidate that Nixon added to his bag of Kennedy grudges." Pat mentally would have added the Brown "consult" to her own private list of Kennedy grievances as well.

The public also sensed that Dick had bigger ambitions than simply being governor of California. In a slip, he "spoke of running for Governor of the United States . . . voters sensed that Nixon's heart was in Washington, not Sacramento." The night before the election, he made another misstep: "Tomorrow, I'm hoping you elect me president of California." Later, Dick himself admitted, "My biggest problem in the campaign was the question of my actual interest in being governor of California. Despite my constant disclaimers of any plans to run for [the] presidency in 1964, I was simply not able to convince many people."

Ensconced in his suite at the Beverly Hilton Hotel on Election Day, exhausted and unshaven, Dick was not planning on speaking to the press after the defeat. He was furious at what he felt was unfair treatment by the press during the contentious race. He had asked his press secretary, Herb Klein, to read his concession speech for him, but reporters were so persistent that Klein came to his hotel room pleading with Dick to come downstairs and meet with the press.

Pat was at home with Tricia and Julie watching events unfold on television. According to historian Will Swift, "She could not tolerate standing at her husband's side for yet another concession speech, having felt humiliated after seeing replays of herself crying at the Ambassador Hotel ballroom on Election Night two years before."

At the Beverly Hilton, Dick's disappointment and frustration exploded when he told Klein, "Screw them. I'm not going to do it. I don't have to, and I'm not going to. You read them my concession message to Brown, Herb, and if they want to know where I am you can tell them I've gone home to be with my family." But as Klein left, the television caught Dick's eye. Reporters were still doggedly asking for him. He had finally had enough.

Thus began one of the most famous concession speeches in American political history. All the years of political disappointment, disillusionment, frustration, and loss came into play. Pat and the girls watched this moment at home, probably not expecting the bitter tirade that poured forth next.

Dick said, "For sixteen years, ever since the Hiss case, you've had a lot of—a lot of fun . . . I leave you gentlemen now and you will now write it.

You will interpret it. That's your right. But as I leave you I want you to know—just think how much you're going to be missing. You won't have Nixon to kick around anymore, because gentlemen, this is my last press conference." At home, Pat cheered. Finally, he might really be done with politics. Julie recalled: "Watching my father on television in the den at home, Mother shouted 'Bravo' at the conclusion. To this day, she does not believe that he made a mistake in expressing his frustration with the biased reporting."

When Dick finally returned home that day, Pat and the girls were waiting for him inside by the front door. Pat tried to reach out to him, saying, "Oh Dick," but he was too upset to speak and headed outside instead. Julie remembered the scene as the "first, and the only, time my parents gave way to their emotions simultaneously, and it bewildered Tricia and me." Pat went upstairs and sat on her bed crying in front of the girls. They cried with her in the darkened room. Everyone in the family was heartbroken. The ever loyal Drowns took the girls for a few days so the couple could process the loss.

Dwight Chapin, the young advance man hired by Haldeman for the 1962 campaign, claimed that after briefly returning home, Dick "vanished. No one, including Mrs. Nixon, knew where he had gone. His family and friends were frantic. There was great concern for his safety, but they managed to keep it out of the media." A week later, Dick returned home; some claimed he had been at the beach house of his friend Tom Duggan. How worried Pat must have been, wondering where in the world her husband had disappeared to. She surely leaned on Helene and Rose Mary Woods as well as some of the other old Nixon hands for support.

ABC News later aired a piece entitled "The Political Obituary of Richard Nixon," which featured Dick's old nemesis Alger Hiss. *Time* magazine crowed, "Barring a miracle, Richard Nixon can never hope to be elected to any political office again."

However, as it would turn out, reports of Nixon's political death were greatly exaggerated.

———

Pat and Dick both agreed that New York City would be the perfect place to start over once again. Julie revealed: "Mother was enthusiastic about a move to New York, since it would be a clean break with politics. There my father would be without a political base and, in fact, in foreign territory, since his longtime rival Nelson Rockefeller controlled the state party." Through his friend Elmer Bobst, Dick connected with the New York law firm Mudge, Stern, Baldwin & Todd. After Nixon joined the firm, it was renamed Nixon, Mudge, Rose, Guthrie & Alexander.

The Nixons soon made the trip to New York to look for a home. They found a suitable apartment on the Upper East Side of the city, a cooperative at 810 Fifth Avenue. They would find out only later that Governor Nelson Rockefeller and his wife were among the tenants. The location featured scenic views of Central Park and the Plaza Hotel, but it had been poorly kept up and needed work. Pat, as always, was enthusiastic about decorating. Now that her husband was making real money in private practice ($250,000 a year), they could afford to splurge. Dick opened his wallet, letting his wife have free rein to fix up the property, and Pat set about remodeling and refurbishing immediately.

The Nixon family arrived in New York only days before setting off on a six-week European tour with Tricia, now seventeen, and Julie, fifteen. Accompanying them on the journey were the Drowns and their twenty-year-old daughter Maureen, who had spent the past year studying abroad in Spain. Maureen recalled many years later that the Nixons had come to "rescue" her after seeing a photo of her flashing her red-wine-stained teeth. (Apparently Maureen was having a little too good a time studying abroad that year.)

Maureen kept a detailed diary of their European adventure, filled with candid glimpses of Pat, Dick, and the girls in relaxed vacation mode. Maureen immediately noticed the high level of recognition Dick was accorded abroad: "People recognize him everywhere, in the car, in restaurants, in tunnels." The Nixons were American celebrities whom everyone wanted to meet. The Nixons and the Drowns were invited to dozens of formal cocktail parties, dinners, and special events over the course of their tour.

One particularly glamorous invite included a visit on July 26 to Greek shipping magnate Stavros Niarchos's ultra-luxury yacht, *The Creole*. Pat, Helene, Julie, and Tricia spent a day-to-evening visit with Stavros, his third wife, Eugenia, and their four children before heading back to Athens. Eugenia, Pat, and Helene hit it off, laughing and chatting for hours. Pat and Helene informed an intrigued Eugenia about the nascent diet cola craze in the United States, and "Pat later sent Eugenia a crate of 150 cans in different flavors of No Cal Cola!" Maureen recalled. Pat's thoughtful "diet diplomacy" won her yet another admirer.

Even in the context of a glamorous European tour, Pat was still thrust into "mother of teenagers" management mode. Maureen recalled that during a visit to Cairo and then the pyramids, "Pat would be pointing things out and making things interesting for teenage girls." However, Tricia and Julie were bored and hot, and from time to time their mother would have to remind them to behave. "I never heard Pat scold her children, but she had riveting eye contact. . . . She had an 'If I were you, I wouldn't do that!' look!"

While the Nixons and Drowns were in Rome, JFK arrived for a state visit. His popularity had been declining in recent days, and Maureen and Jack Drown, who attended his talk, reported that the crowd who showed up was not huge. Despite his packed schedule, JFK called Dick at the hotel just to check in. "Sounding happy and relaxed, he said that he had heard we were in Rome and just wanted to say hello. . . . This was to be the last time I talked to him; five months later he was dead."

This was the longest concentrated period that Dick had ever spent with his teenage daughters. It was a time of reacquaintance and reacclimation for the Nixon family. The pressure-filled political life was gone and their life as private citizens—though prominent ones—had begun. In his memoirs, Dick wrote: "For Pat, Julie, Tricia and me, this trip was one of the happiest times of our lives. What made it so special was that it gave us a chance to be together as a family."

Though Pat had traveled the world many times over at this point, this would be the trip that she would treasure the most. Julie remembered Maureen talking with her mother toward the end of the trip: "Mother told Maureen that the trip was a dream come true—she was with her family, traveling to far-off places. She also said that without parents, her early life had been very difficult, and that now, on this trip, she appreciated every moment."

18

A NEW LIFE ON THE UPPER EAST SIDE

After their summer in Europe, the Nixons returned home ready to settle into their fall routine. Dick threw himself into his new law practice. The girls started their school year at the renowned Chapin School, near their home on the Upper East Side. Founded in 1901, the school had educated generations of elite New Yorkers and boasted an impressive and eclectic roster of graduates, including First Lady Jackie Kennedy, socialite Sunny von Bülow, and the actress Jane Wyatt.

Tricia soon began dating Edward "Ed" Cox, the scion of a prominent New York family, after meeting him at a school dance. As Cox recalled with a laugh: "This very pretty girl from California showed up for a class dance at Chapin where I was at. She was new to New York, and someone had to be helpful to her! We hit it off right away." One of Tricia's escorts at the International Debutante Ball on December 30, 1964, would be none other than Cox.

Pat kept a close eye on her girls as they settled into their new, less public existence. She continued supervising the apartment remodel, and she occasionally joined other ladies for tea or lunch at the Plaza Hotel's Palm Court. "But more often than not, she avoided the round of ladies' social gatherings. She much preferred spending time with a small circle of friends."

Among Pat's old friends in the city were Kathleen Stans, whose husband, Maurice Stans, had worked for Eisenhower as his budget director and would later become the chairman of Nixon's Committee to Reelect the President. Other New York friends included former Eisenhower attorney general Bill Rogers and his wife, Adele. Soon after the Nixons' arrival in town, the Rogerses took them out to 21 for dinner. According to Nixon speechwriter Bill

Safire, "the happiest was Pat, glad to be rid of politics, where not even the victories were sweet."

———

In the early 1960s, New York was *the* epicenter for visual art and culture. In 1962, *Time* magazine ran a cover story on Pop Art, which had begun to challenge the Abstract Expressionist movement of the 1950s. Artists like Andy Warhol, Claes Oldenburg, and Bridget Riley pushed back against the serious tone of artists like Jackson Pollock, Lee Krasner, and Willem de Kooning with a lighter, more playful approach. Portraits of celebrities, comic strips, and giant latex sculptures of household objects would have been commonplace sightings in New York art galleries when the Nixons lived there.

However, Pat and Dick's taste in art ran toward the more traditional. Pat did not connect with abstract art; she much preferred representational painters like Andrew Wyeth. Pat enjoyed visiting the Metropolitan Museum of Art, but the Frick Collection was her favorite, as Tricia recalled, because it was "a home as opposed to a museum, and Mother would introduce friends who were visiting to its unique beauty." Pat and Dick also enjoyed a personal relationship with Helen Frick, who was "a loyal friend through all seasons to our family. And she entertained my parents at dinner several times during the sixties in her personal apartment at the Frick."

In the literary world, the roles of women were being questioned. In May 1962, Helen Gurley Brown published *Sex and the Single Girl*. This advice book was wildly popular, selling two million copies within three weeks. The author was a former secretary who had worked her way up the corporate ladder to become the highest-paid female copywriter on the West Coast. In her book, she encouraged women to experience guilt-free premarital sex. But the equally important message Gurley promoted alongside sexual freedom was female financial independence.

While *Sex and the Single Girl* was lighthearted in tone, Betty Friedan's *The Feminine Mystique* was more despairing. Written after five years of research, the book challenged "the assumption that women should be satisfied by the domestic sphere and traditional roles." Wasn't there something more out there? Wanting marriage and children was natural, Friedan wrote, but so was wanting outside fulfilling employment. "We can no longer ignore that voice within women that says: 'I want something more than my husband and my children and my home.'"

Helen Gurley Brown's emphasis on women's financial independence and Friedan's challenge to the traditional view of women and their domestic role would have resonated with Pat. Both early in her marriage and later as a political wife, she had demonstrated that a woman *could* balance it all—marriage, children, and fulfilling outside work, be it paid or volunteer. However, "having it all" clearly came with a cost.

For Pat, the highest price she paid for being in public life was time away from her girls. Then there was the secondary sacrifice of private self for public image. Added to the loss of family time and the lack of personal privacy was the sheer physical exhaustion of campaigning and the pressure to always be put together. Who could blame Pat for reveling in joyful New York anonymity after all those years under the national microscope?

———

On November 20, Dick flew to Dallas for a business trip. While there, he gave an interview to local reporters. From these journalists, Dick learned that demonstrations were planned to protest the president and vice president's upcoming visit to Dallas on the twenty-second. Early on the morning of the twenty-second, Dick arrived at the Dallas airport to head home. When Jack Kennedy arose that morning at the Hotel Texas in Fort Worth, he read the *Dallas Morning News*, which contained an article in which Dick predicted that Jack would drop LBJ from the ticket for the 1964 election.

The president and First Lady arrived at the Dallas airport and soon departed in their motorcade along with Lyndon and Lady Bird Johnson and Texas governor John Connally and his wife, Nellie. Riding through Dealey Plaza that afternoon, Jack was shot by assassin Lee Harvey Oswald at 12:30 p.m. and was pronounced dead at Parkland Memorial Hospital at 1 p.m.

When Dick pulled up to 810 Fifth Avenue in his cab that same afternoon, the doorman rushed out to meet him. "Tears were streaming down his cheeks. 'Oh, Mr. Nixon, have you heard, sir?' he asked. 'It's just terrible. They've killed President Kennedy.'" Dick was stunned: though he had been critical of some of the president's policies and programs, it was difficult to process that his former rival and friend had just been gunned down in Dallas in broad daylight.

Dick stayed up late the next evening penning a condolence note to the grieving First Lady. Within it, he noted his long friendship with Jack, a relationship that had remained cordial and cooperative despite the 1960 election. "While the hand of fate made Jack and me political opponents I always cherished the fact that we were personal friends from the time we came to the Congress together in 1947." He also took pains to note her contributions as First Lady: "You brought to the White House charm, beauty and elegance as the official hostess for America." The Nixons flew to Washington for the funeral mass and burial at Arlington on November 25. The "brief shining moment" of Kennedy's Camelot was over.

A few weeks later, Dick received a lengthy handwritten reply from Jackie, thanking him for the condolences he and Pat had sent. Her remarks were prescient: "I know how you must feel—so long on the path—so closely missing the greatest prize—and now for you, all the question comes up again—and you must commit all you and your family's hopes and efforts again. Just one thing I would say to you—if it does not work out as you have hoped for so long—please be consoled by what you already have—your life and your family." Pat must have appreciated those words and hoped that her husband took them to heart.

For a time, Dick seemed to heed Jackie's advice. Julie had happy memories of concentrated family time at 810 Fifth Avenue, which often included Rose Mary Woods. "That winter, my father was home for dinner more frequently than ever before. Rose Woods, who had become our unofficial aunt since all our family was in California and hers in Ohio, often accompanied him, coming straight home from the office." Dick would light a fire and immediately put on music, often from the family's favorite Broadway musicals. Such times were precious to Pat, Tricia, Julie, and Rose, but they were not to last for long.

———

After Kennedy's death, his former vice president, now president, Lyndon Johnson, was able to push through legislation that had previously stalled out.

Perhaps the most important piece of new legislation passed under Johnson was the Civil Rights Act of 1964, which he signed into law on July 2. The act forbade racial discrimination in public places, created a formal path toward integration of schools and public facilities, and made employment discrimination based on race illegal. "It was the most sweeping civil rights legislation since Reconstruction."

On the Nixon home front, Hannah Nixon visited the family in New York in the early summer for a lengthy stay. Pat once again took care of her aging mother-in-law, while her husband continued working in his law office. Though Pat was always careful not to complain, even to Helene, it is clear from her letter that she was relieved when Hannah had finally left: "Mrs. N. finally departed after a five week stay. She has aged a great deal, needs assistance walking, etc."

After Hannah's departure, the Nixons left for San Francisco. Dick had been invited to introduce Republican candidate Barry Goldwater at the Republican convention, which began on July 13. Julie recalled her mother having reservations about attending, as the ghost of the 1960 election still hovered in the back of her mind. However, she ultimately accompanied her husband to the events.

Despite his reservations, Dick spent the rest of the summer on the road stumping for Goldwater and for Republican House and Senate candidates. Pat went her own way with the girls, taking Tricia and Julie to Europe with her old friend Louise Johnson, who was then living in England. The teens, their mother, and her friend spent a month traveling by bus through Ireland, Scotland, Belgium, Holland, and Scandinavia. Pat wrote Helene that she was having such a good time, she wasn't sure she was ever coming home.

Tricia started her freshman year that fall at Finch College, just sixteen blocks from her home. She would excel there, majoring in modern European history, and would be elected class president her junior year. Now Pat needed more to do; she would soon fall back on her proficient office skills. Being a lady of leisure had been fun for a bit as Pat settled in, but she was bored with aimless socializing.

"Miss Ryan" began showing up at Dick's office on most weekdays. Dick's biographer Earl Mazo commented: "I've seen her there working her ass off. She'd come to the outer office early in the morning and sit at a desk near

Rose Mary Woods and work like the devil, pecking away at the typewriter." She answered the phone (always as "Miss Ryan"), typed correspondence, and answered the mail. On Saturdays she would often press Julie and Tricia into office service as well.

This office work on her husband's behalf kept her mentally engaged and was good for the marriage. Pat was still a contributing part of the Pat and Dick Team, but now she was a lawyer's wife in a city where she could be relatively anonymous. She could also be the daily hands-on mother she wanted to be for both Julie and Tricia when they came home from school and college. Pat thrived within this New York realm, which allowed her to experience the best of both worlds.

While Pat was not immersed in politics anymore, she still took a keen spectator's interest in that arena. Helene and Jack Drown also remained deeply involved in California politics, so this was a topic Pat and Helene frequently discussed in their letters. Prior to the 1964 election, she wrote Helene: "How are the Goldwaterites today? I am slaving 14 hours a day for 'the cause' helping Loie [Gaunt, one of Dick's secretaries] answer the requests from all the panic-stricken campaigners who want *help*."

Despite Dick's hard work on the campaign trail on behalf of Goldwater, and Pat's best efforts in his office, Johnson won by a landslide on November 3 with 61.1 percent of the popular vote and 486 electoral votes to Goldwater's 52 electoral votes. The Republican Party, which had traditionally had the stronger female voting bloc, was trounced in that area too. "For the first time since winning suffrage in 1920, women turned out to vote in higher numbers than men, and for the first time in a presidential election, more women voted Democratic than Republican."

The Republican Party would have to regroup and reformulate a new strategy going forward. Dick meant to be part of that reform, perhaps running again for president in 1968. He realized the demands another political run would make on Pat and the girls. He seemed to regret putting them back in the spotlight. But it was an irresistible urge he could not deny. He found legal work, even at its best, soul-crushing. By early 1965, he had made an important decision, but "I did not reveal to my family or anyone else that this was what I had in mind. I knew that Pat and the girls would again be disappointed. But I had finally come to the realization that there was no other life for me but politics and public service." The push-pull between his home and family life and his love of politics may have been the source of Dick's tension, an undercurrent of which ran throughout the Nixons' New York household as well.

1965, like the preceding year, was to be defined by the civil rights struggle, which continued to intensify. In February, civil rights crusader Malcolm X was gunned down at the Audubon Ballroom in Manhattan. He had advocated violent means if necessary to secure civil rights, saying, "There can be no revolution without bloodshed." His prediction was prophetic and presaged not only his own death but also the assassinations of other civil rights leaders in the coming years.

When spring arrived, however, "something happened that gave a rebirth of vigor to the movement": the famous March from Selma to Montgomery. During this mobile demonstration, Martin Luther King Jr. "called for more marches—on ballot boxes, segregated schools, poverty, 'until race baiters disappear from the political arena.'" Later that summer, real progress was made in this area when Congress passed the Voting Rights Act, which led to close to one million African Americans registering to vote between 1965 and 1970. This law would come up for renewal in 1970, when Dick would become more directly involved.

Though revolutions of all sorts were taking place around them in New York and nationwide, Pat's mothering duties were in the forefront of her mind in 1965. That May, Pat wrote Helene that "the gals [her affectionate term for Julie and Tricia] only have two more weeks of school. The years fly so fast—a good sign of old age. Those rocking chairs are beckoning." Pat would often refer wistfully to the rocking chairs she hoped she and Helene would one day occupy together. Those days, however, were still far in the future.

In the fall of 1966, Julie would become reacquainted with David Eisenhower, whom she had last seen in 1957. David was a freshman at Amherst College, not far from Smith, which Julie was attending. Both David and Julie were invited to speak at the Hadley, Massachusetts, Republican Women's Club; both declined after speaking to each other by phone. A few days later,

David would drop by to see Julie. A romantic relationship soon blossomed between the two young people.

The matchmaker behind the scenes? Mamie Eisenhower. The former First Lady met Julie again about a month before David went off to college and was very impressed with the young woman. As David recalled: "She sort of pestered me a bit to call her. Then there was the immediate chemistry." David noted that "the relationship was a big lift for my father and grandfather." He also realized that Pat was worried about a potential breakup in the spotlight.

Even so, David "felt accepted very fast" by the Nixon family, and the relationship progressed quickly. When Julie made her own debut at the International Debutante Ball in December, David was by her side as her civilian escort.

That summer, Dick surprised Pat with a romantic twenty-fifth-anniversary trip to Mexico. Well, as romantic an anniversary trip as it could be with two teenage girls accompanying them and Dick's best friend, Bebe Rebozo, meeting them at the Mexico City airport. The group stayed at La Reforma Hotel, where the Nixons had spent just one night of their budget honeymoon. Richard Nixon clearly cared about his wife, and he made efforts like this throughout their marriage to celebrate important dates in their relationship.

But he always had his eye on the political arena.

When they returned home, Dick was soon back to his punishing travel schedule. Even in this election off-year of 1965, Pat told Helene they couldn't take a vacation with the Drowns, as "Dick is traveling constantly it seems, boys' clubs, firm, politics, none of which is holidayish." The next year was even busier, with Dick traveling constantly in support of Republican candidates.

Julie noted that her mother worried about not going with her husband on his many political jaunts, "wondering aloud at one point to Tricia and me during a vacation in Key Biscayne over the Fourth of July whether she was 'a failure to Daddy.'" The longtime political wife must have known what was coming. "The handwriting was clearly on the wall and Pat was reading it. He had not left politics; he was not dead politically; he would rise from the ashes, and the old, familiar, rigorous routine would begin all over again."

Then a lull arrived before the storm. In 1967, Dick declared a "moratorium on politics." He stopped traveling and campaigning for others, staying home to read history, politics, and political philosophy. In August Pat escaped to California, where she spent three weeks alone with the Drowns.

Helene, always a straight shooter, told Pat that she and Jack still felt Dick had more to do on the national stage, and his rising popularity was evident in the political polls they avidly followed. Over many conversations that summer, the Drowns "gently turned aside her protests that she wanted 'peace of mind' and to 'live a normal life.'" Hadn't she left provincial Whittier to see the world and live a more meaningful existence?

Helene told Julie years later that "I sensed strongly that Pat still had a deep belief in your father's unique talent. She was sure that he alone was capable of solving some of the problems we were facing in the country then." But Pat's inner conflict was evident. She knew exactly what her husband wanted, and she wanted him to have that. However, it was not the life she wished for herself; she had been there and done that, and she knew the costs to the family.

There was more soul-searching on Dick's part when his mother passed away in the early fall of 1967. Hannah had suffered a stroke in 1965, and she had spent the past two years at a nursing home in Whittier. She died on September 30, 1967, at the age of eighty-two. Pat, Dick, and the girls immediately flew from New York to Los Angeles to attend the funeral.

Popular evangelist Billy Graham spoke at the funeral, held at Whittier Friends Church with nearly four hundred mourners filling the pews and spilling outside as well. Dick's brothers Don and Ed were there with their families, celebrating the quiet but spiritually strong woman who had such an impact on all their lives.

While Tricia and Julie were standing in front of Hannah's grave after the service, their uncle Tom Ryan led them quietly to another set of graves marked for Kate and Will Ryan: Pat's parents were buried in the same cemetery, just yards from Hannah and Frank Nixon's graves. Tom told the girls to make sure to "tell Pat." There is no record of Pat lingering there or visiting her parents' graves that day. For her, the past was the past, and in this case it was probably too painful to revisit it.

Dick, in contrast, was the more emotional spouse. His bottled-up emotions finally burst forth after the service as he wept with Billy Graham. Years later Dick would recall how he had encouraged his mother not to give up after a particularly painful operation in her last years. He recalled that she had struggled to sit upright in her bed, and "with a sudden strength in her voice she said, 'Richard, don't *you* give up. Don't let anybody tell you you are through.'" While Dick didn't listen to Jackie Kennedy's advice, he *would* take his mother's advice. One can only imagine Pat's dismay that her mother-in-law got the last word regarding Dick's career.

———

By Christmas, the matter had come to a head. After months of internal debate and many notes to self, written upon his favorite yellow legal pads, Dick had almost convinced himself that "I don't give a damn." But in truth he did want to run, to try again for what he thought was the greatest prize: the presidency.

It wasn't just Pat he had to convince, though; it was the girls too, and David Eisenhower, to whom Julie had recently become engaged. Even Dick's best friend, the laid-back Rebozo, was wary of yet another campaign. He feared for Dick but was much more concerned about the emotional welfare of the Nixon girls and their mother. "To me it was a personal thing," Rebozo said. "I didn't want him or the family to get hurt again. I'd seen what had happened in 1960 and especially in 1962. It just wasn't worth it."

Dick left the family after Christmas to mull over the potential run once more before making a final decision. Pat stayed home with the girls. He remembered, "As I left on December 28, Pat took my arm and kissed me. 'Whatever you do, we'll be proud of you,' she said. 'You know we love you.'" Dick spent days walking on the beach with Rebozo and Billy Graham hashing matters out. It speaks volumes that Pat did not go with him. Perhaps she hoped that if she left him alone and avoided a confrontation he would make the right choice for their family. This was the couple's long-term habit: nonconfrontation, and putting distance or space between them when big decisions loomed.

Ultimately, the pattern of past campaigns repeated itself. The family's initial reluctance and apprehension about being back on the public stage gave way to situational acceptance from the girls and grim resignation from Pat. Dick admitted to a *Good Housekeeping* reporter that running again "is a rough deal for the family." He insisted that "if the family had strongly resisted . . . I wouldn't have done it. Tricia, Julie and David, however, were definitely for it. Pat was neutral."

Pat's being "neutral" was Pat trying to say no but not being able to bring herself to do so. Pat remained a woman of her time and era in some ways. She told the same reporter at *Good Housekeeping* that "I don't care about politics one way or another, but a man has a right to make his own decision about his career. A woman should support that decision." Dick would always make a pretense of consulting her and the girls before each election, but everyone knew that he would end up in the race. "Her man would say that he was ready to give up all hopes and ambitions for her, if that was what she wanted, and she would reply that his destiny was her fate." In this way, Pat was a classic midcentury wife: her husband's career was her "career" too, and her wagon was hitched to his star.

The happy New York years marked significant steps forward in Pat's quest for a private family-centered life. But by January 1968, Pat and Dick would step back into the glare of the national spotlight—reluctantly, on Pat's part—to wave to the crowds during yet another campaign.

19

A TOGETHER COUPLE BUT
NOT TOGETHER AT TIMES

On January 9, 1968, Dick met a key figure who would raise his political profile using the still relatively new medium of television. This person would later become a major player in American cable television news. That evening, Dick was scheduled to be a guest on *The Mike Douglas Show* in Philadelphia. When he arrived at the studio, Dick dispatched his new assistant, Dwight Chapin, to find someone to brief him. Chapin would make an introduction that day that changed the media game both for Dick and for his 1968 campaign.

The twenty-seven-year-old executive producer whom Chapin introduced to his boss that day was none other than Roger Ailes, destined to later become the CEO of conservative media giant Fox News. Ailes, confident even at this young age, informed Dick: "Television is what you need to get elected. You have to make television your friend." Dick had already used television in the past to get his messages across. This had worked both to his advantage (in the Fund Crisis speech) and to his disadvantage (in the 1960 Nixon-Kennedy debates). This go-round, he wanted expert guidance on how to master the medium.

By the end of the month, Ailes had signed on to the campaign as Dick's television producer. Ailes would be working with television consultant Harry Treleaven, who hailed from the same glossy Madison Avenue ad agency, J. Walter Thompson, as Bob Haldeman and thus had instant credibility. The team would be headed up by former CBS division chief Frank Shakespeare. The candidate "gave this team carte blanche: 'We're going to build this whole campaign around television. You fellows just tell me what you want me to do and I'll do it.'"

Pat seemed innately suspicious of the whole enterprise, especially of Ailes. Joe McGinnis noted this antipathy in his classic *The Selling of the President*, documenting an interaction between Ailes and Pat in September 1968. The two entered an elevator together after Dick's televised appearance in Philadelphia, and though Ailes tried to chat with her, Pat did not speak or respond to him. It was clear from this interaction that Pat didn't like or trust Ailes. Something instinctive inside her recoiled from him and his brand of televised self-promotion. Her distrust of the young producer and her dismissal of his pleasantries may have indicated her inner turmoil. This campaign was taking a different direction, one she did not feel comfortable with at all.

In addition to Ailes, many of those whom Dick was gathering around him came from the advertising and media world. Bob Haldeman, Dwight Chapin, Ron Ziegler, and Larry Higby all came from J. Walter Thompson. This New Nixon team believed in the power of television, through which the campaign could reach large numbers of voters with relatively minimal effort. Eight years after the 1960 election, technology had changed, and so had the kind of men Dick was hiring to keep up with the times.

Shakespeare was advising Dick to get rid of his "Old Nixon" hands, who, he claimed, only knew how to fight using "Old style politics." "The key to the campaign," he continued, "will be how successfully the candidate resists the advice of the old political types." The "tour manager" in 1968, John Ehrlichman, also supported this approach, writing dispassionately in his 1982 book *Witness to Power*, "In the staffing of the 1968 campaign, many old Nixon loyalists were shunted to insubstantial or honorary roles to make room for more able and efficient newcomers." As it would turn out, Pat too was considered an "old hand" and thus someone whom the new guard sought to minimize.

While Ehrlichman had had little interaction with Pat in the 1960 and 1962 campaigns, he intersected with her frequently in 1968. His early assessment of Pat was not flattering. "By 1968 she was telling her husband's staff what to do; she obviously saw herself as an experienced campaigner with an ability to sense what voters might be thinking." Ehrlichman claimed the staff took their cues from her husband, who "seldom included her in his deliberations on strategy or scheduling. He treated her as a respected but limited partner." From Ehrlichman's point of view, Pat's most intense dislike was reserved for Haldeman, who "bore the brunt of Pat's dissatisfaction over campaign arrangements."

Haldeman and Pat did not start out well as the 1968 campaign kicked off. Daughter Julie noted that Haldeman forgot not once but twice to introduce her mother at 1968 campaign rallies. Only when The Boss took Haldeman to task did he correct the issue. This was not a small detail, and it was one that caused understandable resentment on Pat's part. "Haldeman had been on the periphery during the vice-presidential days, and thus underestimated my mother as a political asset."

Dwight Chapin had a foot in both the Old Nixon and New Nixon camps. He had first been hired by Haldeman in 1962 for the California gubernatorial campaign. Chapin had been offered a job with ABC, but his career mentor, Haldeman, made him another offer. Haldeman moved Chapin, his wife, Susie, and their two girls to New York City for a job with J. Walter Thompson, ostensibly so Chapin could learn the ad business. The other sweetener to the deal: "If you're back east, I think we can get you involved working with Nixon."

In 1967, Chapin was hired as Dick's personal assistant, and he began working out of the Nixons' Fifth Avenue apartment. Chapin's "office" was a small desk in the closet of one of the guest bedrooms. Around noon every day, Pat would come in and ask if he wanted lunch, a sandwich or something simple. Chapin recalled Pat's "graciousness and warmth towards me as just Dwight." She became both his tutor and mentor for the campaign's office work. "She's checking me out, she's getting to know me, she's trusting me." The young employee barely saw Nixon for the first few months of his new job. Pat was doing Dick's due diligence on his recruit. She "was a hurdle I didn't even know existed."

The other guardian of the Nixon galaxy was the "Fifth Nixon," Rose Mary Woods. Like Pat, Rose had been devastated by the 1960 election's outcome. Chapin called her "a verifier of that trauma. She knows the 1960 election was stolen. She knows all the gossip." Rose naturally functioned as "the linchpin to all the old friends." As the New Nixon team assembled and began to sideline the old hands, "Rose was answering all the calls from old friends bitching about losing contact with him."

Dick's soon-to-be presidential aide Steve Bull remembered Rose Mary as "a political celebrity during the 1968 campaign." She was treated as such by the advance men on that campaign. Steve attended a big meeting for the 1968 campaign advance team where Ehrlichman told them all: "Rose Woods is one of the best, she's a political figure in her own right." But Rose Mary's perch was now being challenged by the new regime and by Haldeman in particular. The two eyed each other warily, both vying to be The Boss's right-hand person in his second presidential campaign.

Chapin had a bird's-eye view of both factions. The young man observed that as the 1968 election approached, his boss wanted "all the young people and their energy for the next administration." Dick was bringing fresh talent in, but this displeased some of the old-timers. "The older people were sabotaging the newer people coming in." At the same time, Haldeman was instructing Chapin: "Don't go to Rose's parties. Keep quiet." A toxic environment was brewing, with Rose reporting back to Pat about the drama.

It wasn't just those on the inside of the campaign who noticed radical changes in the Nixonian entourage. Feminist activist and reporter Gloria Steinem, who covered the 1968 campaign, wrote that with a few notable exceptions the 1968 Nixon campaign staff "is almost totally new since '60." These young Turks had a merchandising and sales approach instead of the previous traditional political approach. "Top aides do not speak of policy briefings but of 'programming the candidate.'"

Joe McGinnis noted the same sea change. The bottom line? Strategic commodification of the candidate. McGinnis noted "a striking new phenomenon—the marketing of political candidates as if they were consumer products." This image-based approach would not be limited to the candidate; the image-making would apply to his wife and daughters as well. The difference was that the Nixon women hadn't agreed to the New Nixon team's packaging deal.

Helen Thomas, chief of United Press International's White House bureau, had been covering Pat Nixon and the Nixon campaigns since 1960. She too noticed the phalanx of young men Dick had gathered around him, as well as their disregard for Pat and her significant political experience:

When I met Mrs. Nixon again in 1968, I saw a much more sophisticated, confident woman. She was clearly not gung ho about campaigning and would solo stump as little as possible. Her daughters took over where she had left off. Mostly she just went along for the ride, while Nixon's bright young public relations men ran a smooth campaign with much fla[ir] and little substance. They did not seem to care whether she was around or not. Women had no place on their high-powered team.

Pat intensely disliked this Madison Avenue approach. Despite her teaching and acting experience, she had never felt comfortable on television, shunned the spotlight, and studiously avoided too much publicity. This didn't mean she had no opinions or was ignorant of election strategy and tactics. Decades of political experience put her light-years ahead of the new team in many ways. But this wisdom was often discounted due to her age and her gender. She was considered "old-fashioned" in her political approach, *and* she was a woman—two strikes, in the minds of some of the young male staffers. *What could she possibly know?* they thought, routinely underestimating her.

———

On January 31, 1968, Dick officially announced his candidacy for president. On February 2, Dick made his first official remarks as a candidate at the Holiday Inn in Manchester, New Hampshire. This press conference would be much different from his last, infamous one in 1962, after he lost the California gubernatorial race. This time, the New Nixon joked a bit with reporters, quipping: "Gentlemen, this is *not* my last press conference!"

Due to foggy conditions, Pat and Tricia arrived later that evening, as did Julie and her fiancé, David Eisenhower. Dick worried about putting his son-in-law-to-be in an awkward position due to his grandfather's tradition of candidate neutrality prior to the convention. Ultimately, though, David attended the press reception and "was quietly baptized into the presidential campaign."

David fit seamlessly into the entourage. Like Tricia and Julie, he soon had a chartered campaign plane named after him. Writer Gloria Steinem took note, quipping, "Having that [name] painted on a plane seems a big strain on a 20-year-old's engagement." David seemed to take it all in stride, joining Julie that spring for a thirty-state campaign tour that focused on smaller cities. Tricia frequently stumped solo for her father. The whole family worked hard for the cause.

But it was Pat, "the family member who least wanted to be involved," who "ended up working the hardest." She was still doing the mundane tasks, the daily meet-and-greets with everyday people that no one else wanted to do. "While her husband rested or worked in his hotel room, she went to the factories, schools, and shopping centers." Even when the family took weekends off in Key Biscayne, she would write up to fifty handwritten letters a day. Here Pat's daily political drudge work—the personal signatures, the public appearances, the GOP women's coffees and teas, disdained by some on the New Nixon team—paid dividends.

Though Pat was not a fan of Eleanor Roosevelt, she had a similar "eyes and ears" approach in regard to filling her husband in on women's issues. "I fill him in on what women think. They're thinking peace at home and peace abroad." Pat and his daughters were his best connection to women and the women's vote, something many on the New Nixon team either dismissed or devalued. This even though the ratification of the ERA was again a plank of the GOP campaign. Nixon himself pointed out its importance prior to the August convention: "All Republican Conventions since 1940 have supported the long-time movement for such equality."

The one thing Pat and the New Nixon team agreed upon was a less punishing campaign schedule. The 1960 run had taken a real mental and physical toll on both Dick and Pat. This time they would not make that mistake. "They did not want to end up with a candidate as exhausted and ill as the Nixon of 1960. . . . He would travel to fewer states (twenty-seven) and would refrain from presidential debates—which would have benefitted his challenger."

Overseas, the unpopular Vietnam War continued to diminish the power and credibility of President Johnson. Beginning on January 31, the Tet Offensive in Vietnam brought the conflict to a head. And while this massive Vietcong-led offensive resulted in a monumental defeat for the communist forces, popular *CBS Evening News* anchor Walter Cronkite announced—much to LBJ's chagrin—that the United States was now in a no-win situation. After a visit to Saigon, the formerly balanced newsman was so discouraged at what he had seen, he gave the American people one of journalism's first on-air op-eds, saying, "It seems now more certain than ever that the bloody experience of Vietnam is to end in a stalemate."

Former national security advisor under President Donald Trump and military historian H. R. McMaster explained: "This is exactly what the Vietnamese Communists wanted out of Tet. They really got defeated militarily. They took losses that they could not replace in terms of the Vietnamese communist infrastructure in the South. It was a defeat of the Viet Cong. . . . But that story, the narrative became that the war is futile . . . it's had a big impact on U.S. enemies and adversaries, the idea that if you can mount a large-scale offensive, then America will just quit."

While bombs continued to be lobbed on both sides in Southeast Asia, bombshells also fell in the domestic press. On March 16, Robert F. Kennedy stepped into the fray, announcing his candidacy for president. A mortal enemy of Johnson's, RFK heartily opposed Johnson's Vietnam War policy. In March 1967, RFK had given a significant speech on the issue. After that, he was "thoroughly identified as the major spokesman on that issue against Johnson at that point."

To both Dick and Pat, the déjà vu of RFK's candidacy must have been unsettling. Pat mistrusted the Kennedys perhaps even more than her husband did; would RFK steal this election from them as well? After watching RFK's announcement on television, both Ehrlichman and young speechwriter Pat Buchanan "recalled a gloom settling over the Nixon campaign."

On March 31, Lyndon Johnson, "who had gone to such great lengths to ensure a crushing defeat of Barry Goldwater in 1964, declared he was withdrawing from the race for his party's presidential nomination." Vietnam had suffocated his chances of reelection. His efforts to ignore Vietnam-related issues such as the POW/MIA problem had also backfired on him. He was deeply unpopular at this point, and he knew his hopes of winning another term were gone.

Then, on April 4, civil rights leader Martin Luther King Jr. was murdered on the balcony of the Lorraine Motel in Memphis. "When he was murdered, it seemed that nonviolence went to the grave with him, and the movement was 'free at last' from restraint." In the wake of the murder, riots broke out in the streets, and chaos reigned. Dick would fly to Atlanta to pay his respects to MLK's wife, Coretta, and would attend his funeral, marching in the procession with the likes of Jackie Robinson, RFK, and Marlon Brando in a show of respect and support. MLK's murder was only the beginning of the season of violence that would mark 1968.

On June 4, the night of the California Democratic primary, the Nixon family and Julie's fiancé David Eisenhower gathered at the Nixons' Fifth Avenue apartment to watch the returns. RFK triumphed over Senator Eugene McCarthy, and the family retired to their beds. David, however, stayed up a bit later and soon woke the family with the news that RFK had been shot while giving his victory speech at the Ambassador Hotel. By June 6, Kennedy was dead.

———

In July Dwight Eisenhower did something he had resisted doing in the past: he endorsed Richard Nixon for president on July 18, ahead of the convention. The Nixon family was elated. The former president's endorsement would help the team sail confidently into the nominating process.

On August 7 at the GOP convention in Miami, Dick won the nomination against challengers Nelson Rockefeller and Ronald Reagan on the first ballot. Maryland governor Spiro Agnew would be his running mate. Though most of the Nixon entourage was ecstatic, Julie recalled that her mother's reaction was muted: "In contrast, Mother was subdued. Burned by her overconfidence in 1960, she was taking each day of the campaign as one, simply to get through until the final test."

Perhaps this less frantic, calmer approach improved her image with the press as well. Reporters covering the Republican convention in Miami gushed about the "new Pat Nixon." Marie Smith from the *Washington Post* filed a glowing report after a sit-down at the convention with Pat. "Pat Nixon at 55 has a new sophistication that goes well with her old friendliness. She has a more relaxed smile, a confident sparkle in her brown eyes. . . . She has more self-assured poise as she answers questions about her public and private life."

Reporter Betty Beale confirmed this take on the "new Pat Nixon" in her own convention profile for the *Boston Globe*. "When you talk to Pat Nixon alone, you wonder why anyone ever thought that Pat was a stiff woman with a masked smile. She is warmly approachable and laughs frequently and easily."

By October, however, some of the goodwill from the women's press seemed to be diminishing. And Pat's patience with what she considered their silly questions was wearing thin. Steinem caught a glimpse of this resentment in October 1968, in the last, exhausting days of the Nixon campaign. Her piece "Patricia Nixon Flying" may have overexaggerated Pat's chagrin with her line of questioning, but it revealed Pat's deep-seated resentment of the press and those she and her husband considered Eastern establishment types.

Steinem interviewed Pat on one of the Nixon campaign planes en route to St. Louis. She began the piece by opining that Pat had "shared all the vilification and praise without ever emerging in public as an individual. I was eager to meet her, but all her other interviewers said Mrs. Nixon had put them straight to sleep." According to Steinem, she and Pat went back and forth while Mrs. Nixon gave her bland answers to questions she had likely been asked hundreds of times already.

When asked whom she admired most in history, Pat cited Mamie Eisenhower "because she meant so much to young people." Steinem disputed this idea, noting that she had been in college when Mamie was First Lady and hadn't noticed her influence on that segment of the population. Pat pushed back, saying, "I never had time to think about things like that—who I wanted to be, or who I admired, or to have ideas. I never had time to dream about being anyone else. I had to work. My parents died when I was a teenager, and I had to work my way through college. . . . I worked in a bank while Dick was in the service. . . . I haven't just sat back and thought about myself or my ideas or what I wanted to do. . . . I don't have time to worry about who I admire or who I identify with. I've never had it easy. I'm not like all you . . . all these people who had it easy."

What Steinem's snapshot showed was a woman weary of what she considered trivial and unimportant questions. Pat had developed a standard set of press responses, and when Steinem pitched her a fastball ("Who do you most admire in history?"), she blanked. Mamie Eisenhower was probably top of mind for other reasons such as her daughter Julie's engagement, but it is doubtful that she was truly the person Pat most admired from history. Due to her daughter's relationship with Mamie's grandson, she also would not have wanted to offend Mamie by naming another First Lady.

There were several reasons that Pat appeared less than authentic to Steinem. First, Pat was legitimately tired of reporters trying to pick her apart, trying to "analyze" her. Second, the quotes she doled out to the press were carefully thought out so as not to be inflammatory or controversial. She knew from previous campaigns that one misstep on her part could result in lost votes. By giving out innocuous replies, she could ensure that she would not be the cause of problems for the campaign. Steinem was just doing her job here, but so was Pat as a practiced political wife.

Unfortunately for Pat, stories like this one tended to reinforce her "Plastic Pat" image. Honest answers would have served her better. But they also would have given away private pieces of herself that she did not feel comfortable sharing. As Julie observed during the 1968 election cycle, "In the spotlight of the press . . . my mother sought increasingly to preserve a core of privacy when interviewed. She kept the focus on Nixon programs and on the volunteers. When she was asked about her childhood, invariably she recited two or three unchanging stories."

The Nixon marriage was another constant source of speculation in the press. On the campaign trail, some staffers were able to observe the relationship at close range. During the many months on the road with Pat, Dick, and the Nixon entourage, Chapin for one became "keenly aware of the sensitivities between the President and Mrs. Nixon." The Nixon team would all stay together in a motel, "not the Ritz like a Howard Johnson's." A typical evening after a rally would involve Dick ordering a hamburger to eat in his room so he could keep working. He would eventually ask Chapin to "tell Mrs. Nixon she should have dinner with Rose."

Chapin would knock on the door of Pat's hotel room, where Pat and Rose would often be having a cocktail together. Pat would look up and say, "Dwight, I know, Rose and I should get some dinner." It all made for an awkward interaction. To Dick, campaign season was "a committed, highly intense thing, winner takes all, meaning the presidency." But when drafted as the couple's intermediary, Chapin found these situations uncomfortable. "I can't tell you how much I dreaded these kinds of encounters."

Jack Carley, who was Pat's driver during the 1962 campaign, explained their dynamic this way: Nixon was "one track . . . this was often interpreted as him being insensitive to his wife. But she was his best friend." Chapin also remarked, "When Pat or the girls came to his office, everything stopped so he could talk to them." It was clear to everyone that Pat and Dick's relationship was complicated. Chapin's take in 1968? The Nixons were "a together couple but not together at times."

———

There were two major campaign planks during the 1968 election. First and foremost was the Vietnam War quagmire. Republicans would focus on ending the Vietnam War honorably, pulling American troop numbers down while helping train the South Vietnamese to take over their own fight for democracy. The second plank was domestic. Dick and his administration would restore law and order to a troubled America, tamping down violence on the home front.

Dick tapped into a gold mine of votes during the campaign with his characterization of "forgotten Americans." These voters were against hippies, against radical causes; they were "'the non-shouters, the non-demonstrators' who constituted the majority." He and Pat fit this same mold. They both detested scenes, shouting, and public demonstrations of emotion. He was referring to a group he and his wife had always identified with.

Dick's Democratic challenger, Hubert Humphrey, was LBJ's vice president. Though Humphrey also received his nomination on the first ballot, the Democratic National Convention in Chicago in late August suffered from rashes of violence and intraparty strife. A televised clash between antiwar protestors and Chicago police on the night of Humphrey's nomination cast a pall over his run that would be hard for him to shake.

Another fly in the election ointment was southern segregationist and former Alabama governor George Wallace, who ran for president in 1968 on the American Independent Party platform. He set both Dick and Humphrey on edge during the final months of the campaign. Shockingly, October 1968 polls indicated Wallace had captured 23 percent of the electorate. As the three candidates raced to the campaign finish line on November 5, a tense and troubled country held its collective breath.

On Election Day, the Nixon family boarded one of their campaign planes, the *Tricia*, en route from Los Angeles to New York. Pat and Dick had voted already via absentee ballot. Even though Dick felt confident he would win, he called Pat, Tricia, Julie, and David to his private office compartment on the plane to prepare them just in case he lost. "I told them how proud I was of their tireless campaigning. I said how it would be almost impossible for me to lose this election by popular vote. But it *could* happen, and I wanted them to be prepared just in case." Ever sentimental, Dick marked the occasion by giving Pat a diamond and pearl pin with matching earrings.

The Nixon family, David, and the campaign team disembarked at Newark Airport and headed to the Waldorf Towers to settle in for a long election eve. Pat and the girls had their own separate suite. The staff gathered in a large communal suite to await the returns. Dick stayed sequestered with his advisors Haldeman and John Mitchell. Helene and Jack Drown, their old faithful friends, stayed with the women throughout the long, tense evening, bringing some much-needed calm to everyone's frayed nerves.

Pat, Julie, and Tricia had no contact with Dick during those nerve-racking hours of vote counting. It was a curious arrangement, separating the women from the campaign staff and their operations. Julie recalled that other than Jack Drown, "we spoke to no one who was in authority in the campaign who might have brought us up to date on any information that was not being reported on television."

Things got so strained in the family quarters that David left around 2 a.m. "Election night in 1968 I was in the family suite at the Waldorf. When this thing got close and it looked like it was going to be a redo of 1960, I just realized that I was in the presence of something I was really not part of. . . . She [Pat] might have been skeptical in 1968, but she was part of it and wanted it to succeed."

Though Pat took a short nap, no one really went to bed that evening. It looked at various points as though Humphrey might win. With no communication from the higher-up staff, the Nixon women had no clear idea during the late night and early morning what the outcome might be. Pat's nerves were completely shredded by 6 a.m. The television commentary sparked traumatic memories of the 1960 election, and Julie, Tricia, and the Drowns heard her being sick to her stomach in the bathroom.

Around 8:30 a.m. Chapin saw the announcement on television: Richard Milhous Nixon would be the next president of the United States. He ran down to the hall and was the first to give Dick the news: "Sir, ABC just announced that you have won!" The staff all poured into the suite's living room area, wildly cheering at the news. Dick then made his way down the hall, still in his bathrobe, to give his family the news now that he was 100 percent sure of the outcome.

When Dick arrived and told them the news, the family almost collapsed with both relief and joy, the tension had been so great. Pat asked him with trepidation if he was sure about the votes from Illinois. When he reassured her that they indeed had the votes there they needed, Pat "cried with relief and happiness. It was only then that she allowed herself to feel elated." And called her good friend Priscilla Kidder, the designer who was then in the midst of creating Julie's wedding gown, to tell her jubilantly, "We won!"

Humphrey conceded at 11:30 a.m. By noon, Dick, Pat, Tricia, Julie, David and the entire Nixon team filed into the Waldorf ballroom for Dick's acceptance speech. With a twinkle in his eye, Dick joked: "Having lost a close one eight years ago and having won a close one this year, I can say this—winning's a lot more fun."

After a small private reception and a trip home to pack, the Nixons were back on another plane—this time Air Force One, lent to them by President Johnson, headed to Key Biscayne. Here they would rest and regroup but also plan for their future in the White House. Julie recalled her parents' uncharacteristic actions as they stood on the threshold of the aircraft. "Once under the shelter of the plane, they turned to each other. Simultaneously, they embraced, and my father swung Mother around in a pirouette."

Soon after the election, a beautiful handwritten note arrived by hand for Pat with a 1040 Fifth Avenue return address. The note was from Jacqueline Kennedy Onassis, congratulating her and sending her best wishes to her and her family on their "new life. You are such a close family that I know you will be able to be happy, in spite of the pressures and the absence of privacy."

PART III

LEADING LADY

20

THE HARDEST UNPAID JOB
IN THE WORLD

Dick's presidential election win was not the most important thing on Pat's mind in the late fall of 1968. She had a momentous occasion to plan, and it had nothing to do with the upcoming inauguration in January. Julie and David Eisenhower had been engaged since December 1967, but they had decided to wait to announce their wedding date until the presidential election was over. Once Dick won, he urged them to consider waiting to wed until after the inauguration, when he and Pat could host their nuptials at the White House.

Although Pat liked David very much, she had mixed feelings about Julie marrying so young. She confided her feelings to Helene, who wrote down snippets of their conversation while on the campaign trail: "I wish J & D had waited until after college because then they'd be adults—easier." Pat also worried that there would be "no other married students on campus" and the two would be "isolated . . . all the fun is gone."

As for David, after so much time on the road with his fiancée and his in-laws, the young man knew exactly what he was getting into. He quickly re-alized that Pat and her daughters "were incredibly tight" and that respecting the mother-daughter relationship was critical to getting along with his future mother-in-law. He caught glimpses of Pat that others didn't often see. "She had a good sense of humor, very wry, very smart in a low-key way. She didn't offer a lot of opinions but the ones that she did were very well considered and bore up. Particularly on people."

Despite their young age, both Julie and David had firm ideas regarding their wedding day. David recalled, "I put my foot down on a White House wedding. I felt encasing a wedding in a White House ceremony was really too much." Julie emphasized that once she and David decided on a non–White House wedding, there was no pressure from her parents to change their minds. "My parents never questioned our decision, nor did they try to make the wedding a political thank-you party."

The ceremony would be held at the Marble Collegiate Church in New York City, where the Nixons regularly attended services. The young couple selected the church's pastor, famous theologian Dr. Norman Vincent Peale, to perform the ceremony.

All went as planned except for one unexpected twist: press coverage. Traditionally, the weddings of presidential children had been covered widely. Julie and David bucked past conventions by not allowing the press to cover their church ceremony. "Our decision not to allow the press coverage of the ceremony seemed heretical." This was akin to not being able to cover a royal wedding or coronation, and it sorely aggrieved the media. The New Nixon press team aggravated the situation further with its disorganization and attempts to control news coverage of the wedding reception.

More than a thousand spectators were standing outside the church, hoping to catch a glimpse of the bride and groom. This huge crowd included members of the press, including Judith Martin, a young *Washington Post* reporter who would later achieve fame as the etiquette columnist Miss Manners. (Martin would also be portrayed in the 2017 movie *The Post*.) Judith and her friend and fellow *Post* reporter Myra McPherson were issued press passes for the church and the reception following. However, due to David and Julie's wish for privacy, the press were ultimately only allowed to stand outside the church during the ceremony.

After the ceremony was over, wedding guests were bused over to the Plaza Hotel for dinner and dancing. The Plaza was known as the "Dowager Queen of American Hotels" and had hosted New York's social elite for over sixty years. Despite the hotel's glamorous reputation, the night of the Eisenhower wedding the Plaza felt decidedly dressed down. The wedding reception had no reserved tables and no head table, a more casual arrangement. Like the church, the Plaza was decorated for Christmas without additional flourishes.

Martin and McPherson were among other invited members of the press who had been told they could attend the reception. However, the Nixon communications staff soon changed the game plan. They "herded us into a room with a big bar, a lot of liquor. Get 'em drunk, right?" remembered Martin. "And they said we couldn't go into the reception, but they would come out every once in a while and brief us about what was going on. I ask you, as a journalist, would you want the Nixon spokesperson covering the event and telling you what to write? So Myra and I just went in, but we had credentials to do so."

Martin and McPherson "sneaked down a back stairwell, slipped their wedding rings into their purses and emerge[d] with the rest of the guests, pretending to be friends of Julie's." When the two women were recognized, they made a quick exit. But they had their scoop. Regardless of the minor press skirmish behind the scenes, Dick recalled the day in his memoirs fondly: "That night, Pat and I sat in front of the fire in our apartment and talked about the day and how beautiful Julie had looked and about how perfect the ceremony had been. But I know we were both thinking about time: about how fast it goes, and about how little of it there is to do the important things with the people who really matter to you."

Just before and soon after Julie and David's wedding, Pat began to absorb her duties as First Lady and think about her impending move to the White House. Wearing a green-and-white-checkered dress from Mignon originally purchased by her daughter Julie, Pat arrived for a tour of the White House hosted by Lady Bird soon after the election. Lady Bird and Pat were already acquainted through their membership in the Ladies of the Senate and were on friendly terms. Pat, Tricia, and Julie would be back and forth to the White House several times before the inauguration to prepare the family quarters for their residency.

The Johnsons and the Nixons, despite the political rivalry of the past, put their differences behind them on Inauguration Day. They met that morning for coffee in the Red Room in front of a cheery fireplace. LBJ welcomed Pat with a kiss. The Humphreys also joined the conversation, and the wives and husbands chatted amicably together. LBJ had thoughtfully made sure that the Nixon dogs, Vicky and Pasha, were on hand, groomed and eager to greet their family after a good night's rest in the White House kennels.

The Nixon women sported colorful Mignon-designed winter coats in cyclamen pink, pale blue, and apple green at the inauguration ceremony, standing out against the wintry backdrop and delighting the fashion press. Pat held up the two Milhous family Bibles for her husband to take his oath of office, followed by Dick's inaugural address focusing on peace both at home and abroad. Jo Haldeman, chief of staff Bob Haldeman's wife, remembered that Pat seemed ill at ease that freezing cold day. From her seat, Jo noticed a "tight smile is frozen on her face, I wonder what she is thinking."

Perhaps the discomfort Jo Haldeman noticed on the new First Lady's face was due to the domestic unrest percolating just behind the scenes that day. The pageantry and historic nature of the inauguration were undercut by the ugliness of the antiwar protests taking place all over Washington that day. The vitriol that had been reserved for Johnson was immediately transferred to the new president: he would enjoy no honeymoon period on the Vietnam War issue.

Demonstrators lined Pennsylvania Avenue, and the new president and First Lady were soon grateful to have a bullet-proof sunroof protecting their presidential limousine. "This was the first disruption of an inaugural parade or ceremony in 180 years of the American Presidency. . . . It was so bad that when the Nixons' limousine got to 13th Street, a barrage of sticks, stones, beer cans, bottles and obscenities hit the vehicle." This time the Nixons were not in Caracas facing communist demonstrators; they were in their own country facing a divided nation. This marred an otherwise monumental day for the couple and likely brought back traumatic memories. A conflict between the protestors and the police occurred later that day, and a total of eighty-one people were arrested.

Still, the show had to go on. After a candlelit steak dinner in the White House Family Dining Room, the Nixon family attended six inaugural balls together. Helene and Jack Drown were also present to witness their friends' spectacular success. Pat's Southern California fashion palette would extend to her inaugural dress—a golden-hued showstopper in "mimosa silk satin," designed by Karen Stark for Harvey Berin in New York with a matching bolero jacket and cummerbund embroidered with Swarovski crystals. Julie and Tricia sported gowns of white and pink, respectively, by designer Priscilla Kidder, their longtime family friend.

When Pat, Dick, Julie, Tricia, and David finally returned home to the White House together just before 2 a.m., David showed them the secret place where he had stashed a note inscribed "I shall return" eight years before, when his grandfather was president. Tricia and Julie discovered that the Johnson daughters had left a stock of butter brickle ice cream and Dr Pepper soda in the White House refrigerator. Dick, ever sentimental, played a song he had composed in honor of Pat before they were married on the grand piano in the Family Quarters.

As the staterooms were dark and quiet, Pat suggested, "Dick, let's turn on all the lights in the White House and make it cheery." Her wish was granted, and the White House glowed like a gem. They had finally won "the greatest prize," as Jackie Kennedy had called it. At least it seemed so in the post-inaugural glory of that first evening.

———

Dick began his presidency facing Democratic control of both the Senate and the House—the first president in 120 years confronting this scenario. He had to lead a country bitterly divided over the war in Vietnam; Inauguration Day had already forced both Dick and Pat to stare antiwar activists in the face. One unifying factor was the growing concern for American prisoners of war and those missing in action. Just a few days into his new administration, the new president received over two thousand telegrams from the POW/MIA wives' lobby "reminding him to put the POW/MIA situation at the very top of his agenda."

Pat had her own constituencies to win over, the first one being the women of the press. Pat's press secretary, Gerry Van der Heuvel, had barely begun her job for the First Lady when she was also called upon to speak at the Women's National Press Club luncheon honoring Lady Bird's press secretary, Liz Carpenter, on February 7. Van der Heuvel's humorous remarks focused on White House décor, the First Lady's wardrobe, and whom Tricia would be allowed to date. But underneath the jokes, she laid down some parameters as well as expectations for both the press and the West Wing.

The biggest question of all from the female press was what the First Lady's "project" would be. Until Jackie Kennedy, First Ladies did not usually have specific projects. However, Jackie's refurbishment of the White House and subsequent televised tour were so popular that ever after, First Ladies were pushed by the media and their administrations to come up with a signature program. Lady Bird followed with her well-publicized beautification efforts.

Following this relatively new tradition, Pat was also expected to come up with something to stamp her First Lady status. Van der Heuvel's play here was to give her boss some time and wiggle room to make up her mind on this issue. "Mrs. Nixon has given a great deal of thought to what her efforts can accomplish in this area of concern. What that area is and what direction her efforts will take, she—herself—will reveal."

It wasn't just the press pushing Pat for a signature project, though; pressure was coming at her from the West Wing staff as well. As Julie pointed out, "The attitude of the President's aides towards the First Lady—and her East Wing staff—was divided into two groups: on one hand, her presence has little to do with us; on the other hand, a keen interest in her activities. Those who did take an interest in the First Lady's role in the Administration were agreed that she should, as the press inquiries mounted, focus on one project above all others."

Presidential speechwriter Bill Safire confirmed this push behind the scenes, noting, "All the image types would pull their beardless chins about Mrs. Nixon's 'Project'—that is, something that she would become identified with. . . . 'Volunteerism' was the thing, and we envisioned her traveling the country like a new Florence Nightingale, reawakening the spirit of volunteer service." It was another advertising campaign, and it made Pat uncomfortable. She disliked being "programmed" by the West Wing, the press or anyone else.

Thus, female members of the Washington press corps were shocked and delighted when the new First Lady invited them all to a February 17 "sit-down luncheon at a big table in the State Dining Room. They drew numbers for seats at the table, and Pat drew a number too. The women reporters could hardly remember the last press conference given by a First Lady in the White House, back in Eleanor Roosevelt's time."

When Pat announced her First Lady "project" at the luncheon, it did not fit neatly into one slot. She had decided to focus on volunteerism in a broad sense, first by undertaking a tour of ten "'Vest Pockets of Volunteerism' programs that addressed pressing social problems that fell outside the purview of legislation." That summer she would kick off her First Lady initiative.

Pat was also able to incorporate educational initiatives under the volunteerism umbrella. Her correspondence secretary, Gwen King, noted that "Mrs. Nixon was intensely interested in the Right to Read program" due to her background as a teacher. Other programs later would include tours at the White House for the handicapped and the blind.

Pat was involved in so many different projects that choosing just one thing as her signature issue was too confining. She again showed her dislike of being pigeonholed by choosing a much broader "project" than previous First Ladies. She was able to put her personal stamp on the efforts, thus pushing back against the "beardless image types" Safire described. As she would often say, "People are my project."

Pat's varied roles both within and outside of the White House and her encounters with individuals could not be limited to simply "volunteerism." She saw the most important part of her role as First Lady as connecting with people. Her warmth and authenticity were not commodities to be sold and packaged for public consumption like a candy bar.

Little more than a month after Pat's announcement, on March 28, Haldeman informed the president that Eisenhower had just died. Dick broke down in tears. He was the one the former president had chosen to deliver the eulogy. The president went over to Walter Reed to see Mamie immediately. She, Julie, and David had been with Eisenhower when he died. When Mamie and Dick talked later on the phone, she made sure to tell him her husband's final words: "I have always loved my wife. I have always loved my children. I have always loved my grandchildren and I have always loved my country."

Dick would use these exact words in his eulogy to the great general and president. Though he and Pat had had their differences with the Eisenhowers in the past, the two families were now inextricably linked through the marriage of David and Julie. This unification and Eisenhower's willing support of Dick in the presidential election had gone a long way toward healing old wounds.

As newly minted East Wing staffer Debby Sloan remembered, "One of the first 'events' in the White House was a reception for all of the world leaders who were coming to Washington for his (Eisenhower's) funeral. It was a very big deal, of course, and quite a 'test' for a new administration, but Mrs. Nixon and Lucy Winchester, Pat's social secretary, were up to the task."

In June, Pat made good on her February announcement. She went on the road, touring ten local grassroots volunteer initiatives. One "Vest Pocket" example was her support of the Greenfingers Project in Portland, Oregon, where local volunteers took an empty urban lot in an at-risk neighborhood and turned it into a community garden. She also visited the Wesley Social Center of Love and Concern in the Watts neighborhood of Los Angeles with Julie. The center hosted cultural programs for inner-city youth. In newsreels of these visits, it is evident how much Pat loved children. She would pick them up, hug and kiss them, and get down on their level to talk with them. The children hugged her back willingly, sensing an authenticity in her that other government officials rarely possessed.

Pat also visited college campuses where students were involved in social improvement projects. "I was going out to see the students in action" she proclaimed, "so I had to go where the action was." The First Lady connected well with young adults, listening to their thoughts and comments intently. With two young adult daughters of her own, she understood many of their concerns. She also felt that young Americans were the key to continuing the volunteer movement. "We have to build generations to take over the lead" in this area, she commented.

In July of that year, Dick and Pat made an important—and secret—visit to Vietnam during a presidential world tour. The tour was code-named "Moonglow" to honor NASA's successful Apollo 11 moon landing. During this around-the-world tour, the Nixons would visit Guam, the Philippines, Indonesia, Thailand, India, Pakistan, Romania, and Britain. Dick and Pat would also make an unannounced stopover in Vietnam for five and a half hours on July 30.

This was the first time ever that a First Lady had dared to visit a combat zone. Historian H. R. McMaster noted how important the First Lady's presence in a combat zone was in 1969 and still is today. "It's immensely important to recognize that the President and the First Lady are committed to seeing a fight through. . . . There's been this narrative these days about ending endless wars. . . . But I really think what soldiers want more than anything are leaders who are committed to fighting the war as hard as they are so they can achieve a worthy outcome. . . . I think the First Lady going forward (here in Vietnam) communicates that the government is behind this effort. That the administration is behind this effort and the community is behind the effort."

Pat continued where she had left off as Second Lady, choosing to highlight the problems of women, children, and the needy by visiting orphanages and hospitals. While the president was visiting the troops, Pat insisted on visiting the 24th Evacuation Hospital, where she could meet and talk to wounded American servicemen. She also went to an orphanage to comfort children there, putting her Secret Service agents on edge. She had no worries for her own safety, but she was upset when the children at the orphanage were scared by the noise of military helicopters and jets. "Pat remained cool and composed, but she was furious, and vowed never to subject children to such an ordeal again."

Pat herself had a close call with a helicopter while in Vietnam. Military staff were flying the First Lady to a hospital to spend time with wounded American servicemen. Staff were paying attention to the president but ignoring the First Lady. As General Don Hughes told the story: "You know, when the President is involved, he gets the attention, and Mrs. Nixon sometimes was sort of left out." She almost walked into the rotor blades of the helicopter. If Gene Boyer, the pilot, hadn't been looking out for her, she might have had a terrible accident.

Overall, however, the Vietnam visit and the world tour were a huge success. "Moonglow was a public relations triumph. Every stop brought out huge crowds, and later headlines back home." More importantly, America's South Vietnamese allies felt reassured by the president and First Lady's presence. UPI reporter Helen Thomas recalled: "Mrs. Nixon was praised by Madame Nguyen Van Thieu, wife of the South Vietnamese President, for 'disregarding the dangers to come here. She and her husband have intensified our morale by coming here.'"

After their triumphant trip, the Nixons also spent a three-week "working vacation" at their new "Western White House" in San Clemente, California. This stately Spanish-style hacienda was built in 1926 by Hamilton Cotton, who had worked for FDR as the Democratic National Committee national finance chairman. Dick had named the new home La Casa Pacifica, the

Peaceful House, and it was intended to be their refuge from Washington and their home base while in California.

Pat's Vietnam helicopter incident highlighted an attitude regarding the First Lady that only got worse as 1969 turned into 1970 and the tendency of some of the West Wing staff to overlook Pat's power as a political asset to her husband grew. Often at major events she was an afterthought, if thought of at all. She rarely complained about this, but others on staff took note of it.

Ron Walker was the first director of the White House Office of Presidential Advance. Beginning in 1969, he worked with Pat, Julie, and Tricia as well as the president. He tried to the best of his ability to protect and showcase Mrs. Nixon as an integral part of the Nixon team. But he noticed, from early on, the tendency of the New Nixon team to ignore her presence. "More often than not, people [West Wing staff] had not thought about the First Lady." He found himself growing upset at some of the treatment he witnessed regarding Pat. "It was very emotional for me to be with her. To make sure she was okay, to make sure she wasn't left behind, which was more often the case than not."

Unlike Haldeman and some of his staff, Walker wanted to ensure that Pat was a prominent presence at events, "to make sure she was recognized along with the president. . . . She was as important as anyone because when she was there, we could tell the positive reaction in the audience."

Debby Sloan saw immediately from her desk in the East Wing that "the men in the West Wing really ran the show." Chapin, now deputy assistant to the president under Haldeman, had remained friendly with the women of the East Wing, including Rose Mary Woods and Pat, who had trained him. From his desk in the West Wing, he saw the same thing Debby saw from hers: "The overarching attitude was that the East Wing was a pain in the ass . . . they were not viewed as an asset."

Though Chapin had worked well with Pat in the past, neither he nor Haldeman was a good fit as West Wing liaison to the First Lady. Alexander Butterfield, the president's deputy assistant from 1969 to 1973, was hired by Haldeman and eventually took on this role. He recollected: "That was a pretty important job hardly anyone knew about. [Chapin] would solve problems that came up between the President and the First Lady so that they didn't have to argue with one another." Butterfield remembered that Haldeman had held the position first but he later told him, "I flunked the course because Mrs. Nixon couldn't stand me. . . . I put Dwight Chapin in that job, and I thought he'd be perfect for Mrs. Nixon . . . [but] Chapin flunked the course too!" The liaison position then went to Butterfield. The third try was apparently the charm.

Butterfield related, "I liked Pat a lot. I met with her every week, sometimes twice a week, whatever it was, up in the residence up in her little living room off her bedroom. And we got along well, and I understood her things and I tried to argue her case oftentimes with the president. We won some and lost some. I got to know Pat well, and pretty soon I was meeting with her twice a week."

Why did Butterfield seem to succeed where Haldeman and Chapin had failed? "I didn't always take her side. I would try to explain to her how the president was viewing the thing or how important this particular social event coming up or state dinner [was]. I gave a little more thought visibly to Pat and she saw that. She knew I was not trying to automatically say what the president wanted."

21

WEST WING VS. EAST WING:
BATTLE OF THE SEXES

Early on in her tenure as First Lady, Pat established a rigorous daily routine. Unlike previous First Ladies, Pat's schedule did not include breaks to watch soap operas, play bridge, or ride horses. Other than seeing her daughters, David Eisenhower, and Ed Cox, for whom both she and the president always made time, and occasional visits from her dear friend Helene Drown, the First Lady placed her focus squarely on her official duties.

Rising by 7–7:30 a.m. each day, the new First Lady scanned the newspapers and began reading over her staff messages and outside correspondence. She then worked with Lucy Winchester on her social events, went over her shopping lists with the head housekeeper, discussed her menus with head White House chef Henry Haller, and helped plan floral arrangements for in-house events with the White House florist.

After lunch, most often enjoyed with Tricia, the First Lady had ceremonial events to attend to. Her evenings were filled with more formal social events such as state dinners and receptions. She still had correspondence to work on in the evenings, so bedtime was generally late, around midnight to 1 a.m. Pat continued to show the same remarkable stamina, discipline, and hard work that had defined her for her entire life. Her previous role as Second Lady served her well: she was better trained than any previous First Lady for the position.

Anita McBride, former chief of staff for First Lady Laura Bush's East Wing operations, has seen firsthand how the East and West Wings work together and has also studied their historical partnership. She noted that in

1969, during the first Nixon term, these side-by-side White House operations were "a bellwether of changes to come" in the 1970s. The transition of the First Lady from pure support role to a more active position had only just begun with Lady Bird Johnson. (Eleanor Roosevelt, an outlier First Lady with her activism, was considered highly unusual for her time.)

Lady Bird had hired Liz Carpenter, a former journalist, as her press secretary, and "a separate East Wing office was established with specialists in print and broadcast media." Pat continued this same structure and arrived in the White House expecting to run her own show in the East Wing. Ill feeling was building, however, between the two wings, entities that had been almost completely separated before the Johnson era. McBride noted that Pat "was the center of that tension going on." Pat and her East Wing staff were fighting an uphill battle to establish their territory. These were still pioneer days for the First Lady's office. Pat's side of the residence had to be constantly on guard against empire-building and power grabs emanating from the West Wing in the early days of the new administration.

Adding to the layers of tension between the two wings were worries in the West Wing about Dick's presidential image. While Pat's popularity could have been used to further the president's goals by involving her more directly in administration publicity, East Wing staffer Penny Adams noted that West Wing staff often showed "worry about the First Lady getting more positive press than the president." Over time, Pat and her staff would push back on this issue. Veteran UPI reporter Helen Thomas noted, "When Haldeman tried to curtail [her] press coverage, she often countermanded him. She was so much more sophisticated than the Palace Guard I wondered why her husband did not listen to her more often."

Then there was the feminist press, who routinely diminished Pat. Noted Anita McBride, "The feminists never gave her credit. They saw her as being subordinate." Instead of seeing Pat as an advocate for women who was "moving the needle" toward a more modern First Lady role, they viewed her as a bourgeois 1950s housewife subservient to her husband and his staff. Pat was far more sophisticated about women's issues than the feminist press gave her credit for.

As McBride noted: "She understood her place and was playing the long game" for women. "You don't change people's minds overnight by beating them over the head with it." Given her era and the attitudes toward women at the time, Pat worked silently in the background to change things for women. "She was a savvy behind-the-scenes influencer."

Both the West Wing staff and the feminist press underestimated the new First Lady. They misread her silence as acquiescence, and they were unaware of her iron will. Gloria Steinem had caught a glimpse of Pat's resistance to being placed in a media box when she interviewed her in 1968. Soon enough, the West Wing would encounter flashes of the First Lady's steely determination as well.

———

From 1969 until 1970, some in the West Wing, perhaps even including the president, felt that the new First Lady and the East Wing staff were adrift and in need of rescue. Chapin watched as "the West Wing was moving at warp speed. The president was deciding how to govern, how to get the presidency under way. . . . The amount of time he was giving to East Wing was minuscule" at this point, "but Pat is still expected to perform." Presidential aide Steve Bull added: "There wasn't a role for Mrs. Nixon during the first years."

West Wingers were "probably reflecting the president's point of view that it's going to be difficult to ask anything of Pat," explained David Eisenhower. After years of political hurts, Pat was emotionally wounded and apprehensive about being First Lady. "After the California governorship is lost in 1962, she says [to Dick], 'Promise me you'll never run for anything again.' So, in 1967, we have to revise that deal. She felt she was going to set the terms . . . but what you notice is when she's in the thick of events, the light comes on and she's on program."

Pat's East Wing staff who saw and worked with her daily saw a different First Lady. Debby Sloan noted: "I never saw any evidence of her being unsure of herself. The West Wing was just trying to give an excuse for why they were attempting to control Mrs. Nixon and the East Wing . . . a never-ending struggle!" Susan Porter Rose, Pat's appointment's secretary, concurred: "The disparagement between West and East Wing was strong. It was NOT equal!"

Patti Matson, who worked in Connie Stuart's press shop, echoed this view, remarking that the West Wing in the early 1970s was a microcosm of the nation's sexist climate. "Those were the days of chauvinist pigs. . . . There had been NO awakening" about women at this point. Like her other East Wing colleagues, Matson felt minimized by the West Wing attitude, which also regularly diminished Pat. "They thought they were the ones who were important. They just wanted the East Wing to stay out of trouble."

Chapin's take was that the new First Lady felt "alienated . . . she was odd person out in her mind." "The president was trying to wallpaper over it," meaning Pat's hurt and resentment, to cope with the situation. The president's deputies on both sides of the residence acted as proxies between the president and the First Lady—shuttling between the two camps, trying to facilitate cooperation and understanding between them. The president's approach, according to Chapin, was as such: "In order to bring a solution, he brings in other outside people to solve it," thus complicating the situation further and widening the gap between them.

The Nixon White House staff-as-proxies situation calls to mind the Nixons' engagement ring episode. Pat had received her ring from a third party, Nixon's cousin. This showed a pattern Dick would continue to display throughout their marriage: using intermediaries—friends, his mother, Father Cronin, Rose Mary Woods, his daughters, and even the West Wing staff—to smooth over hurts or perceived slights with his wife. Son-in-law David Eisenhower noticed this dynamic between his in-laws as well: "He may have put her on a pedestal. . . . I think that may have made him shy, made it difficult to test the relationship, he didn't want to offend her. So he had intermediaries, and he left her notes."

Alexander Butterfield was coached by Haldeman himself on how to manage the delicate relationship between the president and the First Lady within the walls of the White House. "When they had some difference in opinion, I asked, why couldn't they just solve it themselves? Haldeman thought it was a very stupid question. He said, 'No, *we* do that—we have to step in and solve it.'" Butterfield added: "His point was they don't talk that much at home."

Today, a therapist might have been called in to deal with what was partially a communication issue. But instead, Pat's hurt and resentment over the 1968 election was papered over and patched up. The couple's core issues relating to their joint life in the political spotlight remained untended. Resentment would often pop up on both sides—most frequently in the early days of the new presidential administration.

———

Early on, the new First Lady initiated a major shift in tone regarding the residence itself. She preferred to refer to the presidential home not as "the Mansion" but as "the White House," a house for all Americans. This new way of thinking and talking about America's seat of power also reflected Pat's goal to open the White House to more visitors: she felt deeply that it was the People's House, something to be shared—not a palace to be savored only by a privileged few. Debby Sloan recalled that early on the new First Lady "admonished us all that this was the 'People's House' and we were to refer to it as 'the White House' and *not* 'the Mansion'!" This working-class viewpoint led directly to several important First Lady projects.

The nightly illumination of the White House became a major goal for the First Lady. Pat began this important work soon after the inauguration after receiving numerous letters asking her why the Mansion was not lit up at night like other national monuments. On November 25, 1970, these lights were switched on for the first time officially. Thanks to her efforts, the White House can still be seen shimmering in the darkness after dusk descends on Washington. The illumination project was undertaken as a surprise for the president; he would not find out about this until August 1970.

Another enduring tradition also begun in 1969 was her White House Christmas candlelight tours. Though the intent was partly atmospheric, opening the residence for holiday tours from 6:30 to 9 p.m. also allowed working Americans to enjoy the People's House. An illuminated White House, bedecked with wreaths, garlands, and specially decorated Christmas trees, greeted tourists as Christmas music wafted through the public rooms. Visitors also delighted in viewing special gingerbread houses commissioned by Pat and first created by assistant chef Hans Raffert in 1969 for display in the residence.

A more important program Pat put in place in 1969 featured White House tours that catered to the disabled and the blind. Not only Pat but also Julie and Tricia were heavily involved in the development and implementation of these efforts. From 1969 onward, under the umbrella of "volunteerism" but also under the roof of residence renovation initiatives, "the Nixon White House had tried to establish its reputation for being particularly open to the handicapped. In addition to encouraging special tours for the blind and disabled, Mrs. Nixon initiated a Talking Book Tour of the White House." Ramps and other wheelchair-accessible alterations were installed to help this population experience the White House safely and comfortably.

As far as the daily work of First Lady duties is concerned, Pat's 1969 schedule shows a woman who never canceled an event and always arrived on time for her duties. She attended 115 in-house activities that year. Highlights included her luncheon for the ladies of the press on February 17, a state dinner for Canadian prime minister Pierre Trudeau in March, and a dinner for the Apollo 9 astronauts, also in March. In April Pat hosted six different teas—for NATO wives, diplomatic corps wives, and the Defense Advisory Committee on Women and Service, among others.

Pat's schedule that spring continued to be a whirlwind of obligations. May was packed with luncheons and teas. There was only a slight slowdown in the summer, which included a dinner for the Apollo 10 astronauts and a Rose Garden celebration for the anniversary of the presidential nomination. By fall, Pat was back in full swing with a September cabinet dinner with wives as well as a reception for the National Federation of Republican Women. In October alone Pat participated in fifteen events, one of which involved hosting 670 guests.

Pat traveled often with the president in 1969, journeying to Colorado, California, Hawaii, Los Angeles, and the Apollo 12 launch in Florida. She spent eleven days on the president's around-the-world trip with the secret side visit to Vietnam. She also attended a groundbreaking ceremony in Cerritos (formerly Artesia), California, for Pat Nixon Park.

On top of all these one-off activities, there were the almost-monthly Sunday services, instituted at the president's behest, beginning the first Sunday after the inauguration. Although Pat didn't attach herself strongly to one denomination, she revealed to Helen Thomas: "I'm a very religious person. . . . It isn't exactly praying. I follow the golden rule. I was taught it when I was young, and I never lost it. I also have great faith and live life based on that philosophy." Pat's East

Wing staffers Debby Sloan and Susan Dolibois, both of whom worked on coordinating the services, recalled a strong push from both Nixons that everyday Americans be invited to the services. Dolibois noted: "It wasn't just all VIPs."

Lucy Winchester added that these services were created with the president's strong encouragement so the First Family could worship inside the White House. There were so many Vietnam antiwar protestors in Washington at the time, it would have been difficult for the Nixons to go out to church without being followed or hassled. These services also allowed for a wide variety of religious denominations to be represented, without showing favoritism to one over the others.

The new First Lady seemed to have her duties well in hand as 1970 approached. She soon would become comfortable with the latest fashion trend for women as well. White House fellow and staff assistant Bobbie Kilberg remembered an early encounter with the new First Lady in the East Wing.

> Fairly early on in my fellowship year fall of 1969, pantsuits had just come out and I wore a pantsuit to work. I had no idea it was a radical concept. And that was one of the days that Mrs. Nixon was around. She later herself wore one and was very proud of it. But that day, she happened to see me [as] I was walking through the portico from the West Wing to the state rooms and the East Wing. . . . Maybe to her that made it more offensive. She said to me, "Young lady," and I said, "Yes, ma'am," [and] she said "We don't wear pantsuits in the White House. Please go home and change!"

The young West Winger promptly complied.

However, as Kilberg recounted, a few months later the First Lady also began to wear pantsuits. "She obviously changed her mind about that!" Perhaps Pat's encounter with Kilberg—a woman working in the West Wing—reminded her that times were changing. Women's visibility in public life was growing, and wardrobes reflected that shift.

———

In the summer of 1969, Gallup polls showed a wildly popular First Lady, giving Pat "an amazing approval rating of 9–1, which was far higher than Jackie or Lady Bird ever achieved." Newspapers reported eye-popping numbers: "The Nixons set a record for White House entertaining in 1969, receiving 44,000 guests and more state visitors than any other president in that year's time." But despite Pat's hard work and popularity as the new First Lady, the West Wing continued to micromanage her operation.

Pat's longtime secretary Bessie Newton was overwhelmed and unequipped to deal with the massive amounts of mail the First Lady routinely received. The East Wing received an average of 1,000–2,000 letters a week during Pat's tenure and as much as 4,000 letters a week after a high-profile appearance or trip by the First Lady. Gwen King had been on staff at the White House since the Eisenhower administration, working in the correspondence area. When she received a distress call from Ehrlichman, now the counsel to the president, asking her to consider moving over to the East Wing to help the new First Lady with her correspondence, she assumed it would merely be a temporary gig to help the new operation get up to speed. King liked working with her new boss so much, she decided to permanently accept the position as head of correspondence.

Ehrlichman was assigned by Haldeman and the president to deal with the First Lady directly on "the mail issue." According to Ehrlichman, he was also empowered by the president and Haldeman to talk to the First Lady about what the West Wing perceived as her adjustment issues to her new role. When the president's new domestic affairs advisor walked into his late afternoon meeting with Pat, he found her "wary and tense, but she tried to be gracious and attentive as I began my rehearsed explanation: the President was concerned, as were her friends, as to how she was adjusting to her new situation. . . . Perhaps she would feel the need of someone to talk to, even to share problems with. There was the mail for example, I would be happy to try to ease that burden."

Pat's reaction was cool. Ehrlichman was self-aware enough to realize he had crossed the line with her, and he also noted her intelligence. "Pat bristled; she saw easily what this chat was all about, and she didn't like it. She explained icily that she had an obligation to all the people who cared enough to write her. She might be slow and old-fashioned, but she believed everyone deserved a personal answer and a personal signature."

However, Ehrlichman was *not* smart enough to know when to quit. He had to add his concern over Pat's health to this already tense conversation. "She was very thin, and I hoped she would pay attention to her nourishment. . . . If she was lonely or depressed, I hoped she would feel free to call my wife (whom she said she liked) or me."

Pat did not react and said nothing in response. Ehrlichman left feeling like a "clumsy intruder." And the First Lady went back to doing exactly what she planned to do: answering her mail and personally signing each piece of correspondence to constituents, eschewing automatic signing devices.

A short time later, when Gwen King received a memo from Haldeman and Ehrlichman putting a West Wing umbrella over the East Wing correspondence operation, she went directly to her boss. "I didn't think this would be at all to Mrs. Nixon's liking." The next morning, Gwen got a call from the First Lady, telling her, "Business as usual." As Gwen noted, "The West Wing discounted us. . . . I think they looked upon us as social butterflies mainly." Penny Adams went a step further with her recollections: "Haldeman was the [West Wing] role model. He enabled the others and gave them license to act like absolute barbarians."

This incident, far from being the end of internecine warfare in the residence, was but a harbinger of more battles to come.

————

In September 1969, an East Wing study by thirty-two-year-old White House staffer Chuck Stuart would yet again attempt to subvert the authority of Pat and her East Wing operation. Stuart was directed by Haldeman to study the East Wing, on the grounds that things were not functioning smoothly. As Stuart later explained, "The reason for Bob's current angst was the President's displeasure at the quality of work coming out of the East Wing." Two targets for immediate removal in the East Wing were Pat's press secretary, Gerry Van der Heuvel, and her social secretary, Lucy Winchester.

Van der Heuvel was a well-regarded former journalist recommended by Nixon's communications director, Herb Klein. She had been a columnist for the Newhouse News Service, and she had most recently served as president of the all-female Washington Press Club.

Lucy Winchester, a well-educated young woman from an old Lexington,

Kentucky, family, had been working as Pat's social secretary since January 1969. The college graduate had worked in New York for the advertising firm Leo Burnett and at the United Nations in the protocol department. After meeting with and impressing Richard Nixon himself, Winchester was offered the job as the First Lady's social secretary three separate times after the election. She turned the offer down twice, citing her daughter at home and her business running her family's multiple farms in Kentucky. However, Winchester finally decided it was her patriotic duty to accept the position, and she moved to Washington, leaving her daughter temporarily in the care of her mother and a governess until she could find suitable housing. As a working, divorced mother raising her daughter alone, Winchester had sacrificed much to come work at the White House.

The thirty-two-year-old social secretary was whip-smart and socially astute. She knew her way around both a foxhunt and the ballroom and was family friends with the ultimate Washington bad girl (and Nixon confidant) Alice Roosevelt Longworth. During her short time in her new role, she had already organized and thrown Tricia's Masked Ball, "one of the swingingest, most fabulous parties ever held in the executive mansion," with much fanfare from the Washington press.

Winchester also had a wicked sense of humor. Like Helene Drown, Lucy was able to bring out Pat's sense of fun and silliness. Early in her tenure as social secretary, Winchester was in the White House mess eating when she overheard a group of Secret Service agents laughing hysterically. When she asked what was going on, the men revealed that one of the Secret Service guys had bought "a blow-up sex doll as a gag gift at a place called Le Sex shop." Winchester instantly knew she *must* have that doll for a special group. The Daughters of the American Revolution were coming for a tour of the second floor of the residence, and Winchester decided to make sure that a special guest was waiting for them.

Winchester soon showed up at Mrs. Nixon's door in the family living quarters with the inflatable blond woman. Pat laughed and exclaimed, "Oh, no, Lucy, they will think that is me in the bathtub!" But the two women left the doll in the bathtub of the Queen's Bedroom bathroom to await the DAR. Though the two women were not able to observe the surely horrified reaction of the tour group, just the thought of the prank kept them laughing for months afterward. Haldeman especially disliked Winchester and her subversive sense of humor, and he would have been apoplectic had he known about the sex doll in the bathtub. She stood up to his bullying, and she insisted on running her own show. This put her squarely in his crosshairs.

In his report, Stuart recommended firing both Van der Heuvel and Winchester despite their stellar qualifications and high-quality work. Stuart also made recommendations in his report regarding Pat and her image in the press. These suggestions were often insulting (and at times unintentionally hilarious). Stuart suggested that one way the First Lady could court good publicity was by drawing upon her farming roots. "Mrs. Nixon was once a member of the 4-H Club and raised a prize-winning hog. She should relate the story of her 'Piggy Wiggy' [the sow's name] at the next 4-H convention. She should present the prize sow award."

Even though both Pat and her staff had their hands full with their current duties, Stuart devised a new suggested roster of activities. He encouraged the staff to host "a fashion show in the East Room. Throw a lawn party with Circus acts for entertainment. Screen more movies and ask friends to watch. Have house guests. Have a dog show for Congressional children's dogs."

Debby Sloan noted that the "list of suggested activities for Mrs. Nixon prepared by the West Wing would be amusing if it were not so totally misguided. Mrs. Nixon always had 'gravitas' in all she did in politics and being First Lady provided the perfect platform for her interests and influence." Pat was a serious person who wanted to undertake projects that would make a difference in people's lives. Suggesting her primary activities should involve prize pigs and dog shows belittled her status as an active First Lady and a woman of substance.

So why did Pat not go to her husband earlier and more often with her complaints regarding the West Wing? Nixon historian Bob Bostock explained that after years of life in the spotlight, Pat was used to handling much on her own. She was a seasoned political wife "who felt she could take care of herself. She didn't want to bother her husband with what she considered office politics not worth his valuable time."

East Winger Pat Howard was a longtime White House staffer who began her career at the White House as a writer for Lady Bird's beautification campaign in February 1966 at age twenty-one. She remained on staff under Mrs.

Nixon as Winchester's assistant social secretary. She echoed Bostock's comments on Pat's approach to the West Wingers. "Mrs. Nixon didn't say much about the West Wing trying to control [the] East Wing at times because you don't complain, you move ahead and stay focused. . . . The First Lady felt that you don't get involved in cattiness that is beneath you. The public is not expecting that."

There was one instance, though, when Pat clearly and firmly put her foot down regarding West Wing encroachment on her domain. According to Lucy Winchester, Stuart nominated himself to become Mrs. Nixon's chief of staff. Winchester recalled the meeting she had with Stuart where he revealed his plan to her: "He was sitting with his profile facing me, smoking a pipe, thinking far-away big thoughts. He announced he was going to be Pat's chief of staff! I told Mrs. Nixon, who didn't know a thing about this. She said, 'That's *not* happening!' She picked up the phone and said, 'Please get my husband!' 'Dick, I will *not* have a male chief of staff!'"

The West Wing solution for their East Wing headaches? Instead of Chuck Stuart becoming Pat's chief of staff, Haldeman suggested a woman named Connie Stuart. As Winchester recalled: "They [the West Wing] searched the world over and finally found Chuck's wife!"

Connie Stuart was a tall, attractive redhead from Wheeling, West Virginia. Her niece Cassie Price remembered that Stuart was the local beauty queen and "the antithesis of a shrinking violet." Smart and accomplished, the stylish Stuart "didn't suffer fools gladly. She wanted to get things done and you better not get in her way!" Stuart was unusual in the late 1960s and early 1970s. She was an ambitious woman who didn't plan to give up her career. "She was very strong and very definite in an era when women were not well represented in the halls of power."

Stuart arrived at the White House with solid media credentials. She had worked for both AT&T and C&P telephone companies in New York and D.C. as a film producer. She had met the new First Lady on several occasions when her husband was working for the Nixon campaign. In September 1969, as Connie recalled, her husband came to her with an intriguing job proposal: would she like to become the First Lady's new chief of staff? Pat was not invited to these discussions. Soon the deal was sealed, and Connie became Haldeman's East Wing equivalent.

Connie met with the president within a few days of beginning her new job to discuss Mrs. Nixon. "He wanted to take the time to tell me how important she was. How much she deserved to have good press and good staff support . . . it was probably half-an-hour's worth of his concern for her. He wanted to make sure that it wasn't, 'Bob and I' or 'Bob thinks . . .' That was Richard Nixon saying, 'She's important, she matters. She matters to me. She matters professionally, and you work hard, young lady. . . . But make sure you don't become a lightning rod.'"

Connie had been given her marching orders, not by the First Lady but by the president's side of the house, before she even discussed her new position with Pat. Despite the president's meeting with Connie, the underlying message from Haldeman was that he was her real boss. One task Haldeman seemed intent on was getting rid of Lucy Winchester. (He had already gotten rid of Van der Heuvel.) Said Winchester, "The first thing Connie was told to do was get me fired."

The East Wing environment soon became divided over this unwanted reorganization. Stuart and Winchester were at odds, as Stuart was widely regarded as a West Wing spy. Recalled Pat Howard, "It was not a comfortable time . . . we knew they were after Lucy. If Connie had her way, Lucy would have been let go." Fortunately for Winchester, the loyal East Wingers who had worked with her in the early days had her back. The Nixon women, Pat, Julie, and Tricia, also admired Winchester's social finesse and work ethic and wanted her to remain in her job.

Winchester, who had been nicknamed (fondly) "Lucifer" by Bill Gulley, director of the White House Military Affairs Office, was there to stay. But so was Stuart, the new East Wing chief of staff. They would have to coexist and work together in support of the First Lady. The atmosphere was bitter at first. But despite Stuart's brusque manner and rough start with the East Wing ladies, she would also end up pushing back against Haldeman's iron rule as things progressed.

22

A WARTIME WHITE HOUSE

While the East and West Wings skirmished, war in Southeast Asia raged in the background. The endless Vietnam War dominated daily headlines and television broadcasts in 1969. Draft numbers were picked, and young men flew to Southeast Asia on airplanes and came home to America in body bags. The atmosphere in the residence was tense and edgy, mirroring the disruption in the country outside its gates.

As David Eisenhower explained: "It's not a White House that's going to work like the Ford White House. The 800-pound gorilla that's not in the room during the Ford administration is the Vietnam War. . . . It's true of Korea, it's true of World War Two. Wartime is a different ambiance." Debby Sloan, on the East Wing social staff, remembered one Senate ladies' luncheon that was held during antiwar protests, with protestors tipping over cars: "It was very, very scary."

Winchester, Sloan's boss, had been asked to spend the night before the luncheon just to make sure she could get to the White House that day as the protests clogged the capital. But Winchester remembered that Pat wanted the Senate wives to see the chaos when they came to the luncheon so that they would fully understand how the war was affecting daily life at the White House.

Eisenhower recalled the change in tone once his father-in-law took office. Under LBJ, as "a wartime procedure you don't see casualties, you don't hear about POWs . . . that changes with Nixon." Johnson had applied the "keep quiet" policy of his presidential predecessors to the POW/MIA issue, earning him the ire of POW/MIA families but effectively tamping down his bad press domestically in the early days of the war.

The new Nixon administration decided to take a different "go public" tack with the POW/MIA wives and families. Noted Eisenhower, "The idea is that we are on a downward trajectory and other styles become possible. And we made the POW return a major objective."

While bringing home the POWs was a unifying issue, the war itself continued to divide the country and to impede daily functions at the White House. Hundreds of thousands of war protestors filled D.C. in the fall of 1969. The Moratorium Marches on Washington in October and November put the nation's capital on edge. The antiwar movement swelled for several key reasons. According to McMaster, failures of leadership, policies of not mobilizing the reserves and the National Guard, and student deferments all fueled these massive antiwar protests.

Due to these enormous crowds invading the nation's capital, the White House was on high alert regarding the safety of its occupants. Bill Gulley, director of the White House Military Affairs Office, recalled the violent undercurrent of the protests and the measures taken to ensure the safety of the First Family, the staff, and the residence itself. "In October and November of 1969, we felt seriously threatened by the demonstrations. To deal with the real possibility of violence, to organize and run an operation to put it down if it did erupt, we set up a control center in the bomb shelter under the East Wing of the White House." Within this center, direct phone lines were installed to the chief of police, the mayor, the National Guard, the FBI, and the Pentagon. Along with this, a closed-circuit television system was installed, and during major protests, the control center was manned twenty-four hours a day.

Julie Eisenhower vividly described the scene on October 15, Moratorium Day. "As a quarter million people converged peacefully on Washington, Mother kept her originally planned schedule, presenting awards at a luncheon given by the American Association of Nurserymen, a tea for members of the Soroptimists, a service club, and a meeting with Señora Aurora Juárez de Oporta, mayor of Uyuni, Bolivia." Pat kept calm and carried on, as was her way. She was not rattled, and she remained in public view: a stable presence that the country could rely on. There was no sense of withdrawal or lack of participation from the First Lady, even during some of the country's darkest days. According to David Eisenhower, "She was in full flow by the fall of '69 when things became so serious" due to the Vietnam War protests.

On November 3, President Nixon's "Silent Majority" speech captured the nation's attention. The speech and Nixon's stance on Vietnam received an outpouring of support from those in middle America who applauded the administration's position. As historian Evan Thomas put it, "Nixon was not wrong when he told Haldeman that his speech was the greatest turnaround since the Checkers speech (or as Nixon preferred, the Fund Speech) in 1952. Polls showed that more than three out of every four Americans approved of the speech, and Nixon's approval rating shot up from 52 to 68 percent." A Gallup poll of television viewers of the "Silent Majority" speech found that 77 percent supported the president's position.

The speech provided the new administration with a much-needed system reboot. David Eisenhower commented that the "Silent Majority Speech of November 1969 is the reset . . . ownership of the Vietnam policy passes to Nixon emphatically after that. The Johnson policy has expired. . . . This is when the business of the White House becomes very serious. This is when Pat Nixon and everybody else came alive." Indeed, Pat believed so strongly in her husband's Vietnam policy that she would tell deputy director of the White House writing and research staff Lee Huebner and others following a state dinner the following year that if her husband had won the presidency back in 1960, the Vietnam War might never have happened at all.

On Saturday, November 15, both Washington and San Francisco faced more gigantic protests. This Vietnam Moratorium (also known as the "New Mobe") brought an estimated 250,000 protestors to the capital for a rally and march up Pennsylvania Avenue. Marchers carried placards with the names of soldiers killed in Vietnam. The protests were not limited now to D.C. and San Francisco: "All over the country, sober faced men and women gathered with students to listen to speeches, carry placards, wear black armbands, light candles, toll church bells, read the names of the dead."

The White House protection plan kicked into high gear. The residence was "encircled by a protective barricade of fifty-seven city buses parked end-to-end. Sharp-shooting soldiers were stationed behind the balustrade of a tall building nearby, and another three hundred soldiers were in the basement of the White House and the Executive Office Building next door."

As the president nonchalantly watched a football game on television, Secretary of Defense Melvin Laird worried that the administration did not realize "the extent of the feelings of those young people. . . . I couldn't get the White House to understand that." Miraculously, the D.C. Moratorium passed peacefully and with little incident.

In San Francisco, however, some speakers urged extreme violence against the president. Julie remembered that Black Panther leader David Hilliard told a crowd of 125,000, "'We will kill Richard Nixon. We will kill any [one] that stands in the way of our freedom.'" The president may have displayed bravado in public, but in private it would have been nearly impossible for Pat, her daughters, and White House staff not to be concerned by the constant mobs surrounding the residence—and the frequently violent rhetoric—that dominated the news through the fall of 1969.

It was a season of domestic unrest and tension not unlike our 2020s historical cycle. While Vietnam was perhaps uppermost in the minds of the American public, other movements also grabbed headlines. Racial tensions focused at this time on busing issues, and student protests and the feminist movement were front and center. As Julie recalled in an oral history, "It was rough and tumble and a lot of anger below the surface on the part of some women because women had been excluded for so long and not given a fair share. There were a lot of wrongs to be righted, and there was sort of an edge to the women's movement . . . this was an area that had to be looked at seriously, it was all part of the unrest in this country."

———

Only a few weeks later, the Nixon family celebrated their first Thanksgiving in the White House with 280 local seniors. In addition to Pat and the president, Tricia, Julie and David, David's sister Susan, and Mamie Eisenhower and her ninety-year-old uncle Joel were all on hand to eat with their elderly guests. Tables were set up in the East Room and the State Dining Room.

What could have been a lovely but unremarkable affair turned out to have historic consequences for women in the military. Colonel Jack Brennan, one of the president's military aides, noted: "Although Mrs. Nixon may have thought about it and wanted it sooner, the origins of military 'female social aides' did begin on Thanksgiving Day in 1969."

During the event, Brennan remembered, "an aged woman had an issue in the ladies' room. An embarrassed male Marine social aide had to go in and help her. That is when Mrs. Nixon asked General (then Colonel) Hughes in my presence why we did not have female social aides. There was no answer, and we (the military office of the White House) started the process of selecting and getting top secret clearances for the nominees. All were interviewed by the Military Office and the Office of the Social Secretary."

After months of scrutiny and background checks, Navy lieutenant Chris Alberts and four other women would make history in November 1971 when they replaced five male aides to become the first female military social aides in White House history—thanks to Pat Nixon's practical eye. As Alberts recalled, she and her fellow aides acted as "assistant hosts to the President and First Lady at all military and social events at the White House."

While Pat had made great strides for women just by noticing the need for them as White House social aides, another attempt to diminish her influence in an area that traditionally fell to the First Lady was afoot. Camp David, the presidential retreat in Maryland (named for President Eisenhower's grandson and Julie's husband, David), was being taken over by an unwanted—and tasteless—decorator: Haldeman. Though Mrs. Nixon had gotten a say in decorating the presidential cabin, known as Aspen, her opinions were not consulted regarding the other cabins of Camp David, according to Bill Gulley, director of the White House Military Affairs Office who had an insider's view of the Camp David refurbishing.

As Gulley recalled, Pat had asked to be consulted before the peripheral cabins were redone. Haldeman, however, told Gulley this would not be necessary and hired a New York decorator to work directly with him instead. After the Haldeman-chosen decor arrived and was installed, Pat came up to Camp David for a visit and was told the cabins had been completely redone. She asked to go see the cabins; when she saw what had been done, she was none too pleased.

Gulley revealed: "She took violent exception to the furnishings. So did just about everybody else who had a chance to see them. They were atrocious. The President became aware that Mrs. Nixon was upset about this, because she told him she was, and all the furnishings went out. We redid the whole place, this time with Mrs. Nixon's approval." Architectural historian Patrick Phillips-Schrock also confirmed this story, noting that Pat "ordered the New York materials removed and began redecorating anew from scratch. It appears she relied on her own taste and judgment for the interior appointments, many of which were to remain in place for several decades."

Haldeman's Air Force One revamp in 1970 was another bone of contention. The chief of staff "helped redesign Air Force One so that the large staff section was directly behind the President's office and before the First Lady's sitting room . . . with the redesign, every time a family member wanted to go to the lounge, he or she would have to walk through the staff compartment," where Haldeman acted as watchdog over the presidential section. It took only one flight before Pat complained, and the plane soon reverted to its original floorplan, with rooms in front of the plane that included both the president and his family members.

The Air Force One revamp was an expensive mistake, costing taxpayers around $750,000. East Winger Pat Howard also noted that Haldeman "insisted his luggage be marked with big tags so he would be first off the plane. The tags got bigger and bigger as time went on! He seemed to want to be equal to the president."

Haldeman's wife, Jo, and John Ehrlichman's wife, Jeanne, were warned to stay away from Pat Nixon and not engage with her socially. As Jo recalled, Jeanne Ehrlichman questioned the privacy arrangement: "Was there more we could do for Pat Nixon? We felt she was lonely. Perhaps we could do some informal activity with her." However, both of their husbands firmly said no to this idea. "Bob told me what he expected, and I was so used to conforming, I didn't think much about it."

Helen McCain Smith, Pat's press secretary, claimed that from the first Nixon administration onward, she heard "echoes of ugly jokes made by members of the President's staff at the First Lady's expense. H. R. Haldeman, always an opportunist, apparently felt that Pat was a political liability, and that the President would do well to dump her. At the time, I couldn't believe Haldeman could be that stupid. I knew that if the comments ever got back to the President, he never would have tolerated them."

Several other White House staffers who prefer to remain anonymous also heard these rumors. One former staff person claims Haldeman told them directly that the president should divorce his wife or put her in a mental institution.

Losing Pat would have been a huge blow to the president's image. During this era, a divorce could very well have cost him an election. That the cold and calculating Haldeman would express such an opinion defies explanation. However, proximity to power seemed to be foremost on Haldeman's mind—as well as keeping those who used to be on the inside, out.

———

On February 19, 1970, the First Lady and the president would host the first one-man show of paintings ever held in the White House. Their choice of artist for this historic happening? Andrew Wyeth, the heralded Pennsylvania painter who "represents unofficially a vast silent majority of his countrymen who know what they like." Andrew was part of the famous Wyeth family of artists, which included N. C. Wyeth, Jamie Wyeth, and Henriette Wyeth Hurd. (Years later, Henriette would paint Mrs. Nixon's official portrait.) Australian art critic Robert Hughes perceptively placed Andrew's work in the context of the time: "Just as the vanishing of the mythic West only made its fictive images vastly more popular, so the massing and incorporation of American culture produced intense nostalgia for 'old' and 'real' America, its folkways and idiosyncrasies, its threatened values."

This kind of art, harkening back to the rural America where both Pat and Dick grew up, appealed greatly to them both. Wyeth was the artist whose work meshed well with Nixonian values. The president would toast the featured artist as the painter who "caught the heart of America." Pat's favorite painting was Wyeth's painting of his wife, *Distant Thunder*. The show was a massive success, with 140,000 visitors enjoying the small show (just twenty-one paintings) in the East Room during its short run.

Pat's next project would also reflect these solid American values on a much larger scale. The Nixon White House redo would stamp the residence as distinctly American, separating it from Jackie Kennedy's French-influenced White House decor. Pat would help create the decor of the White House as we know it today: a residence with a unique flavor reflecting the early days of the American Republic, inspired by Colonial Williamsburg.

When the Nixons moved in, Pat was instantly struck by the shabby state of their new home. The residence looked more like a gigantic, dingy motel, with its tattered upholstery, frayed curtains, and threadbare wallcoverings. "When Pat Nixon moved in five years after President Kennedy's death, she was astonished to find the mansion looking run-down and seedy. The heavy traffic of more than a million and a half sightseers and fifty thousand invited guests every year for almost ten years had taken their toll, and the Lyndon Johnsons had done little or no work to keep up the appearance of the downstairs public rooms."

However, Pat was hesitant to make White House decor one of her major endeavors, due to the rising tide of second-wave American feminism. "She was reluctant as well to undertake the decorating because she knew the news media, riding the . . . wave of the women's movement, were eager to focus on issues more substantial than decorating."

However, practicality soon won out. Winchester could often be found frantically cutting stray threads off chairs before state dinners, trying to disguise the shabby state of the furniture. Lady Bird had held back on any redecoration, in part due to lack of funds, but also out of fear of backlash if she changed any of the Kennedy decor. It was as if the White House had been frozen in time, a sacred spot preserved as an untouchable shrine to the Kennedys. However, by the time the Nixons arrived, enough time had elapsed. Presumably, the new First Lady could start over without (much) fear of political backlash. White House refurbishment was now imperative for reasons of national image.

Haldeman wasted no time getting involved in this area (traditionally the purview of the First Lady) by recruiting Clement Conger, the State Department's assistant chief of protocol and curator of the State Department reception rooms, to help oversee the project. He arranged for Conger to meet the president and Mrs. Nixon at a State Department reception, where the First Couple were impressed by his work there. The president himself asked Conger to help the First Lady. Although reluctant at first to take on such a politically charged position, Conger could not refuse a presidential summons. He soon accepted the job of White House curator, working in the residence in the afternoons but keeping his State Department job in the mornings.

Conger was a flamboyant personality and for some an acquired taste. A member of the so-called FFVs (First Families of Virginia), Conger not only grew up with a distinguished lineage but also was raised around beautiful and costly English period furniture, thus developing his love of antiques. S. Dillon Ripley, secretary of the Smithsonian Institution, dubbed him "The Grand Acquisitor," while Undersecretary of State Elliot Richardson described Conger as "having the talents of an Oriental rug dealer, a horse trader, and a Florentine merchant."

Conger brought an A-list team with him to the White House job: Edward Vason Jones, a neoclassical architecture expert, and Berry Tracy, curator of the American Wing at the Met and a specialist in American period interiors. Pat would become good friends with all the men, especially Conger. Pat and Conger shared a birthday and a similar appreciation for an all-American approach to redoing the White House. The White House curator and the First Lady soon developed a mutual admiration society, and they would always have birthday lunches for each other complete with their shared favorite: coconut cake with lemon filing.

Pat's first major project within the public parts of the White House was the Oval Office, where Pat employed her New York decorator Sarah Jackson Doyle's aesthetic eye. The centerpiece of the room was a new and imposing rug sketched out by the First Lady and her decorator, "a large oval expanse of rich, deep blue bordered with dark yellow stars and the insignia of the president in the center." Dramatic yellow silk curtains formed an impressive backdrop behind the mahogany Wilson Desk, which the president had also used as vice president. This backdrop would become iconic to Americans during the Nixon years.

Haldeman took care of the West Wing office redo, in the style referred to by many as "Colonial Williamsburg Office." The president's chief of staff cultivated deep ties with Colonial Williamsburg itself and was able to procure many items of value for the office spaces directly from Colonial Williamsburg collections. Conger himself was deeply entrenched with Carl Humelsine, the president of Colonial Williamsburg; the two had worked together at the State Department. As Al Louer, the former director of principal gifts at the CW Foundation, who worked with Conger, explained, there was "a deal between Carl and Conger" that focused needed attention on Williamsburg.

Luminaries such as Britain's Queen Mother, the young Queen Elizabeth, King Mohammed of Morocco, Indian prime minister Indira Gandhi, and scores of other famous personages had flocked to Colonial Williamsburg for years. There was the presidential seal of approval too. General Eisenhower and Mamie visited in 1946 with Clementine and Winston Churchill, then again together in 1953 after he became president. (Eisenhower would re-turn in 1957 for a solo visit.) Conger and Haldeman had seized on a unique branding opportunity with a then-glamorous Colonial Williamsburg, a way to showcase American power and history in a neat marketing package.

Perhaps the First Lady and Conger's most significant collaboration was the renovation and redecoration of the three state reception rooms, with the Green, Blue, and Red Rooms being special highlights. Berry Tracy would call out the Green Room as "the finest example of a federal period furnished room in America" with its museum-quality examples of American cabinet-maker Duncan Phyfe furniture. The Blue Room, which under Mrs. Kennedy was a "Boudin masterpiece" styled as a circa 1801 reception room, was re-styled by the Conger team into a more "lounge-like" sitting room, with chairs in conversational groupings and wallpaper replacing the Kennedy striped silk on the walls.

The Red Room was redone in American Empire style, utilizing a new, more "American" red paint that Mrs. Nixon called "Dolley Red" in honor of the background color in First Lady Dolley Madison's portrait, which she would later acquire for display in the Red Room. Much of the Kennedy fur-niture was retained but was supplemented with important new acquisitions, including a priceless Charles-Honoré Lannuier secretary-bookcase.

Jacqueline Kennedy had started the acquisition process for White House–appropriate art, furniture, and rugs. Former White House curator Bill All-man notes, "Mrs. Kennedy obviously gets enormous credit for starting the museum focus, the Curator's Office and the White House Historical Associ-ation" in 1961. Mrs. Kennedy's 1962 televised tour of the White House was a sensation, bringing much-needed attention to the White House as a historic residence that needed preservation. As historian Betty Boyd Caroli noted, the First Lady's televised tour "signaled the possibility that a president's wife could bring some of her own interests to the job . . . it marked a change from Mamie Eisenhower's unwillingness to show she could think and Bess Truman's reluctance to be seen."

Mrs. Kennedy was *toujours* a Francophile. She hired the famous French designer Stéphane Boudin, president of international decorating firm Maison Jansen, to help her decorate the Mansion, as well as American designers Albert Hadley and Dorothy "Sister" Parish. Famed architect Norman Askins worked on the Nixon redecoration project as a young employee of Colonial Williamsburg. As Askins noted, during the Kennedy administration "French decorative arts were the thing. But the White House is really nineteenth century."

Conger frequently disparaged the Kennedy-era decor and acquisitions due to a long-held grudge the curator had toward Boudin. "In the 1950s Maison Jansen (with Boudin as its president) was called upon by the General Services Administration (GSA) to redecorate (among other spaces) the American embassy in Paris. The cost was naturally high and American designers were incensed at being bypassed in favor of a foreigner. 'After that, Boudin was persona non grata at the State Department.'"

Thus, Williamsburg was a logical point for the reorientation of the White House decor as the 1970s dawned. Askins recalled: "Everybody had 'Williamsburg-itis' at the time. The tone was anti-ranch, anti-modernism." This all fit in perfectly with the Nixon administration's push toward homespun American values.

The Nixon redecoration and acquisition project was also inspired by the upcoming American Bicentennial of 1976, but the "fervor started earlier than that; in the late 1960s there was a big push" toward Americana. A White House decorated in the American style with American period antiques, furnishings, and art was a key image the Nixon White House wanted to cultivate and project, not only to the American public but also to the international community. It was brand-building—something Haldeman understood well and was able to turn to the White House's advantage. The decor anticipated Bicentennial fever, and it might also help harvest patriotic votes in the 1972 presidential election.

Fortunately, the match Haldeman facilitated between Conger and Pat was one made in decorating heaven. Previous West Wing attempts to foist staff upon her had failed due to staffers' age, temperament, and lack of experience. However, at fifty-eight and with a proven track record, Conger was the First Lady's contemporary, and he treated her as an equal partner, consulting her in depth on all White House decorating decisions. The Pat Nixon–Clement Conger team was effective, efficient, and motivated. Thanks to their dedication and hard work, the residence redo was a smashing success.

As few are aware today, it was Pat Nixon who did the bulk of acquiring period-appropriate antiques for the White House. Decorative arts historian William Seale gave tremendous credit to Pat and Conger in terms of acquiring top-notch antiques for the White House, calling items acquired by the Nixon team "the Citizen Kane lode of furnishings." All in all, Pat and Conger secured a total of $1,897,245 from foundations and individuals in service to the Nixon White House restoration and redecoration project. This encompassed 252 pieces of furniture, 61 paintings and drawings, 21 chandeliers, 28 period rugs, and a treasure trove of other art objects. This is more than any other administration has amassed before or since.

The sale of White House guidebooks was the only source of funds for the project: the government paid nothing toward redecoration and acquisition efforts. This is where Conger's talents at coaxing both money and artifacts from wealthy donors and foundations came to the fore. He attributed "his success to the fact that 'people love to be patriotic, love tax deductions, and love to be invited to the White House and State Department for dinner.'" Conger the "horse trader" used all these tools adroitly in service to the White House and the First Lady's renovation project. At times, though, he tangled with Winchester and her staff by trying to add too many of his donors to the White House dinner party lists. He could be "annoyingly persistent," noted Winchester, who jokingly referred to him as "Inclement Conger."

One highlight of the program was the loan/acquisition of President James Madison's wife Dolley's beautiful portrait, subsequently installed in the Red Room in 1971. Gilbert Stuart's work portrayed the popular and vivacious First Lady "with her hair arranged in a neoclassical style and wearing a fashionable high-waisted Empire-style dress."

The portrait originally hung in the White House during the Madison administration, but it was lost temporarily when the British burned the Mansion in 1814, at the end of the War of 1812. Dolley was "too busy during the fire saving Stuart's famous full-length portrait of George Washington to be bothered about her own picture." The portrait was loaned to the White House by the Pennsylvania Academy of Arts, and a memorable reception was held when Dolley arrived to thank the academy for bringing the former First Lady back "home."

Pat told ABC reporter Virginia Sherwood that she felt a kinship with this brave First Lady, who was forced to flee the White House when the British invaded. "Dolley Madison always intrigued me. She was always quite a hostess, and I have read many biographies on her. And apparently, she was quite a character with her turbans and her high sense of style."

Dolley's choice of what precious White House item to save from the British indicates she was a First Lady who put others above her own interests, as Pat always did. Dolley and Pat also shared high-level diplomatic skills, which both women employed on behalf of their husbands' administrations. "Aside from arranging social events, Dolley also acted as a political liaison for her husband," even going so far as to dip snuff with Madison's political colleagues to help him.

While you would never catch Pat dipping snuff (or even sharing a cigarette) with her husband's political cronies, she clearly admired her predecessor, and she wanted to include Dolley's image in her personal White House representation of the American feminine spirit. In all, Pat added seven portraits of First Ladies to the residence. The First Lady's significant effort at putting women back into the White House narrative with these portraits was both a great achievement and a sign of her interests that is far too often overlooked.

23

WHAT MAKES PAT NIXON TICK?

While David Eisenhower saw the fall of 1969 as the beginning of his mother-in-law's deeper engagement in her First Lady position, Nixon aide Chapin's view was that "Peru is a line of demarcation . . . Mrs. Nixon's asset appreciation rose dramatically after Peru."

Pat's historic trip to Peru was the result of a terrible natural disaster. On May 31, 1970, the Great Peruvian Earthquake hit the coastal town of Chimbote. Seventy thousand Peruvians died, and fifty thousand were injured; eight hundred thousand were left homeless. Landslides after the quake destroyed whole villages. A wall of ice, mud, and snow came loose from Peru's highest mountain after the quake and buried the entire town of Yungay. All that remained was a statue of Christ above the city cemetery and the tops of four 90-foot palm trees. The only residents spared were a group of schoolchildren attending a circus that day, and all of them were orphaned by the landslide.

Pat Nixon witnessed these horrific events on television in the United States. She was so deeply disturbed by the scenes of devastation she saw that she felt she must do something personally to help. The president encouraged her to go solo to Peru as his personal ambassador.

On June 28, 1970, Pat flew to Peru on Air Force One with another jet in tow carrying ten tons of relief supplies. The First Lady also brought members of the U.S. press with her and $25,000 in relief checks written to her personally. The goal of the trip was to bring food, medical supplies, and other useful items to those in need. Pat was able to use her platform as First Lady to focus world attention on the Peruvians' plight. This would (and did) encourage other countries to send relief to Peru.

After arriving in Lima, Pat was greeted by Consuelo Velasco, the First Lady of Peru. Mrs. Nixon's prior global travels and love of people allowed her to make an instant warm connection with Mrs. Velasco. The two women hit it off and often walked arm in arm together during the trip.

The next morning, the supplies were loaded onto a cargo plane taking Pat, Mrs. Velasco, and a few members of the press deep into the Andes Mountains, where they made a dangerous landing on a dirt strip. Pat sat on a kitchen chair bolted to the floor of the plane, with no seat belt, while Mrs. Velasco sat in the copilot's seat. From here, the two women took a Marine helicopter to the worst-hit areas and spent five hours picking through the rubble of demolished homes.

Pat hugged children, held the hands of villagers, met people on the ground, and empathized with their situation. Mrs. Velasco, who had been used to more formal interactions with the Peruvian people, followed the American First Lady's lead, also hugging children and talking person-to-person with those she encountered.

The next day the two women met with the leaders of volunteer agencies as well as more everyday people affected by the quake. At the Hospital del Niño, Pat hugged children orphaned and traumatized by the disaster.

As she had demonstrated on her many previous international trips as Second Lady, Pat was much more interested in one-on-one interactions with locals in hospitals, orphanages, schools, and village squares than she was in formal dinners, banquets, or teas. Now, as First Lady, Pat's genuine care and concern for the victims of the Peruvian earthquake exemplified her person-to-person humanitarian efforts. After this devastating catastrophe, she used her platform as First Lady to model not only the volunteerism that was her signature project domestically but also Americans' empathy and concern for those in need globally.

The personal nature of Pat's trip, her sincere interest in the welfare of the Peruvian people, and her authentic warmth won hearts. The *Dallas Morning News* wrote: "She could have been above all the tragedy, but instead, for a few hours, she became part of the tragedy, and her face and voice showed it."

The First Lady's helicopter pilot in Peru, Gene Boyer, related what one of the Peruvian generals told him as they prepared to return home: "'I must tell you,' he said, 'this visit by Mrs. Nixon has done more to improve relations with our country than anything the United States has done in a hundred years.'"

The First Lady's volunteer efforts in Peru were an international success, and in June 1971, Pat was awarded the Grand Cross of the Order of the Sun, the Peruvian government's highest honor, for her earthquake relief work. She was the first North American woman to win this distinguished award.

Chapin noted that the First Lady's "confidence level went up after that." David Eisenhower was there to greet her when she came back from her mercy mission: "She was very proud of what she had done. It was a hazardous trip. Peru must have made her aware of the impact that a First Lady can have." Chapin concurred with Eisenhower's assessment of the First Lady's relief mission to Peru: "It's a stage setter . . . the dam breaks, and then she becomes very available to come out and do things."

———

In stark contrast to the international acclaim that greeted her return from the Peru trip were the nationally traumatizing events occurring among American student populations in response to the horrors of the Vietnam War. In the spring of 1970, the conflict in Southeast Asia continued to splinter the country.

In an address given on April 30 in the Oval Office that has since become known as the "Pitiful Helpless Giant" speech, President Nixon declared his intent to use U.S.–South Vietnamese joint operations to clear out North Vietnamese "sanctuaries" in Cambodia. The address described the fate of the United States if the country failed to act against the communists in Cambodia: "If, when the chips are down, the world's most powerful nation, the United States of America, acts like a pitiful, helpless giant, the forces of totalitarianism and anarchy will threaten free nations and free institutions throughout the world." As a precaution, the president had "summoned Julie and David down from Smith and Amherst, where they were shortly scheduled to graduate, because he feared a violent campus reaction to his speech."

After a Pentagon briefing the next morning, the president made the mistake of saying, "You see these bums, you know, blowing up the campuses. Listen, the boys that are on college campuses are the luckiest people in the world, going to the greatest universities, and here they are burning up the books, storming around about this issue." The "bums" comment was instantly picked up by the press and widely reported.

Then the unthinkable happened. On May 4, 1970, National Guardsmen at Ohio's Kent State (under the control of the governor of Ohio, not the president) fired upon unarmed student protestors, killing four students and wounding nine. The president later admitted that "[t]hose few days after Kent State were amongst the darkest of my presidency. . . . I felt utterly dejected." Julie vividly remembered "my mother's reaction was disbelief. She was appalled by the tragic deaths, and tremendously upset that my father's 'bums' statement had been so distorted."

The mood on campuses nationwide turned hostile, and Julie wrote presidential advisor John Ehrlichman, fearful of the danger her father would face if he went through with plans to attend her Smith graduation. "'I truly think the day will be a disaster if he comes . . . the temper up here is ugly.' She mentioned a rally with thousands of people chanting 'Fuck Julie and David Eisenhower.'" The decision was reluctantly made for both Julie and David to forgo their graduations for their own security as well as that of the president.

———

In mid-June 1970, the American press learned that Prince Charles and Princess Anne would be guests at the White House for several days in July. Even in the 1970s, Americans were obsessed with British royalty—a fascination that continues to this day. Today we have a cancer-stricken King Charles III, at long last married to his longtime mistress (and now queen), Camilla. But in 1970, Prince Charles was young, handsome, and eminently single. All America held its breath and hoped for a fairytale royal romance between beautiful blond First Daughter Tricia and the courtly English prince.

Unbeknownst to the public, Tricia was secretly engaged to her beau of several years, Edward Cox. But the seriousness of this relationship was still under wraps. Reporter Helen Thomas claimed that a protective Pat told her, "Tricia has boyfriends in every port." The engagement cover-up was the First Lady's attempt to provide a protective screen around the young couple's relationship.

Exciting as the royal visit news was for the American public, it created a huge amount of work for Mrs. Nixon's press office. Martha Doss, Connie Stuart's assistant, noted, "What a lot of work. The staff assignment and duties list was a monster." Connie Stuart also noted the massive coordination efforts needed, as there were "something like seventeen different motorcades in three days, and they visited . . . fifteen different locations." The biggest issue, however, was not the mind-boggling logistics but managing the American press. "The Prince and the Princess were not all that used to that type of press coverage, and it provided for certain problems in itself."

Indeed, as soon as Princess Anne stepped off the plane, nattily attired in a "bright chartreuse mini dress and a white broad brimmed hat that had a yellow green sash," she faced the flash bulbs of an excited press corps. "I didn't know they made so many cameras," she said incredulously.

The next day she was so put off by the press throngs that she refused to talk to the reporter Helen Thomas at a Lincoln Memorial outing. "I don't give interviews," the princess said frostily. When Thomas tried again for a comment, she was stopped by Anne's protection officer. Charles seemed much more at ease with the press and the informality of the visit. As Julie recalled, Charles came across as "a thoughtful human being, not a royal robot. He had a gift for putting people at ease." At a Camp David cookout on the royals' first evening in the United States, Charles charmed twenty young guests; "it was almost as if the Prince were the host."

The highlight of the three-day extravaganza was the 8 p.m. supper-dance on the South Lawn of the White House hosted by Julie, David, and Tricia. Seven hundred guests enjoyed the music of the Canadian rock band the Guess Who under a canopy of twinkling lights. Julie recalled that at this point, Anne had loosened up and now seemed to be enjoying herself. This turnaround perhaps ensued because guests in the receiving line were mistakenly curtseying to Julie and calling her "Your Royal Highness," as she was positioned next to Charles. Anne found that situation hilarious.

Julie revealed that it was she, not Tricia, who had the first dance with the prince. This was a deliberate attempt to tamp down the Tricia-Charles romance rumors floating around in the American press. "My sister was embarrassed by rumors and news stories of a romance between her and Prince Charles, especially since she and Edward Cox, whom she married a year later, were secretly engaged at that time. We thought that if Tricia had the first dance that night with Charles, it might increase speculation."

The night of the ball, Charles gave Julie some rare insight into his thoughts on the marriage he must make as heir to the British throne: "The head must rule the heart. . . . Falling in love is not enough. His wife must also be his best friend. And his marriage must last forever." (We all know how that one ended up.)

The royal visit and related events marked a happy occasion for both Pat and Dick, who kept their distance from the dance and the other activities, allowing the young people to enjoy each other without interference. They had confidence in their two poised and lovely daughters as well as their son-in-law. And, of course, Pat had her superb East Wing staff, headed by Winchester and Stuart, to run the show.

Despite Anne's initial fit of pique, the British invasion of the White House overall was a splendid success. Anne's thank-you note to Tricia echoed the sentiments Julie had voiced at the supper dance. Anne told her that it had been "tremendous fun" and she thought "a great success." She also expressed the hope that "you were able to enjoy it as much as your guests certainly did."

Charles's warm thank-you note to Tricia showed that Edward Cox need not have worried. He was "in" on their secret engagement and wished them "a wonderful wedding and honeymoon."

———————

On September 27, 1970, the Nixons headed to Europe for an eight-day sojourn, including a visit to Ireland and Pat's long-lost Ryan relatives there.

Novelist and Nixon cousin Jessamyn West accompanied the Nixons on their trip to Ireland and was granted a private interview with Pat for *Good Housekeeping*. Her profile of Pat, whom she had known well for many years, revealed a very private First Lady whom West compared to the mysterious German movie star Marlene Dietrich. "Her life, like Dietrich's, is, insofar as the public can see, a performance; but hers is a performance in which she is not the star, but a supporting actor. It is difficult to see how this role could be performed better. But is it a role? Or is it Pat?"

Pat told West that she was never tired. And everyone observed that Pat always looked perfect, unwrinkled, and fresh even after fourteen-hour days. How did she pull this off? wondered the writer. To West, Pat was "mystifying" and the cause of "bafflement." Previous First Ladies fit into certain molds, West wrote, roles that were expected and easily understandable. Pat, however, defied easy categorization. She would not be put in a box.

This is frustrating to the public, because "bafflement in a First Lady is something we feel cheated by. 'What makes Pat Nixon tick?' we want to know. So, we ask. And Pat Nixon doesn't say." Even to a cousin she had known well for decades, Pat didn't reveal herself fully. But she did show flashes of herself, brief, tantalizing glimpses, like the ones she showed (more unwillingly) to Gloria Steinem in 1968. The West interview is a rejoinder to that one, where Pat resented what she considered Steinem's silly question about whom she most admired.

Here, Pat tells West, "Many of the women I meet are important in their own right. They are women who are themselves bankers, presidents, vice-presidents, investment counselors, bank lawyers." When West tells the First Lady, "Women's Lib will thank you for making that clear," Pat responds (as if talking to Steinem directly): "I wasn't doing that for Women's Lib. Just for accuracy. I think people are able to judge others by what they do. A person is what he does. That's what's important and interesting, not character analysis or personality assessment."

Only a few weeks later, Pat would demonstrate her philosophy by her own actions. On October 17, Pat would take the unusual step of campaigning for a female GOP candidate in Detroit: Lenore Romney, wife of Michigan's former governor George Romney, Nixon's secretary of housing and urban development (and the mother of future Massachusetts governor, Utah senator, and Republican presidential candidate Mitt Romney), who was running for a Michigan Senate seat.

Romney was a well-liked Michigan First Lady who "did not shy from encouraging women to take a more active role in government. 'Why should women have less say than men about the great decisions facing our nation?' she said in one 1966 address, adding that women 'represent a reservoir of public service which has hardly been tapped.'" Lenore Romney and Pat shared similar philosophies about women in government.

Despite a strong campaign, Romney suffered a crushing defeat. Her attempt to dethrone Democratic senator Philip A. Hart failed (despite the First Lady's support), in large part because she was female. Romney (like Pat before her), "encountered a predominately male press corps that often wrote about her in a paternalistic way, as if her run were little more than a housewife's lark."

The former First Lady of Michigan "found in my campaign that many men and women openly resented the fact that a woman would even try to unseat a man . . . I take exception. It's the real world, and women have every right—and duty—to be in it." One can imagine Pat applauding those remarks. She had lent her valuable presence to the Romney campaign, only to see her friend's quest go down in flames. The experience left a bitter aftertaste. The debacle was still on her mind in January 1972 when she gave a rare televised interview with young CBS reporter Barbara Walters. The First Lady told Walters with conviction in her voice:

> I know there are not very many women who are elected members of Congress, I think there should be more—but many women don't want to run because it's very difficult to get elected in as much as other women won't support them. For example, Mrs. George Romney in Michigan told me that the women did not come forward as she expected they would. So, I think we need to give lessons to women to support other women.

On camera, the First Lady's eyes lit up while she spoke her mind. Getting women in higher-level government roles was an issue that Pat was passionate about.

———

On January 7, 1970, Pat received a letter from an old acquaintance, Jacqueline Kennedy Onassis. After her husband's assassination in 1963, Jackie had remained visible on the world stage. His martyrdom only piqued interest in her postpresidential life, and a series of high-profile romances kept her in the gossip columns. In October 1968, she had married Greek shipping magnate Aristotle Onassis, a notorious playboy who had previously dated her sister, Lee Radziwill. Onassis had also been involved in a long-term romantic relationship with the American opera diva Maria Callas before he ditched her (temporarily) for Jackie.

A few years after her wedding to Onassis, Jackie politely declined an invitation from Pat to attend the Committee of the Preservation of the White House's January 28, 1970, meeting. But she graciously agreed to continue serving on the committee from afar, expressing her thanks to Pat and her husband for "asking me to continue to serve" and indicating that she would "be most honored and happy to do so as long as you both shall wish."

Jackie was certainly aware of the diligent renovation and restoration work that Pat and Clement Conger had taken on at the White House, building upon the foundation that she had so carefully begun. Despite the bitter defeat of 1960 and her suspicions that the race had been stolen from Dick, in deference to the former First Lady Pat had scrupulously avoided both publicity about her extensive work on the White House and comparisons to Jackie's work in this area. Jackie concluded her letter by acknowledging Pat's commitment and adding, "I know that the White House has a great defender in you."

Perhaps it was due in part to Pat's solicitous caretaking of the White House that the former First Lady agreed to return there with her children John and Caroline in February 1971. The major impetus for the visit, however, was to privately view the portraits of the two Kennedys that had been recently completed by New York artist Aaron Shikler. Jackie had let it be known she would not participate in any formal ceremony, but she sent "a personal note to the Nixons asking, 'Could the children and I slip in unobtrusively to Washington, and come pay our respects to you and to see the pictures privately? . . . And the children could see their father's portrait in the rooms they used to know, in a quiet way.'"

Both the president and Pat thought it important that Jackie and her children be given the chance to view the portraits within an atmosphere of comfort and privacy. Plans were set in motion immediately for the clandestine visit. The president sent his personal pilot in a small military jet to pick up Jackie and her children in New York on February 3. The halls of the White House were blocked off when the family arrived so as to ensure their total privacy.

Julie remembered, "My mother was determined that the visit be as private and as happy as possible. Only four members of the White House staff who would be directly involved in the visit were informed and they were sworn to strict secrecy. No one in either the East or West Wings was briefed."

Only UPI's White House Bureau chief Helen Thomas's sharp radar picked up signals of a Jackie visit. Pat's assistant press secretary, Helen Mc-Cain Smith, was forced to make a deal with Thomas to keep the secret viewing off the wires. Thomas recalled: "I was working late in the White House press room when I got a tip that Jackie was coming. I confirmed my information with Mrs. Nixon's press secretary Helen Smith. . . . When she confirmed the story, she asked if I would hold it off the ticker for a certain time to give Jackie a chance to leave. I agreed, as long as I could have the story exclusively."

The First Lady, Tricia, and Julie met Jackie and her children at the second-floor elevator upon their arrival in the White House. The first order of business was to visit Jackie's portrait, which Clement Conger had hung on the ground floor outside the Diplomatic Reception Room. JFK's portrait was hung in the Grand Hall and prominently displayed. After viewing the portraits, the group ranged all over the White House, exploring the newly renovated rooms, admiring newly acquired antiques and objects, and enjoying the new Jacqueline Kennedy Garden dedicated under the Johnson administration.

That evening, Jackie, John, and Caroline had a gourmet dinner in the Nixon family quarters (surely Pat's idea to keep the evening as warm and casual as possible). The president then led the special guests on a tour through the West Wing and the Oval Office, where John Jr. was able to sit behind the presidential desk where his father had once sat.

Pat's innate understanding of the value of privacy protected Jackie and her children from what could have been a media circus. This still relatively unheralded event is a striking example of her thoughtful nature and lack of interest in publicity for herself or for its own sake. Due to Pat's precautions, the visit remained secret, allowing the former First Family to tour the White House—the only home Jackie's children remembered with their father—in total peace, with no invasive press corps documenting their reactions. "Despite knowing what extensive publicity it would generate, the Nixons made sure no photos were taken and every effort was made to ensure complete privacy for the Kennedy family."

Jackie's heartfelt note thanking Pat for "the gift you gave me" was worth more than a million columns of text in the newspapers to Pat. Jackie was thrilled to be able to "return to the White House privately" with her children "while they are still young enough to rediscover their childhood." She asked Pat to thank her daughters, "such extraordinary young women," for serving as guides. A day Jackie had "always dreaded turned out to be one of the most precious ones I have spent with my children."

A few days later, JFK's mother Rose Kennedy wrote Pat after a telephone call from Jackie, saying that she had been "deeply" moved by Pat's "warm-hearted welcome" on a day that "might have been difficult for Jackie and the children." She added that Pat's "daughters completely captivated the children" and gave them "an opportunity to see again the places in the White House which were familiar to them." Despite the defeat of 1960 and those bitter memories, Pat did not hesitate to create a safe environment for the Kennedy children and their mother to return to the White House. As a result, she conquered the hearts of the Kennedy women with her kindness.

Pat received another letter from the Kennedy matriarch that summer. On June 9, Rose wrote to thank Pat for hosting her for tea at the White House to view her son and daughter-in-law's portraits herself, saying how interesting it was "to see the widely discussed portraits." JFK's mother concluded the letter with: "If you or any members of your family are ever near me here in Palm Beach, I shall be most honored to welcome them to my home."

24

A FEW GOOD WOMEN

On February 6, 1969, President Richard Nixon faced a room packed with reporters for the second press conference of his new administration. He fielded questions on a wide range of topics. But when Vera Glaser, Washington bureau chief for the North American Newspaper Alliance, got her turn, she asked him a question no one had expected: "Mr. President, in staffing your administration, you have so far made about 200 high-level Cabinet and other policy position appointments, and only three have gone to women. Can you tell us, sir, whether we can expect more equitable recognition of women's abilities, or are we going to remain a lost sex?"

Glaser's question became part of the push that the new administration needed to ramp up efforts to include women in government. Under Nixon, this push would occur not just at the lower levels, as previous administrations had halfheartedly done, but with the appointments of women to high-level government posts. The woman who deserves credit for being the front woman leading this effort in the White House is Barbara Hackman Franklin. One of her backers behind the scenes? First Lady Pat Nixon.

After a prestigious college career at Penn State, Hackman was one of only twelve women among the 632 in her Harvard Business School class of 1964, one of the first classes to admit women. After graduation from Harvard, Hackman, now Barbara Hackman Franklin, worked at the Singer Company, and then at First National City Bank (now Citibank) as assistant vice president. But when she got a call from her former HBS classmate Fred Malek, who was working for President Nixon as his special assistant for personnel, she was intrigued.

Malek wanted her to spearhead a program recruiting women for high-level government jobs under the new Nixon administration. At the time, Franklin did not have much support for her decision to go into government work. "I was told by almost everybody—all my friends in New York—don't do that. That administration will never do anything for women, and you will set back your career. But I decided to do it anyway." She took a six-month leave from the bank—and never looked back.

———

Franklin's first day on the job as staff assistant to the president on April 12, 1971, proved challenging. Her title was announced as "staff assistant to the president for executive manpower." Vera Glaser, and other veteran members of the female press, were appalled and immediately jumped on the disconnect. Franklin cringes a bit when she remembers that day. "This did *not* go over well with the female press. They asked, 'How can you be a recruiter for women when your title is executive assistant for *manpower?*' . . . It shows you the mindset of the men who were there."

Franklin knew she had to show results quickly. By May 15, a presidential directive was issued requiring action plans for advancing and appointing women within each executive department and agency. The directive included both high-level government appointments and mid-level ones. Advisory boards and committees with vacancies needed more female appointees as well. Franklin was the overall supervisor, or in her words the "monitorer," of all these plans as well as the administration's head cheerleader and a prominent example of its female leadership.

One major focus of her work was developing a "talent bank" of women, as Franklin called it, for different roles across the new administration. Prospecting for these women required Franklin to travel to the ten U.S. federal districts that stretch across the country seeking out names. Franklin's eagle eye identified many women whom Americans would come to know later, with Sandra Day O'Connor, Juanita Kreps, and Carla Hills among them. The talent bank would also identify qualified women whose names we may not know today but who changed history all the same: female tugboat captains, forest rangers, sky marshals, and FBI agents, roles formerly closed to women that were now unlocked.

As was evident by the initial "manpower" title, Franklin often faced an uphill battle with her male West Wing colleagues. She had to use humor to deflect some of the nasty commentary that often surrounded her. A bust of Susan B. Anthony "lived" for a time in Franklin's office closet. Franklin laughed as she recalled: "She would steal out of there sometimes in the middle of the night and land on the desks of someone who had done something detrimental to women. The spirit of Susan B. Anthony roamed around the West Wing at night" until she was formally presented to the First Lady in early 1973.

There was little pressure from within the West Wing for the president to do anything for women. Neither of the past two presidential administrations had made women a priority group. Franklin commented: "It was a kind of a vacuum. There was a bit of force building up there." Although the women's movement and female reporters like Vera Glaser were crucial to women's issues moving forward, Franklin also thought a few good women behind the scenes gently pushed the president along as well: "I think Mrs. Nixon had a lot to do with this . . . in addition to his two daughters and the lasting influence of his mother Hannah. There was beginning to be a political need or rationale for supporting women's roles outside the home."

Without serious support from the president, Franklin claimed, her efforts would have been muted. "I don't believe that the advances that were made and the barriers that were broken could ever have happened at that particular time in our country if a president of the United States hadn't made the effort to advance women." And Franklin added, "Who [Mrs. Nixon] was and how she felt about some of these key issues at the time and the advancement of women had a lot to do with where he was. He was more open to advancing women than he might have been had he just been surrounded by the usual guys. I think she really made a difference."

Henry Kissinger also felt that the president was supportive of this push. "Nixon wanted to make sure women were given an opportunity. Even in his dealings with me, when I told him about staff hirings, he would say, 'Make sure you consider some women for this, particularly some recent college graduates.'"

In the end, these efforts paid serious dividends for the advancement of women in government. "Thanks in large part to [Franklin's] outstanding leadership in this area, by 1972 the White House had almost tripled the number of jobs for women in policy making positions (from 36 to 105) and had promoted 1,000 additional women into mid-level federal jobs. . . . The number of women on presidential commissions and boards was also greatly expanded." Pat's often-stated goal of getting more women into the workforce and into government roles was beginning to be realized.

————

While Franklin was diligently working on ramping up roles for women in the administration, the country had its eyes on two very different brides and their wedding ceremonies, both of which would take place in 1971. The two women and their styles couldn't have been more different, but both were equally captivating.

The first of these iconic ceremonies took place among rock-and-roll royalty on May 12, 1971, in St. Tropez, France. Here Rolling Stones lead singer Mick Jagger married his Nicaraguan girlfriend, Bianca Perez-Mora Macias, in a hippie atmosphere notable not only for its colorful participants (including rock gods Eric Clapton, Paul McCartney, and Ringo Starr) but also for the uncontrolled press frenzy the nuptials invoked. Pregnant bride Bianca became a bohemian style icon due to her choice of an Yves St. Laurent white satin Le Smoking jacket paired with a silk skirt and floppy brimmed hat with tulle veil. The marriage wouldn't last, but the images of Bianca and her unusual bridal outfit most certainly did.

Exactly one month later, an equally stylish but much more traditional and family-oriented wedding would take place at the White House, this time among American political royalty. On June 12, 1971, Tricia Nixon married Edward Finch Cox of New York in the Rose Garden. This was to be the first outdoor wedding in White House history and the eighth presidential daughter to be married at the White House.

Bob Bostock, Nixon historian, noted, "Tricia and Ed wanted it to be a family event, but they knew there would be intense interest both at home and abroad." A deal was struck to accommodate both the American public and the private family element. "The couple gave many interviews and sat for countless photographs prior to the big day. They also allowed the television networks to film the ceremony which was broadcast after the event." Ultimately, 110 million Americans would tune in to watch. The broadcast to millions would prove to be a triumph, helping to humanize the president and to connect the Nixon family with the American family in a relatable way.

The band in the East Room played music all evening for dancing. The Nixons didn't dance together in public often, but on this day, the presidential couple did just that. The First Lady even revealed that "Dick is a wonderful dancer. In fact, he's my favorite partner." Television coverage shows a radiant First Lady embracing and then dancing with a smiling president.

The next day, photos of the president and the new Mrs. Cox were splashed across the front pages of all the national newspapers. Tricia looked radiant, and her father beamed next to her with pride. *Washington Post* reporter Judith Martin, who had been banned from the wedding due to her perceived gate-crashing of Julie's wedding, was not allowed to cover Tricia's nuptials. Despite this boycott, Martin was the one who nabbed the wedding byline in the *Washington Post* the next day. As Martin remembered, Haldeman had called Kay Graham, publisher of the *Post*, to tell her Martin would not be allowed to cover the Rose Garden wedding. However, women from other newspapers were outraged, and they all called in details to help Martin write the story.

Martin was the least of the president's problems that day. In the *New York Times*, the wedding headline "Tricia Nixon Takes Vows in Garden at White House," on the left side of the front page, was juxtaposed with another, more jarring headline: "Vietnam Archive: Pentagon Study Traces 3 Decades of Growing U.S. Involvement." This headline was the beginning of a damning story for the U.S. government concerning the Vietnam War.

The secret study, soon to be widely known as the "Pentagon Papers," had been leaked by Daniel Ellsberg, a consultant for the Rand Corporation. The papers gave an inside view of previous administrations' cynical, qualitative analysis of the war, and its seeming willingness to expend titanic amounts of blood and treasure on an unwinnable conflict. The country would be horrified by what they read: many would conclude that this war was an unconscionable waste of human lives, matériel, and money.

The president was not implicated in this analysis, which focused on the Kennedy and Johnson administrations. However, Kissinger persuaded the president that leaks of this nature could very well ruin the administration. They were on the verge of several major diplomatic breakthroughs with both the Russians and the Chinese. "Kissinger was convinced, because [those diplomatic initiatives] were secret. If the newspapers continued to publish the Pentagon Papers, the Communist governments might well conclude that the U.S. government was incapable of keeping a secret, and break off negotiations."

Much to the administration's horror, Ellsberg soon began a media tour, appearing on television programs and radio shows. The president ordered his staff to "try to find out what other secrets he might reveal." Ehrlichman headed up this effort and ordered his underling Bud Krogh and his team of "plumbers" to plug such security leaks. During Labor Day weekend of 1971, the "plumbers" broke into the office of Ellsberg's psychiatrist to try to get more information on him and his operation, if he indeed had an organized one. They found nothing.

———

The First Lady and her family made great use of the presidential retreat in 1971. Set among the Catoctin Mountains, the haven was only a hundred miles from Washington (thirty minutes by helicopter, two hours by car) and offered the privacy Pat craved. First christened Shangri-La by President Franklin Delano Roosevelt, the woodsy, rustic camp was renamed Camp David by President Eisenhower in honor of the grandson who would one day marry the Nixons' daughter Julie. Camp David, with its 134 walled and guarded acres, provided more space for the family to move around and allowed the Nixon family members generous breathing room between themselves and their security details.

The peaceful presidential haven also gave Pat the chance to exercise—something she craved but was rarely able to do in the nation's capital. Here she could walk for hours without being closely guarded. She could also bowl, swim, read, and hang out with her daughters and the beloved family dogs without interruption. At the presidential retreat, Pat and the girls were always top priority. Socializing with aides there was never on the president's agenda.

(Above) Britain's Prince Charles and Princess Anne, accompanied by President Nixon, the First Lady, and David and Julie Eisenhower, wave to onlookers from the White House balcony on July 16, 1970. The royal visitors were hosted primarily by Julie, David, and Tricia, and rumors of a romance between Charles and Tricia captivated the public. However, Tricia was already secretly engaged to her own Prince Charming, Edward Finch Cox, whom she would marry the following year. *(Courtesy of the Richard Nixon Presidential Library and Museum)*

The First Lady discusses the acquisition of a Mrs. John Quincy Adams portrait with White House art curator Clement Conger. With Conger's expert help, Pat acquired more art and antique items for the White House than any other First Lady before or since her time. Pat rarely receives credit for her extensive work in this area, though the Williamsburg-themed décor of the White House as we know it today was the result of her efforts. *(Courtesy of the Richard Nixon Presidential Library and Museum)*

(*Above*) Pat always felt her greatest accomplishment was her two daughters. American fashion photographer Howell Conant shot this formal group portrait of the First Lady, Julie, and Tricia at the White House on February 5, 1971. (*Courtesy of the Richard Nixon Presidential Library and Museum*)

President Nixon greets his new White House Staff Assistant Barbara Hackman Franklin in April of 1971. One of the first women to obtain an MBA from Harvard, Franklin would be the one to unlock the doors for women in higher levels of government. Pat and her daughters supported Franklin's agenda by pushing for women's rights behind the scenes and at times publicly as well. (*Courtesy of the Richard Nixon Presidential Library and Museum*)

Tricia and Edward Finch Cox's White House Rose Garden wedding on June 12, 1971, captured the imagination of Americans with its romantic outdoor garden party theme. Rain threatened the nuptials, but Tricia held fast, the sky cleared, and the perfect wedding ensued. *(Courtesy of the Richard Nixon Presidential Library and Museum)*

(Below) President Nixon, Pat, Julie, Tricia, and Ed gathering around the White House family Christmas tree with the presidential dogs—Vicky the grey poodle, Pasha the Yorkshire terrier, and King Timahoe the Irish Setter—during a special CBS-TV holiday show taping on December 12, 1971. The Nixon family adored their dogs: each one had their own canine Christmas stocking at the White House. *(Courtesy of the Richard Nixon Presidential Library and Museum)*

Pat in Monrovia, Liberia, on January 4, 1972, wearing a traditional lappa cloth dress and turban near a Liberian women's dance troupe, while attending a National Cultural Center performance in Liberia's Presidential Executive Mansion Garden. The First Lady was touring Africa as a solo goodwill ambassador. *(Courtesy of the Richard Nixon Presidential Library and Museum)*

Pat Nixon touring the grounds of the Evergreen People's Commune in China on February 23, 1972. Pat's red coat was seen by the Chinese as a symbol of good fortune, and her warm engagement with the Chinese people won her many admirers as well as two Chinese pandas for the Washington Zoo. The First Lady thus began a half century of "panda diplomacy," thanks to her positive interactions with Chinese premier Chou En Lai. *(Courtesy of the Richard Nixon Presidential Library and Museum)*

Pat addressing the GOP convention in Miami, Florida, on August 23, 1972. The First Lady was introduced by Hollywood legend, actor Jimmy Stewart (far left), and was supported by Kansas senator Bob Dole and California governor (and future president) Ronald Reagan. Pat was the first Republican First Lady to address a national convention. *(Courtesy of the Richard Nixon Presidential Library and Museum)*

(Above) Pat became the first First Lady to wear pants to a public event on September 19, 1972, when she toured Yellowstone National Park accompanied by Secretary Rogers Morton and park officials. Pat sported a stylish blue pantsuit accessorized with a jaunty red, white, and blue scarf. *(Courtesy of the Richard Nixon Presidential Library and Museum)*

Mamie, Julie, and Pat laughing together at the inaugural gala for the Kennedy Center on January 18, 1973. Mamie had delighted in playing matchmaker between her grandson David and Julie before their marriage in 1968. The former First Lady enjoyed a close relationship with Pat and Julie, especially in her later years. *(Courtesy of the Richard Nixon Presidential Library and Museum)*

On March 1, 1973, President Nixon and the First Lady held a high-profile state dinner for their friend and ally Israeli prime minister, Golda Meir. Just months later, on October 6, 1973, Egypt and Syria launched a surprise attack on Israel later known as the Yom Kippur War. Israeli troops were seriously outnumbered and faced almost certain defeat. President Nixon ordered an emergency airlift of supplies and matériel, telling Dr. Henry Kissinger, his national security advisor and secretary of state, "Send everything that will fly." The American airlift enabled Israel to launch a decisive counterattack and to ultimately win the war. *(Courtesy of the Richard Nixon Presidential Library and Museum)*

Pat with her East Wing staff. The First Lady's loyal "East Wingers" adored their boss and often did battle with the West Wing on her behalf. The women also closed ranks around Pat during Watergate and helped her to conduct "business as usual" until the resignation. Pat is pictured sitting on the floor next to Lucy Winchester, her social secretary, whose witty sense of humor amused the First Lady—and infuriated the humorless Haldeman. Winchester often had to do battle with Haldeman and the West Wing on her boss's behalf. *(Courtesy of the Richard Nixon Presidential Library and Museum)*

"The Berlin Wall": Haldeman and John D. Ehrlichman were two of the president's closest advisors. Due to their Germanic names, the men were dubbed "The Berlin Wall" and were accused of isolating the president from his family, friends, staff, and the outside world. Haldeman frequently ignored or diminished the contributions of the First Lady and the East Wing and treated Pat as a liability instead of an asset. *(Courtesy of the Richard Nixon Presidential Library and Museum)*

On May 24, 1973, the President and the First Lady hosted the largest dinner ever held at the White House for American prisoners of war just returned from Vietnam and their female guests under giant tents erected on the South Lawn. Composer Irving Berlin, shown above onstage, called the White House asking if he could sing his patriotic classic, "God Bless America," with the returned POWs. The evening was a highlight of the Nixon presidency despite the clouds of Watergate. Left to right: Phyllis Diller, Joey Heatherton, President Nixon, Irving Berlin, Sammy Davis Jr., Pat, and Bob Hope. *(Courtesy of the Richard Nixon Presidential Library and Museum)*

(Above, left) August 9, 1974. The President and the First Lady walk down a red carpet toward their waiting helicopter with Vice President Gerald Ford and Second Lady Betty Ford after President Nixon's resignation from office due to the Watergate scandal. As she left for her life post-presidency in San Clemente, California, Pat warned the new First Lady. "Well, Betty, you'll see many of these red carpets, and you'll get so you hate 'em." *(Courtesy of the Richard Nixon Presidential Library and Museum)*

(Above, right) Pat and Dick at their home, La Casa Pacifica, in San Clemente in 1975. The couple grew closer as they spent more time together out of the political spotlight. Pat cherished what she called the "blessed aloneness" that she finally enjoyed in the post-presidential years. *(Courtesy of the Richard Nixon Presidential Library and Museum, photo by Manolo Sanchez)*

Pat's First Lady portrait by Henriette Wyeth Hurd (of the famous Wyeth family of artists) is technically beautiful, but it failed to capture her animated, warm spirit. Though the work was completed in 1978, Pat refused to have her portrait hung at the White House until her husband's portrait was also completed and displayed there in 1981. *(Courtesy of the Richard Nixon Presidential Library and Museum)*

The Nixons celebrated their 50th wedding anniversary on June 21, 1990. Their daughters and their families joined them for a family portrait. Pat's grandchildren were among her greatest joys in her later life. Back row: David and Julie Eisenhower, the Nixons, Tricia and Ed Cox. Second row: Jennie and Alexander "Alex" Eisenhower, Christopher "Chris" Cox. Front row: Melanie Eisenhower. *(Courtesy of Maureen Drown Nunn Personal Collection)*

When the Nixon Presidential Library and Museum was dedicated in Yorba Linda, California, on July 19, 1990, four Presidents and First Ladies were on hand to celebrate the day with the Nixons. Left to right: Nancy Reagan, Barbara Bush, Pat, and Betty Ford. *(Courtesy of the Richard Nixon Presidential Library and Museum)*

Jo Haldeman, chief of staff Bob Haldeman's wife, remembered her husband giving her and their four children, Hank, Peter, Ann, and Susan, ironclad rules to follow whenever they were at Camp David at the same time as the president, Pat, and their daughters. She recalled having "strict orders not to talk to them . . . to give them a complete sense of privacy as this was the only place they could find that privacy."

One woman who was an important exception to the family privacy rule was the "Fifth Nixon," Rose Mary Woods. Rose Mary continued her long-term practice of socializing with the Nixon women at Camp David. She was always the president's close companion there as well. "He was always close to Rose, and if she was at Camp David, she was always asked to dinner with Nixon." Although she was a staff member, she was also family, a status none of the men in the West Wing ever achieved.

As the summer ended and Camp David activities wound down for the season, a rested and confident Pat was feeling more and more comfortable in her public role. She even sat for a series of television interviews with ABC reporter Virginia Sherwood that took place both at the White House and at La Casa Pacifica.

The Washington part of the interview featured a more open First Lady, one who was willing to discuss her husband's defeat in 1960 and how she had coped. "I have a practice which I've had all my life of picking up the pieces and keeping busy." She also admitted that her husband never had any intention of getting out of politics, even after the loss of that election. "Knowing him, I was positive he would get back in . . . he was never really out of politics." She also frankly discussed the total lack of privacy her role entailed: "The most difficult task of all is to be so guarded to be surrounded all the time. You don't have enough of what I call 'blessed aloneness.'"

As the ABC special with Sherwood showed, the First Lady was becoming more confident with her press appearances and was giving reporters more authentic remarks. She would now begin speaking on record more often in support of women and initiatives to promote women's equality.

That same September, while chatting with women of the press, Pat became the first First Lady to state her desire to see a woman named to the Supreme Court. She assured reporters, "Don't you worry; I'm taking it up. . . . If we can't get a woman on the Supreme Court this time, there'll be another time." In another public statement, she declared, "Our population is more than 50 percent women, so why not? A woman will help to balance the Court."

This wasn't something Pat had just thought of, either. In 1969, Justice Abe Fortas had resigned. The new First Lady began her push to find a woman to sit on the Supreme Court right away. "This nomination opportunity was the first time that women candidates had ever been discussed, and as evidenced by the First Lady asking Vera Glaser for a list of potential names, it is generally accepted that Pat Nixon urged her husband to appoint a woman to the Supreme Court."

A June 18, 1969, memo shows that President Nixon was considering a female candidate for the Supreme Court much earlier than previously thought. Perhaps this was partially due to his wife's insistence on this issue at the time. Historian Dr. Luke Nichter stated his belief that "Nixon genuinely wanted to be the first to appoint a woman to the SCOTUS. It wasn't just a gesture, but a genuine first—like the Moon, China, the gold standard . . . he first thought about it in mid-1969 before all of those other 'firsts.'"

Ehrlichman's memoir, *Witness to Power*, claims that the president considered this issue even earlier than the June 1969 memo indicates. He wrote that the president had been creating his personal Supreme Court dream team ever since he first set foot in the Oval Office. "From the time Nixon arrived at the White House, he continually played his shuffle-the-people game with the Supreme Court . . . Jewel Lafontant of Chicago came up repeatedly."

Though hers is not a name that is well-known today, Jewel Stradford Lafontant was a prominent Black Chicago lawyer and GOP supporter whose father, renowned U.S. Supreme Court attorney C. Francis Stradford, had "carefully groomed her to be a pioneer in the male-dominated area of law." In 1946, Jewel Stradford became the first African American woman to graduate from the University of Chicago law school. In 1955 President Eisenhower named Stradford (now married, with the last name of Rogers) as assistant U.S. attorney for the Northern District of Illinois, making her the first African American woman to hold the job.

She remained visible in Republican politics, seconding Nixon's nomination at the 1960 GOP convention. Due to her expertise, she was asked to serve as Henry Cabot Lodge's civil rights advisor for the remainder of the campaign. Though Nixon lost the race, he would continue to hold her in high regard. Lafontant began her own law firm in 1961 with her new husband, Ernest Lafontant, and her father. In 1963 Lafontant argued and won her first case before the Supreme Court.

Despite an outstanding legal career, Lafontant lost two campaigns: one for superior court judge in Illinois in 1962, and one for appellate state court judge in 1970. Her son, Ariel Investments CEO John Rogers Jr., notes that Cook County, where his mother ran, was a Democratic stronghold. As a Republican woman, she didn't have a chance. However, Lafontant's years of legal work and her continued support for the Republican Party kept her on the president's radar.

A Supreme Court second chance came in 1971. Justice John Marshall Harlan, who was ill, resigned, and Justice Hugo Black also resigned, dying a week later. With two slots open, both the president and Pat knew that now was the time for another pass at the matter.

Helping the president find qualified women for the Supreme Court fell under Franklin's jurisdiction. As she traveled the country prospecting for candidates, she wrote how she was "attacked" and "bombarded" by both career women and housewives, who demanded representation through a female Supreme Court justice. On October 6, 1971, Franklin's boss Fred Malek noted that "the mail to the President on this issue has been heavy, and approximately one third of the letters recommend the appointment of a woman to the Court."

In an October 11 memo, Franklin noted: "The appointment of a woman to the Supreme Court. This is far and away the most crucial issue of concern to women at this moment. The appointment of a woman would go a long way toward changing the President's image on the women's equality question." In all, Franklin identified thirteen female candidates for the Supreme Court in 1971. Two of these women, Jewel Lafontant and Constance Baker Motley, were Black. Of the thirteen candidates identified, eight were Democrats and five were Republicans.

Mildred Lillie, a state appellate judge from California, was among the thirteen, and her name rose to the top. Hers and the names of other top Nixon choices were leaked to the press, undermining the potential nominees. The Nixon administration claimed the leaks came from the American Bar Association (ABA), whose Standing Committee on the Federal Judiciary evaluates and rates potential federal court nominees. The ABA committee promptly rated Lillie as "unqualified" by a vote of 11–1. "The 12 male lawyers . . . said Justice Lillie, who had by then presided over various courts for 24 years, lacked experience." This opinion was no surprise due to the prevailing "belief of male lawyers in those years that women were too emotional to sit on the Supreme Court."

The validity of Lillie's rating was questioned by many who suggested that "by labeling Mildred Lillie as 'unqualified,' the ABA panel was simply masking its 'discomfort' with the notion of a woman on the high court." The lack of gains for women on the federal bench in 1971 was clearly not due to a lack of female lawyers: "There were over six thousand women practicing law in 1950 who by the 1960s would likely have had the necessary experience to be professionally qualified for appointment."

Pat's hopes of appointing a woman Supreme Court justice were thwarted not by her husband but by the ABA's unofficial policy in 1971 of keeping women out of high-level judicial appointments. Tricia felt that both her parents were deeply disappointed over this matter. "Of course, my parents were very disappointed by the ABA's thumbs down verdict on these candidates . . . which squandered a significant opportunity to push the equality ball forward."

Pat was rightly suspicious of the committee's judgment, and she didn't accept the argument that Lillie was unqualified. According to Haldeman, the president confided in him: "'Boy is she [Pat] mad.' Apparently Mrs. Nixon really hit him on his failure to appoint a woman, because she felt she had a commitment that he would do so and didn't buy the argument of the Bar turning her [Lillie] down." Nixon ended up nominating two men, lawyer Lewis Powell and the Justice Department's William Rehnquist, to fill the vacancies.

Julie recalled that the issue of putting a woman on the Supreme Court was of great importance to her mother: "She did things in a quiet way, she tended to be very supportive of my father, and she really didn't think it was her role to argue policy with him, but I remember she was very strong about a woman on the court. This was one instance where she really spoke up. I remember a family dinner where she didn't tell him off, but she said I think there should have been a woman, and I'm very disappointed, etc." In a separate conversation, the president told Tricia, "We are preparing a woman for the next spot."

There is much evidence that his wife's disappointment drove President Nixon to keep trying on this hot-button issue. The only recently unsealed personal papers of John Ehrlichman at the Hoover Archive reveal notes from December 1972 regarding the idea of putting a woman on the Supreme Court the next time a slot opened. This time the president and his aides circled back to Nixon's dream pick: Jewel Lafontant.

In an Oval Office meeting on December 12, item number thirty-four on Ehrlichman's long list of to-do items was the generation of a "List of Black Women for S/Court." The Nixon tapes of the meeting not only match Ehrlichman's notes but also catch the president mentioning Lafontant twice as a possible Supreme Court nominee. On the tapes, Nixon says, "It's going to be a black woman. I've decided that. That's exactly the right way to handle two problems."

Nichter contributed: "I interpret it to mean he was seriously considering Lafontant for a high judicial post. They seem to almost suggest that [Thurgood] Marshall might step down." Appointing Lafontant once Marshall departed his post could provide the Court with both the gender and race diversity it sorely needed.

The president also thought about appointing Lafontant to a federal appeals court judgeship. However, as with Lillie, "the ABA Committee on Federal Judiciary found [Lafontant] unqualified despite her being a graduate of the University of Chicago Law School and having a professional career of distinction." Once again, the ABA seemed to close ranks, blocking another qualified woman from entry into America's federal courts.

Though the ABA showed its racial bias and sexism with the rejection of both Lillie and Lafontant, the president had more faith in female ability and experience. He soon appointed Lafontant as deputy solicitor general in the Justice Department, where she served from 1973 to 1975. Years later, in 1988, the former president would confirm his inclination yet again, expressing his thoughts on Lafontant to a reporter for an article about her:

Because of her excellent qualifications as an attorney and as deputy solicitor general, Jewel would have been a serious candidate for nomination to the U.S. Supreme Court regardless of the fact that she was a woman and black. I recall particularly that Bill Rogers, our Secretary of State who served as Attorney General in the Eisenhower Administration, recommended her strongly. If I had had the opportunity to name a fourth Justice, she would have been very high on my list of potential nominees.

Despite many obstacles, the seeds of Supreme Court gender and race equality were planted during the Nixon administration with the strong support of the First Lady herself. An important conversation had begun, one that hadn't even been a discussion point in the past. Julie Eisenhower believes this all goes back to her mother's positive influence on this issue.

I am not surprised for one single moment that an African American woman would have been considered along with other qualified women for the position on the Supreme Court . . . my father was at his core, a visionary thinker and a progressive politician. He was color blind when it came to finding important talent. I am so glad that my mother kept his feet to the fire . . . his heart was in the right place all because of my mother.

While Pat remained in the background, she continued her push for women in government through Franklin, through her own public statements about women and their capabilities, and through her positive influence on her husband. Thanks in part to her Western frontier mindset, the First Lady believed that if they had the right qualifications, women of any race could achieve any goal they set their minds to—including gaining their rightful seats on the United States Supreme Court.

In 1981, a decade later, Sandra Day O'Connor finally became the first woman Supreme Court justice. She was identified by none other than Barbara Franklin through her diligent development of a talent bank of qualified female candidates for high-level government jobs.

25

NOT EVEN A LION COULD BREAK IT

As 1972 dawned, Pat remained in frequent communication with her old friend Helene Drown. Their letters had diminished as their conversations transitioned more often to phone calls. Helene's daughter Maureen remembered that ever-thrifty Pat still worried about their long-distance bills. "For God's sake, Pat!" Helene would remark when her old friend would not let her pay for any phone calls. Pat paid out of pocket for all her long-distance calls even when she was in the White House.

Helene also frequently came to the White House from California for visits. Simply put, these reunions helped Pat cope. With Helene, she could relax and be her authentic self. When she was with her, she was just Pat from Artesia.

Right before the New Year, Pat and Helene had chatted at length about Pat's upcoming solo visit to Africa. The First Lady would be visiting Liberia, Ghana, and Ivory Coast. This foreign trip would be much like her Peru trip; the First Lady would be traveling solo as an official representative of the president. As always, Pat studied the briefing books and prepared herself diligently for her diplomatic role.

When Pat arrived in Monrovia, Liberia, for the January 3 inauguration of Liberian president William Tolbert, her charm and person-to-person diplomatic skills were on full display. In his welcoming remarks, Tolbert noted the "warm friendship between our two families going back many years." There was an important American connection between the two countries, as Liberia had been founded in 1822 by former enslaved Africans, and Tolbert was the grandson of slaves from South Carolina.

Accompanied by family friend and famous evangelist Billy Graham, the

First Lady more than held her own at the celebrations, returning presidential toasts, chatting with foreign dignitaries, and dancing with local women who wrapped her in traditional cloth. Photos of Pat swathed in blue African fabric were soon featured in newspapers all over the world. "Mrs. Nixon's simple gesture of respectfully and exuberantly embracing the fashion style of a culture other than her own was a deft political move." She also received a high Liberian honor: the Grand Cordon of the Most Venerable Order of Knighthood of the Pioneers of the Republic of Liberia.

Pat's next stop was Accra, Ghana. She had been here before with her husband in 1957 for the inauguration of another African leader, Prime Minister Kwame Nkrumah. Pat and Dick had been the first Americans to visit Ghana in an official capacity that year. It was also here that she had first met Martin Luther King Jr. and Coretta Scott King when they too attended Nkrumah's inauguration.

In Accra, Pat became the first First Lady of the United States to speak to a foreign parliament when she spoke to the Ghanaian National Assembly. Pat's sly sense of humor shone as she addressed the lively crowd: "Your assembly is a little different from ours," she quipped. "There [in the U.S.] they don't have half as much fun." Of particular interest to Pat in Ghana were job programs for women. She made a point of being filmed at one of these training facilities to highlight women's issues.

The president and Pat had also kept in touch for the past fifteen years with the Ghanaian tribal chief Nana Osae Djan II. Pat trekked to the hills of Aburi to show her respect for the now much older ruler. A delighted Djan proclaimed that, thanks to the First Lady, the American-Ghanaian friendship was now "so strong not even a lion could break it."

———

The First Lady's last stop was Ivory Coast, and here she focused on the country's primary-school children. She can be seen in newsreels hugging the younger children, shaking hands with the older ones, and observing how educational television programs were helping there with the teacher shortage.

Marine military aide Jack Brennan was on the African trip with Pat. "Kids ran to her," he said. He noted that veteran UPI reporter Helen Thomas, who was on Pat's press detail for that trip, told him that kids "always know a phony from a real person." Brennan agreed with Thomas. The children "could feel the warmth she exuded. She was that way with everyone." As the first First Lady to visit Africa, Pat prioritized the American relationship with Africa and its peoples that she and her husband had first begun in 1957.

When Pat returned home, presidential aide Charles Colson wrote up a seven-page memo compiling all the glowing publicity she had received during the trip. He went so far as to admit that after years of the West Wing trying to humanize the presidency, "Mrs. Nixon has broken through where we have failed. She has come across as a warm, charming, graceful, concerned, articulate, and most importantly—a very human person." Pat sent a copy of the memo to Helene Drown, writing, "Thought you'd be amused at the late recognition!" However, not everyone in the White House was willing to acknowledge her African triumph.

After the First Lady conversed separately with both Haldeman and Ehrlichman upon her return, neither brought up the African trip or her successes there. When Pat complained to her husband about this omission, he replied, "I told her that Haldeman, in particular, had spoken of the fact that there had been nothing which had been done in the course of the Administration that had received more universal approval than her trip." Pat replied, "Well, at least they should tell me."

This was exactly the problem: Haldeman, Ehrlichman, and most of the other presidential staff rarely bothered to tell her what a good job she was doing as First Lady in her many different capacities. It was a case of taking an invaluable team member for granted. Pat was the administration's best diplomatic weapon, but all too often her contributions, so obvious to the outside world, were minimized and undervalued by many on the West Wing staff.

When the West Wing suggested that a biography of her be written, with the express purpose of supporting the 1972 presidential election, she balked. Pat's former student Gloria Seelye had been selected and seemed like the perfect fit. Seelye was also good friends with Helene Drown. The issue was likely not Seelye but Pat's negative feelings about being packaged and commodified for public consumption. Once again, the West Wing wanted to use her primarily as a prop to further other goals.

Eventually, "Pat said she was too busy to give interviews and protested that she had an aversion to talking into a tape recorder, so the project was dropped." As Pat's former chief of staff Connie Stuart observed, "Mrs. Nixon never wanted a book written about her. We tried twice while I was at the White House to have a book written about her. This was an idea of the men's; this is one of 'those ideas.'" A project that would never fly while Pat was First Lady.

On January 13, just a few days after her return from Africa, Pat had a sit-down interview at the White House with CBS reporter Barbara Walters. Pat had expected that the interview would focus on her diplomacy in Africa, but she was dismayed to find that Walters first asked her several questions on controversial social issues of the day.

A viewing of the interview tape is revealing. Pat visibly tightened up and gave short, clipped answers to many of Walters's questions on foreign policy. However, the First Lady's demeanor changed when the discussion turned to women in politics and the Nixon administration's position on women. When Walters posited that the president might be "old-fashioned" when it came to women's issues, Pat was quick to dismiss that notion. "Oh, I don't think that's true at all, he's always had great faith in women. Ever since I've known him, he's been proud of things I've done. He's often said this would only be half the nation it is without the women. Because women do contribute a great deal to our country in every way."

When questioned about the failure of the administration to name a woman to the Supreme Court, Pat expertly refocused the question, instead noting that "a great number of qualified women have been appointed to positions [in the government] and I would like to see a little more publicity on this." Toward the end of the interview, Pat warmed up to the subject of getting more women into government jobs. Indeed, getting more women into jobs in general seemed to excite her. When asked about a woman running for president, Pat didn't hesitate to express her opinion: "I would support any well-qualified woman for any job: including president!"

———

As spring came to Washington, there was little rest for the in-demand First Lady. Her outstanding diplomatic successes in Peru and Africa were imprinted on people's minds globally. She was now primed for even more important missions.

In 1967, the president had written an article for *Foreign Affairs* in which he urged a rapprochement between China and the United States, foreseeing a day when the world would become globally interconnected. It had taken delicate negotiations and years of work, but on July 15, 1971, President Nixon went on live television to announce he had accepted the invitation of Chinese premier Chou En-lai to visit the People's Republic of China and that he would "seek the normalization of relations between the two countries and also . . . exchange questions of concern to the two sides."

The First Lady felt strongly that she should be part of the historic visit. "Pat lobbied privately and publicly to accompany her husband on the trip, telling reporters, 'I'm putting my name on the sign-up list.'" According to Chapin, at first the Chinese were resistant to the First Lady's presence on the trip. "Initially the Chinese made clear that they did not expect, or even necessarily want, Mrs. Nixon to come. The problem, we knew, was that Chou en-lai's wife was never seen, and Jiang Qing, 'Madame Mao,' was a virulent anti-American." However, Chapin claims that "the President wanted Mrs. Nixon to be there with him, and she wanted to be there; she was actually insistent on it."

On October 26, Haldeman's diary reported that Nixon had determined his wife had to accompany him but that she would "have an advance man to schedule her activities" and that she could "take no women's press along with her" or "ride with the President." Was this Haldeman's advice or the president's wish? This is unclear, but the next phrase regarding Rose Mary Woods's role seems to show Haldeman's heavy hand. "Also, Rose should be lectured cold turkey that she's going along, but she's to work for everybody."

As usual, the First Lady did her homework, attending intensive briefings with Kissinger and his team, studying up on Chinese culture and language, and reading anything she could about the country and its history. She met with advance man Mike Schrauth and military aide Jack Brennan to plan her own separate events and schedule, and had definite ideas on what she wanted to do, including a visit to a children's hospital.

When Pat stepped off Air Force One at the Peking (now Beijing) airport on a frosty late February day in 1972, her clothes made an impression before she herself said a word. Historians agree that Pat's bright red wool coat lined with nutria fur soon became iconic. Fashion paper *Women's Wear Daily* noted that in "China, there was unanimous agreement that she brought sunshine to a drab land with red coats and dresses." As she deplaned, she provided a colorful focal point set against the gray tarmac of the Chinese airstrip. "While communism generally adopted 'red' as its revolutionary symbol, the more ancient Chinese culture viewed it within a larger context; it was simply a sign of good luck."

While her husband, Kissinger, and their team met with Chou En-lai and other high-ranking communist officials behind closed doors, the world watched Pat Nixon on television. Her every move in China was seen by millions all over the world. She was the face of the Nixon administration and the way people connected to the historic opening of China to the West. Brennan accompanied Pat on her solo excursions around China. One outing involved the First Lady shopping for gifts for the president. Brennan noted how she used humor to defuse the tension. "She maintained her personality, smiling and laughing. And to break the ice she said, 'oh look, they're selling pajamas. Oh hey, Brennan, you're the same size as Ricardo,'" Pat's tongue-in-cheek nickname for her husband. "'Try on the pajamas!'"

Brennan, a solidly built, tough Marine, remembered thinking, "What? I had to take off my shirt and try on a pajama top. She laughed and all the Chinese laughed. . . . I think that changed the whole atmosphere. Whenever people saw Mrs. Nixon after that, they wanted to be her friend."

The directive that no female press be included in the trip had been discarded. Still, only a few select press women were allowed to accompany the Nixon entourage to China. Helen Thomas of UPI and Barbara Walters, now reporting for NBC, were among them. This time, however, Pat was spared any in-depth interviews like the recent one she had done with Walters regarding her Africa sojourn.

Still, Barbara Walters pursued the First Lady, and in the view of Nixon staffers, Walters tried to monopolize Pat's time on the trip. Brennan vividly recalled Walters's behavior, which made her unpopular with the other members of the press on the trip. "The worst one, the one who was very much disliked, was Barbara Walters. She was a pushy broad. She was always getting next to Mrs. Nixon and asking questions. Finally, I grabbed her and said, 'This is not the Barbara Walters Show!' And everyone laughed and cheered."

An energetic and perfectly coiffed Pat walked with the vigor and energy of a twenty-five-year-old throughout the trip, never seeming tired or disinterested. Her hostesses would for the most part be made up of high-ranking officials in the Communist Party, including the wives of Mao and Chou En-lai. Just as she had done in other communist countries, the First Lady broke ideological barriers in her approach to people. "At the Shanghai banquet, the wives of some of the Chinese leaders hugged her and told her to return."

The First Lady was a vivid, engaging presence on camera, and she continued to highlight women's and children's issues through the activities she chose. The fact that her hostesses were politically opposed to democracy did not inhibit her interactions with them at all. In fact, "she noted with pleasure that Chinese women were taking an active part in government and had major roles on the Revolutionary Committees." Just as she had welcomed Democrats to Nixon campaign rallies in the past, she welcomed these women without regard to their political persuasion.

During her stay in Peking, Pat toured the Evergreen People's Commune, an acupuncture clinic, Chinese classrooms, the Peking Summer Palace, the Peking Children's Hospital, and the Peking Hotel on her own, as well as the Ming tombs and the Great Wall with her husband. Schrauth, who was new to the advance job, learned a lesson about the First Lady's style while on the China trip. On one occasion, he "got in front of her to look for a little separation" between the First Lady and the crowd. "Well, this was not something she wanted done!" The young aide got a gentle "chewing out," as Pat "wanted to be with the local folks." She didn't want to be treated like a fragile doll or be isolated from meeting the Chinese who flocked to see her.

Bill Hudson, who became Pat's lead Secret Service agent in 1972, remembered the First Lady's stoicism when they visited an acupuncture clinic in China. When she watched a teenage boy having his abdomen sliced open without any anesthesia other than acupuncture, she did not flinch. When she visited a Chinese village and was invited into the mud hut of a Chinese peasant family, she treated its inhabitants with the same respect she would have given to a high-ranking Chinese government official. While social distinctions registered with her, they did not affect her approach or behavior to individuals. "She'd been at this a long time . . . she always did and said the right thing." The one word that best described her behavior in China and on all foreign trips, Hudson noted, was "poise."

Despite her packed schedule, Pat subsisted on a meager diet of green tea and tangerines during the day to make room for multi-course evening feasts with her Chinese hosts. Perhaps Pat's most significant diplomatic coup would take place during one of these banquets on her first evening in Peking. This unexpected triumph involved the acquisition of a pair of adorable creatures that would eventually help found a furry dynasty in the United States within the confines of Washington's National Zoo.

That first night, Pat was seated next to Premier Chou En-lai and noticed a beautifully decorated cylindrical cigarette tin adorned with pandas at her place.

"Aren't they cute?" she said as she picked up the tin. "I love them."

Zhou replied: "I'll give you some."

"Cigarettes?" she asked.

"No," Zhou said. "Pandas."

At the end of the trip, the premier made good on his promise, sending two giant pandas to the National Zoo as a thank-you to the Nixons. The eighteen-month-old pair were named Hsing-Hsing (the male) and Ling-Ling (the female). They would begin a family and have five cubs, though sadly none lived more than a few days. However, other pandas would arrive from China to take their place, and eventually four cubs would be born in captivity at the zoo. At the request of the Chinese, the United States would send a pair of musk oxen in return; the animals were not nearly as photogenic as the pandas, however.

This diplomacy lived on through other Chinese pandas' descendants at the zoo. In 2022, the zoo's director, Brandie Smith, "praised Pat Nixon for raising the issue of pandas with Zhou. 'She took an opportunity to make this comment and turn it into something else,' Smith said. 'For me, it's the power of one woman's voice.' She added, 'I love that fact that this is all the result of a woman speaking up.'"

Pat had proved during the VP years before and now again during the presidential years on her trips to Peru, Africa, and now in communist China that she was much more than just window dressing: she was a diplomatic force to be reckoned with. In the case of China, her presence alone had helped breach the "great wall" between the two countries and cement a new phase of Chinese-American relations. Her next foreign trip would prove to the world (and those staffers who doubted her importance) that she had both guts and high-level diplomatic skills to help her husband seal a major international deal—this time, one that would contribute mightily toward world peace.

———

On May 2, FBI director J. Edgar Hoover died in his sleep. The president had considered asking him to resign the previous year but could not bring himself to do it, largely because of his long personal friendship with Hoover. He and Pat had socialized with Hoover and his partner Clyde Tolson for twenty-five years and were fond of them both, but the president's old friend was becoming a political liability. David Eisenhower recalled: "Nixon thought of Hoover as a problem because he had stayed on too long. More than once I heard him say—respectfully—'he really should step aside.'"

As Hoover biographer Beverly Gage explained of Hoover, at the time "he was seventy-six, and showing his age, napping for hours in his office in the afternoons. He was also showing, in Gage's words, 'increasing levels of vitriol and instability,' informing the White House, for instance, that the four student demonstrators shot to death by National Guardsmen at Kent State had 'invited and got what they deserved.'"

Less than a week later, on the evening of May 8, the president announced the mining of Haiphong Harbor in North Vietnam on national television. This location was the conduit through which Russian military supplies flowed to the North Vietnamese communist forces. In addition to mining the harbor, communications would be cut off and bombings of military targets would also continue.

Due to an upcoming summit with the Russians in Moscow, this decision was not made lightly. The president was aware of what his congressional leaders would tell him: "Don't risk the summit—don't escalate." He didn't ask for their permission, but he informed them of his announcement before airtime, hoping they would support this high-stakes gamble.

The president had retreated to Camp David a few days prior to contemplate such actions. He took both his wife and his younger daughter with him. Julie worried aloud to her father that Americans might not support mining the harbor. When he talked to Tricia, however, she "was immediately positive as she felt we had to do something." When the president returned very late to Aspen, the presidential cabin, that night, he wrote in his diary of Pat's warm support during this difficult time. "She got up and came over, and put her arms around me, and said, 'Don't worry about anything.'"

When the going got rough, the president often turned to the women in his life for both consolation and advice. He solicited and listened to their opinions at critical times. He didn't always follow their suggestions, but he did want to know what they thought, and he valued their input.

In the end, the president's gamble paid off. Thanks in no small part to productive back-channel exchanges between Kissinger and Soviet ambassador to the United States Anatoly Dobrynin, the Soviet-American relationship remained intact. When Kissinger saw Dobrynin shortly after Nixon's on-air pronouncement, the ambassador made no mention of canceling the Soviet-American summit set for May. A delighted Kissinger crowed to his boss, "'I think we are going to be able to have our mining and bombing and have our summit too.'"

Pat had done her part behind the scenes to keep the Soviet-American relationship functional. The month prior, the president had encountered Dobrynin at a State Department ceremony. He did not hesitate to tell the ambassador that the First Lady "had greatly appreciated Mrs. Dobrynin's recent invitation to get together for a talk about our trip to Moscow." Kissinger arranged the meeting for the ladies and briefed Pat beforehand. When the meeting between the two women took place shortly thereafter, it was a success, according to the president. "Pat showed great skill and subtlety. When she raised the point that we did not want anything like Vietnam to interfere with the summit, Mrs. Dobrynin squeezed her hand and vigorously nodded in agreement."

Such "soft diplomacy" was critically important to maintaining the promising but tenuous relationship being slowly and painstakingly built between the two global superpowers. Pat's work in this area, honed by years of global travel and intense and committed studies on her part, was an important contribution to the development of the American-Soviet relationship that has too often gone unmentioned.

———————

On May 22, the president, the First Lady, and their entourage landed in Moscow. The president would meet with Secretary General Leonid Brezhnev, while the First Lady pursued her own separate schedule. Pat had been here before in 1959 as Second Lady. At that time, she had charmed Soviet premier Nikita Khrushchev's wife and other Soviet leaders' wives. She was well prepared to deploy the same charm offensive on the new premier's spouse.

Louise Hutchinson was a respected *Chicago Sun-Times* reporter and former president of the Women's National Press Club in D.C. She was part of Pat's press entourage for the Moscow summit and was with the First Lady on the first day of the trip when she met with Mrs. Brezhnev. As Hutchinson noted, in those days Soviet leaders' wives were still rarely seen in public and almost never written about in the press or photographed. According to the reporter, the secretary general's wife was frightened by the 250 or so press surrounding her meeting with the First Lady. Hutchinson's description of the meeting between the two women is classic Pat Nixon:

> Mrs. Nixon looked wonderful. She had on a red suit. She was smiling and we mobbed them. Asked Mrs. Brezhnev questions through an interpreter. I think Mrs. Brezhnev came close to fainting. She had never in her life been exposed to this sort of thing. With generosity and kindness, Pat Nixon took her hand. They could not communicate without an interpreter. Mrs. Nixon patted her hand and led her to the side of the room and sat her down in a chair and then she talked to her in a motherly way. It was really quite an astonishing event.

As Julie wrote, her mother had never been more heavily guarded than by the Russian KGB on this trip. "Wherever she went, the KGB agents, some of them burly women, formed a human shield around her and would not budge." Hutchinson recalled this as being a major problem for American reporters, and she feared for her own safety at several points during the trip. During an event at Moscow University attended by Pat and the press pool,

Hutchinson was physically removed from the event by three Soviet agents. Pat displayed her customary cool as the scene played out. Hutchinson later recalled screaming to alert the First Lady of her precarious situation: "'Mrs. Nixon,' I yelled. 'It's all right Louise,' she said. I remember fervently praying that she knew what she was talking about." Thanks to Pat, Hutchinson escaped scared but unscathed when the agents deposited her in an adjoining room and left her there.

Hutchinson was not alone in experiencing rough treatment by the Soviet KGB and police. Mrs. Nixon's visit to the GUM department store in Moscow was fraught with tension as the police blockaded their charges, the First Lady and the Soviet foreign minister's wife, Mrs. Gromyko, from the American press. Bill Hudson recalled that despite the large crowds there, the First Lady remained cool and collected. "She was fine. I was nervous!"

Connie Stuart, Pat's chief of staff, was also on the Russia trip. She praised her boss for taking care of her Russian counterparts, who were not used to dealing with the press. The First Lady "got so she was trying to look out after the hostesses, to make sure they were not being pushed, shoved, harmed, and at the same time she was trying to give the press an opportunity to get a picture here, or a little quote there. That's hard work folks. She was masterful at it."

Despite such efforts, shouting and jostling among the crowd still ensued, and AP reporter Saul Pett was smacked down by a security guard. Pat shouted out, "'Leave him alone, he's with me.'" She invited Pett into her inner circle, sharing her ice cream with him in an attempt to defuse a tense scenario. Once again, Pat's "keep calm and carry on" attitude saved both the day and another reporter.

Soon Pat and Mrs. Brezhnev were talking, walking arm in arm through Moscow, affectionately calling each other "sister." With Mrs. Brezhnev, Mrs. Gromyko, and Mrs. Dobrynin, Pat toured a secondary school, rode the Moscow subway, and attended the Bolshoi Ballet. The First Lady even shook hands with a Russian bear that gallantly extended its paw to her on cue. Once again, Pat's person-to-person diplomacy had worked its magic and she had acquired a second Soviet "sister," bonding the Soviet-American relationship with her own unique treaty of understanding and friendship.

Despite the antagonistic relationship between Soviet security and the American press at times, the summit was a stunning success for President Nixon. He signed the Antiballistic Missile (ABM) Treaty with Brezhnev, regarding each country's missile defense systems. This agreement, in addition to an interim agreement freezing both countries' production of strategic missiles, began the first stage of American-Soviet détente, dramatically improving the relationship. Known as SALT I, this treaty was the foundation for the administration's arms limitation talks going forward and the most extensive attempt to limit nuclear arms between the two powers to date.

Despite her First Lady status, Pat was not invited to the signing of the ABM Treaty. Women were still treated as second-class citizens in Russia, and none of her Soviet counterparts were included in the ceremony either. However, at her husband's suggestion, Pat kept out of sight between the large columns of St. George's Hall in the Kremlin as a silent witness to the signing of the treaty there. She had earned her view.

Pat's active participation in the successful summit, smoothing the path for her husband behind the scenes both before and during the Russian visit, helped bring about a much-hoped-for conclusion for millions on both sides of the arms issue. As Hollywood star Jimmy Stewart noted of the First Lady's role in both the Chinese and Russian visits of 1972, "She represents best the president's policy of reconciliation—the desire for a people-to-people bond that reinforces the universal desire for peace."

Two weeks after the Nixons' triumphant return from the Russian summit, there was still no rest for the First Lady. She was already gearing up for the upcoming 1972 presidential election and had taken off on a three-state barnstorming trip, visiting Texas, California, and South Dakota.

It was Father's Day weekend, and the president decided to spend some downtime with his good friends Bebe Rebozo and Bob Abplanalp on Grand Cay, Abplanalp's private island in the Bahamas. The president swam and walked. He also went boating with Rebozo and Abplanalp that afternoon. Sunday morning the president and Rebozo left for Key Biscayne, where he noticed a small news item on the front page of the *Miami Herald*. Though the story provided minimal details, the headline was ominous: "Miamians Held in D.C. Try to Bug Demo Headquarters."

Elsewhere in Key Biscayne, Haldeman and his wife, Jo, were staying in a villa at the Key Biscayne Hotel, close to the Nixons' home. That Sunday, they also noticed the same story in the *Miami Herald* about a break-in at Democratic National Committee headquarters at the Watergate office and apartment complex in Washington. The night before, five men had been arrested in D.C. for this crime. One of the men was a former CIA employee working in Washington.

Jo asked her husband, "What's the deal on this crazy break-in at the Watergate?" Haldeman replied, "The whole thing's ridiculous. . . . I can't imagine why anyone would want to bug the Democratic headquarters. It's the last place in the world to get inside information."

Two days later, Ron Ziegler, the president's press secretary, did his best to tamp down speculation concerning any connection between the White House and the break-in attempt. "On June 19, 1972, only two days after the break-in, Ziegler refused to comment on the incident and called it a 'third-rate burglary attempt,' adding, 'This is something that should not fall into the political process.'"

Julie's recollection was that her mother "barely noted the news about the break-in . . . her attention as June ended was on the long political campaign ahead." However, Preston Bruce, longtime doorman at the White House from the time of the Eisenhower administration, thought he noticed Pat's anxiety when he saw her soon after the Watergate news broke. Bruce was surprised when the president, Mrs. Nixon, and Julie returned to the residence early from their weekend away.

Like everyone else in the country, the doorman of the residence had been reading the newspapers regarding the Watergate burglary, wondering what had really happened there. When the helicopter landed on the South Lawn, Bruce escorted the First Lady and Julie upstairs, noticing immediately that "Mrs. Nixon was far from her usual self—she seemed disturbed and unhappy."

Bruce was no fan of Haldeman or Ehrlichman. Since they had arrived in 1969, he and many of the other household staff had experienced their micromanaging. Haldeman's memos rained down on Bruce and his colleagues, many of whom had been working in the residence for years. "There was a steady stream of memos like that telling us what to do. We had years of experience to guide us, and, as far as we knew, never before had political aides to a President interfered this way with the household staff of the White House."

In his memoirs, Bruce wrote, "It was obvious these men were more interested in their power and objectives than in the President's future. . . . I felt a deep foreboding. I told my friends I feared these men might double-cross everybody, even including the President. I feared the worst."

26

ELEGANT BUT NOT ALOOF

Whatever worries regarding the Watergate burglary that might have plagued her earlier in the summer had likely been relegated to the back of Pat's mind by August 1972. At this point, she and the president had far more pressing issues to tackle, with the upcoming GOP convention in Miami and the presidential race to follow. She had to gear up mentally for yet another campaign. Once more she jumped into the political fray, this time with a more prominent role than in 1968.

When the convention opened in Miami on August 21, Pat was one of the stars of the show. Hollywood actor Jimmy Stewart, a Nixon supporter, deftly narrated her political life story in a nine-minute documentary entitled *A Tribute to First Lady Pat Nixon*. The focus was on the famous Pat and Dick Team. Stewart's distinctive voice intoned, "For thirty-two years, it is a partnership. She believes in him, she's always there, companion, helpmate, campaigner."

However, the highlight reel also showed Pat's solo successes. She was pictured first inaugurating the Legacy of the Parks program, including footage from a Legacy program at the California-Mexico border where she insisted that the fence separating the two countries be cut down so that she could meet Mexican citizens. Scenes of her relief work in Peru and her historic visit to Africa were featured. Stewart heralded her visits with the president to China and Russia as "a new beginning in international diplomacy."

Pat would next appear in front of a massive, cheering crowd at the Miami convention hall, escorted by two of the GOP's best-looking politicians, Senator Bob Dole and California governor Ronald Reagan. After being introduced by a gallant Stewart, she would achieve another historic first by becoming the first First Lady to speak at a GOP convention. Her address was delayed for over five minutes while the boisterous crowd clamored for her attention. Chants of "We love Pat!" were followed by "Four more years!" and whistles, hoots, and hollers from the Young Republican masses, while a smiling Pat attempted to bring the crowd to order with an enormous gavel. She eventually shrugged and gave up, allowing the adulation to wind down on its own.

The First Lady was finally able to give a concise speech, playing down her enormous popularity. "I stay in the wings and don't come out in front too often, so this is quite unusual for me . . . thanks to the young people, this is a great welcome." Julie, David, and Tricia can be seen on camera smiling and clapping, blending in with the gigantic flood of young people who all seemed to love Pat.

At this point it seemed that the presidential campaign strategists might have finally realized what an asset the First Lady was. This time Pat also seemed to be on board with being a supporting star of the show. It was quite a change from 1968. Now she seemed at ease, energized, and ready to shine. She could afford to rest on her laurels a bit. In 1972, she was at the pinnacle of her popularity, with Gallup polls rating her number one in its "Most Admired Woman" category. She would remain on this list for the next ten years straight.

Both daughters were also assets on the 1972 campaign trail. Tricia and Ed traveled extensively in support of the campaign. Tricia spoke frequently on the election circuit about her parents' support for traditional American values. She stated that her father "has transformed America since 1969, moving it back from the brink of breakdown and back to traditional principles and progress."

Though David could not campaign in 1972, as he was serving as a Navy officer at the time, Julie was even more active in this election cycle than she had been in 1968. One of the big issues the Nixons' younger daughter chose to highlight when speaking was "the fact that there was for the first time in history a presidential assistant who was trying to make sure that if a woman was qualified, she was considered." This assistant, of course, was Barbara Hackman Franklin.

Franklin was on the White House staff and not part of the Committee to

Re-Elect the President (CRP). However, Franklin and other prominent Republican women also hit the campaign circuit in what she called all-female "flying squads": the women would fly together to campaign dinners and destinations to support the Nixon effort. As in past elections, the Nixon administration relied heavily on GOP women to get out the campaign message and to see and be seen at events.

Franklin recalled: "I was involved in the planning, but Barbara MacGregor [wife of Clark MacGregor, Nixon's chief campaign advisor] was out front, assisted by Margaret Hodges. My recollection is that this campaign approach was her idea. . . . I was one of the surrogates, one of the Administration women, who flew with 2 Cabinet wives. That was the 'flying squad.' I flew with Ann Richardson and Joyce Rumsfeld." This was not the only female squad working to reelect the president, Franklin remembered. "There were a bunch of other squads sent to different parts of the country" as well.

This group was officially known as the Women's Surrogate Program, a "CRP effort coordinated by Margaret Hodges. The group included prominent Nixon administration wives such as Barbara Bush, Lenore Romney, and Jill Ruckelshaus, along with presidential assistants Franklin and Virginia Knauer."

Ehrlichman's notes regarding the 1972 campaign highlight the importance of these squads of Republican women, an elite feminine campaign force. His memo from July 1972, a few weeks prior to the Republican convention in August, shows that women were *not* an afterthought in the Nixon campaign; they were an integral part of internal strategy.

And, in a final coup, Pat saved the day for the ERA at the Republican convention. Julie noted that her mother had been the one to push hard for her husband's inclusion of the ERA again in 1972 as part of the GOP platform. Though Nixon had supported the ERA for decades, as a lawyer, he worried that "legally it might open a Pandora's box, but he knew that the symbolism of it was so important that he did agree that the Republican convention would endorse the ERA . . . but that was a push from my mother."

Though the Republican convention proved to be a smashing success for Pat, on the campaign trail the First Lady had to confront tough questions on controversial issues as well as the growing scandal of Watergate. Connie

Stuart accompanied Pat on a 5,400-mile cross-country campaign in September, "billed as her longest solo campaign trip ever." The First Lady shook thousands of hands, hugged children warmly during photo ops, and dutifully performed yet again the role she knew so well. However, things were much different than they had been in 1968, when the press kept a more respectful distance from her.

The younger generation of press women were not content to simply shake the First Lady's hand and ask for her famous meatloaf recipe. This go-round, they wanted to discuss more serious topics. Though a press reception at the Nixon Chicago campaign HQ had been planned and "carefully programmed to present Mrs. Nixon in a social setting," the event quickly turned to queries about abortion, the Vietnam War, Watergate, and the colorful Martha Mitchell, outspoken wife of Attorney General John Mitchell. Pat tried to field all the questions neutrally, but reports depicted her as uncomfortable and glad to wrap up the session after fifteen minutes.

The Watergate incident, which had seemed worrisome but manageable in June, was beginning to mushroom. When asked by a reporter, "'Are you concerned that the investigation of the Watergate bugging incident will hurt your husband in the election?' . . . she replied that she was not. Then, showing she was studying the barometers carefully, she added, 'The polls haven't indicated that. They know he has no part in it.'"

Martha Mitchell was another thorn in Pat's side. Martha was a flamboyant southern belle from Pine Bluff, Arkansas, aptly described in the press as "a cross between Archie Bunker and Scarlett O'Hara." Famed for years for talking out of turn to reporters in an amusing way, by 1972 Martha began making late-night alcohol-fueled calls to journalists. Reporters Helen Thomas and Winnie McLendon were among her favorite confidants.

In the early days of the first Nixon administration, Martha had seemed to be a useful tool to reach out to a southern Silent Majority. She made for good copy. "From the beginning she was the darling of the press; among all those drab, button-down Nixonians she provided a gaudy splash of color. Her iconoclastic if conservative views, uninhibited style, and honeyed Southern charm . . . added up to an astonishing degree of celebrity." At first, her visibility had benefitted the administration. But once Watergate hit, Martha became a liability.

In the fall of 1972, Martha claimed she had been restrained, beaten, and tranquilized by bodyguards while on a June trip to California so that she would not speak out about the Watergate break-in and the secrets surrounding it. When Pat was asked about this incident during her fall campaign trip, she responded that she wasn't in the room and had no idea what had happened. At this point, Martha claimed to be a "political prisoner" of the administration.

Prior to the events of Watergate, presidential aide Chapin had the unenviable job of trying to handle Martha's outlandish requests. He recalled her frequent drunken calls to the White House asking to speak to the president. Chapin claims the president knew of her issues but that "they didn't really become a political problem until she began drunk calling reporters at night. The reporters enabled and emboldened her. They used her and turned her into a character who became well known to the public." Chapin was not alone in having to deflect such calls. Lucy Winchester also often had to field drunken late-night calls from Martha as she tried to reach the First Lady.

As her husband's staunchest supporter, Pat could not have countenanced Martha's behavior or her unsubstantiated, alcohol-fueled claims. Though we will never be able to separate Martha's truth from her fiction (and there were likely elements of both in her late-night confessionals to reporters), one thing is certain. "Unlike other political wives, Martha never learned the rules—smile and speak only when spoken to. It's ironic to remember that Nixon himself used to say in the early pre-Watergate years, 'Right on, Martha!'"

———

Although she disdained Martha Mitchell's outbursts regarding the Nixon administration and Watergate, Pat did evince concern in October 1972 about the way the new campaign was being run. She confided in her daughter Julie that "it worried her that more and more power seemed to be vested in the handful of men around my father and that he had so little direct involvement in the campaign. The Committee to Re-Elect the President staff was huge—an empire unto itself. My father was more insulated from his Cabinet and the majority of his staff in the 1972 campaign than ever before."

The media had certainly noticed this handful of men and reduced the group down further to its two most prominent members, Haldeman and

Ehrlichman, the president's chief of staff and his domestic policy advisor, respectively—known as the "Praetorian Guards" and also as "Hans and Fritz" and "The Berlin Wall." Though they were seen by the public as Siamese twins, the two men were quite different. Bobbie Kilberg, the White House fellow and Yale law school grad who worked for Ehrlichman and knew Haldeman, defined them this way: "Haldeman was the enforcer and John was the domestic policy maven and they had very different personalities."

Both Haldeman and Ehrlichman had discounted Pat and butted heads with her in the past. However, after his early attempts at an East Wing takeover and his failed attempt to manage Pat's mail operation, Ehrlichman had largely stayed out of Pat's orbit. Unlike Haldeman, Ehrlichman also had female friends in the White House. Lucy Winchester was very fond of him—both were Christian Scientists, and they attended the same church in Washington for a time. Kilberg worked closely with Ehrlichman on domestic policy for two years, first as a White House fellow and then as Ehrlichman's staff assistant. Kilberg felt that "he treated me just the same as he would treat anyone else in his staff. And there was never on his part any distinction based on the fact I was a woman."

Kilberg also remarked that Ehrlichman "spent a fair amount of unnecessary time protecting me from Bob Haldeman." Kilberg noted Haldeman's "very cold and unwelcoming demeanor to me. I never felt comfortable with him. I don't think I ever had a full conversation with him. If he came in one direction, I walked in the other direction." Even Kilberg's Yale law degree and status as a West Winger didn't shield her from Haldeman's suspicious glare.

As he himself put it, Haldeman was happy to act as "Richard Nixon's son of a bitch." *Newsweek* described him in 1973 in the same manner that the household staff, the East Wing staff, and even some from the West Wing had perceived him since 1969: "He sits 100 gold-carpeted feet down the hall from the Oval Office, glowering out at the world from under a crew cut that would flatter a drill instructor, with a gaze that would freeze Medusa."

Alexander Butterfield, Haldeman's deputy assistant, concurred with the general press assessment of his boss, whom he had known since and even double-dated with in their days together at UCLA. Haldeman was "very controlling, abrupt, and rude. He didn't seem to care. He was the Grand Mughal there" in the White House. For Pat, a frontier woman to the core who hated hierarchy, the idea of a Mughal gatekeeper isolating her husband must have been hard to stomach.

Kissinger also confirmed this image of Haldeman as the gatekeeper to the president. "Bob Haldeman thought his job was to protect the president from his own tendency of acting off the top of his head. And so he set up a very strict system and it was hard to get to the president with any specific request . . . this made [Haldeman] highly unpopular with people who thought they could get into the Oval Office."

Even Kissinger occasionally had a hard time getting to the president. Events concerning the Apollo 13 mission provided an example of Haldeman's inflexible personality and management style. Kissinger recounted:

For example, there was a night when two American astronauts were in an emergency vehicle going around the moon. And this happened after Nixon's bedtime. So, I called him—I could call the president afterwards, but it had to be a foreign policy problem. So, I called Bob and he said, "What's the problem?' I said, "These astronauts are maybe lost; we need to recover them eventually." But he said, "That's not a foreign policy problem, therefore you can't get through." . . . I said to him, "So, Bob, if I have to explain to the press tomorrow that two astronauts are going around the moon and it's not a domestic or foreign policy problem, what kind of problem is it?"

Kissinger speculated, "It's possible that Haldeman applied this [closed-door policy] also to Mrs. Nixon. That would not have been appropriate towards the president's wife. . . . I did not see this one way or the other, but it's conceivable that if she wanted to do something that he had problems with, that he would not be very easy to deal with."

Despite Haldeman's dour image in the press, his continued hostility toward the First Lady, the Watergate break-in, and Martha Mitchell's far-out claims, the 1972 election was a roaring success for the president. On November 7, Nixon won reelection against the Democratic candidate, George McGovern, by a landslide: 47,169,841 votes to 29,172,767—a whopping 60.7 to 37.5 percent.

The Nixon approach on Vietnam and many other domestic issues appealed to far more Americans than McGovern's stance, and the election was won with relative ease. Yet, the president recalled, he had a sense of foreboding that overtook him that historic November evening. "I am at a loss to explain the melancholy that settled over me on that victorious night. . . . To some extent the marring effects of Watergate may have played a part, to some extent our failure to win Congress, and to a greater extent the fact that we had not yet been able to end the war in Vietnam."

However, the end of the conflict in Southeast Asia was near. As Margaret Truman noted, "For the Nixons, the real victory came in January, when the North Vietnamese finally accepted the terms that ended the war." This was a milestone at which the entire family rejoiced. When Kissinger called Nixon to congratulate him, Pat also got on the line to congratulate him for his skillful negotiations. In his memoirs, Kissinger described the First Lady:

> With pain and stoicism, she had suffered the calumny and hatred that seemed to follow her husband. . . . She was totally without illusions and totally insistent on facing her trials in solitude. Her dignity never wavered. And if she seemed remote, who could know what fires had had to be banked in her stern existence. She made no claims on anyone; her fortitude has been awesome and not a little inspiring because one sensed it had been wrested from an essential gentleness.

On January 27, the Paris Peace Accords, which officially ended the war and instituted a cease-fire, gave Americans much to celebrate. The agreements included the repatriation of the American POWs and the best accounting possible for the MIAs thanks to Nixon, Kissinger, and the tireless POW/MIA wives who had spent years working to ensure that this provision would be part of the deal. The inauguration victory parties on January 20 may have seemed minimal in comparison to the joy and pride both the First Lady and the president felt with the end of the years-long bloody conflict.

As the second Nixon administration began, two other historic events took place on the same day. On January 22, Lyndon Johnson, Nixon's predecessor and sometime rival, died of a heart attack at his ranch in Texas. The relationship between the two men had mellowed after the 1968 election. The president claimed to have seen LBJ's better side in the last four years of his life. "He was courteous, generally soft-spoken, and thoughtful in every way. He was not the pushing, prodding politician, or the consummate partisan of his earlier career."

The same day as LBJ's death, the momentous *Roe v. Wade* decision was handed down from the Supreme Court, giving American women control over their reproductive rights. Though Pat did not believe in "abortion on demand," she was strongly in favor of women making their own reproductive choices and publicly supported their right to do so. She "was the first First Lady to use the word 'abortion.' She said it in the context of being pro–abortion rights."

Pat's exact words, uttered in 1972, almost a year before *Roe v. Wade*, were, "I think abortion should be a personal decision." She wholeheartedly believed in an individual's privacy and ability to make her own reproductive choices. One wonders what Pat would think of *Roe v. Wade* being dismantled today, placing what she thought should be a woman's personal decision into the hands of state governments. In this area, she was a First Lady ahead of her time—and now perhaps ours as well.

———

On January 8, 1973, four of the five men charged in the Watergate break-in of June 17, 1972, pleaded guilty before Judge John Sirica. As Nixon historian Bostock noted, "The Watergate case seemed to come to a close shortly before the President was sworn in for his second term. . . . In fact, the crisis was taking on a new life." The five men were sentenced on January 30. On February 7, the Senate established the Ervin Committee to investigate both Watergate and the 1972 presidential campaign. Things were beginning to heat up in the West Wing.

During the reelection campaign Pat had expressed concern to her daughters about some of the men around the president and their tendency to isolate him. As noted earlier, household staffer Preston Bruce had observed Pat's anxious demeanor after news of the break-in hit the papers the previous June.

From the perspective of Connie Stuart, the First Lady's chief of staff, "there was a sense among the family that Haldeman was keeping the staff too distant from the President. That the President wasn't getting the kind of information, the kind of access to staff that he should be having."

Pat had also been distressed by what appeared to be a systematic weeding out of long-term Nixon hands from 1969 onward. The old loyal gang of supporters, friends, and aides had become walled off from the president, mostly due to the efforts of the president's chief of staff. Julie and Tricia had noticed this isolation as well. Julie wrote, "By the time of the second inauguration, most of my father's original band of aides and supporters had little contact with 'the boss.' My father wanted Bob Haldeman to be the sole conduit to him, and Haldeman seemed to want that even more."

However, as Pat told Julie later, watching the intricate and years-long Vietnam War negotiation process had made her wary of second-guessing her husband's decisions. His hard work in that area with Kissinger had finally paid off. When the Watergate affair continued to reveal itself, daughter Julie related, "only one person could know all the facts and all the pressures that were being brought to bear. That is why, as Watergate unfolded, she was reluctant to probe. Her husband had handled the big problems well in the past; he could handle this one."

Meanwhile, the First Lady was undergoing an East Wing changing of the guard. After four years, Connie Stuart was leaving in the spring for a job in the State Department. The West Wing plot contrived when Stuart first arrived on staff to control the East Wing through her had collapsed in short order. The dueling interoffice exchanges between Stuart and Haldeman became famous among her staff, who called his memos "H grams." Haldeman had met his equal in Connie Stuart. Though Stuart wasn't always well liked by some of the East Wing staff, she did manage to get the First Lady in front of the media on a consistent basis, generating more positive press for her. This was not something Pat was keen on, but it had paid off.

According to Stuart, her boss told her that she wanted to enjoy her second term as First Lady. She would not work as hard, and she would relax and spend more time with her daughters and her friends. Pat told Stuart, "I've been campaigning all my life for Dick or somebody else and I'm not going to do that anymore. I'm going to enjoy these last four years." She decided not to replace Stuart with another chief of staff; instead, Stuart's deputy press secretary, Helen McCain Smith, took over as communications director.

Smith was the widow of McCain Smith, a lawyer and relative of Senator John McCain's family who died young in a flight training accident. After her husband's untimely death, she embarked upon a long career as the executive secretary for the Washington bureau of the *New York Daily News*.

Where Stuart's PR approach had been splashy and out front, Smith's style was refined and low-key. The new communications director was a team player who fit in well with the other women. She was also more willing to scale back the First Lady's interaction with the press. Patti Matson, who became Smith's deputy press secretary, noted, "Helen was a peacemaker" with the press and "so sweet, an old Washington, social kind of person." Matson saw Smith and the First Lady as a good fit for each other. "Helen kept Mrs. Nixon out of the press, which is what she wanted."

White House journalist Helen Thomas had much respect for Smith, especially considering West Wing press secretary Ron Ziegler's sometimes boorish behavior toward the press. Thomas was quoted in an article as saying, "People trust Helen, which is more than you can say for other press secretaries around here." The article went on to say that "Ron Ziegler is notorious for his general hostility and inaccessibility."

Smith would face the same poor treatment from many in the West Wing that her predecessors had faced. Years later she revealed that she and Ziegler did not get along and that "she was not even informed when Nixon was going to give a speech. She would often send memos to Z and get no answer; she couldn't get him on the phone. Z would always lay down what was going to happen and never ask her opinion." Mrs. Nixon at this point was not pushing back as much as she had under Connie Stuart. Smith noted, "On many things Mrs. Nixon would just say, 'Dick's too busy.'"

One thing Smith commented on, and many East Wing staff agreed upon, was the loyalty to the First Lady that prevailed among her staff and their willingness to work toward a common goal. During her tenure, Smith claimed, "unlike the President's staff, we who served Mrs. Nixon were united by a common respect for her that obliterated any personal ambitions or rivalry that might have divided us. There were no internal politics in the East Wing, no concealed weapons. We had no Haldeman or Ehrlichman. We were a happy, harmonious team."

While the East Wing had a smooth, professional operation that supported their First Lady above all, the West Wing continued its implosion. Chapin, Haldeman's deputy, was sacked in an effort to contain the burgeoning scandal. He vacated his job at the White House in March, but that was not to be the end of his problems related to Watergate.

The scandal soon began to consume others within the West Wing. Pat and her daughters watched as the tension began to mount. On March 21, the president's White House counsel, John Dean, who had been managing the Watergate cover-up from its earliest days, told the president of "a cancer—within—close to the presidency that's growing. It's growing daily. It's compounding." It would turn out that Dean himself was inextricably bound up in the Watergate scandal, delivering bags of cash to Watergate defendants and possibly even possessing knowledge of the June 17 break-in. Though his hands were far from clean, Dean would make a deal later to save his own skin. Others, like Chapin, would not be so lucky.

———

By April, the papers were filled with headlines regarding Watergate, and what initially had been treated as a public relations problem was now clearly something more. The president remained distant, walled off, in a solitary mood. Perhaps Pat and his daughters thought they could approach him better at the Nixons' seaside compound in Key Biscayne, Florida. Sunlight, swimming, and walks on the beach might restore some balance to the situation and provide a private place for the family to talk.

However, a photo of the president, the First Lady, Julie, David, and Tricia in Key Biscayne on Easter Sunday of 1973 illustrates the charged atmosphere of the date. In the photo, Pat, perfectly coiffed and dressed in a pale green Easter suit, looks off into the distance from one end of the photo. In the middle of the image, Julie and David stand under a tree together; Julie has her arms crossed as if shielding herself from the glare of the press. Tricia stands between a military aide and her father. The president, standing far away from his wife, looks downcast, with his arms crossed. The tension in the photo is palpable. The Easter weekend passed miserably without much penetration of the shell the president had built around him. However, over the next week the Nixon women, along with David Eisenhower, would unite and try to do something to help.

Midmorning on Saturday, April 28, the president was at Camp David working in the library of the Aspen cabin when he entered the living room in search of a cup of coffee. He was surprised to see Tricia sitting on the couch in front of the fireplace. She had come to Camp David early that morning, driven by the Secret Service from the White House.

Tricia, normally stoic, was clearly upset. The president wrote in his memoirs, "She said she had been awake all night talking about Watergate with Julie and David and the decisions that had to be made. They had talked with Pat for a long time early in the morning, and they wanted me to know that they all agreed that there was no choice but to have Haldeman and Ehrlichman resign." This, Tricia said, was an objective decision and was not influenced by her own negative feelings toward the two men. The family would understand if he chose not to take their advice, and they would support him regardless.

By the next day, Sunday, April 29, the president had made up his mind: it was time to make a clean break. Ziegler called Haldeman, informing him that the president wanted resignations from him and from Ehrlichman. They were to meet with the president at Camp David at 2 p.m. that afternoon. The "Germans," glum and largely silent, arrived at the mountain retreat by helicopter in what was to be their last meeting with the president.

The president met with each man separately. In anguished and emotional terms, he told them he had to let them go. Haldeman recalled looking at the gorgeous tulips in bloom just off Aspen's porch. The president told him he needed to enjoy that view "because I may not be alive much longer." He also told Haldeman that, as president, he prayed on his knees every night and that he had prayed hard over the decision to ask for his resignation. Ehrlichman remembered the president "crying uncontrollably" and telling him "he had prayed he might die the night before."

The next day, an exhausted-looking president gave his first televised address on Watergate. He expressed his great regret at having to ask for the resignations of Haldeman and Ehrlichman, "two of the finest public servants it has been my privilege to know." He also announced the resignation of his friend Richard Kleindienst, the attorney general, noting that Kleindienst was not involved in the Watergate affair. John Dean's resignation (really, firing) was flatly announced. The president explained that his other great regret was having delegated many of the 1972 election campaign duties to subordinates. He explained that "the Presidency should come first, and politics second." Still, he declared, "the man at the top must bear the responsibility."

At this point, the possibility that the Nixon presidency might meet a premature end began to seem real to Pat and her daughters. According to David Eisenhower, his mother-in-law, wife, and sister-in-law "realize[d] that this may not work out at all; in fact, it would be surprising if he completes the term when Ehrlichman and Haldeman resign." Despite the Nixon women's negative personal feelings about the so-called Praetorian Guards, the family and remaining staff now questioned whether "a Nixon White House could really go forward, as they were so much part of the operation."

With Haldeman and Ehrlichman finally dispatched, the Pat and Dick Team was ready to show the world a united front. The family hunkered down together to try to ride out the storm. The popular press narrative at the time was that the president and the First Lady were estranged during the Watergate era. Son-in-law Eisenhower disagreed. "I'm completely contrary as far as Watergate goes. I think that's where I really saw them draw together. It was protective. . . . I felt more solidarity in that period than ever."

Two months after Haldeman and Ehrlichman's departure, the president promoted Rose Mary Woods from his personal secretary to his executive assistant. Finally, Rose had won the battle for control that she and Haldeman had waged for years. (Reported the *Washington Post* in July 1974, citing an anonymous source, "'She had more savvy,' says someone still at the White House, 'than all those p-r types put together.'")

The Old Nixon team was reassembling to fight together what some called "the last campaign."

27

GOOD AFTERNOON, MRS. FORD'S OFFICE

Less than a month after the departure of "the Germans," the president and First Lady hosted an event that would be the culmination of years of negotiations between the United States and the North Vietnamese. A gala in honor of the returning American prisoners of war—some of whom had been in captivity for as long as eight years—took place on May 24 on the South Lawn of the White House. After many years of heroic resistance and sacrifice, these courageous servicemen were finally back on home soil. The heavy rain that soaked the grounds that day and evening would not dampen anyone's spirits. To the contrary, the evening would be joyous, celebratory, and triumphant.

Lucy Winchester recalled that the White House staff was told repeatedly by the military that "the White House dinner was never going to work because of the poor POWs and all their health conditions." The thought was that many would not be mentally or physically strong enough to attend a White House event that soon. However, Pat didn't let that opinion stop her. Winchester remembered the First Lady saying, "Anyone who needs to come with a nurse, tell them to bring them!"

There were also issues with some of the POWs' marriages dissolving, so a blanket invitation to the POWs' wives would not have been appropriate. Pat had a solution for that too. She told her social secretary that "of course, they may bring whoever they like" to the dinner. Assistant social secretary Pat Howard noted, "When a POW called and said a Playboy Bunny was going to be his date, Lucy [Winchester] called Mrs. Nixon about it. Mrs. Nixon told her, 'If she's his guest, that's his guest, Lucy!'"

Presidential aide Steve Bull worked directly with the First Lady on the POW dinner and noted that "Pat was very much the architect of the POW program." Bull worked on the entertainment side of the dinner and recalled a call he got from famous American composer Irving Berlin the day before the gala:

> I get this call from Irving Berlin, and he said, "Mr. Bull, I want to come and sing my song to my boys." I said, "Of course." So we added him to the program . . . he sings the first verse of "God Bless America," and he stops, and he starts again, and the Marine orchestra that's there joins him in accompaniment, and he gets through the second time, and he starts again the third time, everybody in the room—in the tent, 1300 people with the rain coming down, and the tears streaming down from their eyes, were singing and holding hands, "God Bless America."

Returned POW Mike Brazelton remembered, "After dinner, we were allowed to wander anywhere in and around the White House that we wanted. Quite a few of us even were allowed into the personal quarters of the President. . . . The party lasted well into the night. Nobody ended it at 11pm or midnight. It was probably between 1am and 2am that we finally caught the last bus back to the Hilton Hotel."

Though it was a night never to be forgotten by the POWs or the Nixon family, the president was beginning to succumb to despair. He later wrote in his memoirs, "The contrast between the splendid lift of this night and the dreary, daily drain of Watergate suddenly struck me with almost physical force."

At 1 a.m., after Pat had gone to bed, he called David and Julie and Tricia to the Lincoln sitting room. He asked them all if he should resign. They assured him he should not. He had brought the subject up at Camp David three weeks before, and Pat had insisted he continue to fight. The president may have wanted the young people's opinions alone for comparison. They also continued to urge him to fight. Tricia summed up the evening visit best in her diary later: "And so the evening concluded—an evening representing great historical and personal achievement for Daddy, marred by a great personal tragedy."

That summer things went from bad to worse for the embattled president. The media focused on Watergate to the exclusion of almost anything else.

On May 25, Archibald Cox was sworn in as the Watergate special prosecutor, and the Senate opened its investigation. In June, former White House counsel John Dean appeared as a witness, implicating the president with his testimony.

In mid-July, presidential aide Alexander Butterfield revealed the existence of a voice-activated taping system in the White House. Though taping systems had been used for decades by former presidents, Roosevelt, Truman, Eisenhower, Kennedy, and Johnson among them, this revelation hit the press like a bombshell. Now the public's attention became riveted on the presidential tapes and what was on them.

The president argued that the doctrine of executive privilege gave him "the right to maintain the confidentiality of his papers." However, Cox and the Senate Watergate Committee filed suit to force the release of the tapes. Some of the president's advisors urged him to destroy the tapes. Pat too believed the tapes should be destroyed. She told Helene Drown that they were comparable to "private love letters" and should not be shared with the public.

Rose Mary Woods then became embroiled in the tape controversy when it seemed she might have inadvertently erased several minutes of an eighteen-and-a-half-minute conversation between the president and Haldeman on June 20, 1972, during her transcription work.

Woods was called to testify at a court hearing before the grand jury—a painful ordeal for someone so committed both to The Boss and to the Nixon family. "A picture of her re-creating the moment—dubbed the 'Rose Mary stretch'—that showed her leaning back and stretching to reach the phone with her hand while her foot was on the recorder's pedal sparked skepticism of her explanation."

No charges were ever brought against Woods, and the mystery of the gap was never solved. But the psychological upset to Woods was significant and traumatic. Steve Bull, who was also called to testify about the taping incident, explained that Rose was "ridiculed publicly for the tapes. She was very upset." The situation also added fuel to rumors that she had deliberately erased the tapes on her boss's behalf.

As if things were not bleak enough for the Nixon administration, in early October Vice President Spiro Agnew resigned in disgrace due to tax evasion charges. The Nixons' old friend Gerald Ford assumed the vice presidency.

Agnew's resignation would be the least of the president's problems that fall. In the Middle East, he faced an unexpected war when both Syria and Egypt attacked Israel on October 6. Despite resistance from his military advisors, the president sent war matériel and air support to the beleaguered Israelis, saving the day. "Nixon's decisiveness saved Israel. It was his last major international achievement."

Despite Nixon's triumph in the Middle East, the long shadow of Watergate remained over the White House. When Cox continued to insist that the president turn over the White House tapes, the president ordered his attorney general, Elliot Richardson, to fire Cox. Richardson refused to do so, resigning in protest. Deputy attorney general William Ruckelshaus also resigned. Finally, the solicitor general, Robert Bork, took over as attorney general and fired Cox.

At 8:22 p.m. on the evening of October 20, White House Press Secretary Ziegler went on television to announce the firing and resignations, and all hell broke loose. The so-called "Saturday Night Massacre" riveted Americans. Historian Jonathan Aitken claims that the Cox firing had little impact on the Watergate legal process. However, "its impact on the political landscape was like an earthquake. Nixon's Gallup poll ratings plummeted to an all-time low of 17 percent. All across the country, newspaper columnists and TV commentators called for his impeachment."

Less than two weeks later, Acting Attorney General Bork announced that with the president's approval he had appointed Leon Jaworski, a conservative Texas Democrat, to replace Cox as the Watergate special prosecutor. William B. Saxbe, a Republican from Ohio, would become the president's fourth and last attorney general.

On October 23 Pat called Helene from Camp David. Helene later wrote Julie about her mother's state of mind at that time. "She was fighting mad, said that 'things are getting wild . . . very concerned' . . . she said that Dick had asked Richardson (when he called him after Cox made his TV appearance and he fired Cox) not to resign until after the Israeli and Arab war had been settled, that negotiations were so serious now—and Richardson refused to wait . . . 'Dick was furious . . . I think Dick should go on TV right away and not wait.'"

Pat confided, "'Here he is trying to settle a war and all this stuff is going on.' I (Helene) told her that Jack and I thought things were really going to get rough . . . she said that she 'knew it and that what they want him to do is to get Dick to resign. They don't know him. He'll NEVER do that. We've got to fight.'" Pat's response here echoed both her attitude during the fund crisis of 1952 and her stance in the 1960 election. Right or wrong, Pat always urged her husband not to give up even in his darkest hours.

Pat's negativity toward the press was hard for her to contain at this point. "I'm not going to talk to the press. All they want is Watergate. . . . Helen Thomas is writing me such flowery letters, but when I see her, I just say hi and pass along. I won't give her or any of the press a word. They are so bad."

Pat's old friend Mamie Eisenhower invited her to the farm in Gettysburg to escape the negative press attention. Here, Mamie said, Pat "could rest, walk, read, gossip with me—please everything would be on the QT. What fun we would have—have told Julie and David they could come too—come a running." Despite Watergate and the political firestorm, Mamie's friendship with Pat remained solid.

Administration turmoil and constant press queries continued to put tremendous pressure on the First Lady. Even so, throughout that fall, and during the winter and spring of 1974, Pat would conduct her official White House business as usual. Communications director Helen Smith said, "For Mrs. Nixon work is therapy. And as the pressure mounted, she became even more conscientious than before about fulfilling the backbreaking schedule she set for herself. Until the very end, she made a point of never missing a White House reception, never disappointing an audience, never staying home from a travel assignment."

———

On March 1, 1974, grand jury indictments were handed down for Haldeman, Ehrlichman, and Mitchell, as well as Charles Colson and three other CRP members. Only a few days later, Ehrlichman, Colson, and G. Gordon Liddy were indicted for the break-in at Daniel Ellsberg's psychiatrist's office. On the heels of these developments, Pat left the country for what would ultimately be her last solo tour abroad on behalf of the president. On the six-day journey for presidential inaugurations in Brazil and Venezuela, Pat was hailed with parades, pomp, and ceremony. Upon her arrival at Brasilia's international airport, the First Lady was surrounded by "Brazilian soldiers [who] formed a human chain preventing the American press corps from approaching her." Pat surely wished she had such a guard at home to protect her from the constant domestic press scrutiny.

The First Lady had barely gotten onto her plane to return home when she was thrust back into questions about Watergate, however. The women of the press who had accompanied Pat to South America had decorated the plane for her sixty-second birthday and passed around champagne in honor of the First Lady. Pat reportedly was relaxing and having fun until the inevitable questions about Watergate arose from one of the journalists. The First Lady froze up and the party was abruptly over.

Pat's birthday celebrations did not improve when she returned home. En route to D.C., the First Lady and her entourage, including Helen Smith, stopped in Nashville, Tennessee. There they connected with the president at the opening of the Grand Ole Opry. During a celebratory evening, the president surprised his wife by appearing onstage, playing "Happy Birthday" to her on an upright piano.

The First Lady, who was watching from backstage, emerged to join her husband. Smith watched as, "her face glowing, Pat rose from her chair and moved towards her husband. He apparently wanted to get on with the program. He rose, stepped brusquely to center stage—and ignored Pat's outstretched arms. I shall never forget the expression on her face. It was one of the times some of us winced."

Julie contends that it was due to "mixed signals between two people" and not due to any inherent problems in the relationship. Pat herself commented later that the misrepresentations of the event were much more upsetting to her than her husband's actions that night. However, the optics (as Roger Ailes would have told the president) did not look good, especially during this trying time.

The stress of Watergate certainly had not helped their relationship, nor did the isolation of the president from his wife, which seemed to have begun when the New Nixon team came on board. As Nixon grew more and more insulated by work and by some of his aides, to the public it looked as if a chilling effect had descended upon the marriage. This perception did not begin to thaw until Haldeman and Ehrlichman were gone. As the pressures began to mount, the Pat and Dick Team hunkered down together to face the crisis. Pat was at her best in the most trying times, and protecting her family brought out her fighting spirit.

In April, the White House released the "Blue Book," edited transcripts of the tapes. "With its many omissions, it failed to satisfy anyone, and worse, it began to show the public the real way Nixon spoke in private, with the phrase 'expletive deleted' frequently filling in for vulgarities." The president never spoke that way around his wife and daughters, so the experience of reading the transcripts was painful for his family.

Connie Stuart told her husband, Chuck, that the First Lady "was shocked when the tapes began to come out as she had never heard 'Dick' use such words." Stuart speculated that the president used profanity to toughen his image around his West Wing team, especially in the Oval Office, "a place to flex muscles, a place to bond with other males and assert the pecking order." While the bluster may have impressed the Mad Men of the White House, it certainly did not win the president points with his wife and daughters, nor with the Silent Majority who had elected him.

As the spring continued and the weather improved, Pat began to walk with Julie for exercise—either around Theodore Roosevelt Island before it closed in the evenings or in the evenings around deserted downtown Washington with a contingent of Secret Service agents guarding them. She would often wear dark glasses and a scarf to try to maintain some anonymity. Exercise and the solace of nature had always given her stress relief. She also quit reading the newspapers at this point, relying instead on a news summary prepared for her in-house. She needed buffering as the press began to push the Nixons on financial matters that offended Pat to her core.

The first accusation was an inquiry into the Nixons' finances because of deductions taken for the donation of the president's pre-presidency papers. "Pat, who had to sign the form authorizing an audit of their back tax forms, probably knew little about the convoluted deductions." However, this was yet another public humiliation in an area where the thrifty Pat was especially defensive. When she joined her husband to sign the forms for the tax audit, he said he "could sense her tightly controlled anger." He believed these attacks on their "financial probity and integrity were the ones that hurt most of all."

Also upsetting to Pat were direct accusations from *Washington Post* columnist Maxine Cheshire that she and her daughters had received gifts of diamond jewelry from the Saudi royal family but had not registered the gifts with the White House gift office for almost two years. Pat, who was meticulous about reporting gifts, pushed back sharply when asked by a reporter about Cheshire's claims at a Washington reception. "Oh, that's for the birds, everybody who read it said it from coast to coast." The gifts had in fact been reported on July 1, 1972.

What worried the First Lady most of all, though, was how the lives of her daughters and their husbands were impacted by Watergate. Julie and Tricia too were trapped in the center of the political firestorm. The two daughters had different approaches to help support their father during this time. For Julie, the more extroverted of the two girls, the impulse was to fight, to push back against the negative press reports. She was on the road now constantly in defense of her father; in one week she did as many as six events.

Julie and David eventually held a joint press conference in the East Garden on the White House grounds in May 1974 to address the avalanche of interview requests regarding Watergate and her father's possible resignation. This campaign did help her father's image. Reporter Kandie Stroud wrote Pat praising Julie and David: "Julie and David have warmed the hearts of even the most hardened Democrats. . . . They have done more to reverse the 'unfavorable' polls than anything else."

Julie revealed in her biography of Pat that "Mother was the one who encouraged my appearances," not her father, who worried about her being on the front line of Watergate inquiries so frequently. Helen Smith confirmed this, telling *Washington Post* reporter Bob Woodward that she was sure the president "never wanted Julie out front defending him." After the East Garden press conference, Smith was swamped with calls praising Julie. When she ran into the president in the elevator of the residence and told him this, she noted he had tears in his eyes.

While many members of the press were impressed with Julie's devotion, many others sharpened their knives for her. Journalist Nora Ephron wrote, "In the months since the Watergate hearings began, she [Julie] has become her father's First Lady in practice if not in fact." She also claimed that journalists who believed Julie's impassioned defense of her father "have been around Nixon so long that they don't recognize a chocolate-covered spider when they see one."

This surreal conceit of describing the younger First Daughter as a "chocolate-covered spider" delighted Nixon critics and confounded anyone who knew the young woman. (It's an understatement to say that Ephron, who would soon marry *Washington Post* reporter Carl Bernstein, cannot be considered an unbiased source.) Just as her mother was unfairly tagged "Plastic Pat," so Julie became "the chocolate-covered spider." Both appellations were untrue and mean-spirited, but they were reductive enough to be retained easily in the public consciousness. The only truth in the commentary was that Julie had taken on a more active role while Pat remained on the sidelines of the Watergate defense. The First Lady continued her other First Lady duties, however.

Due to Tricia's more reserved nature, she was often dubbed "the Mystery Girl." She was much like her mother in this regard, though she dismissed the notion, saying, "I don't think I'm mysterious at all."

The East Wing staff women also drew together in a protective huddle during the spring and summer of 1974, wanting to both comfort and shield "Mrs. N" from further upset. Joni Stevens, who worked in the appointments office, remembered that "the staff were all devoted to Mrs. Nixon . . . We were like a sorority because we all went through a difficult time together." Stevens and the Nixon daughters' assistant, Cindy Vanden Heuvel, lived next door to each other, and they often commuted together to work. During Watergate Stevens felt "we didn't want to be around other people as others wouldn't understand what the staff were going through."

Pat Howard, in the social secretary's office, noted, "Mrs. Nixon was always the one who was so upbeat, strong, encouraging, and positive, especially during those days near the end of the Nixon Administration. When I say upbeat . . . one thing that comes to mind immediately is Mrs. Nixon sending fun things down to Lucy [Winchester] with her funny comments. I felt that she knew it was a trying and tough time for us and she wanted our spirits to be uplifted."

Susie Dolibois, who also worked in the social secretary's office, remembered, "Mrs. Nixon kept on keeping on, being the best First Lady, despite the political swirl." Dolibois's diary notes show that "May and June of 1974 were filled with receptions and dinners." Dolibois and the East Wing staff interviewed for this book were eyewitnesses to Pat's schedule and behavior, and the women all dismiss the still prevalent mythology that the First Lady became a recluse at this time.

In addition to her full domestic calendar of events that summer, the First Lady accompanied her husband to both the Middle East and Russia in June for key foreign policy summits. On June 10, the Nixons left for a peace-seeking trip to the Middle East, where they met with leaders in Saudi Arabia, Egypt, Syria, Israel, and Jordan. Though the trip was a success, helping to reduce tensions in the region between Israel and the Arab nations, it cost the president healthwise.

During the journey, the president suffered another attack of his old malady, phlebitis. The couple made it home to D.C., but they had less than a week before they left again—this time for Moscow to meet with Soviet premier Leonid Brezhnev for the third summit. While no major breakthroughs occurred at that summit, the current détente between the two nations held and the president's phlebitis was kept at bay. As they winged their way home, bone-tired after a strenuous trip, the president, the First Lady, and their entourage, including Rose Mary Woods and Bebe Rebozo, worried what new tribulations would greet them on the ground.

————

On July 12 the First Lady, the president, Tricia, and Ed flew to San Clemente for a tense two-week vacation. On July 28 Helene Drown flew from California to the White House to be with Pat. Her old friend stayed at the residence until August 2 to distract her and try to keep her spirits up. Helene was Pat's constant and consistent source of support. She had been there with her during all the many crises of the Nixons' political life, taking care of her friend when Dick was too wrapped up in his political life to do so himself. It was women who gave the First Lady her strength during this awful time. Pat's girls, Helene, and the women of the East Wing formed a protective force field around her while the West Wing collapsed around them.

Within this protective cocoon, Pat continued to work with the White House curator, Clement Conger, on the ongoing White House renovation and restoration projects. Plans were under way to update the Garden Room, the East Hall, and the Queen's Bedroom. Pat showed Helene some of this work in progress during her stay at the White House.

Conger had held a meeting with White House staff on July 22 to discuss the design of the Nixon china service. Both Pat and the president had long admired the Wilson china pattern with its outer gold band and inner wider lapis border. They had planned to order something similar, perhaps with a decorative golden eagle in the center. The design and the order of 250 plates were still pending Pat's approval on the twenty-second.

However, when Helene left Pat on August 2, she knew the end was near. She later told Julie that her mother looked fragile and forlorn when she left, "as if a little puff of wind could have blown her away. . . . She had always been a doer and now there was nothing we could do." Helene cried in the backseat of the White House car that took her to the airport. That same day, Pat called her good friend Conger with a quaver in her voice: "I won't explain, Clem, but don't go ahead with the porcelain. Call it off."

That evening the president called the family together for a meeting. Tricia and Ed had just arrived from New York, and Julie and David were already at the White House with Pat. Bebe Rebozo had come into town from Florida the night before. After about twenty minutes, Manolo Sanchez (he and his wife Fina had been with the Nixons as trusted members of their household staff since their days in California) handed out transcripts from one of the presidential tapes for all to read. It would be released the following Monday, and the president wanted the family's reaction. Julie could see her mother's "rocklike solidarity with my father and a fierce protectiveness. I am not sure she even looked at the transcript."

After reading the transcript, Julie, Ed, and Tricia all felt the president should continue to fight. Pat also continued to urge her husband to fight. David felt his father-in-law should take whatever he thought was the best course of action. When Pat, Julie and David, and Tricia and Ed retired for the evening, Tricia noted in her diary: "We all broke down together, and put our arms around each other in circular, huddle-style fashion. Saying nothing."

After an agonizing weekend at Camp David, the family returned to Washington. On Monday, August 5, the so-called smoking-gun tape was released to the public.

The Oval Office conversation between the president and Haldeman from June 23, 1972, had taken place just six days after the break-in at the Watergate complex. During the conversation, Haldeman passed on John Dean's recommendation that the CIA and FBI be instructed to curtail their investigation on the grounds that Watergate was a matter of national security. Nixon agreed with his staff's recommendation to hold back the CIA and the FBI from interviewing two important witnesses.

The special prosecutor, Jaworski, believed that the tape indicated the president "had entered a criminal conspiracy to obstruct justice." Once the public heard the tape, almost all of the president's political support vanished.

Dolibois wrote vividly about the days directly following the tape's release in her 1974 journal: "Tuesday and Wednesday were days of speculation, disappointment, and deep gloom for everyone. Instead of will the President resign, it was when will the President resign? All the petty differences were forgotten in the East Wing—It was an amazing time, everyone helping and supporting each other. . . . Then on Thursday morning everyone was in high spirits because Julie called late Wednesday afternoon and said that she and Tricia had just spent time with their father, and he was going to fight. In the middle of Thursday morning, we were told that Julie was packing!" Events were moving so fast, it was difficult for even White House staff to know from minute to minute what would ultimately take place.

Little did the women know that on Tuesday, August 6, the president had already made the decision to resign. Rose Mary Woods, now his executive assistant, was tasked with telling the First Lady and their daughters the crushing news. "I needed her help in telling the family. . . . There was no need for them to worry over something that we could no longer do anything about." Woods took on this duty with dignity, but she was shattered by the decision. In her diary Tricia recalled, "Rose in tears that afternoon told us (Mama, Julie and me) in the Solarium that Daddy had irrevocably decided to resign. . . . We must not collapse in the face of this ordeal. We must not let him down." Julie left him a note on his pillow that night, however, still asking him to "wait a week or even ten days before you make this decision . . . millions support you."

On August 8, Pat Howard took notes about the whirlwind of activity going on around her in the East Wing. Even in these final days, the conscientious

First Lady was thinking about her correspondence and how much it would mean for Americans who wrote her to hear from the Nixon family during this troubled time. Cards were sent out until 8 p.m. on August 8, the night that the president resigned. Howard wrote in her personal notes, "The phones rang all day, people begging the President not to resign. As soon as people called, we were mailing out these cards. Everyone was taking calls, and hand-addressing these cards—marvelous 'team spirit' with a lot of tears."

Joni Stevens remembered "one call on 8/8 from a nurse whose patient was on oxygen but he so wanted to speak with Mrs. Nixon so the nurse took the tubes out of his nose so he could dictate his message to me. Another was [comedian] Jerry Lewis not understanding that I couldn't put him on the phone with the First Lady, and one who wanted me to go on the PA system and announce that he was waiting to talk to Mrs. Nixon and having to explain that the White House didn't have a PA system!"

The East Wingers were so frantically busy, they could not allow themselves to be sad until President Nixon made his resignation speech that evening at 9:01 p.m. Eastern time. As the nation watched, the thirty-seventh president gave his thirty-seventh and final speech from the Oval Office: "I have never been a quitter. To leave office before my term is completed is abhorrent to every instinct in my body. But as President, I must put the interest of America first. . . . Therefore, I shall resign the Presidency effective at noon tomorrow. Vice President Ford will be sworn in as President at that hour in this office."

Only then did Howard and the other women have time to "think about the reality of what the President had just announced. I remember thinking amidst all of my emotions that night that I must be strong as I knew that Mrs. Nixon would want all of us to be strong."

Stevens summed up the surreal nature of the situation the morning of August 9: "We were writing envelopes until we left for the State Floor [to hear the president's farewell speech to staff]. It was so odd to get to work in the morning and answer the phone 'Good morning, Mrs. Nixon's office'—and return from the mansion to watch the swearing in and the phones being answered 'Good afternoon, Mrs. Ford's office.'"

During all this chaos, Pat had not forgotten even the smallest details. Through the chief usher, Rex Scouten, she had ordered thirty-eight red roses for the Fords (Ford being the thirty-eighth president), to be delivered to them as they moved into the White House. The Nixon presidency was now officially finished. Pat and Dick were back together as a team, but their trials were far from over.

28

TRUE GRIT

J ack Brennan, the president's Marine military aide, was on Army One with
the Nixons as they took off on their next to last flight as president and First
Lady. Just after takeoff, he recalled, "Everyone's in tears, especially all the ladies
on the staff . . . and Mrs. Nixon looked down and just said, 'It's so sad. It's
so sad.'" Still, she did not cry. Inside the helicopter a solemn silence reigned.
Passengers included Tricia and Ed Cox, Manolo and Fina Sanchez (with their
pet bird), Jack Brennan, Steve Bull, the president's personal physician Walter
Tkach, Ron Ziegler, and two Secret Service agents. Gene Boyer, the Nixons'
longtime helicopter pilot, who had flown Pat around Peru on her 1970 mercy
mission, wept quietly. David, Julie, and Rose Mary Woods stayed behind in
D.C. to pack and organize the Nixons' belongings and papers.

As the soon-to-be ex-president flew over Washington, his thoughts were
already on the future. He had suffered many defeats before and still had
risen from the ashes. Even on Army One as he and Pat flew off into exile,
he remained hopeful. He was pondering not "the past but the future." His
political obituary had been written many times before, and he had always
proved them wrong in the past.

For the soon-to-be former First Lady, however, political life was forever
finished. Watergate took whatever last bit of enjoyment she had out of her
White House role. While she would finally have the "blessed aloneness" in
San Clemente that she had always sought, it came at an extraordinarily high
price. This fact registered bitterly with the president. He wrote in his memoirs
of his wife, "Now she would not receive any of the praise she deserved. There
would be no round of farewell parties by congressional wives, no testimoni-

als, no tributes. She had been a dignified, compassionate First Lady. She had given so much to the nation and so much to the world. Now she would have to share my exile. She deserved so much more."

The Nixon entourage landed at Andrews Air Force Base just outside D.C. for their last presidential flight. During their four-hour-plus journey on Air Force One to California, Pat and Dick stayed in adjacent compartments separated only by a sliding panel. "Both were totally drained, content for a few hours to live in a state of suspended reality." Neither Pat nor Dick watched as Ford took the oath of office or gave his first address as president, in which he declared that "our long national nightmare is over." Ford also asked Americans to pray for peace for the former president and his family.

When the flight landed at El Toro Marine Base near San Clemente, Dick and Pat came back together. Upon opening the door from his small office, Dick found Pat, Ed, and Tricia waiting for him in the aisle. Pat instinctively reached out to grasp her husband's hand. After facing a crowd of five thousand well-wishers at the Marine base, Pat, Dick, Ed, and Tricia boarded another helicopter bound for the Coast Guard station next to Casa Pacifica.

Bill Hudson, who had acted as the First Lady's lead Secret Service agent since 1972, was among those waiting for them on the helipad at the Coast Guard station. Hudson, who had been transferred out to San Clemente as the deputy to the Western White House detail, remembered, "It was sad, really sad." Though both Nixons waved and smiled to the small crowd that had assembled near the house, Mrs. Nixon went straight into the home. The president got in a golf cart and went right to his office. Hudson knew well from his many years working for the First Lady that she was always a consummate professional. On this day, however, it must have taken her last reserves of strength to maintain her poise until the doors of Casa Pacifica at last shut behind her.

While her husband continued toiling in his home office, Pat spent her first weeks back in California unpacking, arranging their belongings, and planting a garden. However, her overriding concern was her husband's state of mind, and she kept close watch over him in those early days. Tricia and Ed also stayed on for three weeks to facilitate the move and help the now former president and First Lady ease into retired life. Rose Mary Woods soon arrived as well to help with the transition.

On September 7, Pat and Dick slipped out of Casa Pacifica under cover of darkness for their first trip outside the compound. A few hours later, they arrived at Sunnylands, the palatial estate of their old friends Walter and Leonore Annenberg, for a five-day visit. Annenberg had served as Nixon's ambassador to the Court of St. James (England) from 1969 to 1974, and Leonore was a world-renowned hostess, who would later become President Ronald Reagan's Chief of Protocol.

The Nixons had visited Sunnylands numerous times since 1968, most recently in January and July 1974. The Rancho Mirage estate, built between 1963 and 1966, was a pink Mayan-temple-inspired fantasia in the desert. Only ten miles from Palm Springs, the Annenbergs' "private dreamworld and winter home" looked out over an artfully designed golf course, set in the foothills of the majestic San Jacinto Mountains.

Perhaps the lush, secluded setting in the desert and time with their old friends and supporters the Annenbergs were what finally lured the former First Couple out of their gloomy seclusion in San Clemente. Dick would write a poignant note in the Sunnylands guestbook on September 8: "When you're down, you find out who your real friends are—We shall always be grateful for your kindness and your loyal friendships."

That same day, September 8, Dick received word that he had been pardoned by President Ford. The family had not been told in advance that a pardon was forthcoming. Pat was especially offended by the concept. "A pardon for what?" she exclaimed furiously. To receive the pardon, the former president had been required to submit a statement of contrition as well, which only added to Pat's upset. The former president did not want to prolong the misery of his situation. He decided to move forward quickly, thus avoiding emotional discussions of the pardon with his family.

Julie wrote that she only learned of the pardon that same day along with the public. Her father did not return her phone call to him that day. When she finally reached her mother that night, "she was obviously upset and uncommunicative." Pat then confessed that Dick had told her, "'This is the most humiliating day of my life.' Months later, she would explain that it was for her the saddest day. In her eyes, my father had done nothing to require a pardon and his acceptance of it would imply surrender to his enemies." The nightmare would continue, however, for both the ex-president and the former First Lady.

The same evening as the pardon, Nixon suffered another attack of phlebitis. Dick and Pat ignored the problem for weeks until their family doctor, Jack Lungren, finally convinced Dick to enter the hospital in Long Beach on September 23, where he would remain for treatment for five excruciating days. Pat visited him daily.

Dick was released on October 4. He was too ill to attend the trial of Haldeman, Ehrlichman, and Mitchell in D.C., but a cynical press disputed whether his illness was serious enough to warrant his absence, depressing him further. (Haldeman, Ehrlichman, and Mitchell would all be convicted, serving eighteen, eighteen, and nineteen months, respectively. Chapin would serve nine months. As a key witness for the prosecution, John Dean would be sentenced to only four months; he would never serve a day in a traditional jail.)

Dick was readmitted to the hospital just a few weeks later, where he soon faced emergency surgery. After the surgery, he woke up briefly, only to pass out with Pat sitting beside him. After receiving a massive blood transfusion, Dick regained consciousness and asked to see his wife. He told her weakly he didn't think he would make it. Her response was classic Pat. As Dick later described the scene: "She gripped my hand and said almost fiercely, 'Dick, you can't talk that way. You have got to make it. You must not give up.' As she spoke my thoughts went back to the Fund crisis in 1952. . . . I told her, 'I just don't think I can go through with this one.' She grasped me firmly by the hand and said, 'Of course you can.'"

A year later, Dick spoke to *McCall's* about the crisis and had nothing but praise for his devoted spouse. "I think it's her immense capacity to comfort and encourage that pulled me through. Pat's devotion kept me alive—I doubt I would have made it without her. Her love, her strength, her constant reassurance, her faith in me as a human being and as her husband led me out of the depths."

Pat had nursed others many times before: her father, her TB patients, her girls through all their childhood illnesses. Though she never permitted herself to be ill, she always selflessly took care of those around her. Soon it would be Dick's turn to take care of her.

While Dick continued his slow but steady recovery, Pat read and gardened. She saw Helene and Jack Drown frequently, the two couples resuming their old habit of double dates, now at Casa Pacifica. Helene and Pat even took off together for Tijuana one memorable day. The former First Lady kept up with former staffers Lucy Winchester and Gwen King, speaking to them often on the phone. She and Dick enjoyed daily pool swims and poolside dining as well as watching new films sent to them directly by their Hollywood friends.

The couple finally had time to spend together, and the marriage seemed to renew itself. Without the demands of political life, both halves of the couple could enjoy each other and savor the little things that made their life together sweet. At Dick's insistence, Pat agreed to attend the late May 1975 dedication of the Pat Nixon Elementary School in Cerritos (formerly known as Artesia), California, where she had grown up. This would be her only solo public event during her entire stint in California postpresidency.

In 1975 Dick sold his memoirs for $2.5 million. A few years later, in 1977, he would also sell exclusive interview rights to British television personality David Frost, generating much-needed funds to pay off legal bills and replenish the family coffers.

In February 1976, the former president and his wife were invited to visit Chairman Mao in China. Military aide Jack Brennan also accompanied the Nixons. The trip buoyed Dick's spirits—he was slowly but surely getting back into the political game through his expertise in foreign policy, the area where he shone brightest. Both presidents and politicians would come calling for his advice in the years that followed.

Despite these positive developments, however, a series of events took place next that would negatively impact Pat's health and well-being. In May, Bob Woodward and Carl Bernstein's sensational book about the last days of the Nixon presidency, *The Final Days*, was published, quickly becoming a bestseller. Without naming sources, the book portrayed Pat as a recluse and a heavy drinker crushed by the Watergate scandal.

The two reporters claimed that Pat returned from her South American goodwill trip in April 1973 "distraught and even more underweight than usual. She was becoming more and more reclusive, and was drinking heavily. On several occasions members of the household staff came upon her in the pantry of the second-floor kitchen, where the liquor was kept, in the early afternoon. Awkwardly, she had tried to hide her tumbler of bourbon on the rocks."

No specific attributions were given for either of these claims. When interviewed for this book, Woodward was still unwilling to attach any source names to this description of the First Lady. (Bernstein initially agreed to be interviewed for this book in 2022, but he never responded to subsequent emails.)

Woodward and Bernstein's characterizations of the former First Lady couldn't be confirmed. First, Pat was anything but reclusive from April 1973 until the end of her husband's presidency. White House records show an active First Lady for whom showing up to work was almost a religion. Her motto, which she repeated often throughout her public life, was "I do or die, I never cancel out." As Helen Smith noted: "Until the very end, she made a point of never missing a White House reception, never disappointing an audience, never staying home from a travel assignment."

The claim that she was hiding out in the residence runs contrary to all her previous conduct and also contradicts her published schedule. For example, in April 1973, the month Woodward and Bernstein claim the First Lady's "reclusiveness" started, she attended a total of eighteen events: sixteen in-house and two out of town with the president. That month she also inaugurated the first-ever public tours of the White House grounds.

A sample calendar from April 1974, a year later, shows an *increase* in activity. That month, the First Lady attended twenty-four official events. Only in the very last days of her husband's presidency in June and July 1974 does the slowdown of outward-facing activity become noticeable. Still, the First Lady continued to host official functions until less than three weeks prior to the resignation, her last event being a reception for the National Council of Negro Women on July 12, 1974.

Hudson, who was with the First Lady on her foreign trips during this time, said that his charge (whose Secret Service code name was "Starlight") always showed up on time and did her job in a professional manner: "She kept up every day on foreign trips." He also noted that during the Watergate era, Pat "kept up her normal schedule with no change." Hudson added emphatically: "I was with her on many on the record as well as off the record appearances and I certainly never saw any evidence of a drinking problem."

304 | THE MYSTERIOUS MRS. NIXON

Pat's schedule may have slowed during the last weeks before the resignation, but she never became reclusive. Her East Wing staff interviewed for this book noted that she was always present and visible inside the residence, working hard with her East Wing staff on projects (such as the continuing work with Clement Conger) and her voluminous correspondence until the literal last moments of her husband's presidency. The only "reclusiveness" was her unwillingness toward the end to speak to a hostile press about Watergate (including Bob Woodward, who did ask for an interview with the First Lady; Pat declined).

It is notable that out of the many subjects interviewed for this book, not a *single* source among the East Wing staff, West Wing staff, friends, family, or other outsiders, saw any behavior that would lead them to believe that the First Lady had a drinking problem. Lucy Winchester, who was with Pat from dusk until dawn every day during her time as First Lady, recalled many days where she would call the First Lady at 7:30 a.m. and say, "'May I come up and see you?' Mrs. Nixon would say, 'I haven't even got my face on yet but yes, come on up!' . . . She was always ready. You cannot cover up being hung over or an alcohol problem. It's not possible."

Steve Bull was with the president and First Lady daily for years. In the White House he described his role this way: "I was almost like an invisible person." He was there 24/7 and also in the residence. "I saw them in private settings often. . . . I never saw any indication of alcohol abuse." Helen Smith was one of the few White House staffers who had agreed to talk to Woodward. In July 1976, just a few months after the release of *The Final Days*, she categorically denied the "heavy drinking" stories in the book regarding her former boss:

> I do know that liquor was never a problem to the First Lady—before or during or after the Watergate crisis. Of course, she had a highball on occasion, just as she smoked off duty (she is no prude), but we who also worked with her daily never saw a sign of dissipation in her face—even in the morning before she had time to put on her makeup. There was never the slightest thickness in her speech; never the smell of liquor on her breath . . . she is too strong and self-reliant to resort to any kind of crutch.

Alexander Butterfield, who worked closely with Pat as the West Wing's liaison with the East Wing, was concerned when he heard the Woodward-Bernstein claim about her heavy drinking. "Absolutely not true. And the same thing about the President . . . RN couldn't handle more than one drink."

In 1976, after *The Final Days* was published, both of the Nixons' sons-in-law denied "having held views or made statements attributed to them" in the book. Both Eisenhower and Cox went on record saying that Woodward and Bernstein used "distorted facts, rumors and untruths . . . without giving them a chance to set the record straight."

In 2023, both Eisenhower and Cox maintained their positions regarding *The Final Days* account. Cox flatly denied ever talking to either Woodward or Bernstein. "His henchman called me, and I told him I wasn't going to interview, and he threatened me." Cox also revealed that the famous passage in *The Final Days* that described an alcohol-fueled, potentially suicidal president talking to presidential portraits on the walls of the White House was wrongly attributed to him.

Instead, Cox related, Senator Robert Griffin of Michigan (the second-ranking Republican in the Senate) called *him* and "spun a story about President Nixon looking at pictures, and I denied it completely . . . he then ascribed to me what he said and not what I said to him. He in fact wanted to undermine the president of the United States so that his man, Ford, could get the presidency." Cox stated he never had any of those conversations with the authors of *The Final Days*.

Cox, like Eisenhower, had a close relationship with Pat. "She was just a wonderful mother-in-law. . . . We always just had a terrific relationship in a very warm sense. She made me feel that I was a member of the family right from the start. . . . She's always been the person who holds the family together, quietly in the background." Cox also denied claims in *The Final Days* that his mother-in-law was drinking heavily to cope. "That's ridiculous. I've known her since 1963 and I never saw her as a heavy drinker at all. At *all*."

Eisenhower contributed: "There are a lot of 'imaginings' in the Nixon world. . . . One of the prevalent things in the media . . . the family was some sort of cabal to keep Nixon in power. It was absolutely not the case. I would say that Mrs. Nixon repairing to her room and drinking would be the same sort of thing. In other words, you have a staff person imagining that the family must be doing that, and Mrs. Nixon must be doing this."

Compounding the injury to Pat's character and reputation, on May 8, 1976, *Saturday Night Live* featured a sketch, also called "The Final Days," that used the book as the basis for its portrayal of the former First Lady as an alcoholic mess, speaking next to a half-drained bottle of gin and slurring her words. Written by comedian (and later humiliated Minnesota senator) Al Franken, the sketch also portrayed the former president as drunk and mentally unfit.

Finally, many Americans seem to conflate First Ladies Betty Ford and Pat Nixon. Ford courageously acknowledged her dependence on prescription drugs and alcohol, later conquering her addictions and founding the Betty Ford Center in Rancho Mirage, California, in 1982. Due to their First Lady terms running together and the fact that Betty and Pat were old friends, the confusion/conflation of the two women here is not surprising.

In sum, the perfect storm of questionable journalism, mean-spirited satire, and conflation of the two First Ladies has contributed to a portrait of Pat that has little basis in fact. Much like "Plastic Pat," this version of the former First Lady as an alcoholic recluse was based on media "imaginings" with no on-the-record eyewitnesses or conversations from family members that can be verified as accurate. Woodward and Bernstein's claims regarding Pat fly in the face of much conflicting evidence. The only remark Woodward would allow to be published in this book? "I always had a lot of sympathy for Pat Nixon. You may quote me on that."

———

In Julie's recollection, Pat read portions of *The Final Days* the morning of July 7, 1976; "despite my father's protests, she had finally borrowed from one of the secretaries in his office." In addition, that morning Dick had shared the upsetting news that the next day he would be disbarred in New York State. Julie and David were staying with the Nixons, and Julie noticed unusual behavior from her mother that evening.

The next morning, Dick became concerned. A Camp Pendleton base doctor examined Pat and determined she had suffered a small stroke. At her husband's insistence and despite Pat's protests, she was taken to Memorial

Hospital Medical Center in Long Beach by ambulance. Her left side became paralyzed during the ride to the hospital, and doctors there diagnosed her with a hemorrhage of the right cerebral cortex.

Fortunately, the stroke had been caught and dealt with immediately, and after several weeks of medication and physical therapy she was discharged from the hospital. A frail-looking but outwardly cheerful patient was shown on the television news being wheeled out by her husband, accompanied by her daughters. Pat was wearing a yellow pantsuit, smiling, and waving to onlookers. But the following weeks at home were exhausting as Pat struggled to regain her physical capacity. During Pat's grueling recovery, her husband watched over her and cheered her on. Now he was the one encouraging her. As Tricia recalled: "Family members, especially my father, were her partners in her recovery—working with her on her physical therapy and always praising and encouraging her efforts."

Maureen Nunn related how her mother, Helene Drown, "visited Pat many times and they cheered each other up—walking on the beach; swimming; listening to music; playing darts . . . Pat became really good and beat my mom! The sound of laughter permeated their visits—I remember this as I went with my mom on many occasions." Nunn also emphasized: "She was a fighter and had tremendous self-will to 'never give up.'"

Through hard work and steely determination, Pat regained the full use of her left side with only a slight limp remaining. Though she stayed close to home, she enjoyed her tight circle of friends, her shopping and dining trips into town, and having her husband to herself. Historian Jonathan Aitken, who knew both Nixons, wrote of this time: "The scary intimations of mortality which they had both passed through bonded husband and wife together in a closer relationship than had existed since the early days of their marriage. They spent more time together; communicated better; and became more closely attuned to one another's emotions."

The president became even more protective of his wife, telling Bill Gulley, still acting director of the White House military office, that he blamed Woodward and Bernstein for her stroke. Especially hurtful were their "speculations in it about her drinking and their relationship. He said, 'I don't care what the bastards say about me. But Mrs. Nixon never did anything to anybody, and she doesn't deserve to be treated—to have speculations like that about her.'"

In late 1978, Pat reluctantly consented to have her portrait painted by Henriette Wyeth Hurd, the oldest daughter of painter N. C. Wyeth and sister of the Nixons' favorite painter, Andrew Wyeth. The former First Lady looks beautiful in the portrait, wearing an aquamarine chiffon evening gown and her favorite piece of jewelry: a three-strand choker of pearls with a platinum and diamond rose-shaped pin that she and Dick designed together. Still, the portrait failed to capture Pat's animated, laughing spirit. When complaints about the work reached Hurd, she refused to change Pat's expression, saying her subject had "a very sensitive mouth that to me looks sweet and strong but also rather hurt." The artist (like so many reporters before her) was not able to access the real Pat Nixon. Her depiction in oil only served to reinforce old stereotypes.

Yet some of Pat's greatest joy was still to come. The Nixons' first grandchild, Jennie Elizabeth Eisenhower, was born in 1978, followed by Christopher Nixon Cox in 1979, Alexander Richard Eisenhower in 1980, and Melanie Catherine Eisenhower in 1984. As Pat told her friend Adele Rogers when Christopher was born, "This is what life's all about, children and grandchildren, isn't it, Adele?" She said it not once but twice. Dick also adored being a grandparent, showing off the grandchildren at every opportunity. The grandchildren affectionately called their grandparents "Ma" and "Ba."

In 1980, the Nixons moved back east to be closer to their daughters and their young families. Julie and David lived in Berwyn, Pennsylvania, and Tricia and Ed resided in New York City. Pat had loved living in New York City in the 1960s: that period out of politics was perhaps the happiest time in her married life. It was no surprise that the Nixons again selected New York as their home base, settling upon a townhouse on 65th Street just blocks away from the Coxes.

However, the New York sojourn did not last long. The Nixons were too often recognized in the city, and Pat had trouble with the steep stairs in the townhome and the city noise. In the fall of 1981, they moved to Saddle River, New Jersey, to a contemporary home with acreage for the grandchildren to play. The home had both a tennis court and a black marble swimming pool—the perfect playground for the grandchildren.

In 1983, Pat had a second, smaller stroke, followed by a series of hospital stays for bronchitis, pneumonia, and other pulmonary infections. She also suffered from emphysema. Pat tired easily and needed to take naps and rest for much of the day. Still, she spent as much time as possible with her daughters and their children, continuing to display flashes of her dry sense of humor. Betsy Reimer, who helped Julie with her children in the early 1980s, when Pat still had her Secret Service detail, remembered Pat asking her to explain to the children about her First Lady past, quipping, "They must wonder why I am running around with all these handsome men in dark suits!" Pat Nixon gave up her Secret Service protection in 1984 with Dick giving up his detail a year after in 1985, all in the interests of saving American taxpayers money.

In the spring of 1985, Pat and her daughters held a reunion luncheon for women on Pat's East Wing staff. The group included Connie Stuart, Penny Adams, Patti Matson, Cindy Vanden Heuvel, Gwen King, Lucy Winchester Breathitt, Coral Schmid, Helen McCain Smith, Julie Robinson, and Susan Porter Rose. Penny Adams reflected: "After lunch President Nixon served us Mimosas and told us stories about Churchill and Brezhnev."

The year 1990 proved to be a banner year for the Nixons. It was their golden anniversary year, Dick had a bestseller, *In the Arena*, and the Nixon Presidential Library was dedicated. On July 19, Pat and Dick attended the dedication ceremonies and events in Yorba Linda, Dick's birthplace. Pat arrived wearing a pale green suit and leaning on her husband's supportive arm. Later that day, Dick was honored by three other living presidents: Ronald Reagan, George Bush, and Gerald Ford. "All three praised former First Lady Pat Nixon, with Reagan calling her a 'true unsung hero of the Nixon administration.'" Barbara Bush, Nancy Reagan, and Betty Ford all attended with their husbands in a show of First Lady support. A crowd of fifty thousand surrounded the library, and three thousand invited guests attended the dedication.

Perhaps the strangest sighting of the day was the encounter between old enemies Rose Mary Woods and Bob Haldeman. Aitken, who attended the dedication, observed Rose in a forgiving mood. "Resplendent in a green silk dress, she was meeting and greeting like a Hollywood hostess, even giving her old adversary Bob Haldeman a warm embrace, after he whispered, 'I'm so sorry, Rose, and for so many things.'" Did Haldeman also try to make amends with the former First Lady that day? If so, there is no record of the exchange. However, according to Dwight Chapin, Haldeman did express remorse for his treatment of many old staffers, telling his former aide that he wished he had acted differently while in the White House.

The Nixons downsized to smaller quarters in 1990, moving to a Park Ridge luxury condominium just a few miles away. Monica Crowley, who worked for the former president as his foreign policy assistant starting in 1990, had ample opportunity to observe both Nixons in these smaller quarters. Crowley experienced the same warmth and concern from Pat that the East Wing staff had enjoyed. Crowley recalled: "Every once in a while, she would come to the office to make sure things were running well. She would always ask me, 'How is Dick treating you? If he's not treating you right, let me know and I'll straighten him out!' Always with a warm smile and often with a squeeze of my hand."

In terms of the Nixons' partnership, Crowley saw how solicitous the former president was of his wife's well-being. Crowley would notice "the little things he would do for her to keep her comfortable. He would make dinner for them when their housekeeper was gone. He would bring her treats and tea and make sure the pillows were propped up for her, check on her all the time. Little gestures that showed he was constantly thinking about her."

Pat's last public appearance was at the Ronald Reagan Presidential Library dedication in Simi Valley on November 4, 1991. Fragile and needing assistance to walk, Pat collapsed due to the heat. Over the next few months, her condition worsened, and by March she was in the hospital, her health declining rapidly.

In the spring of 1993, Pat received a diagnosis of terminal lung cancer. Her husband was distraught; he coped in the manner that helped him most: by setting his thoughts down on his yellow legal pad. Two pages of Dick's handwritten notes from May 8 show a husband fully conscious of his spouse's immense devotion. He detailed every phase of her personal life: childhood to adulthood, marriage to motherhood. Then he described how Pat was his political backbone, his best advisor, and his sounding board. During the 1952 campaign, he wrote, Pat "made the critical decision to urge RN not to give up." He also noted, "Eisenhower told RN, 'Pat is your biggest asset!'"

During the White House years, Dick wrote, among her greatest achievements were her coordination of the POW gala, her visit to Peru after the earthquake, her work on the White House restoration, and her "Evenings at the

White House," which included those who were everyday citizens, "not just the beautiful people." During Watergate, he declared, his wife was "heroic."

Postpresidency, Dick wrote, his wife had saved his life "when he was ready to give up." And that she never gave up on herself either when she had her own health issues.

He praised her as a mother and grandmother, referring to her as a model for their daughters, and noting that Pat's grandchildren "never thought of her as *old*." And, her husband wrote, she was "above all—always a lady. Pro-ERA, women's rights but never obnoxious, never made an ass of herself." Though she had been out of the public eye for the most part since 1974, "for a record 25 years [she had been] among the 16 most admired women in the world."

Now, toward the end of their tumultuous lives together, it seemed as if Dick had finally realized the truth of Jackie Kennedy's advice to him in late 1963: to "be consoled by what you already have—your life and family." While the presidency ultimately became "the tragedy of getting what you want and finding it to be a poison chalice," Dick's relationship with Pat and his daughters proved to be the "greatest prize," one that had been there with him all along, in both good times and bad.

The last two days of Pat's life, the family gathered around her in a tight protective circle at the Nixons' Park Ridge home. The beginning of the end for the former First Lady came on June 21, the Nixons' fifty-third anniversary. From her bed, she could see a gorgeous anniversary arrangement of lilies and orchids. When Julie arrived, Pat kept repeating, "Tell me about the children." Even now, she was still fighting, telling Julie, "I've just got to try to get well."

Pat's sense of humor remained intact. When Julie asked her that evening if she wanted her to tell her some stories, she quipped, "No, not unless they are risqué!" Soon the nurse told the family Pat was slipping into a coma. Tricia told her father to hurry from the den to see their mother. Dick talked to Pat tenderly about that day being their anniversary and bent over her to kiss her forehead. She said simply and clearly, "Thank you." Very early the next day, June 22, 1993, at 5:45 a.m., Pat died, surrounded by Dick, Tricia, and Julie.

Pat's funeral and memorial services took place at the Nixon Library on June 26. Three hundred guests attended the event. As the former president came into view of the attendees, "he broke down. In the audience, Rose Woods exclaimed, 'Oh dear.' Seated, Nixon began sobbing uncontrollably. His torso slumped and his shoulders heaved up and down as Billy Graham tried to comfort him." Later, Dick recovered and reminisced with friends about his beloved Pat. In the funeral program, Dick urged guests to "remember the beauty of the flowers, the superb music, the eloquence of the eulogies. But above all, when you think of Pat, I hope you will remember the sunshine of her smile. She would like that."

Pat's best friend, Helene Drown, died of lung cancer a little less than six months later, on November 21, 1993. She and Pat had spoken often on the phone during Pat's final months, but Helene was too ill to attend Pat's funeral. Her husband, Jack, and daughter Maureen attended the service in her stead.

Richard Milhous Nixon died of a stroke on April 22, 1994, just ten months after Pat's death. Both Julie and Tricia were with their father at the end. Dick's final book, *Beyond Peace*, was published posthumously. The dedication page reads:

For Patricia Ryan Nixon: Ambassador of Goodwill.

Pat and Dick are buried side by side in Yorba Linda at the Nixon Library near the rose garden and reflecting pools that Pat had admired in her later years. The inscription on her gravestone reads: "Even when people can't speak your language they can tell if you have love in your heart."

EPILOGUE: THE ROAD GOES ON . . .

Although Thelma Catherine "Pat" Ryan began her life in Ely, Nevada, on the eastern edge of what came to be known as the Loneliest Road in America, Pat Nixon was truly a woman of Southern California. It is only fitting to end this biographical road trip through her life in the place she considered to be her hometown: Artesia. (Parts of the area Pat Nixon knew as Artesia, including the site of her old home, are now known as Cerritos, California.)

Thursday, March 16, 2023, was Pat Nixon's 111th birthday. It was a bright, sunny morning in Southern California, and the day that First Lady Pat Nixon Memorial Highway was officially dedicated at Pat Nixon Park in Cerritos. The park is built on the site where Pat's childhood home once stood and features a life-sized bronze statue of Pat surrounded by a rose garden. The bricks in the memorial garden were sourced from Pat's old home. An arched canopy of intertwined balloons in yellow, white, and green punctuated the memorial space that day, contributing to the celebratory mood.

California State Senator Bob J. Archuleta (D-Pico Rivera) was the primary sponsor of Senate Concurrent Resolution No. 68, which designated a 2.5-mile portion of the 91 Freeway through Cerritos as First Lady Pat Nixon Memorial Highway. Archuleta was elected in 2018 to represent the 32nd Senate District, which includes swaths of southeastern Los Angeles County and Orange County, including Cerritos.

With Archuleta leading the way, Resolution 68 was approved in 2022 by the California State Legislature. The legislation passed with bipartisan support in both the California State Senate and State Assembly. Seventy-nine members of the Assembly and thirty-six members of the State Senate voted in the affirmative for the resolution: there were no dissenting votes in either legislative chamber.

One might ask: why, in this era of extreme political division and separation, did Archuleta, a Democrat, sponsor this resolution for a Republican First Lady? He explained: "For her service, her role to the state, to the nation, and to men and women everywhere regardless of party. This is a woman, an American, who has given so much to open doors for women."

Archuleta pointed to Pat's Western frontier upbringing as the key to her legacy: "I think at that time she was growing up, it was 'the strong will survive' attitude . . . she had a strong-willed personality, a lot of courage. . . . As Second Lady of our nation and the First Lady, she had to stand up and say things that perhaps weren't as popular as they were, as they should be, but stand up for women to appoint a Supreme Court judge, get more women in public office."

Archuleta emphasized: "We're also proud of her contributions as a Second Lady and First Lady promoting volunteerism, diplomacy, and as an educator. Those are timeless issues to acknowledge her role in history—that is so important. . . . There are a lot of Pat Nixons across this country right now who are giving to children, to education, for the betterment of our freedom and our states. In our state of California, we're very proud of her. . . . Women are now taking a leadership role, and I think now we can turn the clock back and say thanks for Pat Nixon—thank you for opening up those doors."

———

Today in hindsight we can see the sum of Pat Nixon's achievements. She was America's first modern First Lady: a bridge between women of the old school, like Mamie, Jackie, and Lady Bird, and First Ladies of a new, more visible mold, like Betty Ford and Rosalynn Carter. Only now, many years after her death, can we truly understand how she moved the needle toward women's rights in a subtle but profound way. Pat wasn't loud and forceful, and she was not a "feminist" in the second-wave sense. But she was inherently pro-women in her outlook due to her Western upbringing. She believed a qualified woman of any race could do anything, *be* anything, including a Supreme Court justice or the president of the United States.

Behind the scenes, she was quietly effective. She set the stage for many more achievements for women both in government and in the private sector with her support and her own example. She refused to be put into a box or to be shaped by the image-makers. She knew exactly who she was and remained true to herself despite public and private pressures. She showed Americans that women could balance marriage and motherhood with public roles, be those positions paid or volunteer. Despite the many outstanding achievements in her public life, however, she always considered her two daughters, Tricia and Julie, to be her most important legacy.

At the Pat Nixon Highway dedication ceremony, Jim Byron, president and CEO of the Nixon Foundation, recalled Pat's sense of adventure, evident from an early age: "She was independent. For example, one of her earliest adventures was at age 20, driving a couple from the East Coast, who spent the winter in California, back to their home in Connecticut. She made the 3,000-mile trek across the country in the couple's 1930 Packard. This was in the days before the interstate highway system, when traversing the vastness of the American continent was no easy task."

Pat's daughter Tricia's remarks that day also noted her mother's love of exploration and underscored her attachment to her California hometown. "My mother loved to drive along the highways and byways of California, discovering new places to see and enjoy. And throughout her life, when her travels took her and my father to the far corners of the earth, she never forgot her roots here in Cerritos."

As Pat used to remind herself before she met with presidents and potentates, kings and queens: "You are just Pat Nixon from Artesia."

In her heart and mind, she was always just the California girl next door.

ACKNOWLEDGMENTS

In May of 2019, I was at the Richard Nixon Presidential Library and Museum (RNPLM) giving a talk with and about the amazing POW and MIA wives in my newly published narrative nonfiction book *The League of Wives*. After the talk, I received a signed copy of Julie Nixon Eisenhower's excellent 1986 biography of her mother, *Pat Nixon: The Untold Story*. That night as I read the first few chapters, I was hooked. I had never considered doing a First Lady biography, but Pat Nixon was so intriguing, and she had not had a new commercial biography since Julie's book in 1986. I decided to pursue her story from an outside perspective and to try to unravel the enigma the American press declared Pat Nixon to be.

I soon found myself back at the Nixon Library, and I would spend weeks there over the next few years, researching within their collections and working with both Nixon Foundation and National Archives staff. However, a major obstacle hit soon after I began my work. COVID would shut things down on-site at the RNPLM for long periods, but the staff would continue to work with me remotely until things finally opened back up.

Thus, my very first thank-you goes to Nixon Foundation president and CEO Jim Byron for his unwavering support of this project and his invaluable help connecting me with so many former Nixon staff, friends, and family who formed the core interviews for the book. All my gratitude goes out to Jason Schwartz, the Foundation's director of research and exhibitions and the Jedi master of the Nixon Foundation archive. His guidance, help, and support were far beyond the call of duty. Foundation research associate Gianluca Allesina was also helpful.

Other Nixon Foundation staff who deserve grateful thanks: Brenda St. Hilaire, Joe Lopez, Chris Nordyke, and Jamison Phelts. Additional thanks to former Nixon Foundation staffers Jonathan Movroydis and Janine Eggers. I am especially grateful to Janine for her wonderful help arranging difficult-to-get interviews. Thanks also to the RNPLM's outstanding supervisory museum curator Christine Mickey for her help with Pat Nixon–related artifacts and exhibits, and to AV specialist Ryan Pettigrew for his help locating NARA photos for the book. Thanks also to Meghan Lee-Parker, Dorissa Martinez, and Greg Cumming for their assistance.

Early in the writing process, I had the great good fortune to meet Nixon historian Bob Bostock. Bob is the bestselling coauthor with Christine Todd Whitman of *It's My Party Too* and a well-regarded political speechwriter. He was the best advisor and sounding board I could have possibly had for my work on Mrs. Nixon. His superb 2012 Pat Nixon Centennial Exhibit was the perfect orientation to her story.

The other guiding light I met early on was Maureen Drown Nunn. Maureen is the daughter of Helene Colesie Drown, Mrs. Nixon's best friend from their early days of teaching at Whittier High School together. Maureen wisely saved and donated the valuable correspondence between Helene and Pat to the Nixon Foundation. Her warm and steadfast support for my work from day one has meant the world to me.

I also welcomed the insights and commentary of historians Luke Nichter and Irwin "Irv" Gellman for this book. Both Luke and Irv went over and above in their efforts to help facilitate my work. Luke generously provided me with additional expert research assistance. Irv connected me with many potential interviewees and made key introductions to some of the archives I would need to access for the project. Many thanks are also due to historian Paul Carter, whose superb new book *Richard Nixon: California's Native Son* provided details I had not seen elsewhere about the early lives of both Pat Ryan and Richard Nixon.

Irv connected me to Whittier College's fly-fishing serials and electronic resources librarian Joe Dmohowski, whose deep knowledge of the Nixons and their time in Whittier proved invaluable. The Whittier College Oral Histories he shared with me provided essential glimpses of Mrs. Nixon as a spirited young teacher in that once-small Quaker town. He also was able to provide copies of the fabulous Alice Martin Rosenberger Collection at the Whittier Public Library. His Whittier College colleague and special collections librarian Paige Harris was a great help with photos for the book as well.

Natalie Garcia, the archivist at the Lawrence de Graaf Center for Oral and Public History at California State University–Fullerton, was also a delight. Natalie made working on the CSU Fullerton oral histories easily accessible. These oral histories, like the ones at Whittier, are an absolute gold mine for anyone studying the Nixons.

Jean Cannon and Samira Bozorgi are two other archivists at the top of my thank-you list. Jean is the curator for North American Collections and research fellow at the Hoover Institution Library & Archives (HILA) at Stanford University. When we first met in 2018, we immediately hit it off with our shared sense of humor and Southern background. Every trip to Palo Alto to work in the Hoover collections is an adventure, thanks to fabulous Jean and her talented and delightful colleague Samira Bozorgi, HILA's senior manager for engagement and outreach.

Thanks are also due to many other wonderful archivists I had the privilege to work with across the country: Anne Rowe at Sunnylands, the Annenberg Estate; Mya Burdick at the White Pine Public Museum; Linda Smith and Mary Bartzloff at the Eisenhower Presidential Library and Museum; Elizabeth Druga and John O'Connell at the Gerald R. Ford Presidential Library and Museum; Lynn Smith at the Herbert Hoover Presidential Library-Museum; and Carl Childs and Sarah Nerney at the Colonial Williamsburg Archives.

My visits to Colonial Williamsburg to research in the CW Archives were facilitated by a former East Wing staffer, Joni Stevens. Joni is one of the most capable and connected people I have ever met. Joni was central to engaging with the other star "East Wingers," Pat Nixon's loyal White House staffers: Pat Howard, Susie Dolibois, Debby Sloan, and Penny Adams. These ladies—plus East Wingers I met separately: Patti Matson, Susan Porter Rose, Cindy Tague, Martha Doss, and Kathleen McCann—were able to give me the bird's-eye view of Mrs. Nixon's smooth and professional operation within the White House.

Martha Doss sadly passed away during the writing of this book, but the personal diaries she sent me of her time in the White House were incredibly useful. She was so generous with her time and her memories. Chris Alberts Holliday, one of the first female White House military social aides (thanks to Pat Nixon), also gave me meaningful observations about the First Lady from her point of view.

I was fortunate enough to enjoy several in-person visits in Lexington, Kentucky, with Lucy Winchester Breathitt, Mrs. Nixon's social secretary. Lucy has a wicked sense of humor that I know Mrs. Nixon admired and appreciated. The female point of view of the White House years that Lucy and the East Wingers provided was key to this narrative, helping me place Mrs. Nixon back in the center of events instead of pushing her to the side as most histories of the era tend to do. I was proud beyond belief to be named an "Honorary East Winger" by Lucy, Penny, Susie, Pat, Debby, and Joni. My framed Certificate of Honorary Appointment now proudly hangs in my office.

Joni also introduced me to Al Louer, the now-retired director of principal gifts at Colonial Williamsburg, who worked on the White House Renovation and Acquisition project instituted by Mrs. Nixon. Al connected me to many others who had worked on this project, including renowned architect Norman Askins. Norman also gave me fabulous inside commentary on his work inside the White House. These contacts also led to important conversations with former White House curators Betty Monkman and Bill Allman, who both confirmed Pat Nixon's significant and often overlooked role in restoring the White House.

I also interviewed many former staffers from the Nixon West Wing for this book. The West Winger whose courageous and tireless work became most important in the context of Mrs. Nixon's life story was the Honorable Barbara Hackman Franklin, who later became the twenty-ninth U.S. secretary of commerce. Barbara's groundbreaking work during her time with the Nixon administration allowed women to advance in government jobs like never before. And that was just the beginning of her long career: she is a women's rights rock star. Thank you also to Barbara's staffers Melissa Coleman and Maureen Noonan for their wonderful assistance.

I am very grateful to Dwight Chapin for being willing to talk about his experiences working with the Nixons before, during, and after the presidency. His excellent book, *The President's Man,* is a must-read. Dwight always gave me his unfiltered and honest take on his time in the White House, yielding fascinating insights—not only into the psyche of the West Wing and his boss Bob Haldeman but also on the relationship between the president and Mrs. Nixon.

Another West Winger who could not have been more warm or gracious was Steve Bull. Steve was with the president 24–7 and also spent much time with Mrs. Nixon. He was able to verify facts and help me dismiss rumors. Steve was also key to the Vietnam POW section in this book as he helped coordinate the POW Gala of May 1973. I am so grateful for his strong recollections of that event and key events leading up to that day.

Dr. Henry Kissinger graciously made time to speak with me specifically about Mrs. Nixon in April of 2022. This was the second time I had the privilege of interviewing this brilliant diplomat. Our conversation regarding Mrs. Nixon yielded some fresh perspectives on her and on the Nixon West Wing that were illuminating. I was lucky to be able to speak to him again for this book before his passing at age one hundred in November of 2023.

A special mention goes out to the kind and thoughtful Bill Hudson, who served as head of Mrs. Nixon's Secret Service detail. His commentary regarding Mrs. Nixon's many trips abroad—especially her trips to China and Russia in 1972—and his eyewitness accounts of the First Lady's professionalism and hard work were invaluable to her portrait.

Other West Wingers who gave me wonderful interviews and research suggestions were Jack Carley, John Ray Price, Don Hughes, Jack Brennan, Alexander Butterfield, Larry Higby, Ken Khachigian, Bobbie Kilberg, Mike Schrauth, and Ron Walker. Thank you all for being so generous with your time and remembrances of Mrs. Nixon.

From the press side, thanks to the fabulous Judith Martin for a particularly memorable interview. Thanks also to Sheila Weidenfeld and Kandie Stroud for their excellent observations regarding Mrs. Nixon. The personal papers of star reporter Louise Hutchinson, loaned to me by her friend Maureen Molloy Morrow, were also an excellent resource for Mrs. Nixon's foreign trips. I owe many thanks to Nancy Rodrigues for connecting me to Maureen.

Other meaningful interviews took place over the course of the research with Linda Hobgood, Jan Ehrlichman, Cassie Price, Rick Perlstein, H. R.

McMaster, Betsy Reimer, Joann Haldeman, Mike Fadden, Monica Crowley, and Linda Detrick. Each of these conversations helped me add compelling details to the story.

With the Nixon Foundation's help, I was able to connect with Anita Mc-Bride, First Lady Laura Bush's chief of staff. Anita is one of the founders of the First Ladies Association for Research and Education (FLARE), established only recently to further scholarly work and awareness of our First Ladies. I am grateful to Anita for her thoughtful commentary regarding both the East and West Wings as well as Mrs. Nixon and how she projected herself as First Lady.

Additional thank-yous are due to FLARE's vice president Nancy Kegan Smith, and to Dr. Diana Carlin, FLARE's treasurer, for their expert assistance during my research phase and their strong support of the book going forward. Thank you also to fellow First Lady biographer and FLARE member Rebecca Roberts, whose superb biography of First Lady Edith Wilson was the perfect inspirational/aspirational reading for me during the writing of my own First Lady bio!

Many thanks to two outstanding researchers who helped me with additional research for this book: Luis Blandon in the D.C. area and Kristina Agopian in the Los Angeles area. The supplementary assistance both Luis and Kristina provided was superb, and I highly recommend them both to other biographers.

The two interviews I had with Pat's son-in-law David Eisenhower were among the most substantial and consequential ones in the book. David kindly spent hours with me discussing the relationship between the Nixons and his grandparents, Dwight and Mamie Eisenhower, as well as his personal relationship with his in-laws and his observations about Mrs. Nixon during both presidential administrations. Edward "Ed" Cox was also most gracious in his discussion with me about his mother-in-law and his recollections of important events during and after both presidential administrations.

Ed connected me to John Rogers Jr., whose mother, Jewel Stradford Rogers Lafontant-Mankarious, played an important role in the second Nixon administration. As my research revealed (and John already knew), his mother's importance extended to the history of women considered for Supreme Court positions as well. John gave me a compelling interview about his mother and provided a wonderful photo of her for the book.

Many thanks are due to California State senator Bob J. Archuleta (D-Pico Rivera). Archuleta was the primary sponsor of Senate Concurrent Resolution No. 68, which designated a 2.5-mile portion of the 91 Freeway through Cerritos as the "First Lady Pat Nixon Memorial Highway." I had an incredible interview with the senator in 2022 that provided me with the perfect ending to the book. Many thanks to the senator for his vision regarding the Pat Nixon Highway, and to his staffers, Cheryl McLachlan and Fred Zermeno, for facilitating my interview with him.

Finally, I could not have done Mrs. Nixon justice without the support and insights of her two amazing daughters, Tricia Nixon Cox and Julie Nixon Eisenhower. Both women were wonderful resources and, of course, experts on their mother's life and times. They connected me to Nixon friends and former staff and shared detailed, highly personal memories of their parents and the family's life together. I know from my own research that Mrs. Nixon considered her girls to be her greatest treasure and her most important legacy. Thank you both for putting up with years of my questions and allowing me access to new papers, letters, and information about your mother. The trust and confidence you placed in me was deeply appreciated.

Thanks to my agent, Katherine Flynn at Kneerim & Williams, for facilitating my second book with St. Martin's Press. A million thanks to my talented editor, Michael Flamini, for his patience, judicious editing, and savvy advice regarding all aspects of this book. Michael is a longtime Pat Nixon admirer, and he believed in the power of her story from day one. Claire Cheek, my wonderful assistant editor, was always cheerful (even under tight deadlines) and willing to answer any question.

Thanks to Jonathan Bush for his inspired cover design, and to Laurie Henderson, production editor for the title. Many thanks also to Michelle Cashman and Jessica Zimmerman in the marketing and PR departments, respectively. I am also grateful for the years of support and advice from my good friend film producer Michael Kelleher, cofounder of the Australian International Screen Foundation. His input helped me to create a much more cinematic story. Additional thanks to my friend filmmaker Steve Mason and his company Red Velocity for working with me on *The Mysterious Mrs. Nixon*'s book trailer. Many thanks to the talented Valerie Hanley for her superb help with the endnotes.

I will end with thanks to my family: my husband Chris, daughter Anne Alston, son James, my mother Anne Hardage, and my sister Morgan Engel, for listening to and encouraging me as I worked on this book over the past four years. Thanks also to all my Biographers International colleagues for your help and support, especially my dear friend Diane Kiesel, and to my Women's Lives BIO group friends for all their encouragement and suggestions. Special thanks to Dolly Parton, my French bulldog and constant writing companion. She is completely unbiased, yet somehow she always finds everything I write to be brilliant.

SELECTED BIBLIOGRAPHY

ABBREVIATIONS

AMR: Alice Martin Rosenberger, Collection of Sixty Interviews for Pat Ryan Nixon at Whitter Public Library.

CCOH: Columbia Center for Oral History, Columbia University.

CSUF: Center for Oral and Public History, California State University, Fullerton.

CWA: Colonial Williamsburg Archives.

HILA: Hoover Institution Library and Archives.

HJDC: Helene and Jack Drown Collection, Richard Nixon Presidential Library and Museum.

HRCWC: Watergate Collection, Harry Ransom Center, University of Texas at Austin.

JNEC: Julie Nixon Eisenhower Collection. Courtesy of Julie Nixon Eisenhower.

LOC: Library of Congress.

NARA: National Archives and Records Administration.

NDA: Notre Dame Archives.

PPS: Pre-Presidential Series, Richard Nixon Presidential Library and Museum.

PRNC: Patricia Ryan Nixon Collection, Richard Nixon Presidential Library and Museum.

RNPLM: Richard Nixon Presidential Library and Museum.

SA: Sunnylands Archives.

SMOF: Staff Member's Office Files.

WHARC: Whittier College Alice Rosenberger Collection.

WCOH: Whittier College Oral Histories.

WHCF: White House Central Files.

WHSF: White House Special Files.

ARCHIVES AND SPECIAL COLLECTIONS

National Archives and Records Administration (NARA)

Bull, Steven. Oral history interview. June 25, 2007. NARA.
King, Gwen. Oral history interview. 1988. NARA.
Stuart, Connie. Oral history interview. August 15, 1988. NARA.

Postpresidential Materials

Nixon, Richard. Oral history, May 4, 1975.
Nixon, Richard. Oral history, May 6, 1975.
Funeral program, Pat Nixon, June 26, 1993.

Richard Nixon Foundation

Hughes, General James "Don," USAF, Ret. Oral history. November 10, 2018.
Klein, Herb. Oral history. February 20, 2007.

Helene and Jack Drown Collection (HJDC), RNPLM

White House Central Files (WHCF), RNPLM

Armstrong, Anne.
Franklin, Barbara Hackman.
King, Gwendolyn B.
Winchester, Lucy.

White House Special Files (WHSF), RNPLM

Chapin, Dwight L.
Ehrlichman, John D.
Haldeman, Harry Robbins (H. R.)

Center for Oral and Public History, CSU Fullerton (CSUF)

Patricia Ryan Nixon Oral History Project
Brennan, Jack. Oral history. Interview by Brenda St. Hilaire. January 9, 2020. OH
#5605.

Richard M. Nixon Project

Ball, Kenneth. Interview by John Donnelly. January 16, 1970. OH #804.

Behrens, Hortense. Interview by Mary Suzanne Simon. May 27, 1970. OH #0811.

Borden, Myrtle Raine. Interview by Sharone Hencey. April 21, 1970. OH #813.

Cloes, Elizabeth. Interview by Mary Suzanne Simon. May 29, 1970. OH #834.

Garman, Grant M. Interview by Mary Suzanne Simon. June 1, 1970. OH #859.

Gwinn, Louis Raine. Interview by Sharone Hencey. June 3, 1970. OH #870.

Holloway, Heber. Interview by Greg Brolin. January 7, 1971. OH #878.

Holmes, Blanche Potter. Interview by Sharone Hencey. June 12, 1970. OH #879.

Montgomery, Vivian Cox. Interview by Steve Guttman. July 3, 1970. OH #913.

Morehouse, Morton. Interview by Nancy Hunsaker. May 28, 1970. OH #914.

Myers, Dr. Mabel. Interview by Mitch Haddad. May 12, 1971. OH #910.

Roach, Nellamena. Interview by Nancy Hunsaker. April 30, 1970. OH #993.

Studebaker, Phil, and Geri Studebaker. Interview by Mary Suzanne Simon. May 11, 1970. OH #960.

Waldrip, Lura Applebury. Interview by Nancy Hunsaker. June 11, 1970. OH #975.

Wray, Marcia Elliott. Interview by Nancy Hunsaker. June 10, 1970. OH #988.

Whittier College Oral Histories (WCOH)

Ball, Kenneth L. Interview by Dr. C. Richard Arena, second interview. October 20, 1971.

Bender, Matthew G. Interview by Dr. C. Richard Arena. October 9, 1972.

Counts, Curtis. Interview by Dr. C. Richard Arena. May 16, 1972.

Counts, Virginia. Interview by Evlyn Dorn, September 10, 1972.

Drown, Jack A. Interview by Dr. C. Richard Arena. August 17, 1972.

Dorn, Evlyn. Interview by Dr. C. Richard Arena. May 8, 1972.

Dorn, Evlyn. Interview by Dr. C. Richard Arena. March 16, 1973.

Day, Roy O. Interview by Dr. C. Richard Arena. November 22, 1971.

Garrett, Ruth, and Waymeth B. Garrett. Interview by Dr. C. Richard Arena. January 20, 1972.

Holt, Edith. Interview by Dr. C. Richard Arena. May 10, 1971.

Kenworthy, Betty Jean. Interview by Dr. C. Richard Arena. October 3, 1972.

King, Gretchen, and Robert L. King. Interview by Dr. C. Richard Arena, March 25, 1973.

Koch, Alyce G. Interview by Dr. C. Richard Arena, March 20, 1972.

Koch, Dr. Eugene. Interview by Dr. C. Richard Arena. May 12, 1972.

Seulke, Thomas T. Interview by Dr. C. Richard Arena. October 19, 1971.

Theriault, Margaret O'Grady. Interview by Dr. C. Richard Arena. September 27, 1972.

West, Miss Jessamyn (Mrs. H. M. McPherson). Interview by Dr. C. Richard Arena. December 5, 1971.

West, Miss Jessamyn (Mrs. H. M. McPherson). Interview by Dr. C. Richard Arena. June 30, 1971.

WATERGATE COLLECTION, HARRY RANSOM CENTER, UNIVERSITY OF TEXAS AT AUSTIN (HRCWC)

Bob Woodward and Carl Bernstein Watergate Papers.

ALICE MARTIN ROSENBERGER COLLECTION OF SIXTY INTERVIEWS FOR PAT RYAN NIXON, WHITTIER PUBLIC LIBRARY (AMR)

Bewley, Kathyrn.
Blake, Robert O.
Daniels, Helen.
Ellis, Geraldine (Gerry) Anderson.
Fantz, Donald.
Gordon, Carol Collins.
Stouffer, Mildred Eason.

NOTRE DAME ARCHIVES (NDA)

Father John F. Cronin audio oral history, 1976.

HOOVER INSTITUTION LIBRARY AND ARCHIVES (HILA)

John D. Ehrlichman Papers.
Allen Weinstein Papers.

COLUMBIA CENTER FOR ORAL HISTORY, COLUMBIA UNIVERSITY (CCOH)

Finch, Robert H. Oral history interview. 1967.
Hollywood Film Industry Project
The Reminiscences of Adela Rogers St. Johns, June 23, 1971. #1422.

Penn State University Libraries

Eisenhower, Julie. Oral history for "A Few Good Women." March 9, 1999. Special
Collections, Penn State University.

Library of Congress (LOC)

Bess Furman Papers.

Colonial Williamsburg Archives (CWA)

Private Collections

Cox, Tricia Nixon.
Doss, Martha.
Eisenhower, Julie Nixon.
Holliday, Chris Alberts.
Howard, Pat.
Kelley, Kitty.
Morrow, Maureen Molloy.
Rogers, John, Jr.

Exhibitions

Life as a Gamble. Park City Museum, September 2021.
The Day Indeed Was Splendid: The Wedding of Tricia Nixon and Edward F. Cox.
Richard Nixon Presidential Library and Museum, June 2021.
The Final Campaign. Richard Nixon Presidential Library and Museum, 1990.
Pat Nixon Centennial Exhibition. Richard Nixon Presidential Library and Museum,
2012.

The Nixon Tapes (www.nixontapes.org)

Sunnylands Archives (SA)

Guest book entries.

White Pine Public Museum

Pat Nixon Scrapbook.

PRESIDENTIAL ARCHIVES

Dwight D. Eisenhower Presidential Library and Museum
Gerald R. Ford Presidential Library and Museum, Betty Ford Papers

UNPUBLISHED WORKS

Carley, Jack. Campaign diary, 1962.
Carter, Paul. *Richard Nixon: California's Native Son*, manuscript.
Dolibois, Susan. 1974 diary.
Haldeman, H. R. Unpublished diaries. RNPLM.
Howard, Pat. Handwritten notes from August 8, 1974.
Nunn, Maureen Drown. European diary, summer, 1963. RNPLM.

FILMS, VIDEOS, MOVIES

Barbara Walters interview with Pat Nixon, CBS, January 13, 1972. WHCA 4968.
"First Lady Pat Nixon Addresses GOP Convention, 1972." Nixon Foundation. YouTube, posted September 10, 2012.
King, Don Roy. "SNL Transcripts: Madeline Kahn: 05/08/76: Final Days." SNL Transcripts Tonight, January 3, 2019. https://snltranscripts.jt.org/75/75snixon.phtml.
The Martha Mitchell Effect. Netflix, 2022.
"Pat Nixon Memorial Service, Pete Wilson Eulogy." YouTube. Accessed April 5, 2023.
Pat Nixon and Barbara Walters interview, January 13, 1972, CBS. WHHA files, Nixon Library.
"President Nixon's Farewell to the White House Staff." Nixon Foundation. YouTube, posted January 16, 2012. https://www.youtube.com/watch?v=32GaowQnGRw.
"President Nixon's First Watergate Speech." April 30, 1973. C-SPAN. https://www.c-span.org/video/?299817-1%2Fpresident-nixons-watergate-speech.
"President Nixon's Resignation Speech." August 8, 1974. PBS. https://www.pbs.org/newshour/spc/character/links/nixon_speech.html.
Small Splendid Efforts: Pat Nixon on Voluntarism. DVD. January 6, 1993. National First Ladies Library.
"Tricia Nixon Rose Garden Wedding." Richard Nixon Foundation. YouTube. Accessed July 1, 2023.
"A Tribute to First Lady Pat Nixon." 1972 GOP convention film. Nixon Foundation. YouTube, posted August 1, 2010.

A Time for Celebration: Highlights from the First Lady's Trip to Africa 1972. DVD. National First Ladies Library.

"A Visit with the First Lady." Pat Nixon Interview with Virginia Sherwood, ABC, September 12, 1971. YouTube, posted by Nixon Foundation, https://www .youtube.com/watch?v=ABfQjJGNQ78.

AUTHOR INTERVIEWS

Adams, Penny. March 29, 2021.

Allman, Bill. August 19, 2020.

Archuleta, Senator Bob. December 13, 2022.

Askins, Norman. November 16, 2020.

Bostock, Bob. June 1, 2023, and July 18, 2023.

Brennan, Jack. July 13, 2023.

Bull, Steve. February 26, 2021, and August 3, 2021.

Butterfield, Alexander. December 8, 2022, and January 12, 2023.

Carley, Jack. June 25, 2020.

Chapin, Dwight. January 29, 2021; February 26, 2021; July 13, 2022; June 16, 2023.

Cox, Edward. August 29, 2023.

Crowley, Monica. April 30, 2021.

Dolibois, Susie. June 20, 2023.

Doss, Martha. April 8, 2021.

Eisenhower, David. March 6, 2023.

Fadden, Mike. August 13, 2021.

Franklin, Barbara Hackman. November 5, 2021.

Gellman, Irwin. December 28, 2022, March 25, 2023.

Haldeman, Joann. May 6, 2020.

Higby, Larry. March 23, 2021.

Hobgood, Linda. September 16, 2020.

Holliday, Chris. September 7, 2022.

Howard, Pat. May 20, 2021, and July 18, 2021.

Hudson, Bill. July 13, 2023; July 28, 2023; August 22, 2023.

Hughes, Colonel Don. February 5, 2021.

Khachigian, Ken. March 30, 2021.

Kilberg, Bobbie. April 11, 2022.

Kissinger, Dr. Henry. April 21, 2022.

Louer, Al. August 11, 2021.

Martin, Judith. April 1, 2022.

Matson, Patti. July 30, 2020, and October 28, 2022.

McBride, Anita. March 5, 2021.

McMaster, H. R. August 2, 2022.

Monkman, Betty. August 20, 2020.

Nunn, Maureen Drown. December 3, 2020, and December 19, 2020.

Perlstein, Rick. May 9, 2023.

Price, Cassie. August 28, 2021.

Price, John Ray. December 3, 2022.

Reimer, Betsy. May 14, 2020.

Rose, Susan Porter. October 20, 2020.

Schrauth, Mike. July 6, 2023.

Sloan, Debby. September 29, 2022, and June 13, 2023.

Stevens, Joni. March 29, 2021.

Stroud, Kandie. July 19, 2022.

Tague, Cindy. April 28, 2020, and October 28, 2022.

Walker, Ron. September 10, 2021.

Winchester Breathitt, Lucy. August 29, 2021; June 17, 2022; June 26, 2021; June 30, 2021; September 20, 2022; September 22, 2022; May 22, 2023.

Woodward, Bob. January 4, 2023.

BOOKS

1969: The Year in Review. New York: Time-Life Books, 1970.

Aitken, Jonathan. *Nixon: A Life.* Washington, DC: Regnery, 1993.

Ambrose, Stephen E. *Nixon: The Triumph of a Politician: 1962–1972.* New York: Simon & Schuster, 1989.

American Press Corps. *The President's Trip to China: A Pictorial Record of the Historic Journey to the People's Republic of China with Text by Members of the American Press Corps.* New York: Bantam, 1972.

Anthony, Carl Sferrazza. *Camera Girl: The Coming of Age of Jackie Bouvier Kennedy.* New York: Gallery Books, 2023.

Anthony, Carl Sferrazza. *First Ladies: The Saga of the Presidents' Wives and Their Power 1789–1961.* Volume 1. New York: William Morrow, 1990.

Anthony, Carl Sferrazza. *Why They Wore It: The Politics and Pop Culture of First Ladies' Fashion*. Yorba Linda, CA: Richard Nixon Foundation/Library/Museum, 2018.

Associated Press, ed. *The World in 1965; History as We Lived It . . .* New York: Associated Press, 1966.

Atkins, Robert. *Art Speak: A Guide to Contemporary Ideas, Movements, and Buzzwords, 1945 to the Present*. New York: Abbeville Press, 1997.

Bassett, Mark S., and J. Joan Bassett. *Nevada Northern Railway*. Charleston, SC: Arcadia, 2011.

Boller, Paul F. *Presidential Campaigns*. New York: Oxford University Press, 1996.

Boyer, Gene T., and Jackie Boor. *Inside the President's Helicopter*. Brule, WI: Cable, 2011.

Brennan, Mary C. *Pat Nixon: Embattled First Lady*. Lawrence: University Press of Kansas, 2011.

Brodie, Fawn McKay. *Richard Nixon: The Shaping of His Character*. New York: W. W. Norton, 1981.

Brower, Kate Andersen. *First Women: The Grace and Power of America's Modern First Ladies*. New York: Harper, 2016.

Bruce, Preston. *From the Door of the White House*. New York: Lothrop, Lee & Shepard, 1984.

Caroli, Betty Boyd. *First Ladies from Martha Washington to Michelle Obama*. New York: Oxford University Press, 2010.

Carter, Paul. *Richard Nixon: California's Native Son*. Lincoln, NE: Potomac Books, 2023.

Celant, Germano. *New York, 1962–1964, Exhibition Catalog, Jewish Museum of New York*. New York: Skira, 2022.

Chapin, Dwight. *The President's Man: The Memoirs of Nixon's Trusted Aide*. New York: William Morrow, 2023.

Collins, Gail. *America's Women: 400 Years of Dolls, Drudges, Helpmates, and Heroines*. New York: HarperCollins, 2009.

Committee on Commerce, U.S. Senate. *The Joint Appearances of Senator John F. Kennedy and Vice President Richard M. Nixon Presidential Campaign of 1960*. Washington, DC: U.S. Government Printing Office, 1961.

Cooper, Charles W. *Whittier: Independent College in California*. Los Angeles: Ward Ritchie Press, 1967.

Cordery, Stacy A. *Juliette Gordon Low: The Remarkable Founder of the Girl Scouts*. New York: Penguin Books, 2013.

David, Lester. *The Lonely Lady of San Clemente: The Story of Pat Nixon*. New York: Berkley, 1979.

Dobbs, Michael. *King Richard Nixon and Watergate—An American Tragedy*. New York: Knopf, 2021.

Edmondson, Madeleine, and Alden Duer Cohen. *The Women of Watergate*. New York: Pocket Books, 1976.

Ehrlichman, John. *Witness to Power: The Nixon Years*. New York: Simon & Schuster, 1982.

Eisenhower, Julie Nixon. *Pat Nixon—The Untold Story*. New York: Simon & Schuster, 1986.

Eisenhower, Julie Nixon. *Special People*. New York: Ballantine Books, 1978.

Ephron, Nora. *The Most of Nora Ephron*. New York: Alfred A. Knopf, 2013.

Farrell, John A. *Richard Nixon: The Life*. New York: Doubleday, 2017.

Friedan, Betty. *The Feminine Mystique*. New York: W. W. Norton, 1963.

Gage, Beverly. *G-Man J. Edgar Hoover and the Making of the American Century*. New York: Viking, 2022.

Gallagher, Winifred. *New Women in the Old West: From Settlers to Suffragists, an Untold American Story*. New York: Penguin Books, 2022.

Gellman, Irwin F. *Campaign of the Century: Kennedy, Nixon, and the Election of 1960*. New Haven, CT: Yale University Press, 2021.

Giorgione, Michael. *Inside Camp David: The Private World of the Presidential Retreat*. New York: Back Bay Books, 2020.

Gitlin, Todd. *The Sixties: Years of Hope, Days of Rage*. New York: Bantam Books, 1987.

Goldman, Sheldon. *Picking Federal Judges: Lower Court Selection from Roosevelt Through Reagan*. New Haven, CT: Yale University Press, 1999.

Gonzales, Donald. *The Rockefellers at Williamsburg: Backstage with the Founders, Restorers, and World-Renowned Guests*. McLean, VA: EPM Publications, 1991.

Gulley, Bill, and Mary Ellen Reese. *Breaking Cover*. New York: Simon & Schuster, 1980.

Haldeman, H. R. *The Haldeman Diaries—Inside the Nixon White House*. New York: G. P. Putnam's Sons, 1994.

Haldeman, Joann. *In the Shadow of the White House: A Memoir of the Washington and Watergate Years, 1968–1978*. Los Angeles: Rare Bird Books, 2017.

Holzer, Harold. *The Presidents Versus the Press: The Endless Battle Between the Presidents and the Media—From the Founding Fathers to Fake News*. New York: Dutton, 2020.

Hughes, Robert. *American Visions: The Epic History of Art in America*. New York: Alfred A. Knopf, 1997.

Hummer, Jill Abraham. *First Ladies and American Women: In Politics and at Home.* Lawrence: University Press of Kansas, 2017.

Karnow, Stanley. *Vietnam: A History, the First Complete Account of Vietnam at War.* New York: Penguin Books, 1984.

Kelley, Kitty. *Jackie Oh!* Secaucus, NJ: Lyle Stuart, 1978.

Kissinger, Henry. *White House Years.* Vol. 1. New York: Simon & Schuster, 1979.

Kornitzer, Bela. *The Real Nixon: An Intimate Biography.* Chicago: Rand McNally, 1960.

Kotlowski, Dean J. *Nixon's Civil Rights: Politics, Principle and Policy.* Cambridge, MA: Harvard University Press, 2001.

Lee, Heath Hardage. *The League of Wives: The Untold Story of the Women Who Took on the US Government to Bring Their Husbands Home from Vietnam.* New York: St. Martin's Press, 2019.

Lepore, Jill. *These Truths: A History of the United States.* New York: W. W. Norton, 2018.

Maddow, Rachel, and Michael Yarvitz. *Bag Man.* New York: Crown, 2020.

Mazo, Earl, Stephen Hess, and Richard M. Nixon. *Nixon.* New York: Harper & Row, 1968.

McCubbin, Lisa, and Susan Ford Bales. *Betty Ford: First Lady, Women's Advocate, Survivor, Trailblazer.* New York: Gallery Books, 2019.

McGinniss, Joe. *The Selling of the President: 1968.* New York: Penguin Books, 1988.

McMaster, H. R. *Dereliction of Duty: Johnson, McNamara, the Joint Chiefs of Staff and the Lies That Led to Vietnam.* New York: HarperCollins, 1998.

Morris, James McGrath. *Eye on the Struggle: Ethel Payne, the First Lady of the Black Press.* New York: Amistad, 2017.

Morris, Roger. *Richard Milhous Nixon: The Rise of an American Politician.* New York: Holt, 1990.

Nixon, Richard M. *Beyond Peace.* New York: Random House, 1994.

Nixon, Richard M. *RN: The Memoirs of Richard Nixon.* New York: Grosset & Dunlap, 1978.

Nixon, Edward C., and Karen L. Olson. *The Nixons: A Family Portrait.* Bothell, WA: Book Publishers Network, 2009.

Perlstein, Rick. *Nixonland: The Rise of a President and the Fracturing of America.* New York: Scribner, 2009.

Phillips-Schrock, Patrick. *Nixon White House Redecoration and Acquisition Program: An Illustrated History.* Jefferson, NC: McFarland, 2016.

Price, Raymond. *With Nixon.* New York: Viking Press, 1977.

Russo, Amy. *Women of the White House: The Illustrated Story of the First Ladies of the United States of America.* London: Welbeck, 2021.

Rymph, Catherine E. *Republican Women: Feminism and Conservatism from Suffrage Through the Rise of the New Right*. Chapel Hill: University of North Carolina Press, 2006.

Safire, William. *Before the Fall: An Inside View of the Pre-Watergate White House*. New York: Belmont Tower Books, 1975.

Schlesinger, Arthur Meier. *Kennedy or Nixon: Does It Make Any Difference?* New York: Macmillan Company, 1960.

Steinem, Gloria. *Outrageous Acts and Everyday Rebellions*. New York: Holt, Rinehart and Winston, 1983.

Stout, Leon J. *A Matter of Simple Justice: The Untold Story of Barbara Hackman Franklin and a Few Good Women*. University Park: Penn State University Press, 2012.

Stuart, Charles E. *Never Trust a Local: Inside the Nixon White House*. New York: Algora, 2005.

Sweig, Julia. *Lady Bird Johnson: Hiding in Plain Sight*. New York: Random House, 2022.

Swift, Will. *Pat and Dick: The Nixons, An Intimate Portrait of a Marriage*. New York: Threshold, 2014.

Taraborrelli, J. Randy. *The Kennedys—After Camelot*. New York: Grand Central, 2017.

Thomas, Evan. *Being Nixon: A Man Divided*. New York: Random House, 2016.

Thomas, Helen. *Dateline: White House*. New York: Macmillan, 1975.

Truman, Margaret. *First Ladies: An Intimate Group Portrait of White House Wives*. New York: Fawcett Columbine, 1996.

Twain, Mark. *Roughing It*. New York: Greystone Press, 1913.

Van Atta, Dale. *With Honor: Melvin Laird in War, Peace, and Politics*. Madison: University of Wisconsin Press, 2008.

Walker, Anne Collins. *China Calls: Paving the Way for Nixon's Historic Journey to China*. Lanham, MD: Madison Books, 1992.

Walker, Nancy A. *Women's Magazines, 1940–1960: Gender Roles and the Popular Press*. Boston: Bedford Books, 1998.

Weidenfeld, Sheila Rabb. *First Lady's Lady: With the Fords at the White House*. New York: G. P. Putnam's Sons, 1979.

Weinberger, Caspar, and Gretchen Roberts. *In the Arena: A Memoir of the 20th Century*. Washington, DC: Regnery, 2001.

Winder, Elizabeth. *Parachute Women: Marianne Faithfull, Marsha Hunt, Bianca Jagger, Anita Pallenberg, and the Women Behind the Rolling Stones*. New York: Hachette Books, 2023.

Woodward, Bob, and Carl Bernstein. *The Final Days*. New York: Simon & Schuster, 1976.

SELECTED ARTICLES

"1976 Republican Platform: Equal Rights and Ending Discrimination." Accessed May 5, 2023. https://www.fordlibrarymuseum.gov/library/document/platform/rights.htm.

Abbott, James Archer, and Elaine Rice Bachman. "The Kennedy Restoration: Historic Interiors with a Past for the Present . . . and Future." *White House Historical Quarterly* 60 (Winter 2021): 35–69.

"Accused Spy Alger Hiss Released from Prison." History.com. https://www.history.com/this-day-in-history/alger-hiss-released-from-prison, last updated November 23, 2020.

Alexander, Kathy. "World War II in San Francisco, CA." Legends of America, January 1, 2022. https://www.legendsofamerica.com/san-francisco-world-war-ii/.

Ambrose, Kevin, and Jason Samenow. "How a Surprise Snowstorm Almost Spoiled Kennedy's Inauguration 60 Years Ago." *Washington Post*, January 19, 2021. https://www.washingtonpost.com/weather/2021/01/19/kennedy-inauguration-weather-1961/.

Anthony, Carl Sferrazza. "Pat Nixon, Stealth Feminist?" *Washington Post*, June 27, 1993. https://www.washingtonpost.com/archive/opinions/1993/06/27/pat-nixon-stealth-feminist/bd46cbf1-575a-4655-9543-f22ac662bd11/.

"Article on Jewels Is 'for the Birds,' Mrs. Nixon Says." *New York Times*, May 16, 1974. http://www.nytimes.com/1974/05/16/archives/article-on-jewels-is-for-the-birds-mrs-nixon-says.html.

Bacharach, Judy. "Rose Mary Woods: Facing Her Two Crises." *Washington Post*, July 7, 1974, sec. H1.

Beale, Betty. "Those GOP Wives." *Boston Globe*, August 3, 1968.

"Bess Truman." Miller Center, August 23, 2023. https://millercenter.org/president/truman/essays/truman-1945-firstlady.

Brown, Gary. "The Monday After: Remembering Sebring's Rose Mary Woods and 'the Gap.'" *Canton Repository*, February 3, 2020. https://www.cantonrep.com/story/news/local/alliance/2020/02/03/the-monday-after-remembering-sebring/1781395007/.

Byron, Jim, and Patricia Nixon Cox. "Jim Byron, CEO of the Nixon Foundation Remarks on March 16, 2023, Dedication of the Pat Nixon Highway." Address presented at the Dedication of the Pat Nixon Highway, March 16, 2023.

Canady, John. "Wyeth Show Opens at White House Today." *New York Times*, February 20, 1970.

"Causeway Coastal Route Is One of the World's Great Road Journeys." Dangerous Roads. https://www.dangerousroads.org/north-america/usa/3755-us-highway -50.html, accessed August 26, 2021.

"Civil Rights Act (1964)." National Archives and Records Administration. Last reviewed February 8, 2022. https://www.archives.gov/milestone-documents/civil-rights-act.

"Clement Conger Proudly Restored American History to Great Settings." *Washington Post*, January 15, 2004.

Contrera, Jessica. "In 1968, Two of America's Most Prominent Political Families United." *Washington Post*, December 22, 2018. https://wapo.st/48rKnJa.

David, Lester. "Pat Nixon's Golden Years." *McCall's* 114, no. 1 (October 1986).

Dennis, Brad. "For Mitt Romney, Mother's Failed Run Offers Cautionary Tale." *Washington Post*, May 19, 2023. https://www.washingtonpost.com/politics /for-mitt-romney-mothers-failed-run-offers-cautionary-tale/2012/02/23 /gIQAXtQAYR_story.html.

"Ely Nevada: Ely Nevada Hotels: Ely Restaurants." *Travel Nevada*, February 8, 2023. https://travelnevada.com/cities/ely/.

Farrell, John A. "What Happened After Nixon Failed to Appoint a Woman to the Supreme Court." *Politico*, June 21, 2020. https://www.politico.com/news/magazine /2020/06/21/pat-nixon-woman-supreme-court-311408.

Feldman, Trude B. "The Quiet Courage of Pat Nixon." *McCall's*, May 1975.

"Financial Calculators." DollarTimes. https://www.dollartimes.com/, accessed August 25, 2022.

"First Daughter-Elect Julie Nixon's Wedding to David Dwight Eisenhower II: Culture Now." Museum Without Walls. https://themuseumwithoutwalls.org/Site ?item Id=20054, accessed April 22, 2023.

"First Lady Biography: Pat Nixon." National First Ladies' Library. http://archive .firstladies.org/biographies/firstladies.aspx?biography=38, accessed May 14, 2023.

"First Lady Pat Nixon Biography." Nixon Library and Museum. https://www .nixonfoundation.org/resources/pat-nixon-biography, accessed August 6, 2023.

Frutkin, Beth, Michal Kranz, and Isabella Zavarise. "This Timeline Shows Exactly How the Day of JFK's Assassination Unfolded." *Business Insider*, last updated November 22, 2022. https://www.businessinsider.com/kennedy-assassination -timeline-2013-11.

Garland, Gregory. "Kennedy, Nixon and the Competition for Mr. Africa, 1952– 1960." American Foreign Service Association, September 2022. https://afsa.org /kennedy-nixon-and-competition-mr-africa-1952-1960.

Glass, Andrew. "Nixon Visits South Vietnam, July 30, 1969." *Politico*, July 30, 2010. https://www.politico.com/story/2010/07/nixon-visits-south-vietnam-july-30-1969-040433.

Glass, Andrew. "Watergate 'Smoking Gun' Tape Released, Aug. 5, 1974." *Politico*, August 5, 2018. https://www.politico.com/story/2018/08/05/watergate-smoking-gun-tape-released-aug-5-1974-753086.

Goldberg, Benjamin Joel. "The Vice Presidency of Richard M. Nixon: One Man's Quest for National Respect, an International Reputation, and the Presidency." Ph.D. dissertation, College of William & Mary, 1998. https://scholarworks.wm.edu/etd/1539623928/.

Goldstein, Allie. "10 Facts You May Not Know About Columbia Heights." *Dcist*, November 5, 2018. https://dcist.com/story/19/01/03/10-facts-you-may-not-know-about-columbia-heights/.

Golus, Carrie. "Legal Precedent: Jewel C. Stradford Lafontant Broke Many Barriers as a Lawyer and Public Servant." *University of Chicago Magazine*, July–August 2013. https://mag.uchicago.edu/law-policy-society/legal-precedent.

Govan, Chloe. "Christian Dior: In Memory of the New Look." *France Today*, December 6, 2019. https://francetoday.com/culture/christian-dior-in-memory-of-the-new-look/.

Griffith, Martin. "Pat Nixon Finally Getting Recognition in Her Birthplace." *Elko Daily Free Press*, March 10, 2003. https://elkodaily.com/pat-nixon-finally-getting-recognition-in-her-birthplace/article_d62cccd8-7140-586e-9013-bbebf13bada1.html.

Haddad, Annette. "Nixon Library Dedicated by Four Presidents." UPI, July 19, 1990. https://www.upi.com/Archives/1990/07/19/Nixon-library-dedicated-by-four-presidents/9509648360000/.

Hansen, Stephen. "Wealth, Power and Status in Dupont Circle During the Gilded Age." *Washington Chronicles*, January 18, 2022. https://www.washingtonchronicles.com/2014/10/wealth-power-and-status-in-dupont.html.

Harris, Eleanor. "The Dark Hours of the Richard Nixons." *Washington Post and Times Herald*, March 4, 1956, sec. AW1.

Herbers, John. "Nixon Names Saxbe Attorney General; Jaworski Appointed Special Prosecutor." *New York Times*, November 2, 1973. https://www.nytimes.com/1973/11/02/archives/nixon-names-saxbe-attorney-general-jaworski-appointed-special.html.

"Historic Mission Inn Riverside CA." http://www.missioninn.com/about, accessed September 7, 2022.

Huebner, Lee. "The Checkers Speech After 60 Years." *The Atlantic*, September 22, 2012. https://www.theatlantic.com/politics/archive/2012/09/the-checkers -speech-after-60-years/262172/.

"International Debutante Ball Is Held at the Astor amid Pink and Silver Decor; 53 Girls from 16 Countries Bow at Spectacular Fete." *New York Times*, December 30, 1964. https://www.nytimes.com/1964/12/30/archives/international -debutante-ball-is-held-at-the-astor-amid-pink-and.html.

"January 20: The Beginning and the End: Ike's First and Last Inaugurations." National Park Service, January 12, 2021. https://www.nps.gov/eise/blogs/january -20-the-beginning-and-the-end-ikes-first-and-last-inaugurations.htm.

King, Don Roy. "SNL Transcripts: Madeline Kahn: 05/08/76: Final Days." SNL Transcripts Tonight, January 3, 2019. https://snltranscripts.jt.org/75/75snixon.phtml.

Larsen, Julia. "Jewel Stradford Rogers Lafontant-Mankarious (1922–1997)." Black Past, July 25, 2020. https://www.blackpast.org/african-american-history /mankarious-jewel-stradford-rogers-lafontant-1922-1997.

Lee, Heath Hardage. "The Ripple Effect of the Landmark Title IX Continues on Its 50th Anniversary." *The Hill*, June 23, 2022. https://thehill.com/opinion /congress-blog/3534426-the-ripple-effect-of-the-landmark-title-ix-continues -on-its-50th-anniversary/.

Lee, Heath Hardage. "Transcript, by Heath Hardage Lee for PN Day of Service at the Nixon Foundation: March 16, 2021." Nixon Library, March 16, 2021.

Lee, Heath Hardage. "The White House Wedding of Tricia Nixon and Edward Cox: The Rose Garden Is Transformed." *White House Historical Quarterly* 65 (Spring 2022): 53–61.

Lewis, Jone Johnson. "Slow and Steady: Women's Changing Roles in 1930s America." ThoughtCo, January 29, 2020. https://www.thoughtco.com/womens-rights -1930s-4141164.

Liu, Karen. "The Long Battle for the Era and Constitutional Equality." Nixon Foundation, August 5, 2013. https://www.nixonfoundation.org/2013/08/does -the-bell-toll-for-the-era/.

Lydon, Christopher. "Charles and Anne Begin Informal Visit to Capital." *New York Times*, July 17, 1970. https://www.nytimes.com/1970/07/17/archives/charles -and-anne-begin-informal-visit-to-capital-charles-and-anne.html.

Marshall, Colin. "Levittown, the Prototypical American Suburb—a History of Cities in 50 Buildings, Day 25." *The Guardian*, April 28, 2015. https://www .theguardian.com/cities/2015/apr/28/levittown-america-prototypical-suburb -history-cities.

McBride, Anita. "The Office of the First Lady: Managing Public Duties, Private Lives and Changing Expectations." *White House Historical Quarterly* 45 (Spring 2017): 5–17.

McCardle, Dorothy. "The Government Curator They Call 'Grand Acquisitor.'" *Washington Post and Times Herald*, January 17, 1971, sec. G1.

McLendon, Winzola. "'Pat Nixon Today.'" *Good Housekeeping* 190, no. 2 (February 1980).

"A Medal for Mme. Nixon." *New York Times*, January 9, 1972.

"The Nation: It's Inoperative: They Misspoke Themselves." *Time*, April 30, 1973. https://content.time.com/time/magazine/article/0,9171,907098-2,00.html.

Newport, Frank, David W. Moore, and Lydia Saad. "Most Admired Men and Women: 1948–1998." Gallup.com, March 21, 2021. https://news.gallup.com /poll/3415/most-admired-men-women-19481998.aspx.

Nichols, Chris. "Just Once a Year, the Public Gets a Chance to Explore This Art Deco Gem on Wilshire." *Los Angeles Magazine*, August 2, 2019. https://lamag .com/lahistory/bullocks-wilshire-public-tour.

Nixon, Patricia. "Crises of a Candidate's Wife." *Ladies' Home Journal* 79, no. 10 (November 1962).

"Nixon's Secretary Takes Riots or Travel in Stride." *The Tribune* (Coshoctan, OH), July 7, 1960.

"November 22, 1963: Death of the President." JFK Library. https://www.jfklibrary .org/learn/about-jfk/jfk-in-history/november-22-1963-death-of-the-president, accessed April 12, 2023.

Oliver, Myrna. "Mildred L. Lillie—55 Years as a Judge." SFGate, October 29, 2022. https://www.sfgate.com/bayarea/article/mildred-l-lillie-55-years-as-a-judge -2758609.php.

"Pat Nixon, the Girl Scouts, and the Spirit of Volunteerism." Richard Nixon Museum and Library, March 18, 2021, https://www.nixonlibrary.gov/news/pat -nixon-girl-scouts-and-spirit-volunteerism.

"Pat Nixon Park." City of Cerritos. http://www.cerritos.us/RESIDENTS/recreation /facilities/neighborhood_parks/pat_nixon_park.php, accessed August 7, 2023.

"Pat Nixon's Lollipops Charm Nursery Children." *Boston Globe*, July 24, 1959.

"Pat Nixon's Yuletide Legacy." Richard Nixon Museum and Library, December 24, 2021. http://www.nixonlibrary.gov/news/pat-nixons-yuletide-legacy.

"Pat Pooh-Poos Jewelry Story." *San Francisco Chronicle*, May 16, 1974.

Pearson, Richard. "Pat Nixon, First Lady in 'Time of Turmoil,' Dies." *Washington Post*, June 23, 1993. http://www.washingtonpost.com/archive/politics

/1993/06/23/pat-nixon-first-lady-in-time-of-turmoil-dies/2fadc435-a3e3 -4e86-9cc9-7dfb91600f28.

Pickens, Jennifer Boswell. "Inside Jackie Kennedy's Secret Visit to the Nixon White House." *Town and Country*, February 3, 2021, https://www.townandcountrymag .com/society/politics/a35381730/jackie-kennedy-secret-visit-to-nixon-white -house/.

"President Nixon's Speech on Cambodia, April 30, 1970." The Wars for Viet Nam, Vassar College, https://www.vassar.edu/vietnam/documents/doc15.html.

"Presidents Nixon and Truman: Reconciliation at the Truman Library." Richard Nixon Foundation. https://www.nixonfoundation.org/2016/03/president-nixon -truman-reconciliation-truman-library/, accessed August 7, 2023.

Radcliffe, Donnie. "Winging Her Way Back Home." *Washington Post*, March 16, 1974.

"Release of Tapes Displeased Pat." *Washington Post*, May 20, 1974, sec. A23.

"Research Starters: Worldwide Deaths in World War II." National WWII Museum, New Orleans. https://www.nationalww2museum.org/students-teachers /student-resources/research-starters/research-starters-worldwide-deaths-world -war, accessed July 24, 2023.

"Revisiting Watergate: John Ehrlichman." *Washington Post*. https://www.washington post.com/wp-srv/onpolitics/watergate/johnehrlichan.html, accessed September 1, 2023.

Ringle, Ken. "But Where Is the Real Pat Nixon?" *Boston Globe*, September 29, 1972, sec. Living.

"Robert F. Kennedy Presidential Campaign, 1968." JFK Library, March 16, 2008. https://www.jfklibrary.org/asset-viewer/archives/MRHPP/001/MRHPP-001-019.

Roe, Dorothy. "Today's Women." *Evening Banner*. August 7, 1959.

Ruane, Michael E. "A Chinese Cigarette Tin Launched D.C.'s 50-Year Love Affair with Pandas." *Washington Post*, March 16, 2022. https://www.washingtonpost .com/history/2022/03/16/pandas-china-nixon-dc/.

"San Clemente's History." City of San Clemente, CA. https://www.san-clemente .org/i-am-a-/visitor/history, accessed September 7, 2022.

Saxon, Wolfgang. "Nixon Sons-in-Law Accuse 2 Authors." *New York Times*, April 3, 1976. https://www.nytimes.com/1976/04/03/archives/nixon-sonsinlaw-accuse -2-authors.html.

Schreiber, Flora Rheta. "Pat Nixon Reveals for the First Time: 'I Didn't Want to See Dick Run Again.'" *Good Housekeeping* 167, no. 1 (July 1968).

Schultz, Colin. "Don't Worry Mr. Nixon, the National Zoo's Pandas Figured Out How to Have Sex." *Smithsonian Magazine*, July 28, 2014. https://www

.smithsonianmag.com/smart-news/dont-worry-mr-nixon-national-zoos-pandas
-figured-out-how-have-sex-180952180/.

Shepard, Geoff. "Geoff Shepard: Author of the Real Watergate Scandal Book."
Shepard on Watergate, June 21, 2023. http://shepardonwatergate.com/.

"The Silent Partner." *Time Magazine* 75, no. 9 (February 29, 1960).

Smith, Helen McCain, and Elizabeth Pope Frank. "Ordeal! Pat Nixon's Final Days
in the White House." *Good Housekeeping* 183, no. 1 (July 1976).

Smith, Marie. "Mrs. Richard Nixon—A Wife Called Pat." *Washington Post*, August
4, 1968.

Smith, Marie. "Julie Nixon Weds David Eisenhower." *Washington Post and Times
Herald*, December 23, 1968.

Steinem, Gloria. "In Your Heart You Know He's Nixon." *New York Magazine*, October 28, 1968.

Stroud, Kandie. "Pat Nixon in China." *Women's Wear Daily*, March 1, 1972, sec.
Issue, 42.

Talbot, Margaret. "J. Edgar Hoover, Public Enemy No. 1." *New Yorker*, November
14, 2022. https://www.newyorker.com/magazine/2022/11/21/j-edgar-hoover
-public-enemy-no-1.

Taves, Isabelle. "Pat Nixon, Problems of a 'Perfect Wife.'" *Redbook* 107, no. 1 (May 1956).

"TB in America: 1895–1954." PBS. Accessed January 17, 2022. https://www.pbs
.org/wgbh/americanexperience/features/plague-gallery/.

"Titanic Sinks." *National Geographic.* https://education.nationalgeographic.org
/resource/titanic-sinks/, accessed October 1, 2021.

"Transcript of Nixon's Farewell Speech to Cabinet and Staff Members in the Capital."
New York Times, August 10, 1974. https://www.nytimes.com/1974/08/10/archives
/transcript-of-nixons-farewell-speech-to-cabinet-and-staff-members.html.

"Treasures of the White House: Dolley Madison." White House History Association. https://www.whitehousehistory.org/photos/treasures-of-the-white-house
-dolley-madison, accessed June 10, 2023.

U.S. National Archives. "Women Unite for Ike!" Google Arts & Culture. https://
artsandculture.google.com/story/women-unite-for-ike-u-s-national-archives
/SQUxMpribfV4KQ, accessed March 5, 2023.

Vogel, Ed. "Ely Celebration Recalls Nevada's Only First Lady, Pat Nixon." *Las Vegas
Review-Journal*, February 26, 2017. https://www.reviewjournal.com/news/ely
-celebration-recalls-nevadas-only-first-lady-pat-nixon/.

Walker, Connecticut. "Helen Smith—Protector and Publicist of the First Lady."
Parade Magazine, August 18, 1974.

"Wallace Quotes." *The American Experience*, PBS. https://www.pbs.org/wgbh/american experience/features/wallace-quotes/, accessed May 1, 2023.

"Walter Annenberg Embarked on His Successful Run as U.S. Ambassador to the United Kingdom 50 Years Ago." Sunnylands, May 20, 2022. https:// sunnylands.org/article/walter-annenberg-embarked-on-his-successful-run-as-u -s-ambassador-to-the-united-kingdom-50-years-ago/.

"Welcome to the DC Greenbook." Welcome to the DC Greenbook, September 1, 2023. http://www.greenbookdc.com/.

West, Jessamyn. "The Real Pat Nixon: An Intimate View." *Good Housekeeping* 172, no. 2 (February 1971).

Widmer, Ted. "The Tapes That Doomed the Nixon Presidency." *Wall Street Journal*, July 22, 2023, sec. C4.

"Woman Suffrage: The Black Spot on the Map." Nevada Women's History Project, November 1, 2014. http://www.suffrage100nv.org.

WEBSITES

The Chapin School. https://www.chapin.edu/. Accessed April 11, 2023.

Ely, Nevada. https://elynevada.net/. Accessed August 23, 2023.

Whittier Museum. https://whittiermuseum.org/timeline/whittier-naming/. Accessed March 20, 2018.

NOTES

PROLOGUE: THE MYSTERIOUS MRS. NIXON

1 *"Oh, Dick"*: Julie Nixon Eisenhower, *Pat Nixon—The Untold Story* (New York: Simon & Schuster, 1986), 426.

2 *She looked painfully thin*: Carl Sferrazza Anthony, *Why They Wore It: The Politics and Pop Culture of First Ladies' Fashion* (Yorba Linda, CA: RNPLM, 2018), 105.

2 *"She will have no books"*: "President Nixon's Farewell to the White House Staff," Nixon Foundation, YouTube, posted January 16, 2012, https://www.youtube.com/watch?v=32GaowQnGRw.

2 *"never made one mention"*: Caspar Weinberger and Gretchen Roberts, *In the Arena: A Memoir of the 20th Century* (Washington, DC: Regnery, 2001), 248.

2 *Daughter Julie Nixon*: Eisenhower, *Pat Nixon—The Untold Story*, 428.

2 *"knew that there"*: Kate Andersen Brower, *First Women: The Grace and Power of America's Modern First Ladies* (New York: Harper, 2016), 298.

2 *"Greatness comes not"*: "President Nixon's Farewell to the White House Staff."

3 *"It was a day"*: Patti Matson, interview with the author, October 28, 2022.

3 *"Well Betty"*: Lisa McCubbin and Susan Ford Bales. *Betty Ford: First Lady, Women's Advocate, Survivor, Trailblazer* (New York: Gallery Books, 2019), 144.

3 *"Have a nice trip"*: Jack Brennan, interview by Brenda St. Hilaire, OH #5605, CSUF, 78.

3 *"Our hearts were breaking"*: Eisenhower, *Pat Nixon—The Untold Story*, 424.

4 *Pat thought women*: Barbara Walters interview with Pat Nixon, January 13, 1972, WHCA 4968, CBS, WHHA files, RNPLM.

5 *"kind of Annie Oakley"*: David Eisenhower, Zoom interview with the author, March 6, 2023.

1: THE LONELIEST ROAD IN AMERICA

9 *Built in 1926*: "US Highway 50 Is the Loneliest Road in America," Dangerous Roads, www.dangerousroads.org/north-america/usa/3755-us-highway-50.html, accessed August 26, 2021; "Ely," Travel Nevada, www.travelnevada.com/cities/ely, accessed September 11, 2021.

9 *One of these settlements*: "US Highway 50 Is the Loneliest Road in America."

9 *Mining boomtowns*: "White Pine County—Its Beginnings," White Pine Public Museum, wpmuseum.org, accessed September 13, 2021.

9 *founding a township*: "Elevated History," Visit White Pine County Nevada, www.elynevada .net, accessed September 12, 2021.

9 *A Wells Fargo office*: "White Pine County—Its Beginnings."

10 *"The Nevada Northern"*: Mark S. Bassett and J. Joan Bassett, *Nevada Northern Railway* (Charleston, SC: Arcadia, 2011), 73.

10 *the metal was utilized*: Ibid., 117.

10 *He was a good-looking man*: Gwendolyn King, Oral History interview, 1988, NARA, 3.

10 *tall, rangy, and blue-eyed*: Eisenhower, *Pat Nixon—The Untold Story*, 17.

10 *"early in life"*: Lester David, *The Lonely Lady of San Clemente: The Story of Pat Nixon* (New York: Berkley, 1979), 21.

10 *The couple had heard*: Ibid., 22–23.

10 *"The miserable living conditions"*: *Life as a Gamble*, exhibition, Park City Museum, September 2021.

11 *Despite their firsthand knowledge*: David, *The Lonely Lady of San Clemente*, 23.

11 *At some point*: Mary C. Brennan, *Pat Nixon: Embattled First Lady* (Lawrence: University Press of Kansas, 2011), 18.

11 *By 1912*: Martin Griffith, "Pat Nixon Finally Getting Recognition in Her Birthplace," *Elko Daily*, March 9, 2003, www.elkodaily.com/pat-nixon-finally-getting-recognition-in her-birthplace/article; Ed Vogel, "Ely Celebration Recalls Nevada's Only First Lady, Pat Nixon," *Las Vegas Review-Journal*, May 11, 2012, www.reviewjournal.com/news/ely-celebration-recalls -nevada's-only-first-lady-pat-nixon/.

11 *Ely remains*: "Mean Number of Days Minimum Temperature 32 Deg. F or Less," Climatic Data for the United States Through 2012, National Oceanic and Atmospheric Administration, 2013; Western Regional Climate Center; ELY WBO, NEVADA—Temperature Summary.

11 *On this day*: Pat Nixon Collection, White Pine Public Museum Ely, Nevada; "The White Pine News Archive," Newspapers.com, https://www.newspapers.com/paper/the-white-pine-news /32044/, accessed December 5, 2021.

11 *She herself would not*: David, *The Lonely Lady of San Clemente*, 23.

11 *The weekend of Pat's birth*: *White Pine News*, March 17, 1912, 5.

11 *The local dry-goods store*: Ibid., 4.

11 *Fifteen hundred passengers and crew*: "Sinking of the Titanic," *National Geographic*, https:// media.nationalgeographic.org/assets/reference/assets/sinking-of-the-titanic-3.pdf, accessed October 1, 2021; "Titanic Sinks," *National Geographic*, https://education.nationalgeographic .org/resource/titanic-sinks/, accessed October 1, 2021.

11 *This organization*: Stacy A. Cordery, *Juliette Gordon Low: The Remarkable Founder of the Girl Scouts* (New York: Penguin Books, 2013), 205.

11 *"focused on the outdoors"*: "Pat Nixon, the Girl Scouts, and the Spirit of Volunteerism," Nixon Library, March 18, 2021, 1, www.nixonlibrary.gov/news/pat-nixon-girl-scouts-and-spirit-volunteerism.

12 *"the most important educative factor"*: Anne Martin, "The Winning of Nevada," *Suffragist*, November 7, 1914, https://suffrage100nv.org/wp-content/uploads/2014/06/The-Winning-of -Nevada-1914.pdf.

12 *"Nevada owed much to"*: "Woman Suffrage: The Black Spot on the Map," Nevada Suffrage Centennial, November 1, 2014, https://suffrage100nv.org/category/nevada-suffrage/.

12 *"Men and women"*: Winifred Gallagher, *New Women in the Old West: From Settlers to Suffragists, an Untold American Story* (New York: Penguin Books, 2022), 229.

12 *"Kate, who hated and feared"*: David, *The Lonely Lady of San Clemente*, 23.

13 *Will, Kate, and the children*: Eisenhower, *Pat Nixon—The Untold Story*, 18.

13 *"ten months out of the year"*: Nellamena Roach, interview by Nancy Hunsaker, April 30, 1970, OH #993, CSUF, Richard M. Nixon Project, 4.

13 *ranch*: Eisenhower, *Pat Nixon—The Untold Story*, 18.

13 *The house initially*: David, *The Lonely Lady of San Clemente*, 23.

13 *Eventually the family added*: Louise Raine Gwinn, interview by Sharone Hencey, June 3, 1970, OH #870, CSUF, Richard M. Nixon Project, 3.

13 *The pride of the house*: Myrtle Raine Borden, interview by Sharone Hencey, April 21, 1970, OH #813, CSUF, Richard M. Nixon Project, 3.

13 *"All his study"*: Brennan, *Pat Nixon: Embattled First Lady*, 3.

13 *"He invested in oil wells or mines"*: Eisenhower, *Pat Nixon—The Untold Story*, 19.

13 *Pat loved stories, reading, and books*: Louise Raine Gwinn, interview by Sharone Hencey, June 3, 1970, OH #870, CSUF, Richard M. Nixon Project, 10.

13 *"He [Will] was quiet"*: Ibid., 4.

13 *"has quite a sense of humor"*: Ibid.

14 *"heavy set"*: Ibid., 3.

14 *"always made real good"*: Myrtle Raine Borde, interview by Sharone Hencey, April 21, 1970, OH #813, CSUF, Richard M. Nixon Project, 2.

14 *Pat was especially close*: Ibid., 3.

14 *"was like many women"*: Morton Morehouse, interview by Nancy Hunsaker, May 28, 1970, OH #914, CSUF, Richard M. Nixon Project, 3.

14 *"She'd make them up"*: Louise Raine Gwinn, interview by Sharone Hencey, June 3, 1970, OH #870, CSUF, Richard M. Nixon Project, 4.

14 *"a mind of her own"*: Myrtle Raine Borden, interview by Sharone Hencey, April 21, 1970, OH #813, CSUF, Richard M. Nixon Project, 14.

14 *"but she never showed"*: Ibid.

14 *"I don't know if"*: Ibid., 15.

14 *Artesia and the countryside*: Lura Applebury Waldrip, interview by Nancy Hunsaker, June 11, 1970, OH #975, CSUF, Richard M. Nixon Project, 8.

14 *"Everybody mixed together"*: Myrtle Raine Borden, interview by Sharone Hencey, April 21, 1970, OH #813, CSUF, Richard M. Nixon Project, 16.

14 *Only if it was raining*: Louise Raine Gwinn, interview by Sharone Hencey, June 3, 1970, OH #870, CSUF, Richard M. Nixon Project, 7.

14 *Each grade*: Ibid., 6–8.

15 *She and her brothers would all*: Ibid., 9.

15 *"She's got that push"*: Myrtle Raine Borden, interview by Sharone Hencey, April 21, 1970, OH #813, CSUF, Richard M. Nixon Project, 7.

2: SOMETHING MORE THAN JUST AN ORDINARY COUNTRY GIRL

16 *Usually an attentive and caring father*: Brennan, *Pat Nixon: Embattled First Lady*, 4–5.

16 *"I detest temper"*: Eisenhower, *Pat Nixon—The Untold Story*, 21.

16 *Her daughter was only thirteen*: Ibid., 26–27.

16 *"It was the first time"*: Marcia Elliott Wray, interview by Nancy Hunsaker, June 10, 1970, OH #988, CSUF, Richard M. Nixon Project, 5.

17 *Though Pat did participate*: Louise Raine Gwinn, interview by Sharone Hencey, June 3, 1970, OH #870, CSUF, Richard M. Nixon Project, 19.

17 *"It wasn't Christian Science"*: Jessamyn West, "The Real Pat Nixon—An Intimate View," *Good Housekeeping*, February 1971, 127.

17 *Buddy*: Brennan, *Pat Nixon: Embattled First Lady*, 3.

17 *She was plumper at this point*: Myrtle Raine Borden, interview by Sharone Hencey, April 21, 1970, OH #813, CSUF, Richard M. Nixon Project, 7; David, *The Lonely Lady of San Clemente*, 28.

17 *five feet five and a half inches*: Eisenhower, *Pat Nixon—The Untold Story*, 29.

17 *"very pretty complexion"*: Morton Morehouse, interview by Nancy Hunsaker, May 28, 1970, OH #914, CSUF, Richard M. Nixon Project, 3.

17 *"We thought she was pretty"*: Marcia Elliott Wray, interview by Nancy Hunsaker, June 10, 1970, OH #988, CSUF, Richard M. Nixon Project, 11.

17 *The young woman did not date much*: Morton Morehouse, interview by Nancy Hunsaker, May 28, 1970, OH #914, CSUF, Richard M. Nixon Project, 13–14.

18 *Kate realized that*: Eisenhower, *Pat Nixon—The Untold Story*, 24.

18 *Neva and Pat were both*: Morton Morehouse, interview by Nancy Hunsaker, May 28, 1970, OH #914, CSUF, Richard M. Nixon Project, 3.

18 *Her grandparents*: Eisenhower, *Pat Nixon—The Untold Story*, 24.

18 *Neva would often take a streetcar*: Lura Appleboy Waldrip, interview by Nancy Hunsaker, June 11, 1970, OH #975, CSUF, Richard M. Nixon Project, 190.

18 *Due to the age difference*: Marcia Elliott Wray, interview by Nancy Hunsaker, June 10, 1970, OH #988, CSUF, Richard M. Nixon Project, 5; Myrtle Raine Borden, interview by Sharone Hencey, April 21, 1970, OH #813, CSUF, Richard M. Nixon Project, 19–20.

18 *It was thirteen-year-old Pat*: Marcia Elliott Wray, interview by Nancy Hunsaker, June 10, 1970, OH #988, CSUF, Richard M. Nixon Project, 5.

18 *"Among the top students"*: Paul Carter, *Richard Nixon: California's Native Son* (Lincoln, NE: Potomac Books, 2023), 60.

19 *Tom promised her*: Eisenhower, *Pat Nixon—The Untold Story*, 33.

19 *"The unemployment rate"*: Jill Lepore, *These Truths: A History of the United States* (New York: W. W. Norton, 2018), 425–26.

19 *Between 1929 and 1932:* Ibid., 425.

19 *Pat took the job*: Eisenhower, *Pat Nixon—The Untold Story*, 33.

19 *The staff was small*: Blanche Potter Holmes, interview by Sharone Hencey, June 12, 1970, OH #879, CSUF, Richard M. Nixon Project, 2.

19 *"A young man came to"*: Ibid.

19 *On May 5, 1930*: David, *The Lonely Lady of San Clemente*, 32.

20 *Pat enrolled as*: Marcia Elliott Wray, interview by Nancy Hunsaker, June 10, 1970, OH #988, CSUF, Richard M. Nixon Project, 13.

20 *Now the ambitious young woman*: Eisenhower, *Pat Nixon—The Untold Story*, 34.

20 *Pat would later tell*: Brennan, *Pat Nixon: Embattled First Lady*, 8.

20 *"Daily at 6 a.m."*: Eisenhower, *Pat Nixon—The Untold Story*, 35; David, *The Lonely Lady of San Clemente*, 32.

20 *This collegiate Cinderella*: David, *The Lonely Lady of San Clemente*, 32.

20 *Still, she managed to snag*: Eisenhower, *Pat Nixon—The Untold Story*, 35.

20 *Mabel Myers*: Dr. Mabel Myers, interview by Mitch Haddad, May 12, 1971, OH #910, CSUF, Richard M. Nixon Project, 7.

20 *She noted Pat's good taste*: Ibid., 10.

20 *"a very personable, attractive girl"*: Ibid., 11–12.

21 *When the car*: Eisenhower, *Pat Nixon—The Untold Story*, 36; David, *The Lonely Lady of San Clemente*, 33.

21 *"sat beside me"*: West, "Real Pat Nixon," 127.

21 *When Pat was offered*: Eisenhower, *Pat Nixon—The Untold Story*, 37.

21 *Good hygiene*: "TB in America: 1895–1954," PBS, https://www.pbs.org/wgbh /americanexperience/features/plague-gallery/, accessed January 17, 2022.

21 *"I wanted to reach out"*: David, *The Lonely Lady of San Clemente*, 34; Brennan, *Pat Nixon: Embattled First Lady*, 8.

21 *While working at Seton Hospital*: Brennan, *Pat Nixon: Embattled First Lady*, 9.

22 *"I didn't want to marry"*: Eisenhower, *Pat Nixon—The Untold Story*, 41.

22 *"Some dump!"*: Pat Ryan to Bill and Tom Ryan, October 1933, Box 2, folder not listed, PPS 265, PRNC, RNPLM.

22 *Thrilled to be*: Ibid.

22 *"only women could lead"*: Lepore, *These Truths*, 433.

22 *She had started her voting*: Eisenhower, *Pat Nixon—The Untold Story*, 85.

22 *"that [Hollywood] life"*: Eisenhower, *Pat Nixon—The Untold Story*, 40.

23 *Pat happily agreed*: Eisenhower, *Pat Nixon—The Untold Story*, 40–41.

23 *"He recalled that"*: "Pat Nixon," *Time*, February 29, 1960, 27.

23 *Virginia later recalled that*: Virginia Counts (1972), Evlyn Dorn (September 10, 1972), WHOC, 3.

23 *in the 1935 film*: Carter, *Richard Nixon: California's Native Son*, 61.

23 *The Great Ziegfeld*: Ibid.

23 *Ben Hur*: "A Visit with the First Lady," Pat Nixon interview with Virginia Sherwood, ABC, September 12, 1971, YouTube, posted by Nixon Foundation, https://www.youtube.com/watch?v =ABfQjJGNQ78.

23 *"Los Angeles' most"*: Chris Nichols, "Just Once a Year, the Public Gets a Chance to Explore This Art Deco Gem on Wilshire," *Los Angeles Magazine*, August 2, 2019, https://lamag.com /lahistory/bullocks-wilshire-public-tour.

24 *She was soon notified*: Eisenhower, *Pat Nixon—The Untold Story*, 48.

24 *Tom would be working*: Ibid., 49.

3: A MAGIC LITTLE CITY

25 *Whittier was incorporated*: Timeline, Whittier Museum, https://whittiermuseum.org/research /timeline/, accessed February 8, 2022.

25 *The citrus, walnut*: Whittier city website, www.cityofwhittier.org, accessed February 8, 2022.

25 *"the magic little city"*: Charles W. Cooper, *Whittier: Independent College in California* (Los Angeles: Ward Ritchie Press, 1967), x.

25 *By the time Pat*: Cooper, *Whittier*, 15; 1940 US Census.

25 *"Whittier was very much like"*: Elizabeth Cloes, interview by Mary Suzanne Simon, May 29, 1970, OH #834, CSUF, Richard M. Nixon Project, 4.

25 *"Whittier was a real, small"*: Phil and Geri Studebaker, interview by Mary Suzanne Simon, May 11, 1970, OH #960, CSUF, Richard M. Nixon Project, 2.

25 *"For many, many years"*: Lura Applebury Waldrip, interview by Nancy Hunsaker, June 11, 1970, OH #975, CSUF, Richard M. Nixon Project, 14; Heber Holloway, interview by Greg Brolin, January 7, 1971, OH #878, CSUF, Richard M. Nixon Project, 7.

26 *Many still used horses*: Lura Applebury Waldrip, interview by Nancy Hunsaker, June 11, 1970, OH #975, CSUF, Richard M. Nixon Project, 15.

26 *Dancing remained*: Samuel G. Warren, interview by Nancy Hunsaker, June 17, 1970, OH #980, CSE Fullerton, Richard M. Nixon Project, 8–9.

26 *She would later famously*: Carter, *Richard Nixon: California's Native Son*, 61.

26 *Margaret taught history*: Margaret O'Grady Theriault, interview by C. Richard Arena, September 27, 1972, WCOH, 2; Margaret Truman, *First Ladies: An Intimate Group Portrait of White House Wives* (New York: Fawcett Columbine, 1996), 190.

26 *The two women soon*: Margaret O'Grady Theriault, interview by C. Richard Arena, September 27, 1972, WCOH, 5–6.

26 *Margaret recalled Pat*: Ibid., 13.

26 *Pat was a natural*: Ibid., 9–10.

26 *"She was very businesslike"*: Betty Jean Kenworthy, interview by C. Richard Arena, October 3, 1972, WCOH, 5, 9.

26 *"She had to be a strict"*: Mildred Eason Stouffer, oral history, AMR, March, 1979, 1.

27 *"All the young people"*: Geraldine Ellis, oral history, AMR, March, 1979, 1.

27 *"Miss Ryan was quite"*: Robert Blake, oral history, AMR, March, 1979, 1.

27 *"We were both interested"*: Margaret O'Grady Theriault, interview by C. Richard Arena, September 27, 1972, WCOH, 14.

27 *"I never spent"*: Eisenhower, *Pat Nixon—The Untold Story*, 54.

27 *"She didn't ever talk"*: Carol Collins Gordon, oral history, AMR, March, 1979, 1.

28 *Cloes was now an*: Elizabeth Cloes, oral history, interview by Mary Suzanne Simon, May 29, 1970, OH #834, CSUF, Richard M. Nixon Project, 2.

28 *"Pat was a very attractive"*: Ibid., 3.

28 *"Pat was there"*: Grant M. Garman, oral history, interview by Mary Suzanne Simon, June 1, 1970, CSUF, Richard M. Nixon Project, 5.

28 *"a striking and beautiful"*: Ibid., 4.

28 *"I sat in the middle"*: Elizabeth Cloes, oral history, interview by Mary Suzanne Simon, May 29, 1970, OH #834, CSUF, Richard M. Nixon Project, 3.

29 *"I met this guy"*: Eisenhower, *Pat Nixon—The Untold Story*, 55.

29 *"Frank was a tempestuous man"*: Miss Jessamyn West (Mrs. H. M. McPherson), interview by C. Richard Arena, December 5, 1971, and June 30, 1971, WCOH, #1 and #8.

29 *"description of his father's"*: Eisenhower, *Pat Nixon—The Untold Story*, 57.

29 *"In her whole life"*: John A. Farrell, *Richard Nixon: The Life* (New York: Doubleday, 2017), 47.

29 *The couple soon had*: Carter, *Richard Nixon: California's Native Son*, 3.

29 *"Richard the Lionheart"*: Michael Dobbs, *King Richard Nixon and Watergate: An American Tragedy* (New York: Knopf, 2021), 83.

30 *In 1922*: Carter, *Richard Nixon: California's Native Son,* 12.

30 *He soon opened*: Dobbs, *King Richard Nixon and Watergate*, 84.

30 *The Nixon boy*: Carter, *Richard Nixon: California's Native Son*, 14.

30 *"Women were recognized"*: Miss Jessamyn West (Mrs. H. M. McPherson), interview by C. Richard Arena, December 5, 1971, WCOH, 32.

30 *"So for QUAKER women"*: Miss Jessamyn West (Mrs. H. M. McPherson), interview by C. Richard Arena, June 30, 1971, WCOH, 33.

30 *Dick graduated*: Carter, *Richard Nixon: California's Native Son*, 35.

30 *Dick graduated second*: Bela Kornitzer, *The Real Nixon: An Intimate Biography* (Chicago: Rand McNally, 1960), 115–16.

30 *Dick took the role*: Carter, *Richard Nixon: California's Native Son*, 59.

4: MISS VAGABOND

32 *Just one month*: Eisenhower, *Pat Nixon–The Untold Story*, 58.

32 *"My Irish Gypsy"*: Thomas, *Being Nixon*, 26; Farrell, *Richard Nixon*, 72.

32 *"Miss Vagabond"*: Thomas, *Being Nixon*, 26; Farrell, *Richard Nixon*, 72.

32 *"Patricia"*: Love Letters, RN PN Navy Folder 9, Box 1, PPS 265, PRNC, RNPLM.

33 *"Someday, let me see"*: Ibid.

33 *But Dick knew*: Eisenhower, *Pat Nixon—The Untold Story*, 58.

33 *"I took the walk tonight"*: Ibid.

33 *"Unaccustomed to dealing with"*: Will Swift, *Pat and Dick: The Nixons, an Intimate Portrait of a Marriage* (New York: Threshold, 2014), 21.

33 *Dick would kill time*: Swift, *Pat and Dick: The Nixons*, 21.

33 *"Remember how I used to"*: Love Letters, RN PN Navy Folder 2, Box 1, PPS 265, PRNC, RNPLM.

34 *"Dear Patricia"*: Love Letters, RN PN Navy Folder 7, Box 1, PPS 265, PRNC, RNPLM.

34 *"I remember him flying"*: Carter, *Richard Nixon: California's Native Son*, 62–63.

34 *"I think you have to"*: Kenneth Ball, interview by John Donnelly, January 16, 1970, OH #804, CSUF, Richard M. Nixon Project, 9.

34 *"Richard was a person"*: Kenneth L. Ball, interview by C. Richard Arena, October 20, 1971, WCOH, 4.

35 *"Pat insisted that"*: Post-Presidential Materials, Richard Nixon oral history, May 4, 1975, RNPLM, 13–15.

35 *"never attempted to compete"*: Eisenhower, *Pat Nixon—The Untold Story*, 62.

35 *"Hannah was convinced Pat"*: David, *The Lonely Lady of San Clemente*, 52.

35 *"Hannah convinced herself"*: Swift, *Pat and Dick: The Nixons*, 26.

35 *"She wasn't really"*: Eisenhower, *Pat Nixon—The Untold Story*, 62.

36 *"When my family and I"*: Edward C. Nixon and Karen L. Olson, *The Nixons: A Family Portrait* (Bothell, WA: Book Publishers Network, 2009), 102.

36 *"That fact alone"*: Nixon and Olson, *The Nixons: A Family Portrait*, 103.

36 *Pat volunteered to drive*: Margaret O'Grady Theriault, interview by C. Richard Arena, September 27, 1972, WCOH, 16–17.

36 *"I felt so sorta' lonesome"*: Love Letters, Letter PN to RN summer 1939, no date, Hotel Whitcomb stationery, Restricted untitled folder 2, Box 1, PPS 265, PRNC, RNPLM.

36 *"I can remember"*: Margaret O'Grady Theriault, interview by C. Richard Arena, September 27, 1972, WCOH, 19.

37 *In this "Straight Note"*: Love Letters, RN PN Navy folder 10, Box 1, PPS 265, PRNC, RNPLM.

37 *"I never really KNEW Pat"*: Alyce G. Koch, interview by Richard C. Arena, March 20, 1972, WCOH, 5–6.

37 *"Dick was like an open-faced sandwich"*: Ibid., 6.

5: FULL AND EQUAL PARTNERS

38 *He was not only*: Carter, *Richard Nixon: California's Native Son*, 63.

38 *As their relationship grew*: Ibid.

38 *They were voracious readers*: Brennan, *Pat Nixon: Embattled First Lady, 15.*

38 *"1920s vision"*: "San Clemente's History," City of San Clemente, CA, https://www.san-clemente.org/i-am-a-/visitor/history, accessed September 7, 2022.

39 *"said something I shall never"*: Alyce G. Koch, interview by Richard C. Arena, March 20, 1972, WCOH, 16.

39 *"As if he would have"*: Kornitzer, *The Real Nixon*, 134.

39 *Dick was president of the Young Republicans Club*: Swift, *Pat and Dick: The Nixons*, 35; Richard M. Nixon, *RN: The Memoirs of Richard Nixon* (New York: Grosset & Dunlap, 1978), 23.

39 *"By the time of her engagement"*: Swift, *Pat and Dick: The Nixons*, 35.

40 *The couple sat*: Eisenhower, *Pat Nixon—The Untold Story*, 66.

40 *"She loved Dick's romantic"*: Ibid.

40 *"What are you marrying"*: Ibid., 66–67.

40 *The set cost*: Invoice, Paul D Walsh Co., Folder 9, Box 2, PPS 265, PRNC, RNPLM.

40 *Adjusted for inflation*: Inflation Calculator, accessed August 25, 2022, dollartimes.com.

40 *Pat chipped in*: David, *The Lonely Lady of San Clemente*, 53.

41 *The best-known account*: Eisenhower, *Pat Nixon—The Untold Story*, 68.

41 *Ricard Nixon himself writes*: Nixon, *RN*, 25.

41 *"He (Dick) asked"*: Thomas T. Seulke (October 19, 1971), interview by C. Richard Arena, WCOH, 6.

42 *"The big question"*: Joe Dmohowski, email to the author, September 13, 2022.

42 *"Dearest Heart"*: Eisenhower, *Pat Nixon—The Untold Story, 68.*

42 *"Through the years"*: Ibid.

42 *On June 9*: Alyce G. Koch, interview by C. Richard Arena, March 20, 1972, WCOH, 20; Carter, *Richard Nixon: California's Native Son*, 67.

42 *A tea and wedding shower*: "Miss Patricia Ryan, Mr. Nixon, Plight Marriage Vows," Folder 9, Box 2, PPS 265, PRNC, RNPLM.

42 *Only when Dick and Pat*: Post-Presidential Materials, May 6, 1975, Oral History, RNPLM, 1.

43 *Though the bride*: David, *The Lonely Lady of San Clemente*, 54.

43 *The couple had previously*: Eisenhower, *Pat Nixon—The Untold Story*, 69.

43 *Adding to the luster*: "Historic Mission Inn Riverside CA," Mission Inn Riverside, accessed September 7, 2022, http://www.missioninn.com/about.

43 *Because Pat had never*: Swift, *Pat and Dick: The Nixons*, 36.

43 *She and Dick also*: "Miss Patricia Ryan, Mr. Nixon, Plight Marriage Vows," Box 2, Folder 9, PPS 265, PRNC, RNPLM.

43 *She would not allow*: Eisenhower, *Pat Nixon—The Untold Story*, 69; Swift, *Pat and Dick: The Nixons*, 36.

43 *The couple rented*: Eisenhower, *Pat Nixon—The Untold Story*, 69.

43 *"in one of the reception rooms"*: Margaret O'Grady Theriault, interview by C. Richard Arena, September 27, 1972, WCOH, 29.

44 *Virginia Shugart and Virginia Hudson*: Alyce G. Koch, interview by C. Richard Arena, March 20, 1972, WCOH, 18.

44 *"This group was"*: Ibid., 19.

44 *Of course, Dick's parents*: Eisenhower, *Pat Nixon—The Untold Story*, 69.

44 *In all*: Nixon and Olson, *The Nixons,* 118.

44 *The wedding was*: Alyce G. Koch, interview by C. Richard Arena, March 20, 1972, WCOH, 21.

44 *Sparkling crystal buttons*: Eisenhower, *Pat Nixon—The Untold Story*, 69; David, *The Lonely Lady of San Clemente*, 54.

44 *At 3:30 p.m.*: Eisenhower, *Pat Nixon—The Untold Story*, 69.

44 *Dick met her*: Swift, *Pat and Dick: The Nixons*, 36; David, *The Lonely Lady of San Clemente*, 54.

44 *"a many-tiered wedding cake"*: Eisenhower, *Pat Nixon—The Untold Story*, 69; Nixon and Olson, *The Nixons*, 118.

44 *"Pat is proud"*: Post-Presidential Materials, Richard Nixon, May 6, 1975, oral history, RNPLM, p. 19.

44 *As there was not a plethora*: Edith Holt, interview by C. Richard Arena, May 10, 1971, WCOH, 3.

44 *"We did the horrible"*: Alyce G. Koch, interview by C. Richard Arena, March 20, 1972, WCOH, 21.

45 *The car in which they drove*: Brennan, *Pat Nixon: Embattled First Lady*, 14; David, *The Lonely Lady of San Clemente*, 55.

6: THE WINDS OF WAR

46 *"We didn't have the honeymoon trip"*: David, *The Lonely Lady of San Clemente*, 55.

46 *"We got to know"*: Post-Presidential Materials, Richard Nixon, May 6, 1975, oral history, RNPLM, 20–21.

46 *Their $200 honeymoon fund*: David, *The Lonely Lady of San Clemente*, 56; Eisenhower, *Pat Nixon-The Untold Story*, 70.

46 *a short-term situation*: Carter, *Richard Nixon: California's Native Son*, 68.

46 *They lived in the rear apartment*: David, *The Lonely Lady of San Clemente*, 57.

46 *Pat's beloved Irish setter*: Ibid.

47 *This school year*: Kornitzer, *The Real Nixon*, 36.

47 *Eventually they would move*: Carter, *Richard Nixon: California's Native Son*, 68.

47 *"there were too many people"*: Brennan, *Pat Nixon: Embattled First Lady*, 16.

47 *Helene remembered*: Kornitzer, The Real Nixon, 36.

47 *Dick's frozen orange juice*: Carter, *Richard Nixon: California's Native Son*, 69.

47 *Pat soon gave her notice*: Eisenhower, *Pat Nixon—The Untold Story*, 73.

47 *the young Dick*: Evan Thomas, *Being Nixon: A Man Divided* (New York: Random House, 2016), 31.

47 *In 1942*: Roger Morris, *Richard Milhous Nixon: The Rise of an American Politician* (New York: Holt, 1990), 230–31.

48 *"Pat has always said"*: Matthew G. Bender, interview by C. Richard Arena, October 9, 1972, WCOH, 4.

48 *Dick interviewed for the job*: Morris, *Richard Milhous Nixon*, 234–35.

48 *The couple headed to*: Eisenhower, *Pat Nixon—The Untold Story*, 74–75.

48 *The young couple packed up*: Kornitzer, *The Real Nixon*, 141.

48 *The California connection*: Morris, *Richard Milhous Nixon*, 236–37.

48 *"hardship cases"*: Eisenhower, *Pat Nixon—The Untold Story*, 75.

49 *"I am for women"*: Carl Sferrazza Anthony, "Pat Nixon, Stealth Feminist?," *Washington Post*, June 27, 1993.

49 *"As a junior lawyer"*: Nixon, *RN*, 26.

49 *They did not try to*: Eisenhower, *Pat Nixon—The Untold Story*, 75; Morris, *Richard Milhous Nixon*, 243.

49 *"I would have felt mighty uncomfortable"*: Kornitzer, *The Real Nixon*, 139–40.

49 *"As a birthright Quaker"*: Joe F. Dmohowski, "Richard Nixon at Whittier College: The Education of a Leader," *Southern California Quarterly* 105, no. 1 (2023): 122.

49 *Pat clearly missed her husband*: WW2 letter, Quonset time period, no date, Box 2, PPS 265, PRNC, RNPLM.

50 *"Sweetie this trip was"*: WW2, no date, Box 2, PPS 265, PRNC, RNPLM.

50 *Both he and Pat*: Nixon, *RN*, 27.

50 *"I never did see him"*: *Des Moines Register*, February 8, 1970, 21.

50 *"Pat Nixon made strong impressions"*: Ibid.

50 *Due to her past work*: Eisenhower, *Pat Nixon—The Untold Story*, 78.

50 *He soon received orders*: Nixon, *RN*, 27.

51 *"We tried to keep the conversation"*: Nixon and Olson, *The Nixons*, 120.

51 *Just two days later*: Nixon, *RN*, 28.

51 *Pat quickly found*: Eisenhower, *Pat Nixon—The Untold Story*, 78–79.

51 *"Arsenal of Democracy"*: Legends of America, LegendsofAmerica.com/san-francisco-world-war-ii/, accessed October 1, 2022, 1–4.

52 *"Restrictions began"*: Lepore, *These Truths*, 494.

7: NEVER JUST A WIFE

53 *By the end of World War II*: "Research Starters: Worldwide Deaths in World War 2," National World War II Museum, www.nationalww2museum.org/students-teachers/student-resources/research-starters/research-starters-worldwide-deaths-world-war, accessed July 24, 2023.

53 *"WILL"*: RMN Last Will and Testament, WW2 Letters, Box 2, PPS 265, PRNC, RNPLM.

54 *Close to six million*: Gail Collins, *America's Women: 400 Years of Dolls, Drudges, Helpmates, and Heroines* (New York: HarperCollins, 2009), 381.

54 *A 1936 Gallup poll*: Nancy A. Walker, *Women's Magazines, 1940–1960: Gender Roles and the Popular Press* (Boston: Bedford Books, 1998), 12.

54 *"The forties was a time"*: Collins, *America's Women*, 388.

55 *"As one seems drawn"*: Gretchen King and Robert L. King, interview by C. Richard Arena, March 25, 1973, WCOH, 3.

55 *Pat wasn't easily thrown*: Ibid., 9.

55 *Hundreds of these letters*: Eisenhower, *Pat Nixon—The Untold Story*, 78.

55 *"Your job is far more"*: WW2 letters, no date, Box 1, PPS 265, PRNC, RNPLM.

55 *"I'm proud Pat"*: Ibid.

55 *"Dear One"*: Ibid.

56 *"Virtually all aspects"*: Walker, *Women's Magazines*, 23.

56 *"Although the magazines"*: Ibid.

56 *"I remember now"*: WW2 Letters, August 31, 1943, Box 1, PPS 265, PRNC, RNPLM.

56 *"let's always go"*: Ibid.

56 *"I love you most"*: WW2 Letters, Box 1, PPS 265, PRNC, RNPLM.

57 *Pat openly professed*: WW2 Letters, Box 1, PPS 265, PRNC, RNPLM; Thomas, *Being Nixon*, 30.

57 *"Here's to say"*: WW2 Letters, undated, Box 1, PPS 265, PRNC, RNPLM.

57 *"The only women"*: Ibid.

57 *Dick's letter to*: WW2 Letters, Thanksgiving Day, 1943, Box 1, PPS 265, PRNC, RNPLM.

57 *"Our first together"*: WW2 Letters, December 25, 1943, Box 1, PPS 265, PRNC, RNPLM.

57 *"Nick's Hamburger Stand"*: Nixon, *RN*, 28; Morris, *Richard Milhous Nixon*, 252.

58 *"So many of the men"*: WW2 Letters, February 6, 1944, Box 1, PPS 265, PRNC, RNPLM.

58 *"On this day"*: WW2 Letters, Valentine's Day, 1944, PPS 265, PRNC, RNPLM.

58 *"Dear one"*: Ibid.

58 *"I'm awfully glad"*: WW2 Letters, undated, spring 1944, Box 1, PPS 265, PRNC, RNPLM.

58 *"You know I always"*: WW2 Letters, August 4, 1943, Box 1, PPS 265, PRNC, RNPLM.

59 *"Today was the most"*: WW2 Letters, April 29, 1944, Box 1, PPS 265, PRNC, RNPLM.

59 *"Jimmie Stuart said"*: Ibid.

59 *"Do you still like"*: WW2 Letters, spring 1944, no date, Box 1, PPS 265, PRNC, RNPLM.

59 *"Being with you"*: WW2 Letters, Box 1, PPS 265, PRNC, RNPLM; Eisenhower, *Pat Nixon—The Untold Story*, 83.

60 *"a kind of epitaph"*: Morris, *Richard Milhous Nixon*, 253.

60 *"Hundreds of times"*: WW2 Letters, Feb. 1944, Box 1, PPS 265, PRNC, RNPLM.

60 *"I was at the airport"*: Nixon, *RN*, 33; Morris, *Richard Milhous Nixon*, 254.

8: THE PAT AND DICK TEAM

61 *"Within two years"*: Walker, *Women's Magazines*, 12.

61 *"The collection was"*: Chloe Govan, "Christian Dior: In Memory of the New Look," France Today, December 6, 2019, https://francetoday.com/culture/christian-dior-in-memory-of-the-new-look/, 5.

61 *While living in New York*: Eisenhower, *Pat Nixon—The Untold Story*, 84.

62 *"Committee of 100"*: Eisenhower, *Pat Nixon—The Untold Story*, 85; Thomas, *Being Nixon*, 31.

62 *"I will be prepared"*: Morris, *Richard Milhous Nixon*, 281.

62 *Dick returned to*: Eisenhower, *Pat Nixon—The Untold Story*, 86; Morris, *Richard Milhous Nixon*, 282.

62 *"Pat said to me"*: Edith Holt, interview by C. Richard Arena, May 10, 1971, WCOH, 6.

62 *Pat also worried*: David, *The Lonely Lady of San Clemente*, 64.

63 *"I really honestly"*: Hortense Behrens, interview by Mary Suzanne Simon. May 27, 1970, OH #0811, CSUF, Richard M. Nixon Project, 21.

63 *Dick's very first*: Carter, *Richard Nixon: California's Native Son*, 107.

63 *"Local Republican"*: Catherine E. Rymph, *Republican Women: Feminism and Conservatism from Suffrage Through the Rise of the New Right* (Chapel Hill: University of North Carolina Press, 2006), 4.

64 *"the housework of government"*: Rymph, *Republican Women*, 133.

64 *"'house meetings' in which"*: Nixon, *RN*, 36.

64 *The Nixons' entire nest*: David, *The Lonely Lady of San Clemente*, 64–65; Brennan, *Pat Nixon: Embattled First Lady*, 64–65.

64 *"advanced age"*: David, *The Lonely Lady of San Clemente*, 67.

64 *A seven-pound baby girl*: Eisenhower, *Pat Nixon—The Untold Story*, 87.

64 *the new baby girl's*: Ibid.

64 *"the only boss"*: *Pomona Progress Bulletin*, March 7, 1946, https://www.newspapers.com/paper /the-pomona-progress-bulletin/22484/.

65 *"It used to bother"*: Ruth Garrett and Waymeth B. Garrett, interview by C. Richard Arena, January 20, 1972, WCOH, 27.

65 *a short three weeks*: David, *The Lonely Lady of San Clemente*, 67.

65 *The problem was*: Eisenhower, *Pat Nixon—The Untold Story*, 87.

65 *"housework of government"*: Rymph, *Republican Women*, 133.

66 *"furious and embarrassed"*: Morris, *Richard Milhous Nixon*, 290–91.

66 *"a bitter blow"*: Eisenhower, *Pat Nixon—The Untold Story*, 90.

66 *"the silk-stocking district"*: Roy O. Day, interview by C. Richard Arena, November 22, 1971, WCOH, 15.

66 *"she was a lovely lady"*: Ibid., 4.

66 *"was nervous, uptight"*: David, *The Lonely Lady of San Clemente*, 67.

66 *"She was a hell of"*: Ibid.

66 *"house meetings"*: Morris, *Richard Milhous Nixon*, 289.

66 *"strongest point"*: Ibid.

66 *"At each event"*: Carter, *Richard Nixon: California's Native Son*, 83–84.

67 *"Pat and Dick Team"*: Eisenhower, *Pat Nixon—The Untold Story*, 88.

67 *"my best helper"*: Nixon, *RN*, 36.

67 *According to Adela Rogers St. Johns*: Thomas, *Being Nixon*, 34.

67 *"I was in his office"*: Donald Fantz, Rosenberger oral history, WHARC, March, 1979, 1.

67 *"One of the most dramatic"*: Ruth Garrett and Waymeth B. Garrett, interview by C. Richard Arena, January 20, 1972, WCOH, 16.

67 *Thankfully, on November 6, 1946*: Eisenhower, *Pat Nixon—The Untold Story*, 92.

67 *But Dick*: Thomas, *Being Nixon*, 37.

67 *"Nothing could equal"*: Nixon, *RN*, 40.

68 *"Well, she'll never be"*: Roy O. Day, interview by C. Richard Arena, November 22, 1971, WCOH, 13.

9: THE GREEN BOOK

71 *In December 1946*: Nixon and Olson, *The Nixons: A Family Portrait*, 127–28.

71 *Hannah and Frank*: Eisenhower, *Pat Nixon—The Untold Story*, 94.

71 *"Mainly from"*: "Wealth Power and Status in Dupont Circle During the Gilded Age," *Washington Chronicles*, accessed November 20, 2022, 2.

71 *By 1932 these pedigreed socialites*: https://thegreenbookdc.com/about-us/, accessed November 21, 2022.

72 *After Hagner's death*: "Welcome to the DC Greenbook," http://www.thegreenbookdc.com/, accessed September 1, 2023.

72 *"it was difficult"*: Eisenhower, *Pat Nixon—The Untold Story*, 94.

73 *"In Washington"*: Ibid.

73 *"While the John F. Kennedys"*: Swift, *Pat and Dick: The Nixons*, 76.

73 *"We were like a pair"*: Thomas, *Being Nixon*, 39–40.

73 *noting his interest*: Eisenhower, *Pat Nixon—The Untold Story*, 96.

74 *"witnessed firsthand"*: Nixon, *RN*, 50–51.

74 *"The Italian industrialists"*: Letter, Richard Nixon to Pat Nixon, September 13, 1947, 2, Congressional Papers, PPS 206, series V, Folder 12, Box 16, PPS 206, series V, RNPLM.

74 *"This may sound like"*: Letter, Richard Nixon to Pat Nixon, September 14, 1947, Folder 12, Box 16, Congressional Papers, PPS 206, series V, RNPLM, 2.

74 *Pat found herself*: Brennan, *Pat Nixon: Embattled First Lady*, 25.

74 *"She stopped faucets"*: David, *The Lonely Lady of San Clemente*, 70.

75 *"stunned when she finally"*: Eisenhower, *Pat Nixon—The Untold Story*, 97.

75 *"What's that thing"*: Ibid., 98.

76 *The suave diplomat*: Eisenhower, *Pat Nixon—The Untold Story*, 99–100; Richard M. Nixon, *Six Crises* (Garden City, NY: Doubleday, 1962), 52–54.

76 *"the most influential"*: Father John F. Cronin, "The Problem of American Communism in 1945: Facts and Recommendations," Report, John F. Cronin Papers, NDA, 49.

76 *"I was able"*: Father John F. Cronin, Audio Oral History, 1976, John F. Cronin Papers, NDA.

76 *Nixon historian*: Irwin Gellman, phone call with the author, December 28, 2022.

76 *"Father John Cronin"*: Tricia Nixon Cox, email to the author, December 15, 2022.

77 *When Alger Hiss*: "Alger Hiss Released from Prison," History.com, last updated November 23, 2020, https://www.history.com/this-day-in-history/alger-hiss-released-from-prison.

77 *Alger Hiss's name*: *Washington Life Magazine*, Holiday 2010, 59.

77 *Only in 1996*: Alger Hiss, "Secrets, Lies, and Atomic Spies," Nova Online, www.pbs.org/wgbh/nova/venona/dece_hiss.html, accessed December 31, 2023.

77 *"believed that the Nixons"*: Thomas, *Being Nixon*, 55.

77 *"The reason people"*: Eisenhower, *Pat Nixon—The Untold Story*, 101.

77 *"I was to be subjected"*: Nixon, *Six Crises*, 70.

78 *two vacations scheduled*: Eisenhower, *Pat Nixon—The Untold Story*, 100–101.

10: HAPPY DAYS ARE HERE AGAIN

79   *"I realize there are mostly"*: Jack A. Drown, interview by C. Richard Arena, August 17, 1972, WCOH, 12–13.

79   *"Dewey's defeat and our loss"*: Nixon, *RN*, 72.

80   *"running for the Senate"*: Ibid.

80   *"the strongest supporter"*: Carter, *Richard Nixon: California's Native Son*, 104.

80   *In April*: Helen Daniels, oral history, WHARC, March, 1979, 1.

80   *"Wherever we took our girls"*: Ibid.

80   *"thought Pat was"*: Ibid.

80   *"one of the most hectic"*: Nixon, *RN*, 73.

80   *"A rarity as a woman"*: Thomas, *Being Nixon*, 59.

81   *"She has shown"*: Eisenhower, *Pat Nixon—The Untold Story*, 107.

81   *"red queen"*: Thomas, *Being Nixon*, 59.

81   *"In the stock"*: Morris, *Richard Milhous Nixon*, 581.

81   *"My mother in particular"*: Eisenhower, *Pat Nixon—The Untold Story*, 107.

82   *The campaign would*: Nixon, *Six Crises*, 73.

82   *one of these dresses*: Kathryn Bewley, Oral History, WHARC, March, 1979, 1.

82   *"This political bit"*: Ibid., 2.

82   *"Driving the dented"*: Thomas, *Being Nixon*, 60.

82   *Pat would give*: Swift, *Pat and Dick: The Nixons*, 103.

83   *"Sometimes your mother's"*: Eisenhower, *Pat Nixon—The Untold Story*, 10.

83   *"Dick, I know you're"*: Nixon, *RN*, 75.

83   *"A young girl"*: Evlyn Dorn, interview by C. Richard Arena, May 8, 1972, WCOH, 3.

84   *According to biographer*: David, *The Lonely Lady of San Clemente*, 78.

84   *"I miss the little girls"*: Newspaper article by Mildred Masterson McNeilly, 1950, Folder 1950 April–December, Box 1, PPS 266, PRNC, RNPLM.

84   *"as she listened"*: Excerpt from "Ladies in the News" with Marjorie Sharpe, November 1, 1950, PRNC Collection 1950, Folder 1950 April–December, Box 1, PPS 266, PRNC Collection 1950, PPS 266, Box 1, Folder 1950 April–December, PRNC, RNPLM.

84   *"Prouder than anything"*: Ibid.

84   *"Plastic Pat"*: Brennan, *Pat Nixon: Embattled First Lady*, 36.

85   *"God she made it"*: Fawn McKay Brodie, *Richard Nixon: The Shaping of His Character* (New York: W. W. Norton, 1981), 234.

85   *"I don't know anybody"*: Adela Rogers St. Johns, Reminiscences of Adela Rogers St. Johns, June 23, 1971, #1422, Columbia Center for Oral History, Columbia University: Hollywood Film Industry Oral History Project, 8.

85   *"You know I don't"*: Morris, *Richard Milhous Nixon*, 593–94.

85   *"Pat exemplified"*: David, *The Lonely Lady of San Clemente*, 83–84.

85   *"as an ornament"*: Brodie, *Richard Nixon*, 234.

86   *Perhaps the toughest*: Eisenhower, *Pat Nixon—The Untold Story*, 110.

86   *Dick won the election*: Carter, *Richard Nixon: California's Native Son*, 112.

86   *Pat remembered*: Swift, *Pat and Dick: The Nixons*, 105.

86 *"No one crossed"*: Ibid., 106.

87 *Even with the proceeds*: Farrell, *Richard Nixon*, 160.

87 *"electric kitchen with dishwasher"*: Letter, Pat to Helene, February 1951, HJDC, RNPLM; Eisenhower, *Pat Nixon—The Untold Story*, 111.

87 *"very pretty and most gracious"*: Letter Pat to Helene, November 3, 1951, HJDC, RNPLM.

87 *"I have moved"*: Letter, Pat to Helene, May 20, 1951, HJDC, RNPLM.

87 *"With it all"*: Letter, Pat to Helene, March 12, 1951, HJDC, RNPLM.

88 *Pat delighted*: Ibid.

88 *"I had a little help"*: Letter, Pat to Helene, November 3, 1951, HJDC, RNPLM.

88 *"Dick is more tired"*: Letter, Pat to Helene, September 4, 1951, HJDC, RNPLM; Eisenhower, *Pat Nixon—The Untold Story*, 111.

88 *In December*: Farrell, *Richard Nixon*, 162–63; Morris, *Richard Milhous Nixon*, 655.

89 *"loves kindergarten"*: Letter, Pat to Helene Drown, November 3, 1951, HJDC, RNPLM.

11: TAKING THE VEIL

90 *This neighborhood*: Colin Marshall, "Levittown, the Prototypical American Suburb," *The Guardian*, April 28, 2015, www.the guardian.com/cities/2015/apr/28/levitttown-america -prototypical-suburb-history-cities.

90 *the Nixons' home*: "Facts You May Not Know About Spring Valley," January 11, 2019, *Dcist*, dcist.com/story/19/01/11/10-facts-you-may-not-know-about-spring-valley/, 2.

90 *Both Pat and Dick*: Ibid.

91 *"We all helped"*: Letter, Margaret Fuller to Julie, July 8, 1978, PPS 267, Box 1, Folder 1953 September–December, PRNC, RNPLM.

91 *Margaret also mentioned*: Ibid.

91 *"She was always a lady"*: Ibid.

91 *"She always took her share"*: Ibid.

91 *The girls would attend*: Brennan, *Pat Nixon: Embattled First Lady*, 50.

91 *"One day Tricia"*: Letter, Margaret Fuller to Julie, July 8, 1978, PPS 267, Box 1, Folder 1953 September–December, PRNC, RNPLM.

91 *Pat had an active*: Morris, *Richard Milhous Nixon*, 654.

92 *"as a senator's wife"*: "Bess Truman," Miller Center, Millercenter.org/Bess Truman, accessed February 1, 2023.

92 *"executive orders and executive privilege"*: "Truman and Nixon Reconciliation," Nixon Foundation, accessed February 1, 2023.

92 *"Since I have never been"*: Letter, Pat Nixon to Helene Drown, 1952 folder, no date, HJDC, RNPLM.

92 *"monkey father"*: David, *The Lonely Lady of San Clemente*, 81.

92 *She couldn't afford*: Swift, *Pat and Dick: The Nixons*, 106.

92 *"It was the meanest"*: David, *The Lonely Lady of San Clemente*, 81.

92 *She wrote to Helene*: Letter, Pat Nixon to Helene Drown, no date, HJDC, RNPLM, 2.

93 *"our kind of people"*: Judy Bachrach, "Rose Mary Woods: Facing Her Two Crises," *Washington Post*, July 7, 1974, H2, Col. 5.

93 *"The Boss" or "El Boss"*: *Marion Star* (Marion, OH), November 11, 1968, 2.

93 *"It was the last carefree"*: Eisenhower, *Pat Nixon—The Untold Story*, 112.

93 *"the duty of a wife"*: Newsletter, PPS 266, Box 2, Folder 1952 August 1–September 21 newsletter, Box 2, PPS 266, PRNC, RNPLM, 2.

93 *"quickly became his party's"*: Earl Mazo, Stephen Hess, and Richard M. Nixon, *Nixon* (New York: Harper & Row, 1968), 84–85.

94 *"Mr. Republican"*: Eisenhower, *Pat Nixon—The Untold Story*, 114.

94 *Dick had met*: Thomas, *Being Nixon*, 67–68.

94 *Alice warned Dick*: Eisenhower, *Pat Nixon—The Untold Story*, 113.

94 *"taking the veil"*: Nixon, *RN*, 85.

94 *"You should talk to"*: Nixon, *RN*, 84–85.

95 *"Eisenhower was tied to"*: Thomas, *Being Nixon*, 69.

95 *"There comes a time"*: Eisenhower, *Pat Nixon—The Untold Story*, 115.

95 *"My mother opened"*: Ibid.

96 *"a pretty, full-skirted"*: Ibid., 117.

96 *"I am amazed"*: Morris, *Richard Milhous Nixon*, 735.

96 *Swept up in*: Thomas, *Being Nixon*, 72; Brennan, *Pat Nixon: Embattled First Lady*, 43.

96 *"I want my Mommy"*: Eisenhower, *Pat Nixon—The Untold Story*, 117; Swift, *Pat and Dick: The Nixons*, 117–18.

96 *"What do you think"*: Tricia Jackie Bouvier article, Folder 1952 October 14–December, Box 2, PPS 266, PRNC, RNPLM.

97 *"5 feet 5" in height"*: Pat Nixon campaign biography, Folder 1952 July–August campaign bio, Box 1, PPS 266, PRNC, RNPLM, 2.

97 *I've campaigned with"*: Ibid.

97 *For the campaign*: Ibid.

98 *"Dear Dick"*: Nixon, *Six Crises*, 91.

12: THE FINANCIAL STRIPTEASE

99 *"shows that try out"*: Mazo, Hess, and Nixon, *Nixon*, 99.

99 *The West Coast*: Nixon, *Six Crises*, 91.

99 *"a lavish car"*: Morris, *Richard Milhous Nixon*, 755.

100 *"My mother's red-gold hair"*: Eisenhower, *Pat Nixon—The Untold Story*, 118.

100 *The fund*: Carter, *Richard Nixon: California's Native Son*, 120.

100 *Many other politicians*: Brennan, *Pat Nixon: Embattled First Lady*, 45.

100 *"I don't care if"*: Brodie, *Richard Nixon*, 278; see also Mazo, Hess, and Nixon, *Nixon*, 118.

101 *"I was completely shaken"*: Kornitzer, *The Real Nixon*, 191.

101 *"There was just no foundation"*: Ibid.

101 *"GIRLS ARE OK"*: Ibid., 192.

101 *"In our family"*: Nixon, *RN*, 96–97.

101 *"Why should we keep"*: Mazo, Hess, and Nixon, *Nixon*, 119.

101 *"Nixon could not be"*: David Eisenhower, Zoom interview with the author, March 6, 2023.

101 *"No mink coats for Nixon"*: Kornitzer, *The Real Nixon*, 194.

101 *"That's absolutely right"*: Mazo, Hess, and Nixon, *Nixon*, 117.

102 *"threw pennies and shook"*: Eisenhower, *Pat Nixon—The Untold Story*, 119.

102 *"You can't quit"*: Ibid., 120.

102 *"You can't think of"*: Nixon, *RN*, 95.

102 *"Thinking always of"*: Brodie, *Richard Nixon*, 279.

103 *Frustrated, Dick told Ike*: Nixon, *RN*, 98.

103 *"stay above the fray"*: Irwin Gellman, phone interview with the author, March 25, 2023.

103 *"From that time"*: Eisenhower, *Pat Nixon—The Untold Story*, 120; Brennan, *Pat Nixon: Embattled First Lady*, 46.

103 *"Why do we have to tell"*: Morris, *Richard Milhous Nixon*, 813.

103 *She had been further incensed*: David, *The Lonely Lady of San Clemente*, 93.

104 *At 5:30 p.m.*: Eisenhower, *Pat Nixon—The Untold Story*, 122.

104 *"GI bedroom den"*: Morris, *Richard Milhous Nixon*, 826.

104 *Dick did not want to*: Carter. *Richard Nixon: California's Native Son*, 125.

104 *"I just don't think"*: Nixon, *Six Crises*, 113.

104 *"I want to feel"*: Morris, *Richard Milhous Nixon*, 826.

104 *Dick was placed behind*: David, *The Lonely Lady of San Clemente*, 94.

104 *Wearing a light brown dress*: Eisenhower, *Pat Nixon—The Untold Story*, 123.

104 *"financial striptease"*: Lee Huebner, "The Checkers Speech After 60 Years," *The Atlantic*, September 22, 2012, https://www.theatlantic.com/politics/archive/2012/09/the-checkers-speech-after-60-years/262172/.

105 *"Well, that's about it"*: Nixon, *Six Crises*, 115.

105 *"We did get something"*: Ibid.

105 *"I don't believe I ought"*: Ibid., 117.

105 *"Pat, I was a failure"*: Morris, *Richard Milhous Nixon*, 836.

105 *"the greatest production"*: Ibid., 839.

105 *"His tabulation"*: Farrell, *Richard Nixon*, 195.

106 *"in a fishbowl"*: Huebner, "The Checkers Speech After 60 Years."

106 *"family struggles"*: Ibid.

106 *"We all admire"*: Letter, Vivian Brashamp to the Nixons, September 21, 1952, Folder 1952 August 1–September 21, Box #2, PPS 266, PRNC, RNPLM.

106 *"I know a guy"*: Letter, September 24, 1952, James du Pont to General Dwight D. Eisenhower, Folder 1952 October 1–13, Box 2, PPS 266, PRNC, RNPLM.

106 *"I hope Pat was allowed"*: Ibid.

106 *When daughter Julie*: Brennan, *Pat Nixon: Embattled First Lady*, 48.

106 *The Fund Crisis*: Eisenhower, *Pat Nixon—The Untold Story*, 126.

107 *Nixon scholar*: Bob Bostock, email to the author, February 3, 2023.

107 *"Mrs. Nixon was quietly"*: Swift, *Pat and Dick: The Nixons*, 122–23.

107 *"I don't know why"*: Thomas, *Being Nixon*, 83.

108 *"how much it had hurt her"*: Nixon, *RN*, 108.

13: THE CINDERELLA GIRL OF THE GOP

109 *"Even your most used stories"*: Letter, Helene Drown to Richard Nixon, Hotel Washington stationery, 1952, no date, HJDC, RNPLM.

109 *"Order of the Hound's Tooth"*: *New York Times*, September 29, 1952.

110 *The Senator said"*: Ibid.

110 *"tax free doghouse"*: Article, "County Turnout Makes GOP Leaders Jubilant," PPS 267, Folder 1953 January 20–February, Box 1, PRNC, RNPLM.

110 *"The Cinderella Girl of the G.O.P."*: Norma Lee Browning, "52 Cinderella Girl of the GOP," September 28, 1952, Folder 1952, September 26–30, Box #2, PPS 266, PRNC, RNPLM.

110 *"makes her own hats"*: Ibid.

110 *"Organizers of Republican women"*: Rymph, *Republican Women*, 133.

110 *"to like a Vice-Presidential"*: Norma Lee Browning, "Still Babes in the Woods: Their Honesty Busts the Campaign Wide Open," September 3, 1952, Folder 1952 September 26–30, Box #2, PPS 266, PRNC, RNPLM.

111 *"Dear Mrs. Nixon"*: Ibid.

111 *After an exhausting journey*: Nixon, *RN*, 111.

111 *The couple's press nemesis*: Eisenhower, *Pat Nixon—The Untold Story*, 127.

112 *"The next 'Mrs. Veep'"*: "Mrs. Nixon's Cinderella Story Reaches Climax," *Washington Evening Star*, Folder 1952 October 14–December, Box #2, 11-PPS 266, PRNC, RNPLM.

112 *The Eisenhower-Nixon ticket's*: Nixon, *RN*, 113.

112 *"I haven't done a thing"*: Letter, Pat Nixon to Helene Drown, December 1952, HJDC, RNPLM.

112 *the temperature registered*: John Joyce, "January 20: The Beginning and the End: Ike's First and Last Inaugurations," Eisenhower: National Historic Site Pennsylvania, National Park Service, January 12, 2021, https://www.nps.gov/eise/blogs/january-20-the-beginning-and-the-end-ikes-first-and-last-inaugurations.htm, accessed February 12, 2023.

112 *"At that moment"*: Walter Lang, "Looking Around: Two Little Girls from Whittier Kept Nation Waiting at Inaugural, *L.A. Examiner*, 1953, Folder 1053 January 20–February, Box 1, PPS 267, PRNC, RNPLM.

112 *As the new VP's wife*: "Social Notes in Washington," March 16, 1953, Folder 1953 January 20–February, Box 1, PPS 267, PRNC, RNPLM.

112 *"Mamie looks as if"*: Letter, Helene Drown to Pat Nixon, January 20, 1953, HJDC, RNPLM.

113 *"Everyone agreed that"*: Letter, Helene Drown to Pat Nixon, 1953, HJDC, RNPLM.

113 *"Mollie Parnis"*: Betty Boyd Caroli. *First Ladies from Martha Washington to Michelle Obama* (New York: Oxford University Press, 2010), 219.

113 *"Mrs. E. invited me"*: Letter, Pat Nixon to Helene Drown, 2-3-1953, HJDC, RNPLM.

113 *"Both were frugal"*: Brennan, *Pat Nixon: Embattled First Lady*, 51.

113 *"intolerant of those"*: Julie Nixon Eisenhower, *Special People* (New York: Ballantine Books, 1978), 188.

113 *Pat also followed*: Brennan, *Pat Nixon: Embattled First Lady*, 51.

114 *"People are marveling"*: Letter, Pat to Mamie, fall 1955, no date, Box 32, White House Social Office, Nixon, Vice-President & Mrs., Dwight D. Eisenhower Presidential Library and Museum, Abilene, KS.

114 *"The staff swiftly found"*: Truman, *First Ladies*, 215.

114 *"She checked for cleanliness"*: Caroli, *First Ladies*, 218.

114 *"Ike trusted her"*: Brennan, *Pat Nixon: Embattled First Lady*, 52.

114 *The West Wing staff*: Carl Sferrazza Anthony, *First Ladies* (New York: William Morrow, 1990), 562.

114 *The Second Lady's only*: Eisenhower, *Pat Nixon—The Untold Story*, 130.

114 *"are very sweet to me"*: Correspondence, Pat Nixon to Helene Drown, April 1, 1953, HJDC, RNPLM, 2–3.

114 *Each Tuesday*: Irwin F. Gellman, *Campaign of the Century: Kennedy, Nixon, and the Election of 1960* (New Haven, CT: Yale University Press, 2021), 7.

114 *"was probably the most faithful"*: Carl Sferrazza Anthony, *First Ladies: The Saga of the Presidents' Wives and Their Power 1789–1961* (New York: William Morrow, 1990), 583.

115 *"a party for fourteen"*: Letter, Pat Nixon to Helene Drown, March 4, 1953, HJDC, RNPLM, 2.

115 *"Tricia lost a front tooth"*: Ibid., 4.

115 *"She needed the help"*: David, *The Lonely Lady of San Clemente*, 96.

115 *"The President asked Dick"*: Letter, Pat Nixon to Helene Drown, June 3, 1953, HJDC, RNPLM.

115 *In September the Nixons were invited*: Gellman, *Campaign of the Century*, 7; Thomas, *Being Nixon*, 89.

115 *"Pat being Pat"*: Isabella Taves, "Pat Nixon, Problems of a 'Perfect Wife,'" *Redbook*, no. 1 (May 1956), 90.

116 *"It was a painful farewell"*: Nixon, *RN*, 119.

116 *"Today the excitement"*: Pat Nixon Diary, October 5–17, 1953, Folder 1953, Box 4, PPS 267, PRNC, RNPLM, 1–2.

116 *In his memoirs*: Nixon, *RN*, 119.

116 *"each took one small"*: Eleanor Harris, "The Dark Hours of the Richard Nixons," *Washington Post and Times Herald*, March 4, 1956, sec. AW1, 2.

117 *"she calmed her nerves"*: Elizabeth Cloes, interview by Mary Suzanne Simon, May 29, 1970, OH #834, CSUF, Richard M. Nixon, 3.

117 *"Queen beautiful"*: Pat Nixon Notes, Folder 1953 October 27–30, Box 2, PPS 267, PRNC, RNPLM.

117 *While in Taiwan*: Letter, Pat to Helene, no date, 1953, HJDC, RNPLM.

117 *"visit schools and institutions"*: Eisenhower, *Pat Nixon—The Untold Story*, 137.

117 *"In many ways"*: Jack Sherwood, "XII Diplomat-Campaigner (Some Interwoven Skills)," JNEC, RNPLM.

118 *"People can sense"*: Handwritten notes, 1953 Trip Folder 4–5, PPS 267, 1953, PNRC, RNPLM.

118 *The visits to schools and orphanages*: Clipping, *Auckland Star*, Folder 1953 October 15, Box 2, PPS 267, PRNC, RNPLM.

118 *"Everywhere I went"*: Eisenhower, *Pat Nixon—The Untold Story*, 142.

118 *"we are happy to be home"*: Clipping, *Washington Times-Herald*, December 15, 1953, Folder News 1953, PRNC, RNPLM.

118 *Pat was brought*: Taves, "Pat Nixon, Problems of a 'Perfect Wife,'" 91.

14: LADY OF FASHION

119 *"Mamie and Ike"*: Eisenhower, *Special People*, 171.

119 *As historian Bob Bostock*: Bob Bostock, interview with the author, July 18, 2023.

119 *"America's Ten Best Dressed"*: Correspondence, Folder Corr. 1954, Box 1, PPS 269, PRNC, RNPLM.

119 *"Grace and charm"*: Article, "August Lady of Fashion," Folder Cor. 1954, Box, 1, PPS 269, 3, PRNC, RNPLM.

120 *"The President and Mrs. E."*: Letter, Pat Nixon to Helene Drown, January 21, 1954, HJDC, RNPLM, 3–4.

120 *"as two of their best friends"*: Swift, *Pat and Dick: The Nixons*, 130.

120 *Fond letters went between*: Mamie to Pat, November 16, 1954, White House Social Office, Box 32 (Nixon, Vice-President & Mrs.), Dwight D. Eisenhower Presidential Library and Museum, Abilene, KS.

120 *Mamie sent warm replies*: Letters from Mamie to Julie and Tricia, November 17, 1954, White House Social Office, Box 32 (Nixon, Vice-President & Mrs.), Dwight D. Eisenhower Presidential Library and Museum, Abilene, KS.

120 *"They had good chemistry"*: David Eisenhower, Zoom interview with the author, March 6, 2023.

121 *"Ike socialized almost"*: Dr. Michael Birkner, email to the author, February 20, 2023.

121 *"What on earth"*: Anthony, *First Ladies*, 583.

121 *Former First Lady Bess Truman*: David Eisenhower, Zoom interview with the author, March 6, 2023.

121 *"an army wife"*: Julie Eisenhower, email to the author, March 3, 2023.

121 *"Mrs. Nixon was very"*: David Eisenhower, Zoom interview with the author, March 6, 2023.

121 *"I would like to do"*: Letter, Pat to Helene, 2-8-56, HJDC, RNPLM.

121 *"Let's face it"*: Anthony, *First Ladies*, 565.

122 *"clear by her every"*: Caroli, *First Ladies*, 215.

122 *Mamie's narrower view*: Ibid., 220.

122 *her grandson, David*: David Eisenhower, Zoom interview with the author, June 5, 2023.

122 *At the White House*: Caroli, *First Ladies*, 220–21; Truman, *First Ladies*, 217–18.

122 *"Mamie was also influenced"*: Truman, *First Ladies*, 217–18; Eisenhower, *Special People*, 182.

122 *"The staff learned not"*: Anthony, *First Ladies*, 557.

122 *"If Mamie Eisenhower"*: Eisenhower, *Special People*, 178–79.

122 *"Everything Mamie"*: Ibid.

123 *"although she still"*: Eisenhower, *Pat Nixon—The Untold Story*, 151.

123 *Chief among his personal reasons*: Richard Nixon note, February 1954, JNEC, RNPLM; Mazo, Hess, and Nixon, *Nixon*, 139.

123 *"We are again enjoying"*: Letter, Pat to Helene, 8-16-54, HJDC, RNPLM.

123 *"Saturday night and all alone"*: Letter, Pat to Helene, 10-23-54, HJDC, RNPLM.

123 *"the official schedule"*: Ibid.

123 *Added to her evening*: Correspondence, Folder Cor. 1954 December, Box 1, PPS 269, PRNC, RNPLM.

124 *The year 1954*: Nixon, *RN*, 159.

124 *"traveled twenty-six thousand"*: Thomas, *Being Nixon*, 88.

124 *"the girls were reaching"*: Nixon, *RN*, 163.

124 *Still, the Democrats*: Mazo, Hess, and Nixon, *Nixon*, 157.

124 *"Once I'm quite sure"*: Father John Cronin audio oral history, NDA, 1976.

124 *"Nixon's marriage was"*: Interview with Father John Cronin, St. Mary's Seminary, Baltimore, MD, November 26, 1975, Folder 77.16, Hoover Archive, Weinstein Collection, 2.

125 *"noticed that Nixon"*: Gary Wills, email to the author, December 18, 2022.

125 *"would telephone his mother"*: David, *The Lonely Lady of San Clemente*, 115.

125 *"on at least one"*: Ibid., 116.

125 *As the calendar pages*: 1955 Itineraries, Nixon Archives, RNPLM.

126 *In San Salvador*: Trip notes, Folder 1955 Central American Trip Feb. 15–17 El Salvador Pat and Children, Box 2, PPS 270, PRNC, RNPLM.

126 *"Pat sought to influence"*: Swift, *Pat and Dick: The Nixons*, 127.

126 *Like the princess*: Ibid.

126 *"No because I honestly"*: Ruth Montgomery, "Pat Nixon Does All Her Own Cooking, Dishes, Housework," *Chicago Defender*, June 23, 1956, Folder, June 1956, Box 1, PPS 271, PRNC, RNPLM.

126 *"arrived poolside in a suit"*: Beverly Gage, *G-Man J. Edgar Hoover and the Making of the American Century* (New York: Viking, 2022), 417.

126 *"Over the course of"*: Ibid., 473.

126 *Pat and Dick sent*: Ibid.

127 *"Dick, the President"*: Nixon, *Six Crises*, 132; Eisenhower, *Pat Nixon—The Untold Story*, 154.

127 *"were on guard"*: Eisenhower, *Pat Nixon—The Untold Story*, 154.

127 *"took over the entertaining"*: Eisenhower, *Pat Nixon—The Untold Story*, 155.

127 *"My problem"*: Nixon, *Six Crises*, 144.

127 *"During the dark days"*: Ruth Montgomery, "Pat Nixon Does All Her Own Cooking, Dishes, Housework," *Chicago Defender*, June 23, 1956, PPS 271, Box 1, Folder June 1956.

128 *"that our thoughts and prayers"*: Letter, Pat to Mamie, no date, White House Social Office, Box 32 (Nixon, Vice-President, and Mrs.), Dwight D. Eisenhower Presidential Library, Abilene, KS.

128 *There were some way*: Ibid.

128 *"warm and encouraging"*: Letter, Mamie to Pat, October 18, 1955, White House Social Office, Box 32 (Nixon, Vice-President and Mrs.), Dwight Eisenhower Presidential Library, Abilene, KS.

128 *"increase in social activity"*: Eisenhower, *Pat Nixon—The Untold Story*, 155.

128 *"Fully engaged in learning"*: Thomas, *Being Nixon*, 93.

128 *"Exceptional circumstances"*: Nixon, *RN*, 163.

128 *"Eisenhower looked at Nixon"*: Thomas, *Being Nixon*, 94.

129 *"It seemed to be"*: Farrell, *Richard Nixon*, 240.

129 *"He [Eisenhower] is terribly cold"*: Ibid., 241.

129 *"Nixon was a much nicer"*: David Eisenhower, Zoom interview with the author, March 6, 2023.

129 *"What [Ike]"*: Ibid.

129 *"more depressed"*: Thomas, *Being Nixon*, 85.

129 *"the trip to Brazil"*: Letter, Pat to Helene, 2-8-1956, HJDC, RNPLM.

130 *In June the Nixons*: David, *The Lonely Lady of San Clemente*, 104; Brennan, *Pat Nixon: Embattled First Lady*, 62–63.

130 *"Pat understood"*: David Eisenhower, Zoom interview with the author, March 6, 2023.

130 *"No one is going to push"*: Eisenhower, *Pat Nixon—The Untold Story*, 158.

15: GRACE UNDER FIRE

131 *"reported back"*: Eisenhower, *Pat Nixon—The Untold Story*, 232.

131 *"With Jesuitical innocence"*: Thomas, *Being Nixon*, 96.

131 *"launched a formal campaign"*: Eisenhower, *Pat Nixon—The Untold Story*, 158.

131 *Stassen had little*": Gellman, *Campaign of the Century*, 12.

131 *"This is not a press*": Article, "Coffee Hour" the Mark Hopkins, 8/20/56, Women of the Press and Pat for Republican Convention, Folder no number, Box 1, PPS 271, PRNC, RNPLM.

131 *"got a roaring*": Article, "Coffee Hour" the Mark Hopkins, "Mrs. Nixon Cheered At Convention," August 20, 1956, Folder no number, Box 1, PPS 271, PRNC, RNPLM.

132 *Finally on August 22*: Eisenhower, *Pat Nixon—The Untold Story*, 159.

132 *"I was so delighted*": Letter, Madame Chiang Kai-shek to Pat Nixon, September 5, 1956, Folder September 1956, Box 1, PPS 271, PRNC, RNPLM.

132 *"she replied with a wry smile*": Eisenhower, *Pat Nixon—The Untold Story*, 159.

132 *The elections of 1952 and 1956*: U.S. National Archives, "Women Unite for Ike!," Google Arts & Culture, https://artsandculture.google.com/story/women-unite-for-ike-u-s-national-archives /SQUxMpribfV4KQ, accessed March 5, 2023.

133 *"Mother's closet door*": Eisenhower, *Pat Nixon—The Untold Story*, 163.

133 *Tricia recalled*: Tricia Nixon Cox, email to the author, January 22, 2024.

133 *"courageous husband*": Letter, Elizabeth Arden to Pat Nixon, December 20, 1956, Folder 1956 December, Box 1, PPS 271, PRNC, RNPLM.

133 *The "errand" Arden*: Richard Nixon Pre-Presidential Materials, Laguna Niguel; Abstract: Subseries D: 1956 Austrian Trip, 8, RNPLM.

133 *"Mrs. Eisenhower or his own wife*": Benjamin Joel Goldberg, "The Vice Presidency of Richard M. Nixon: One Man's Quest for National Respect, an International Reputation, and the Presidency," Ph.D. dissertation, College of William & Mary, 1998, 148.

133 *The new year brought*: Richard Nixon Pre-Presidential Materials (Laguna Niguel), Richard Nixon Presidential Library and Museum. Abstract: Finding Aid Subseries E: 1957 Africa Trip, 8; 1957 Africa trip itinerary.

134 *"Nixon unexpectedly met*": Gregory Garland, "Kennedy, Nixon and the Competition for Mr. Africa, 1952–1960," American Foreign Service Association, September 2022, 3, www.afsa.org /kennedy-nixon-and-competition-mr-africa-1952-1960.

134 *A photo shows MLK*: Eisenhower, *Pat Nixon—The Untold Story*, 167.

134 *Journalist and Nixon acquaintance*: James McGrath Morris, *Eye on the Struggle: Ethel Payne, the First Lady of the Black Press* (New York: Amistad, 2017), 197–98.

134 *King and Ralph Abernathy arrived*: Ibid., 203.

134 *"was the hero of the day*": Ibid.

134 *He was an honorary member*: Garland, "Kennedy, Nixon and the Competition for Mr. Africa," 3.

134 *"good will activities*": Brennan, *Pat Nixon—Embattled First Lady*, 66.

135 *"Both Mrs. Nixon and Vice-President Nixon*": Don Hughes, phone interview with the author, February 5, 2021.

135 *"Colonel, I was happy*": Ibid.

135 *When the Nixons finally*: Richard Nixon Pre-Presidential Materials, Laguna Niguel, 1957 African trip abstract, RNPLM.

135 *Just before leaving*: Morris, *Eye on the Struggle*, 202.

135 *Thankfully, three of*: Eisenhower, *Pat Nixon—The Untold Story*, 168.

135 *"a step up*": Eisenhower, *Pat Nixon—The Untold Story*, 167.

136 *"dead-end street*": David, *The Lonely Lady of San Clemente*, 97.

136 *"The chief conversation*": Bess Furman article, June 5, 1957, Bess Furman Papers, LOC.

136 *"the cookie rug"*: Eisenhower, *Pat Nixon—The Untold Story*, 168.

136 *On November 25, 1957*: Nixon, *RN*, 184–85.

136 *Post-stroke*: Eisenhower, *Pat Nixon—The Untold Story*, 171.

137 *"relatively unimportant"*: Nixon, *Six Crises*, 183–84.

137 *The Nixons would visit*: 1958 Itineraries, Pre-Presidential Materials, Laguna Nigel, 1958 South American Trip Abstract, RNPLM; Nixon, *Six Crises*, 186.

137 *The first stops in Uruguay*: Thomas, *Being Nixon*, 98.

137 *On May 7*: Nixon, *Six Crises*, 198.

137 *"Pat endured a nerve-racking"*: Brennan, *Embattled First Lady*, 64.

138 *"announcing that Vice President"*: Eisenhower, *Pat Nixon—The Untold Story*, 173.

138 *"the State Department"*: Nixon, *Six Crises*, 211.

138 *"We were in a position"*: Ibid.

138 *"knew in advance"*: Don Hughes, phone interview with the author, February 5, 2021.

138 *"At first the spit"*: Eisenhower, *Pat Nixon—The Untold Story*, 174.

138 *"She beat me to it"*: Don Hughes, interview with the author, February 5, 2021.

139 *"my feeling we were"*: Ibid.

139 *Mrs. Nixon had her arms*: Colonel James "Don" Hughes, oral history, interviewed by Frank Gannon and Jonathan Movroydics, November 10, 2018, RNPLM, 9.

139 *"Pat appeared to be"*: Nixon, *Six Crises*, 218.

139 *one of the communist demonstrators*: Eisenhower, *Pat Nixon—The Untold Story*, 175.

140 *"I was in the last car"*: "Nixon's Secretary Takes Riots or Travel in Stride," *The Tribune* (Coshocton, OH), July 7, 1960, 14.

140 *"American soil and a little bit of heaven"*: Eisenhower, *Pat Nixon—The Untold Story*, 175–76; Nixon, *Six Crises*, 219–21.

140 *President Eisenhower had ordered*: Nixon, *Six Crises*, 225.

140 *the Nixon entourage*: Brennan, *Embattled First Lady*, 65.

140 *"welcoming reception"*: Nixon, *Six Crises*, 228; Nixon, *Memoirs*, 193.

140 *"Tricia and Julie were waiting"*: Nixon, *Memoirs*, 193.

140 *"The next two hours"*: Eisenhower, *Pat Nixon—The Untold Story*, 178.

140 *"Lyndon Johnson, then Democratic"*: Brodie, *Richard Nixon*, 373.

141 *"That September"*: Gellman, *Campaign of the Century*, 35.

141 *On November 24*: Pre-Presidential Materials, Laguna Nigel, Itineraries, London, 1958, Working Schedule for the Vice-Presidential Visit to England: November 14, 1958; Department of State Washington, D.C. Office of the Chief of Protocol November 27, 1958, Guest List dinner for Queen Elizabeth II, RNPLM.

141 *"Gals of Fleet Street"*: "Gals of Fleet Street Wowed by Pat Nixon," *Los Angeles Times*, November 27, 1958.

141 *"Mrs. Pat, face to face"*: *The Spectator*, December 22, 1958.

141 *"Russia was still shrouded"*: Nixon, *RN*, 203.

142 *"Mother's role on the trip"*: Eisenhower, *Pat Nixon—The Untold Story*, 181.

142 *"Since the fundamental basis"*: Clippings, Folder, Misc. Material re: USSR American Women Portrayal to the Soviets: U.S. Department of Labor, Women's Bureau, Women of the United States by Mrs. Alice K. Lepold, PPS 274, PRNC, RNPLM.

142 *These notations show*: Ibid.

142 *"Kitchen Debate"*: Nixon, *RN*, 206–8.

142 *At a welcoming luncheon*: Eisenhower, *Pat Nixon—The Untold Story*, 182.

142 *Later that afternoon*: Ibid.

143 *"Children are the same"*: "Pat Nixon's Lollipops Charm Nursery Children," *Boston Globe*, July 24, 1959, 11.

143 *In a stunning turn*: Eisenhower, *Pat Nixon—The Untold Story*, 182.

143 *"the wives of Premier Khrushchev"*: Ruth Montgomery, "The Real Remarkable Pat Nixon," *The Duncan Banner*, Duncan, OK, August 17, 1959, 7.

143 *"the friendly, personable Pat"*: Ibid.

143 *"Afterwards, the four of us"*: Ruth Montgomery, "The Real Remarkable Pat Nixon," *The Duncan Banner*, Duncan, OK, August 17, 1959, 7.

16: 1960 ELECTION: JEWELED JACKIE VS. DRIP-DRY PAT

144 *"Refuse to run in"*: Eisenhower, *Pat Nixon—The Untold Story,* 171.

144 *"dumped from"*: Aitken, *Nixon: A Life,* 271.

144 *"much of the equality"*: Luke Nichter, email to the author, July 15, 2023.

145 *"I couldn't agree"*: Richard Nixon to Helene Drown, May 6, 1959, Correspondence, Box 2, HJDC, RNPLM.

145 *"IF PAT NIXON"*: 1960 election speech, HJDC, RNPLM, 2.

145 *"She traveled with"*: David, *The Lonely Lady of San Clemente*, 115.

145 *"A survey conducted"*: Rymph, *Republican Women*, 132.

146 *"The best advice"*: Nixon, *Six Crises*, 406.

146 *"Inside the party"*: Rachel Maddow and Michael Yarvitz, *Bag Man* (New York: Crown, 2020), 182.

146 *It was the Republican Party*: "1976 Republican Platform: Equal Rights and Ending Discrimination," Gerald R. Ford Presidential Library and Museum, Grand Rapids, MI.

146 *"the task of achieving"*: "All VP Statement, RN," Office of the VP, September 2, 1960, RNPLM.

146 *"I believe that"*: Ibid.

146 *"ringing the doorbell"*: Rymph, *Republican Women*, 133.

146 *"Bess Truman and Mamie Eisenhower"*: Julia Sweig, *Lady Bird Johnson: Hiding in Plain Sight* (New York: Random House, 2022), 110.

147 *"This fall the question"*: Martha Weinman, "First Ladies in Fashion, Too?," Bess Furman Papers, LOC, 33.

147 *"Jackie Kennedy"*: Sweig, *Lady Bird Johnson*, 110–11.

147 *"Met Senator Kennedy's"*: Carl Anthony, *Camera Girl*, 283.

147 *"She's a very glamorous"*: "An Afternoon with a Candidate's Wife," *Washington Daily News*, September 9, 1960.

147 *"While Pat was seen"*: Herb Klein oral history, February, 20, 2007, RNPLM, 7.

148 *"I simply don't like"*: Kitty Kelley, *Jackie Oh!* (Secaucus, NJ: Lyle Stuart, 1978), 90.

148 *"She had never cared"*: David, *The Lonely Lady of San Clemente*, 117.

148 *"I'm sure I spend"*: Nan Robertson, "Mrs. Kennedy Defends Clothes: Is 'Sure' Mrs. Nixon Pays More," *New York Times*, September 15, 1960.

148 *"Good Christ"*: Kelley, *Jackie Oh!*, 90.

148 *"emphasizing that she only"*: Brennan, *Pat Nixon: Embattled First Lady*, 74.

148   *"concerned about"*: Kelley, *Jackie Oh!*, 90

148   *"The contrast between"*: David, *The Lonely Lady of San Clemente*, 116.

148   *"When I first met"*: Kandie Stroud, interview with the author, July 19, 2022.

149   *"When I worked for"*: Ibid.

149   *"I want you"*: Ibid.

149   *"I cannot urge your"*: Fairchild Publications, Inc., Letter, Annette Culler to Bessie Newton, July 22, 1960, Box 275, Folder 10B-PN-1960-Requests for Interviews, PRNC, RNPLM.

149   *"New Nixon"*: Gellman, *Campaign of the Century*, 148.

150   *"In the fall of 1959"*: John Ehrlichman, *Witness to Power: The Nixon Years* (New York: Simon & Schuster, 1982), 17–19.

150   *"had less political experience"*: Brennan, *Pat Nixon: Embattled First Lady*, 87.

150   *"Bob Haldeman was suggesting"*: Ehrlichman, *Witness to Power*, 19.

150   *"Tricia and Julie"*: Eisenhower, *Pat Nixon—The Untold Story*, 188.

150   *"When we see you"*: Letter, RN to Tricia, July 18, 1960, Box 2, PPS 275, PRNC, RNPLM.

150   *Dick not only valued*: Ibid.

150   *"Nixonettes"*: Carter, *Richard Nixon: California's Native Son*, 232.

150   *"pleated dresses"*: Ibid.

151   *"evoked historical precedent"*: Eisenhower, *Pat Nixon—The Untold Story*, 189.

151   *One notable event*: June 17, 1960, Invite from Phyllis Schlafly, Folder Republican National Convention Chicago July 25, Box 275, PRNC, RNPLM.

151   *"Pat Precinct Plan"*: Pat Centered Campaign Plans, Folder, Republican National Convention July 25, 1960, Box 275, PRNC, RNPLM.

151   *"Complete with her own"*: Brennan, *Pat Nixon: Embattled First Lady*, 73.

151   *"presidential campaign previously"*: Committee on Commerce, U.S. Senate, *The Joint Appearances of Senator John F. Kennedy and Vice President Richard M. Nixon Presidential Campaign of 1960* (Washington, DC: U.S. Government Printing Office, 1961).

152   *"I think that women"*: Ibid., 244.

152   *"women not only"*: Ibid.

152   *"Her critics"*: "Pat Nixon," *Time*, February 29, 1960, 25.

152   *"I never have tantrums"*: Ibid.

152   *"I've always been part"*: Ibid.

152   *Pat told a crowd*: Gellman, *Campaign of the Century*, 152.

152   *She made another campaign*: *Atlanta Daily World*, August 28, 1960, 4.

153   *"I am particularly interested"*: Pat, letter to College Women's Activity Chairman, no date but sometime in 1960, Folder 11, PN 1960—Requests to Write Mag, News, Books, Expressions of Opinion Women Key to the Vote in 1960, PPS 275, PRNC, RNPLM.

153   *"In this campaign year"*: Statement by Mrs. Richard Nixon for the Monticello College Alumnae Magazine, October 1960, Folder 11, PN 1960—Requests to Write Mag, News, Books, Expressions of Opinion Women Key to the Vote in 1960, PPS 275, PRNC, RNPLM.

153   *"he functioned as his own"*: Thomas, *Being Nixon*, 112.

153   *"almost cost him"*: Ibid.

153   *Dick's illness*: Swift, *Pat and Dick: The Nixons*, 161.

154   *"Nielson Television Index"*: Gellman, *Campaign of the Century*, 201.

154   *Nixon lent Kennedy*: Ibid., 216.

154 *"the only way he and Mother"*: Eisenhower, *Pat Nixon—The Untold Story*, 192.

154 *"Mamie was plugging at me"*: Gellman, *Campaign of the Century*, 243.

154 *"The First Lady sounded distraught"*: Eisenhower, *Pat Nixon—The Untold Story*, 194.

154 *"I could make no other"*: Nixon, *RN*, 222–23.

154 *"angry—and confused"*: Eisenhower, *Pat Nixon—The Untold Story*, 195.

155 *"It was not until"*: Nixon, *RN*, 222–23.

155 *Election Day came*: Brennan, *Pat Nixon: Embattled First Lady*, 8.

155 *After a brief rest*: Gellman, *Campaign of the Century*, 251.

155 *While Dick watched*: Eisenhower, *Pat Nixon—The Untold Story*, 196.

155 *"had been hearing"*: Thomas, *Being Nixon*, 123–24.

155 *She suspected voting*: Eisenhower, *Pat Nixon—The Untold Story*, 197.

155 *"middle of the road"*: Bob Finch, oral history, 1967, CCOH, 67.

155 *At about 11:00*: Herb Klein oral history, February 20, 2007, RNPLM, 34.

156 *The film footage*: Thomas, *Being Nixon*, 124.

156 *"as I was writing"*: Nixon, *Six Crises*, 386.

156 *"To Pat: She also ran"*: Ibid., dedication page.

156 *"And it is not because"*: Letter, Helene Drown to Pat Nixon, no date, November 1960, Box 2, HJDC, RNPLM.

156 *"courage, and unselfishness"*: Ibid.

156 *"I think the reason 1960"*: Julie Eisenhower, email to the author, March 23, 2023.

17: PEOPLE ARE NOT CATTLE

157 *"Kennedy had won"*: Thomas, *Being Nixon*, 127.

157 *"In Chicago"*: Ibid.

157 *"discouraged any initiative"*: Gellman, *Campaign of the Century*, 272.

157 *On November 11*: Eisenhower, *Pat Nixon—The Untold Story*, 199; Nixon, *Six Crises*, 403.

157 *"They said it was for"*: Herb Klein oral history, February 20, 2007, RNPLM, 36.

158 *"They both berated"*: Nixon, *Six Crises*, 405.

158 *"So on Monday"*: Herb Klein oral history, February 20, 2007, RNPLM, 36.

158 *"the Florida trip"*: Letter, Pat to Helene, no date, Box 2, HJDC, RNPLM.

158 *"Since presidential inaugurations"*: Kevin Ambrose and Jason Samenow, "How a Surprise Snowstorm Almost Spoiled Kennedy's Inauguration 60 Years Ago," *Washington Post*, January 19, 2021, www.washingtonpost.com/weather/2021/01/19/kennedy-inauguration-weather-1961.

159 *The winter weather*: Ibid.

159 *"Dear Diary"*: Eisenhower, *Pat Nixon—The Untold Story*, 201.

159 *"struck by the thought"*: Nixon, *RN*, 228.

160 *He admitted*: Nixon, *Six Crises*, 426.

160 *Dick decided*: Nixon, *RN*, 231.

160 *"JFK called Daddy"*: Note, Tricia to RN re: JFK call, April 20, 1961, Folder 15, 1961, PPS 278, PRNC, RNPLM.

160 *June finally arrived*: David, *The Lonely Lady of San Clemente*, 122.

160 *"water ballet"*: Eisenhower, *Pat Nixon—The Untold Story*, 205.

160 *The Nixons were celebrated*: Brodie, *Richard Nixon*, 451.

160 *The girls were preparing*: Brennan, *Pat Nixon: Embattled First Lady*, 82.

161 *Dick had not made*: Carter, *Richard Nixon: California's Native Son*, 187.

161 *"Long, low, and ranch"*: David, *The Lonely Lady of San Clemente*, 122.

161 *The Nixons also met*: Eisenhower, *Pat Nixon—The Untold Story*, 208.

161 *"I dreaded bringing"*: Nixon, *RN*, 239.

161 *In Dick's telling*: Ibid., 240.

161 *"You voted for running"*: Eisenhower, *Pat Nixon—The Untold Story*, 206.

161 *"if you run"*: Carter, *Richard Nixon: California's Native Son*, 195.

162 *"like a wax figure"*: Ladies' Home Journal, 11, RNPLM.

162 *"Carol, I'm trapped"*: Eisenhower, *Pat Nixon—The Untold Story*, 207.

162 *"Pat campaigned as"*: Brennan, *Pat Nixon: Embattled First Lady*, 84.

162 *"chose the title"*: Eisenhower, *Pat Nixon—The Untold Story*, 209.

163 *Haldeman absorbed some*: Brodie, *Richard Nixon*, 457.

163 *He came from the*: Memo, Bessie Newton to Bob Haldeman re: PN and Women of the Press, PPS 279, PRNC, RNPLM.

163 *"campaign strategists soon"*: "Pat Nixon Memorial Service, Pete Wilson Eulogy," YouTube, accessed April 5, 2023.

163 *"We developed a rapport "*: Jack Carley, phone interview with the author, June 25, 2020.

163 *"The proper cure"*: Jack Carley, unpublished diary summary, 2.

164 *"In 1962, she was"*: Eisenhower, *Pat Nixon—The Untold Story*, 209.

164 *"I saw her treat"*: Carley, unpublished diary summary, 5.

164 *"At some point"*: Ibid.

164 *"I remember that"*: Ibid., 11.

164 *"had distracted the press"*: Thomas, *Being Nixon*, 134.

165 *"spoke of running"*: Brodie, *Richard Nixon*, 458.

165 *"Tomorrow, I'm hoping"*: Dwight Chapin, *The President's Man: The Memoirs of Nixon's Trusted Aide* (New York: William Morrow, 2023), 17.

165 *"My biggest problem"*: Nixon, *RN*, 243.

165 *"She could not tolerate"*: Swift, *Pat and Dick: The Nixons*, 180.

165 *"Screw them"*: Nixon, *RN*, 244.

165 *"For sixteen years"*: Nixon, *RN*, 245.

166 *"Watching my father"*: Eisenhower, *Pat Nixon—The Untold Story*, 213.

166 *"Oh Dick"*: Eisenhower, *Pat Nixon—The Untold Story*, 213–14.

166 *"first, and the only"*: Ibid.

166 *"vanished"*: Chapin, *The President's Man*, 19.

166 *ABC News*: Harold Holzer, *The Presidents Versus the Press: The Endless Battle Between the Presidents and the Media from the Founding Fathers to Fake News* (New York: Dutton, 2020), 253.

166 *"Barring a miracle"*: Thomas, *Being Nixon*, 135.

166 *"Mother was enthusiastic"*: Eisenhower, *Pat Nixon—The Untold Story*, 216.

167 *"After Nixon joined"*: Carter, *Richard Nixon: California's Native Son*, 214.

167 *The Nixons soon made*: Eisenhower, *Pat Nixon—The Untold Story*, 216.

167 *Now that her husband*: David, *The Lonely Lady of San Clemente*, 125.

167 *Maureen recalled*: Maureen Drown Nunn, phone interview with the author, December 19, 2020.

167 *"People recognize him"*: Maureen Drown Nunn, European diary entry, June 21, 1963, RNPLM, 4–5.

168 *Pat later sent Eugenia*: Maureen Drown Nunn, phone interview with the author, December 19, 2020.

168 *"mother of teenagers"*: Ibid.

168 *"Pat would be pointing"*: Ibid.

168 *"I never heard"*: Ibid.

168 *While the Nixons and Drowns*: Maureen Drown Nunn, European diary entry, June 30–July 1, 1963, RNPLM.

168 *"Sounding happy and relaxed"*: Nixon, *RN*, 250.

168 *"For Pat, Julie"*: Ibid.

168 *"Mother told Maureen"*: Eisenhower, *Pat Nixon—The Untold Story*, 217–18.

18: A NEW LIFE ON THE UPPER EAST SIDE

169 *After their summer*: The Chapin School website, https://www.chapin.edu/, accessed April 11, 2023.

169 *"This very pretty girl"*: Ed Cox, interview with the author, August 29, 2023.

169 *One of Tricia's escorts*: "International Debutante Ball Is Held at the Astor Amid Pink and Silver Decor," *New York Times*, December 30, 1964, https://www.nytimes.com/1964/12/30/archives /international-debutante-ball-is-held-at-the-astor-amid-pink-and.html.

169 *"But more often than that"*: Eisenhower, *Pat Nixon—The Untold Story*, 218.

170 *"the happiest was Pat"*: William Safire, *Before the Fall: An Inside View of the Pre-Watergate White House* (New York: Belmont Tower Books, 1975), 22.

170 *In the early 1960s*: Robert Atkins, *Art Speak: A Guide to Contemporary Ideas, Movements, and Buzzwords, 1945 to the Present* (New York: Abbeville Press, 1997), 149.

170 *Pat and Dick's taste*: Flora Rheta Schreiber, *Good Housekeeping* 167, no. 1 (July 1968), 187.

170 *Pat enjoyed visiting*: Tricia, email to the author, April 13, 2023.

170 *"A loyal friend through"*: Ibid.

170 *In the literary world*: Germano Celant, *New York, 1962–1964, Exhibition Catalog, Jewish Museum of New York* (New York: Skira, 2022), 67.

170 *"the assumption that women"*: Ibid., 127.

171 *"We can no longer ignore"*: Betty Freidan, *The Feminine Mystique* (New York: W. W. Norton, 1963), 32.

171 *On November 20*: Beth Frutkin, Michal Kranz, and Isabella Zavarise, "This Timeline Shows Exactly How the Day of JFK's Assassination Unfolded," *Business Insider*, last updated November 22, 2022, https://www.businessinsider.com/kennedy-assassination-timeline -2013-11.

171 *The president and First Lady*: "November 22, 1963: Death of the President," JFK Library, https:// www.jfklibrary.org/learn/about-jfk/jfk-in-history/november-22-1963-death-of-the-president, accessed April 12, 2023.

171 *"Tears were streaming"*: Nixon, *RN*, 252.

172 *"While the hand of fate"*: Ibid., 253.

172 *"You brought to the"*: Ibid.

172 *The Nixons flew*: Eisenhower, *Pat Nixon—The Untold Story*, 219; Brennan, *Pat Nixon: Embattled First Lady*, 91.

172 *"I know how you must"*: Nixon, *RN*, 254–55.

172 *"That winter"*: Eisenhower, *Pat Nixon—The Untold Story*, 220.

173 *"It was the most sweeping"*: "Civil Rights Act (1964)," Milestone Documents, National Archives, https://www.archives.gov/milestone-documents/civil-rights-act, accessed April 17, 2023.

173 *"Mrs. N. finally departed"*: Letter, Pat to Helene, July 7, 1964, Folder 11, HJDC, RNPLM.

173 *After Hannah's departure*: Eisenhower, *Pat Nixon—The Untold Story*, 220–21.

173 *Despite his reservations*: Ibid., 221.

173 *Pat wrote Helene*: Postcard from Scotland, Pat to Helene, August 4, 1964, Folder 11, HJDC, RNPLM.

173 *Tricia started*: Eisenhower, *Pat Nixon—The Untold Story*, 222.

173 *"I've seen her"*: David, *The Lonely Lady of San Clemente*, 126.

174 *She answered*: Stephen Ambrose, *Nixon: The Triumph of a Politician 1962–1972* (New York: Simon & Schuster, 1989), 63.

174 *"How are the Goldwaterites?"*: Pat Nixon to Helene Drown, November 1964, HJDC, RNPLM.

174 *"For the first time"*: Sweig, *Lady Bird Johnson*, 123.

174 *The Republican Party*: Nixon, *RN*, 264.

174 *"I did not reveal"*: Ibid., 265.

175 *"There can be no revolution"*: Associated Press, *The World in 1965: History as We Lived It* (New York: Associated Press, 1966), 37.

175 *"something happened that"*: Ibid., 48.

175 *"called for more marches"*: Ibid.

175 *Later that summer*: Dean J. Kotlowski, *Nixon's Civil Rights: Politics, Principle and Policy* (Cambridge, MA: Harvard University Press, 2001), 77.

175 *"the gals"*: Letter, Pat to Helene, 5-10-65, Box 3, HJDC, RNPLM, 1.

175 *The fall of 1966*: Eisenhower, *Pat Nixon—The Untold Story*, 229.

176 *"She sort of pestered"*: David Eisenhower, Zoom interview with the author, June 5, 2023.

176 *"the relationship was a big lift"*: Ibid.

176 *"felt accepted very fast"*: "First Daughter-Elect Julie Nixon's Wedding to David Dwight Eisenhower, II," Museum Without Walls, www.the museumwithoutwalls.org, accessed April 22, 2023.

176 *That summer*: Eisenhower, *Pat Nixon—The Untold Story*, 225.

176 *"Dick is traveling constantly"*: Letter, Pat to Helene, no date, 1965, Box 3, HJDC, RNPLM, 1.

176 *The next year was even busier*: David, *The Lonely Lady of San Clemente*, 126.

176 *"wondering aloud to me"*: Eisenhower, *Pat Nixon—The Untold Story*, 227.

176 *"The handwriting was clearly"*: David, *The Lonely Lady of San Clemente*, 126.

176 *"moratorium on politics"*: Thomas, *Being Nixon*, 142.

177 *"gently turned aside"*: Eisenhower, *Pat Nixon—The Untold Story*, 231.

177 *"I sensed strongly"*: Ibid., 231–32.

177 *There was more soul-searching*: "Nixon's Mother Is Dead at 82," *Detroit News*, October 1, 1967, Folder 1967, PPS 284, PRNC, RNPLM.

177 *Popular evangelist*: Ibid.

177 *While Tricia and June*: Eisenhower, *Pat Nixon—The Untold Story*, 232.

177 *"Tell Pat"*: Ibid.

177 *Dick, in contrast*: Nixon, *RN*, 288.

178 *"with a sudden strength"*: Ibid.

178 *"I don't give a damn"*: Ibid., 291.

178 *"To me"*: Ambrose, *Nixon: The Triumph of a Politician*, 11.

178 *"As I left on December 28"*: Nixon, *RN*, 292.

178 *"is a rough deal for"*: *Good Housekeeping*, July 1968, 65.

178 *"if the family had strongly"*: Ibid.

179 *"I don't care about politics"*: Ibid., 62.

179 *"Her man would say"*: Ambrose, *Nixon: The Triumph of a Politician*, 111.

19: A TOGETHER COUPLE BUT NOT TOGETHER AT TIMES

180 *"Television is what you need"*: Chapin, *The President's Man*, 53.

180 *"By the end of the month"*: Ibid., 53–54.

180 *Ailes would be working*: Rick Perlstein, *Nixonland: The Rise of a President and the Fracturing of America* (New York: Scribner, 2009), 234.

180 *gave this team carte blanche*: Perlstein, *Nixonland*, 235.

181 *Joe McGinnis noted*: Joe McGinnis, *The Selling of the President: 1968* (New York: Penguin Books, 1988), 111.

181 *In addition to Ailes*: Ambrose, *Nixon: The Triumph of a Politician*, 158.

181 *"Old style politics"*: McGinnis, *The Selling of the President*, 60.

181 *"The key to the campaign"*: McGinnis, *The Selling of the President*, 61.

181 *"In the staffing of"*: Ehrlichman, *Witness to Power*, 48.

181 *"By 1968"*: Ibid., 56.

181 *"seldom included her"*: Ibid.

182 *"bore the brunt"*: Ibid.

182 *"Haldeman had been on"*: Eisenhower, *Pat Nixon—The Untold Story*, 241.

182 *"If you're back east"*: Dwight Chapin, phone interview with the author, January 29, 2021.

182 *"graciousness and warmth"*: Ibid.

182 *"She's checking me out"*: Ibid.

182 *"was a hurdle"*: Ibid.

182 *"a verifier of that trauma"*: Dwight Chapin, phone interview with the author, February 26, 2021.

182 *"the linchpin to"*: Ibid.

182 *"Rose was answering"*: Ibid.

183 *"a political celebrity"*: Steve Bull, phone interview with the author, February 26, 2021.

183 *"Rose Woods"*: Steve Bull, phone interview with the author, August 3, 2021.

183 *"all the young people"*: Dwight Chapin, phone interview with the author, January 29, 2021.

183 *"The older people"*: Ibid.

183 *"don't go to Rose's"*: Ibid.

183 *"is almost totally new"*: Gloria Steinem, "In Your Heart You Know He's Nixon," *New York Magazine*, October 28, 1968, 9.

183 *"Top aides do not speak"*: Ibid.

183 *"a striking new phenomenon"*: McGinnis, *The Selling of the President*, xv.

183 *"When I met Mrs. Nixon again"*: Helen Thomas, *Dateline: White House* (New York: Macmillan, 1975), 166.

184 *"Gentlemen, this is not"*: Nixon, *RN*, 297.

184 *"was quietly baptized"*: Eisenhower, *Pat Nixon—The Untold Story*, 236.

184 *"Having that [name]"*: Steinem, "In Your Heart You Know He's Nixon," 4.

185 *"The family member"*: Ambrose, *Nixon: The Triumph of a Politician,* 152.

185 *"While her husband rested"*: Ibid.

185 *"I fill him in on"*: Ambrose, *Nixon: The Triumph of a Politician,* 153.

185 *"All Republican Conventions"*: Candidate Nixon's July 1968 Statement on the ERA, WHCF, Box 7, Staff Member and Office Files: Anne Armstrong, RNPLM.

185 *"They did not want to end"*: Swift, *Pat and Dick: The Nixons,* 200.

186 *"It seems now more certain than"*: Stanley Karnow, *Vietnam: A History—The First Complete Account of Vietnam at War* (New York: Penguin Books, 1984), 587.

186 *"This is exactly"*: H. R. McMaster, interview with author, August 2, 2022.

186 *"thoroughly identified as the major"*: "Robert F. Kennedy and the 1968 Campaign," March 16, 2008, Kennedy Library Forum, https://www.jfklibrary.org/events-and-awards/kennedy-library -forums/past-forums/transcripts/robert-f-kennedy-and-the-1968-campaign.

186 *"recalled a gloom"*: Thomas, *Being Nixon,* 157.

186 *"who had gone to such"*: H. R. McMaster, *Dereliction of Duty: Johnson, McNamara, the Joint Chiefs of Staff and the Lies That Led to Vietnam* (New York: HarperCollins, 1998), 333.

186 *"When he was murdered"*: Todd Gitlin, *The Sixties: Years of Hope, Days of Rage* (New York: Bantam Books, 1987), 305–6.

187 *Dick would fly to*: Thomas, *Being Nixon,* 158.

187 *On June 4*: Ibid., 160.

187 *In July Dwight Eisenhower*: Ambrose, *Nixon: The Triumph of a Politician,* 161.

187 *"In contrast, Mother was subdued"*: Eisenhower, *Pat Nixon—The Untold Story,* 242.

187 *"Pat Nixon at 55"*: Marie Smith, "Mrs. Richard Nixon—A Wife Called Pat," *Washington Post*, August 4, 1968, G1.

188 *"When you talk to Pat Nixon"*: Betty Beale, "Those GOP Wives," *Boston Globe*, August 3, 1968, 13.

188 *"shared all the vilification"*: Gloria Steinem, *Outrageous Acts and Everyday Rebellions* (New York: Holt, Rinehart and Winston, 1983), 239.

188 *"because she meant so much"*: Ibid.

188 *"I never had time to think"*: Ibid.

189 *"in the spotlight of the press"*: Eisenhower, *Pat Nixon—The Untold Story,* 238.

189 *"Keenly aware of the"*: Dwight Chapin, phone call with the author, January 29, 2021.

189 *"not the Ritz"*: Ibid.

189 *"tell Mrs. Nixon"*: Ibid.

189 *"Dwight, I know"*: Ibid.

189 *"a committed, highly intense"*: Ibid.

189 *"I can't tell you how much"*: Ibid.

190 *"one track"*: Jack Carley, phone interview with the author, June 25, 2020.

190 *"When Pat or the girls"*: Dwight Chapin, phone call with the author, January 29, 2021.

190 *"A together couple"*: Ibid.

190 *There were two major campaign*: Ambrose, *Nixon: The Triumph of a Politician*, 167.

190 *"forgotten Americans"*: Paul F. Boller, *Presidential Campaigns* (New York: Oxford University Press, 1996), 321.

190 *"the non-shouters"*: Ibid.

190 *Dick's Democratic challenger*: Nixon, *RN*, 317.

190 *Another fly in the ointment*: "George Wallace: Settin' the Woods on Fire," PBS.org, accessed May 1, 2023.

190 *October 1968 polls*: Ibid.

191 *"I told them how proud"*: Nixon, *RN*, 330.

191 *Ever sentimental*: Ambrose, *Nixon: The Triumph of a Politician*, 218.

191 *The Nixon family, David*: Eisenhower, *Pat Nixon—The Untold Story*, 246.

191 *"we spoke to no one"*: Ibid.

191 *"Election night in 1968"*: David Eisenhower, Zoom interview with the author, March 6, 2023.

191 *Though Pat took a short nap*: Eisenhower, *Pat Nixon—The Untold Story*, 246.

192 *"Sir, ABC just announced"*: Chapin, *The President's Man*, 84.

192 *"cried with relief"*: Eisenhower, *Pat Nixon—The Untold Story*, 247.

192 *"We won"*: Ibid.

192 *"Having lost a close one"*: Ambrose, *Nixon: The Triumph of a Politician*, 221.

192 *"Once under the shelter"*: Eisenhower, *Pat Nixon—The Untold Story*, 248.

20: THE HARDEST UNPAID JOB IN THE WORLD

195 *Dick's presidential election*: Eisenhower, *Pat Nixon—The Untold Story*, 257.

195 *Once Dick won*: Nixon, *RN*, 358.

195 *"I wish J & D"*: Handwritten notes (Helene) on back of October 10, 1968, campaign itineraries, J&D, Box 7, HJDC, RNPLM, 2.

195 *"no other married students"*: Ibid.

195 *"isolated"*: Ibid.

195 *"were incredibly tight"*: David Eisenhower, Zoom call with the author, March 6, 2023.

195 *"She had a good sense"*: Ibid.

195 *"I put my foot down"*: David Eisenhower, Zoom call with the author, June 5, 2023.

196 *"My parents never questioned"*: Eisenhower, *Pat Nixon—The Untold Story*, 258.

196 *The ceremony would be held*: Marie Smith, "Julie Nixon Weds David Eisenhower," *Washington Post and Times Herald*, December 23, 1968, A7.

196 *"Our decision not to allow"*: Eisenhower, *Pat Nixon—The Untold Story*, 257.

196 *More than a thousand spectators*: Judith Martin, interview with the author, April 1, 2022.

196 *"Dowager Queen of American Hotels"*: Description of the Plaza, Box 18, Gwendolyn B. King Files, WHCF-SMOF.

196 *Despite the hotel's glamorous*: Description of Julie's wedding, Gwendolyn B. King Files, WHCF-SMOF.

197 *"herded us into a room"*: Judith Martin, interview with the author, April 1, 2022.

197 *"And they said"*: Ibid.

197 *"sneaked down a back"*: Jessica Contrera, "Julie Nixon Married David Eisenhower 50 Years Ago—and Refused a White House Ceremony," *Washington Post*, December 22, 2018, 4.

197 *"That night"*: Nixon, *RN*, 361.

197 *Wearing a green and white*: Anthony, *Why They Wore It*, 91.

197 *Lady Bird and Pat*: Brennan, *Pat Nixon: Embattled First Lady*, 107.

197 *The Johnsons and the Nixons*: Ambrose, *Nixon: The Triumph of a Politician*, 243.

197 *They met that morning*: Eisenhower, *Pat Nixon—The Untold Story*, 250.

197 *The Nixon women*: Carl Sferrazza Anthony, *Why They Wore It*, 92.

198 *Pat held up*: Eisenhower, *Pat Nixon—The Untold Story*, 251.

198 *"tight smile is frozen"*: Joann Haldeman, *In the Shadow of the White House: A Memoir of the Washington and Watergate Years, 1968–1978* (Los Angeles: Rare Bird Books, 2017), 48.

198 *"This was the first"*: Ambrose, *Nixon: The Triumph of a Politician*, 245.

198 *This time*: Eisenhower, *Pat Nixon—The Untold Story*, 252.

198 *After a candlelit steak dinner*: Julie Eisenhower, email to the author, May 11, 2023.

198 *Pat's Southern California*: David, *The Lonely Lady of San Clemente*, 131.

198 *"I shall return"*: Ambrose, *Nixon: The Triumph of a Politician,* 245.

199 *Tricia and Julie discovered*: Nixon, *RN*, 366–67.

199 *"Dick, let's turn on"*: Ambrose, *Nixon: The Triumph of a Politician*, 245.

199 *Dick began his presidency*: Boller, *Presidential Campaigns*, 327.

199 *"reminding him to put"*: Heath Hardage Lee, *The League of Wives: The Untold Story of the Women Who Took on the US Government to Bring Their Husbands Home from Vietnam* (New York: St. Martin's Press, 2019), 130.

200 *"Mrs. Nixon has given a great"*: Remarks of Gerry Van der Heuvel Women National Press Club Luncheon Honoring Liz Carpenter and Gerry Van der Heuvel, February 7, 1969, Folder 196, PPS 285, PRNC, RNPLM, 3.

200 *"The attitudes of the President's aides"*: Eisenhower, *Pat Nixon—The Untold Story*, 265.

200 *"all the image types"*: Safire, *Before the Fall*, 608.

200 *"sit-down luncheon"*: David, *The Lonely Lady of San Clemente,* 134.

200 First Lady Biography: Pat Nixon: *"Vest Pockets of Volunteerism"*: archive.firstladies.org /biographies/firstladies/Pat Nixon, page 6, accessed May 14, 2023.

201 *"Mrs. Nixon was intensely"*: Gwendolyn B. King, oral history interview, 1988, NARA, 13.

201 *"People are my project"*: Eisenhower, *Pat Nixon—The Untold Story*, 267.

201 *"I have always loved"*: Nixon, *RN*, 376.

201 *"One of the first"*: Debby Sloan, email to the author, June 13, 2023.

201 *"It was a very big deal"*: Debby Sloan, email to the author, June 13, 2023.

202 *"I was going out to see"*: *Small Splendid Efforts: Pat Nixon on Voluntarism*, DVD, January 6, 1993, National First Ladies Library.

202 *"We have to build generations"*: Ibid.

202 *In July of that year*: Andrew Glass, "Nixon Visits South Vietnam," *Politico*, July 30, 2020, www .politico.com/story/2010/07/nixon-visits-south-vietnam-july-30-1969-040433.

202 *"It's immensely important to recognize"*: H. R. McMaster, interview with the author, August 2, 2022.

203 *"Pat remained cool and composed"*: Ambrose, *Nixon: The Triumph of a Politician,* 286.

203 *"You know, when the President"*: General James "Don" Hughes, USAF, Ret., oral history, November 10, 2018, Richard Nixon Foundation Project, 30–31.

203 *"Moonglow was a public relations"*: Ambrose, *Nixon: The Triumph of a Politician,* 287.

203 *"Mrs. Nixon was praised"*: Thomas, *Dateline: White House,* 134.

203 *"working vacation"*: Eisenhower, *Pat Nixon—The Untold Story,* 271.

204 *"More often than not"*: Ron Walker, phone interview with the author, September 10, 2021.

204 *"It was very emotional"*: Ibid.

204 *"to make sure she was recognized"*: Ibid.

204 *"She was as important as"*: Ibid.

204 *"the men in the West Wing"*: Debby Sloan, phone interview with the author, September 29, 2022.

204 *"The overarching attitude"*: Dwight Chapin, phone interview with the author, January 29, 2021.

204 *"That was a pretty important job"*: Alexander Butterfield, interview with the author, December 8, 2022.

205 *"I liked Pat a lot"*: Ibid.

205 *"I didn't always take her side"*: Ibid.

21: WEST WING VS. EAST WING: BATTLE OF THE SEXES

206 *Early on in her tenure*: David, *The Lonely Lady of San Clemente,* 137; Martha Doss Collection, Mrs. Nixon In House Activities, 1969, 1–4.

206 *Rising by 7–7:30 a.m. each day*: Ibid.

206 *After lunch*: Ibid.

207 *"a bellwether of changes"*: Anita McBride, phone interview with the author, March 5, 2021.

207 *"a separate East Wing office"*: Anita McBride, "The Office of the First Lady: Managing Public Duties, Private Lives and Changing Expectations," *White House Historical Quarterly* 45 (Spring 2017): 14.

207 *"was the center of that tension"*: Anita McBride, phone interview with the author, March 5, 2021.

207 *"worry about the First Lady"*: Penny Adams, interview with the author, March 29, 2021.

207 *"When Haldeman tried to curtail"*: Thomas, *Dateline: White House,* 170.

207 *"The feminists never gave"*: Anita McBride, phone interview with the author, March 5, 2021.

207 *"moving the needle"*: Ibid.

207 *"She understood her place"*: Ibid.

208 *"She was a savvy behind-the-scenes"*: Ibid.

208 *"the West Wing was moving"*: Dwight Chapin, phone interview with the author, June 16, 2023.

208 *"There wasn't a role for"*: Steve Bull, phone interview with the author, February 26, 2021.

208 *"probably reflecting the President's"*: David Eisenhower, Zoom interview with the author, June 5, 2023.

208 *"After the California governorship"*: Ibid.

208 *"I never saw any"*: Debby Sloan, email to the author, June 13, 2023.

208 *"The disparagement between West and East"*: Susan Porter Rose, interview with the author, October 20, 2020.

209 *"Those were the days"*: Patti Matson, interview with the author, October 28, 2022.

209 *"They thought they were"*: Ibid.

209 *"alienated . . . she was the odd person"*: Dwight Chapin, phone interview with the author, June 16, 2023.

209 *"In order to bring"*: Ibid.

209 *"He may have put her on"*: David Eisenhower, Zoom interview with the author, June 5, 2023.

209 *"When they had some difference"*: Alexander Butterfield, interview with the author, December 8, 2022.

210 *"admonished us all"*: Debby Sloan, interview with the author, June 13, 2023.

210 *The nightly illumination*: Eisenhower, *Pat Nixon—The Untold Story*, 304–5.

210 *Another enduring tradition*: "Pat Nixon's Yuletide Legacy," RNPLM, December 24, 2021, www.nixonlibrary.gov/news/pat-nixons-yuletide-legacy.

211 *"the Nixon White House"*: Julie Eisenhower, "Focus on the First Family: Health and the Handicapped," JNEC, RNPLM, 10.

211 *Pat's 1969 schedule*: Martha Doss Collection, Mrs. Nixon In House Activities, 1969, 1–4.

211 *Pat's schedule that spring*: Ibid.

211 *Pat traveled often*: Ibid.

211 *"I'm a very religious person"*: Thomas, *Dateline: White House*, 160.

212 *"It wasn't just all VIPs"*: Susan Dolibois, phone interview with the author, June 20, 2023.

212 *Lucy Winchester added that*: Lucy Winchester, interview with the author, June 26, 2021.

212 *"Fairly early on"*: Bobbie Kilberg, interview with the author, April 11, 2022.

212 *"She obviously changed her mind"*: Ibid.

212 *"an amazing approval rating"*: Ambrose, *Nixon: The Triumph of a Politician*, 318.

213 *"The Nixons set a record"*: Lucy Winchester, "Elegant White House State Dinners Require Extensive Behind-the-Scenes Planning," *Oregonian Day*, September 18, 1970, 2M, WHCF.

213 *Pat's longtime secretary*: Eisenhower, *Pat Nixon—The Untold Story*, 322.

213 *Gwen King*: Gwendolyn B. King, oral history interview, 1988, NARA, 1–2.

213 *"the mail issue"*: Ehrlichman, *Witness to Power*, 58.

213 *"wary and tense"*: Ibid.

213 *"Pat bristled"*: Ibid.

214 *"She was very thin"*: Ibid.

214 *"clumsy intruder"*: Penny Adams, email to the author, May 30, 2023; Bob Bostock, phone call with the author, June 1, 2023; Debby Sloan, email to the author, June 1, 2023.

214 *"I didn't think this would be"*: Gwendolyn B. King, oral history interview, 1988, NARA, 10.

214 *"Business as usual"*: Ibid., 11.

214 *"The West Wing discounted"*: Ibid., 13.

214 *"Haldeman was the"*: Penny Adams, phone interview with the author, March 29, 2021.

214 *"The reason for Bob's"*: Charles Stuart, *Never Trust a Local*, Algora Publishing, New York, 2005. 128; Connecticut Walker, "Helen Smith—Protector and Publicist of the First Lady" *Parade Magazine*, August 18, 1974, 9.

214 *Van der Heuvel*: Walker, "Helen Smith—Protector and Publicist of the First Lady," 9.

214 *"She had most recently"*: Connie Stuart, oral history interview, August 15, 1988, NARA, 7.

214 *Lucy Winchester*: Lucy Winchester, phone call with the author, May 22, 2023.

215 *The thirty-two-year-old social secretary*: Lucy Winchester, interview with the author, August 29, 2021.

215 *"one of the swingingest"*: Kitty Kelley, profile of Lucy Winchester, Junior League newsletter, Kitty Kelley Private Collection, 3.

215 *"a blow-up sex doll"*: Lucy Winchester, interview with the author, June 26, 2021, and September 22, 2022.

215 *"Oh, no, Lucy"*: Ibid.

216 *In his report*: III. East Wing Study, Recommendations, 2–3, WHSF-SMF-Ehrlichman, Box 21, RNPLM.

216 *"Mrs. Nixon was once a member"*: East Wing Study, 11, WHSF-SMOF-Ehrlichman, Box 21, RNPLM.

216 *"a fashion show"*: East Wing Study, 23, WHSF-SMF-Ehrlichman, Box 21, RNPLM.

216 *"list of suggested activities"*: Debby Sloan, email to the author, May 22, 2023.

216 *"who felt she could"*: Bob Bostock, phone call to the author, June 1, 2023.

217 *"Mrs. Nixon didn't say"*: Pat Howard, interview with the author, July 18, 2021.

217 *"He was sitting"*: Lucy Winchester, phone interview with the author, August 29, 2021.

217 *"They [the West Wing]"*: Ibid.

217 *"the antithesis of a shrinking"*: Cassie Price, interview with the author, August 28, 2021.

217 *"didn't suffer fools gladly"*: Ibid.

217 *"She was very strong"*: Ibid.

217 *Stuart arrived at the White House*: Connie Stuart, oral history interview, August 15, 1988, NARA, 2–3.

217 *In September 1969*: Ibid., 3–5.

218 *"He wanted to take the time"*: Ibid., 47.

218 *"The first thing Connie"*: Lucy Winchester, phone interview with the author, August 29, 2021.

218 *"It was not a comfortable time"*: Pat Howard, phone call with the author, May 20, 2021.

22: A WARTIME WHITE HOUSE

219 *"It's not a White House"*: David Eisenhower, Zoom interview with the author, March 6, 2023.

219 *"It was very, very scary"*: Debby Sloan, phone interview with the author, September 29, 2021.

219 *But Winchester remembered*: Lucy Winchester, interview with the author, June 26, 2021.

219 *"a wartime procedure"*: David Eisenhower, Zoom call with the author, March 6, 2023.

220 *The new Nixon administration*: Lee, *The League of Wives*, 135.

220 *"The idea is that"*: David Eisenhower, Zoom call with the author, March 6, 2023.

220 *According to McMaster*: H. R. McMaster, interview with the author, August 2, 2022.

220 *"In October and November of 1969"*: Bill Gulley and Mary Ellen Reese, *Breaking Cover* (New York: Simon & Schuster, 1980), 165–66.

220 *"as a quarter million people"*: Eisenhower, *Pat Nixon—The Untold Story*, 275.

220 *"She was in full flow"*: David Eisenhower, Zoom call with the author, June 5, 2023.

221 *"Nixon was not wrong"*: Thomas, *Being Nixon*, 241.

221 *A Gallup poll of television*: Dale Van Atta, *With Honor: Melvin Laird in War, Peace, and Politics* (Madison: University of Wisconsin Press, 2008), 230.

221 *"Silent Majority Speech"*: David Eisenhower, Zoom call with the author, June 5, 2023.

221 *"All over the country"*: "A Moratorium to March for Peace," *Time Annual 1969 Year in Review*, 49.

221 *"encircled by a protective barricade"*: Van Atta, *With Honor*, 233.

222 *"The extent of their feelings"*: Ibid., 233.

222 *"We will kill Richard Nixon"*: Eisenhower, *Pat Nixon—The Untold Story*, 277.

222 *"It was rough and tumble"*: Julie Eisenhower, oral history for "A Few Good Women," Penn State University Libraries, March 9, 1999, 5.

222 *the Nixon family celebrated*: Eisenhower, *Pat Nixon—The Untold Story*, 278.

222 *"Although Mrs. Nixon"*: Jack Brennan, email to the author, September 17, 2022.

223 *"an aged woman"*: Ibid.

223 *"assistant hosts to the President"*: Kit Cowdrey, "Navy Lieutenant: Assignment: The White House," *Evening Outlook*, February 23, 1973, 16, Chris Alberts Private Collection.

223 *"she took violent exception"*: Gulley and Reese, *Breaking Cover*, 151.

224 *"ordered the New York materials"*: Patrick Phillips-Schrock, *Nixon White House Redecoration and Acquisition Program: An Illustrated History* (Jefferson, NC: McFarland, 2016), 204.

224 *"helped redesign Air Force One"*: Brower, *First Women*, 179.

224 *The Air Force One revamp*: Ibid.

224 *"insisted his luggage"*: Pat Howard, phone interview with the author, May 20, 2021.

224 *"Was there more we could do"*: Jo Haldeman, phone interview with the author, May 6, 2020.

224 *"Bob told me"*: Ibid.

224 *"echoes of ugly jokes"*: Helen McCain Smith as told to Elizabeth Pope Frank, "Ordeal! Pat Nixon's Final Days in the White House," *Good Housekeeping*, July 1976, 127.

225 *One former staff person*: Anonymous Nixon White House staffers.

225 *"represents unofficially"*: Robert Hughes, *American Visions: The Epic History of Art in America* (New York: Alfred A. Knopf, 1997), 507.

225 *"Just as the vanishing"*: Ibid.

225 *"caught the heart of America"*: John Canady, "Wyeth Show Opens at White House Today," *New York Times*, February 20, 1970: 28.

225 *a massive success*: Wyeth exhibit, Box 2.3 PN cor., April 2, 1970, Gwendolyn B. King Collection, WHCF, RNPLM.

226 *"When Pat Nixon moved in"*: David, *The Lonely Lady of San Clemente*, 144–45.

226 *"She was reluctant as one"*: Eisenhower, *Pat Nixon—The Untold Story*, 262.

226 *Winchester often could be found*: Lucy Winchester, interview with the author, June 26, 2021.

226 *Haldeman wasted no time*: Phillips-Schrock, *Nixon White House Redecoration*, 22.

227 *A member of the so-called FFVs*: Dorothy McCardle, "The Government Curator They Call 'Grand Acquisitor,'" *Washington Post and Times Herald*, January 17, 1971, sec. G1.

227 *"having the talents"*: Phillips-Schrock, *Nixon White House Redecoration*, 27.

227 *Conger brought an A-list team*: Ibid., 22–23.

227 *Pat and Conger shared a birthday*: Bill Allman, phone interview with the author, August 19, 2020.

227 *The White House Curator*: "Clement Conger Proudly Restored American History to Great Settings," *Washington Post*, January 15, 2004.

227 *"a large oval expanse"*: Phillips-Schrock, *Nixon White House Redecoration*, 31.

227 *Wilson Desk:* Ibid., 34.

227 *"Colonial Williamsburg Office"*: Ibid., 51.

227 *The president's chief of staff*: Betty Monkman, interview with the author, August 20, 2020.

228 *"a deal between Carl and Conger"*: Al Louer, phone interview with the author, August 11, 2021.

228 *Luminaries such as*: Donald Gonzales, *The Rockefellers at Williamsburg: Backstage with the Founders, Restorers, and World-Renowned Guests* (McLean, VA: EPM Publications, 1991, 90, 151–52.

228 *"the finest example"*: David, *The Lonely Lady of San Clemente*, 149.

228 *"Boudin masterpiece"*: Phillips-Schrock, *Nixon White House Redecoration*, C13–C14.

228 *"Dolley Red"*: Ibid., 105.

228 *Much of the Kennedy furniture*: David, *The Lonely Lady of San Clemente*, 149; Phillips-Schrock, *Nixon White House Redecoration*, C6–C7.

228 *"Mrs. Kennedy obviously"*: Bill Allman, phone interview with the author, August 19, 2020.

228 *"signaled the possibility"*: Caroli, *First Ladies*, 229.

229 *She hired the famous French designer*: "The White House Historical Association Turns Sixty," *White House Quarterly* 60: 39, 2021.

229 *"French decorative arts"*: Norman Askins, phone interview with the author, November 16, 2020.

229 *"In the 1950s"*: Phillips-Schrock, *Nixon White House Redecoration*, 24–25.

229 *"After that, Boudin"*: Ibid.

229 *"Everybody had"*: Norman Askins, interview with the author, November 16, 2020.

229 *"fervor started earlier"*: Ibid.

230 *"the Citizen Kane lode"*: "Two Centuries of Changing Taste," *House Beautiful*, March 1994, Pat Howard Collection, 58.

230 *All in all*: "The White House Historical Association Turns Sixty," 115–16.

230 *The sale of White House guidebooks*: Phillips-Schrock, *Nixon White House Redecoration*, 25.

230 *"his success to the fact"*: "'.furnish the White House and the State Department,'" *American Tradition*, 1978, Collection of Pat Howard, 96.

230 *"annoyingly persistent"*: Lucy Winchester, interview with the author, June 26, 2021.

230 *"Inclement Conger"*: Ibid.

230 *One artifact*: Philips-Schrock, *Nixon White House Redecoration*, 105.

230 *"with her hair"*: White House Historical Association, "Treasures of the White House: Dolley Madison," https://www.whitehousehistory.org/photos/treasures-of-the-white-house-dolley -madison, accessed June 10, 2023.

230 *"too busy during the fire"*: David, *The Lonely Lady of San Clemente*, 147.

231 *The portrait was loaned*: Betty Monkman, phone interview with the author, August 20, 2020.

231 *Dolley Madison always*: "A Visit with the First Lady," Pat Nixon interview with Virginia Sherwood, ABC, September 12, 1971, YouTube, posted by Nixon Foundation, https://www .youtube.com/watch?v=ABfQjJGNQ78.

231 *"Aside from arranging"*: Amy Russo, *Women of the White House: The Illustrated Story of the First Ladies of the United States of America* (London: Welbeck, 2021), 23.

231 *Pat added*: "'.furnish the White House and the State Department,'" *American Tradition*, 1978, Collection of Pat Howard. 97.

23: WHAT MAKES PAT NIXON TICK?

232 *"Peru is a line of"*: Dwight Chapin, phone interview with the author, January 29, 2021.

232 *On May 31, 1970*: Heath Hardage Lee, "Pat Nixon and the Great Peruvian Earthquake of 1970: Transcript, by Heath Hardage Lee for PN Day of Service at the Nixon Foundation," March 16, 2021.

232 *On June 28, 1970*: Ibid.

233 *"She could have"*: Ibid.

233 *"'I must tell you'"*: Gene T. Boyer and Jackie Boor, *Inside the President's Helicopter* (Brule, WI: Cable, 2011), 232.

234 *The First Lady's volunteer effort*: "Biograph of First Lady Pat Nixon," Nixon Foundation, https://www.nixonfoundation.org/resources/pat-nixon-biography.

234 *"confidence level went up"*: Dwight Chapin, phone interview with the author, January 29, 2021.

234 *"She was very proud of"*: David Eisenhower, phone interview with the author, June 5, 2023.

234 *"It's a stage setter"*: Dwight Chapin, phone interview with the author, July 13, 2022.

234 *"Pitiful Helpless Giant"*: "President Nixon's Speech on Cambodia, April 30, 1970," The Wars for Viet Nam, Vassar College, https://www.vassar.edu/vietnam/documents/doc15.html.

234 *"If, when the chips"*: Ibid.

234 *"summoned Julie and David"*: Thomas, *Being Nixon*, 266.

234 *"You see these bums"*: Thomas, *Being Nixon*, 268.

235 *"Those few days after Kent State"*: Nixon, *RN*, 457.

235 *"my mother's reaction"*: Eisenhower, *Pat Nixon—The Untold Story*, 287.

235 *"I truly think the day"*: Brower, *First Women*, 121–22.

235 *The decision was reluctantly*: Thomas, *Being Nixon*, 266.

235 *In mid-June 1970*: Christopher Lydon, "Charles and Anne Begin Informal Visit to Capital," *New York Times*, July 17, 1970, www.nytimes.com/1970/07/17/archives/charles-and-anne-begin-informal-visit-to-capital-charles-and-anne.html.

235 *"Tricia has boyfriends"*: Thomas, *Dateline: White House*, 179.

236 *"What a lot of work"*: Martha Doss, Scrapbook Two, Martha Doss Private Collection, 1.

236 *"Something like seventeen"*: Connie Stuart, oral history interview, August 15, 1988, NARA, 34–35.

236 *"The Prince and the Princess"*: Ibid.

236 *"bright chartreuse mini"*: Lydon, "Charles and Anne Begin Informal Visit to Capital."

236 *"I don't give interviews"*: Thomas, *Dateline: White House*, 178.

236 *"A thoughtful human being"*: Eisenhower, *Special People*, 85.

236 *"It was almost as if"*: Ibid.

236 *The highlight of the three-day*: Misc. Office Memos, 1970 Prince Charles Princess Anne visit, Lucy Wincester, Box 1, WHCF; Lydon, "Charles and Anne Begin Informal Visit to Capital."

236 *"Your Royal Highness"*: Eisenhower, *Special People*, 91.

236 *"My sister was embarrassed"*: Ibid.

237 *"The head must rule"*: Ibid., 95.

237 *"The dance was"*: Princess Anne note to Tricia Cox, July 25, 1970, Tricia Nixon Cox Private Collection.

237 *He was in*: Letter from Charles Prince of Wales to Tricia Nixon, n.d., 1970, Tricia Nixon Cox Private Collection.

237 *"Her life"*: Jessamyn West, "The Real Pat Nixon: An Intimate View," *Good Housekeeping*, February 1971, 68.

238 *"mystifying"*: Ibid., 68.

238 *"bafflement"*: Ibid., 67.

238 *"bafflement in a First Lady"*: Ibid., 67–68.

238 *"Many of the women"*: Ibid., 124.

238 *"Women's Lib will thank you"*: Ibid., 124.

238 *"did not shy from"*: Brady Dennis, "For Mitt Romney, Mother's Failed Run Offers Cautionary Tale," *Washington Post*, February 24, 2012, https://www.washingtonpost.com/politics/for-mitt -romney-mothers-failed-run-offers-cautionary-tale/2012/02/23/gIQAXtQAYR_story.html.

239 *"encountered a predominantly"*: Ibid.

239 *"found in my campaign"*: Ibid.

239 *"I know there are not"*: Barbara Walters interview with Pat Nixon, CBS, January 13, 1972, WHCA 4968.

239 *In October 1968*: Randy Taraborrelli, *The Kennedys—After Camelot* (New York: Grand Central, 2017), 378.

239 *Onassis had also been*: Ibid.

240 *"I am most grateful"*: Letter, Jackie to Pat, January 7, 1970, RNPLM, 2.

240 *"I know that the"*: Ibid.

240 *"a personal note"*: Jennifer Boswell Pickens, "Inside Jackie Kennedy's Secret Visit to the Nixon White House," *Town and Country*, February 3, 2021, https://www.townandcountrymag.com /society/politics/a35381730/jackie-kennedy-secret-visit-to-nixon-white-house/.

240 *"My mother was determined"*: Eisenhower, *Pat Nixon—The Untold Story*, 309.

241 *"I was working late"*: Thomas, *Dateline White House*, 162.

241 *The first order of business*: Eisenhower, *Pat Nixon—The Untold Story*, 310.

241 *That evening*: Thomas, *Dateline: White House*, 162.

241 *"Despite knowing what"*: Pickens, "Inside Jackie Kennedy's Secret Visit to the Nixon White House," 3.

242 *"Can you imagine"*: Letter, Jackie Kennedy Onassis to the Nixons, February 4, 1971, RNPLM.

242 *"Your warm-hearted welcome"*: Letter, Rose Kennedy to Pat Nixon, Box 15, June 9, 1971, JNEC, RNPLM.

242 *"It was a great pleasure"*: Letter, Rose Kennedy to Pat Nixon, Folder unmarked, Box 15, JNEC, RNPLM,

24: A FEW GOOD WOMEN

243 *"Mr. President"*: Leon J. Stout, *A Matter of Simple Justice: The Untold Story of Barbara Hackman Franklin and a Few Good Women* (University Park: Penn State University Press, 2012), xxi.

244 *"I was told by everybody"*: Barbara Hackman Franklin, interview with the author, November 5, 2021.

244 *"This did not go over"*: Ibid.

245 *"She would steal out of"*: Ibid.

245 *"It was a kind of vacuum"*: Ibid.

245 *"I think Mrs. Nixon"*: Ibid.

245 *"I don't believe that the advances"*: Ibid.

245 *"Who [Mrs. Nixon] was"*: Ibid.

245 *"Nixon wanted to make"*: Dr. Henry Kissinger, Zoom interview with the author, April 21, 2022.

245 *"Thanks in large part"*: Heath Hardage Lee, "The Ripple Effect of the Landmark Title IX Continues on Its 50th Anniversary," *The Hill*, June 23, 2022, https://thehill.com/opinion /congress-blog/3534426-the-ripple-effect-of-the-landmark-title-ix-continues-on-its-50th -anniversary/.

246 *The first of these iconic ceremonies*: Elizabeth Winder, *Parachute Women: Marianne Faithfull, Marsha Hunt, Bianca Jagger, Anita Pallenberg, and the Women Behind the Rolling Stones* (New York: Hachette Books, 2023), 225–26.

246 *On June 12, 1971*: *The Day Indeed Was Splendid: The Wedding of Tricia Nixon and Edward F. Cox*, exhibition text, 1, RNPLM.

246 *"Tricia and Ed"*: Heath Hardage Lee, "The White House Wedding of Tricia Nixon and Edward Cox: The Rose Garden Is Transformed," *White House Historical Quarterly* 65 (Spring 2022): 60.

246 *"The couple gave"*: Ibid.

247 *"Dick is a wonderful dancer"*: "A Visit with the First Lady," Pat Nixon interview with Virginia Sherwood, ABC, September 12, 1971, posted to YouTube by Nixon Foundation, https://www .youtube.com/watch?v=ABfQjJGNQ78.

247 *Television coverage*: "50 years ago today—Tricia Nixon and Edward Cox were Married in the White House Rose Garden" June 12, 1971, YouTube, Richard Nixon Foundation, June 12, 2021, https://youtu.be/b1GiA0tvoLU?si=2RAtrpRgHVwWM-iXAccessed July 1, 2023.

247 *As Martin remembered*: Judith Martin, interview with the author, April 1, 2022.

247 *"Tricia Nixon Takes Vows"*: Thomas, *Being Nixon*, 323.

248 *"Kissinger was convinced"*: Ambrose, *Nixon: The Triumph of a Politician*, 446–47.

248 *"try to find out"*: Eisenhower, *Pat Nixon—The Untold Story*, 316.

248 *During Labor Day weekend*: Ibid., 465–66.

248 *Despite Pat's early debacle*: Michael Giorgione, *Inside Camp David: The Private World of the Presidential Retreat* (New York: Back Bay Books, 2020), 24–37.

248 *Camp David with its*: Eisenhower, *Pat Nixon—The Untold Story*, 319.

249 *"Strict orders not to talk"*: Joann Haldeman, interview with the author, May 6, 2020.

249 *"He was always close to Rose"*: Gulley and Reese, *Breaking Cover*, 118.

249 *"I have a practice"*: "A Visit with the First Lady," Pat Nixon interview with Virginia Sherwood, ABC, September 12, 1971, YouTube, posted by Nixon Foundation, https://www.youtube.com /watch?v=ABfQjJGNQ78.

249 *"Knowing him"*: Ibid.

249 *"The most difficult task"*: Ibid.

249 *"Don't you worry"*: Eisenhower, *Pat Nixon—The Untold Story*, 321.

250 *"Our population is"*: Anthony, "Pat Nixon, Stealth Feminist?"

250 *"This nomination opportunity"*: Stout, *A Matter of Simple Justice*, 38.

250 *"Nixon genuinely wanted"*: Luke Nichter, email to the author, December 30, 2021.

250 *"From the time Nixon arrived"*: Ehrlichman, ~~Witness to Power: The Nixon Years~~, 115.

250 *"carefully groomed her"*: "Jewel Stradford LaFontant Biography," https://biography.jrank.org /pages/2625/LaFontant-Jewel-Stradford.html, accessed July 17, 2023.

250 *Rogers remained visible*: Golus, "Legal Precedent: Jewel C. Stradford Lafontant Broke Many Barriers as a Lawyer and Public Servant."

251 *Despite an outstanding legal career*: Julia Larsen, "Jewel Stradford Rogers Lafontant-Mankarious (1922–1997)," Black Past, July 25, 2020, https://www.blackpast.org/african-american-history /mankarious-jewel-stradford-rogers-lafontant-1922-1997/.

251 *Her son, Ariel*: John Rogers Jr., interview with the author, September 2, 2023.

251 *"attacked"*: Memorandum, Barbara Franklin to Fred Malek, October 18, 1971, Box 1, Barbara Franklin, WHCF-SMOF.

251 *"bombarded"*: Ibid.

251 *"the mail to the President"*: Memorandum, Supreme Court Nominee, Fred Malek to John D. Ehrlichman, October 6, 1971, Barbara Franklin, WHCF-SMOF.

251 *"The appointment of a woman"*: "Women's Progress Memorandum," Barbara Franklin to Fred Malek, October 11, 1971, Box 2, Barbara Franklin, WHCF-SMOF; Women Supreme Court Nominees-BHF List, October 5, 1971, John Dean Box 75, WHSF-SMOF.

251 *"In all, Franklin"*: Women Supreme Court Nominees-BHF List, October 5, 1971, John Dean Box 75, WHSF-SMOF.

251 *Mildred Lillie*: Sheldon Goldman, *Picking Federal Judges: Lower Court Selection from Roosevelt Through Reagan* (New Haven, CT: Yale University Press, 1999), 215.

252 *"The 12 male lawyers"*: Myrna Oliver, "Mildred L. Lillie—55 Years as a Judge," SFGate, October 29, 2022, https://www.sfgate.com/bayarea/article/Mildred-L-Lillie-55-years-as-a -judge-2758609.php.

252 *"belief of male lawyers"*: Ibid.

252 *"By labeling Mildred"*: Stout, *A Matter of Simple Justice*, 79.

252 *"There were over"*: Goldman, *Picking Federal Judges*, 182.

252 *"Of course, my parents"*: Tricia Nixon Cox, email to the author, August 9, 2023.

252 *"Boy is she [Pat] mad"*: H. R. Haldeman, *The Haldeman Diaries—Inside the Nixon White House* (New York: G. P. Putnam's Sons, 1994), 367–68.

252 *Nixon ended up*: Stout, *A Matter of Simple Justice*, 79.

252 *"She did things in"*: Ibid., 80.

253 *"We are preparing a woman"*: John A. Farrell, "What Happened After Nixon Failed to Appoint a Woman to the Supreme Court," *Politico*, June 21, 2020, www.politico.com/news/magazine /2020/06/21/pat-nixon-woman-supreme-court-311408.

253 *"In an Oval Office"*: "List of Black Women for S/Court," December 11, 1972, Folder, Box 3, Hoover Archive, JDE Collection, White House, Washington, D.C.

253 *"It's going to be a black woman"*: Nixon Tapes, 3 and 4, December 11, 1972, Oval Office 819–002, unknown time between 10:18 a.m. and 2:25 p.m., www.nixontapes.org

253 *"I interpret it to mean"*: Luke Nichter, email to the author, August 15, 2023.

253 *"the ABA committee"*: Goldman, *Picking Federal Judges*, 224–25.

253 *He soon appointed*: "Jewel Stradford LaFontant Biography"; Goldman, *Picking Federal Judges*, 220; Larsen, "Jewel Stradford Rogers Lafontant-Mankarious (1922–1997)."

254 *"Because of her excellent"*: Letter, Richard Nixon to Mr. Chapelle, July 21, 1988, Collection of John Rogers Jr.

254 *"I am not surprised"*: Julie Eisenhower, email to the author, August 4, 2023.

254 *In 1981*: Barbara Franklin, interview with the author, November 5, 2021.

25: NOT EVEN A LION COULD BREAK IT

255 *"For God's sake"*: Maureen Drown Nunn, phone interview with the author, December 3, 2020.

255 *Helene also came*: Ibid.

255 *The First Lady would be*: A Time for Celebration: Highlights from the First Lady's Trip to Africa 1972, DVD, National First Ladies Library.

255 *warm friendship between*: Ibid.

256 *"Mrs. Nixon's simple gesture"*: Anthony, *Why They Wore It*, 99.

256 *"Your assembly is a little"*: "A Medal for Mme. Nixon," *New York Times*, January 9, 1972.

256 *"so strong not even"*: Eisenhower, *Pat Nixon—The Untold Story*, 329–30.

256 *The First Lady's last stop*: A Time for Celebration, DVD.

256 *"Kids ran to her"*: Jack Brennan, oral history, interview by Brenda St. Hilaire, January 9, 2020, CSUF.

257 *"always know a phony"*: Ibid.

257 *"could feel the warmth"*: Ibid.

257 *"Mrs. Nixon had broken"*: Eisenhower, *Pat Nixon—The Untold Story*, 333.

257 *"thought you'd be amused"*: Ibid.

257 *"I told her that"*: Ibid., 332.

257 *"Well, at least"*: Ibid.

258 *"Pat said she was too busy"*: Ambrose, *Nixon: The Triumph of a Politician*, 520.

258 *"Mrs. Nixon never wanted a book"*: Connie Stuart, oral history interview, August 15, 1988, NARA.

258 *"old-fashioned"*: Barbara Walters interview with Pat Nixon, CBS, January 13, 1972, WHCA 4968.

258 *"Oh, I don't think"*: Ibid.

258 *"a great number of qualified women"*: Ibid.

258 *"I would support any"*: Ibid.

259 *"seek the nomination"*: Nixon, *RN*, 544–45.

259 *"Pat lobbied publicly"*: Swift, *Pat and Dick: The Nixons*, 285.

259 *"Initially the Chinese"*: Chapin, *The President's Man*, 254.

259 *"The President wanted Mrs. Nixon"*: Ibid.

259 *"The President had concluded"*: H. R. Haldeman, unpublished diaries, October 26, 1971, RNPLM.

259 *"Also, Rose should be"*: Ibid.

259 *"As usual the First Lady"*: David, *The Lonely Lady of San Clemente*, 158.

259 *She met with two*: Mike Schrauth, phone interview with the author, July 6, 2023.

260 *"China, there was unanimous"*: Kandie Stroud, "Pat Nixon in China," *Women's Wear Daily*, March 1, 1972, sec. Issue, 42.

260 *"While Communism generally"*: Anthony, *Why They Wore It*, 98.

260 *"She maintained her personality"*: Jack Brennan, phone interview with the author, July 13, 2023.

260 *"What? I had to take off"*: Ibid.

260 *Helen Thomas*: Anne Walker, *China Calls: Paving the Way for Nixon's Historic Journey to China* (Lanham, MD: Madison Books, 1992), appendix, 414.

260 *"The worst one"*: Jack Brennan, phone interview with the author, July 13, 2023.

261 *Her hostesses would be*: American Press Corps, *The President's Trip to China: A Pictorial Record of the Historic Journey to the People's Republic of China with Text by Members of the American Press Corps* (New York: Bantam, 1972), 29.

261 *"At the Shanghai banquet"*: Ambrose, *Nixon: The Triumph of a Politician*, 519.

261 *"she noted with pleasure"*: American Press Corps, *The President's Trip to China*, 31.

261 *"got in front of her"*: Mike Schrauth, phone interview with the author, July 6, 2023.

261 *"Well this was not something"*: Ibid.

261 *"chewing out"*: Ibid.

261 *"wanted to be"*: Ibid.

262 *"She'd been at this"*: Bill Hudson, phone interview with the author, July 13, 2023.

262 *"poise"*: Ibid.

262 *Despite her packed schedule*: American Press Corps, *The President's Trip to China*, 31.

262 *"Aren't they cute?"*: "Don't Worry Mr. Nixon, the National Zoo's Pandas Figured Out How to Have Sex," *Smithsonian Magazine*, July 28, 2014, https://www.smithsonianmag.com/smart-news/dont-worry-mr-nixon-national-zoos-pandas-figured-out-how-have-sex-180952180/.

262 *At the end of the trip*: Ibid.

262 *"praised Pat Nixon for raising"*: Ibid.

263 *"Nixon thought of Hoover"*: David Eisenhower, email to the author, August 30, 2023.

263 *"he was seventy-six"*: Margaret Talbot, "J. Edgar Hoover, Public Enemy No. 1," *New Yorker*, November 14, 2022, https://www.newyorker.com/magazine/2022/11/21/j-edgar-hoover-public-enemy-no-1.

263 *Less than a week later*: Ambrose, *Nixon: The Triumph of a Politician*, 539.

263 *"Don't risk the summit"*: Ibid.

264 *"was immediately positively"*: Thomas, *Being Nixon*, 376.

264 *"She got up and came over"*: Ibid.

264 *"I think we"*: Ambrose, *Nixon: The Triumph of a Politician*, 541.

264 *"had greatly appreciated"*: Nixon, *RN*, 589.

264 *"Pat showed great skill"*: Ibid.

265 *Mrs. Nixon looked wonderful*: Louise Hutchinson oral history, Tape 4, Maureen Molloy Morrow, Private Collection, CCOH, 14.

265 *"Wherever she went"*: Eisenhower, *Pat Nixon—The Untold Story*, 340.

266 *Hutchinson later recalled*: Louise Hutchinson oral history, Tape 4, Maureen Molloy Morrow, Private collection, CCOH, 14.

266 *"She was fine"*: Bill Hudson, interview with the author, July 28, 2021.

266 *"got so she was trying"*: Connie Stuart, oral history interview, August 15, 1988, NARA, 39.

266 *"Leave him alone"*: Eisenhower, *Pat Nixon—The Untold Story*, 340.

266 *Soon Pat*: Eisenhower, *Pat Nixon—The Untold Story*, 341.

266 *The First Lady even*: David, *The Lonely Lady of San Clemente*, 159–60.

267 *Despite the antagonistic*: Nixon, *RN*, 618.

267 *Despite her First Lady*: Thomas, *Being Nixon*, 382.

267 *"She represents best"*: "A Tribute to First Lady Pat Nixon," 1972 GOP convention film, Nixon Foundation, YouTube, posted August 1, 2010.

267 *Two weeks after*: Haldeman, *In the Shadow of the White House*, 189.

267 *It was Father's Day weekend*: Nixon, *RN*, 623.

268 *"What's the deal"*: Haldeman, *In the Shadow of the White House*, 190.

268 *"On June 19, 1972"*: "The Nation: It's Inoperative: They Misspoke Themselves," *Time*, April 30, 1973, https://content.time.com/time/magazine/article/0,9171,907098-2,00.html.

268 *"barely noted the news"*: Eisenhower, *Pat Nixon—The Untold Story*, 343.

268 *"Mrs. Nixon was far"*: Preston Bruce, *From the Door of the White House* (New York: Lothrop, Lee & Shepard, 1984), 154.

268 *"There was a steady stream"*: Ibid., 144.

269 *"It was obvious these men"*: Ibid., 153.

26: ELEGANT BUT NOT ALOOF

270 *"For thirty-two years"*: "A Tribute to First Lady Pat Nixon," 1972 GOP convention film, Nixon Foundation, https://www.youtube.com/watch?v=-w6rmPWJ-gY, posted August 1, 2010.

270 *"a new beginning"*: Ibid.

271 *"I stay in the wings"*: "First Lady Pat Nixon Addresses GOP Convention," 1972, Nixon Foundation, https://www.youtube.com/watch?v=-w6rmPWJ-gY, posted September 10, 2012.

271 *"Most Admired Woman"*: Frank Newport, David W. Moore, and Lydia Saad, "Most Admired Men and Women: 1948–1998," Gallup, March 21, 2021, https://news.gallup.com/poll/3415/most-admired-men-women-19481998.aspx.

271 *"has transformed America"*: Thomas, *Dateline: White House*, 183.

271 *"the fact that there"*: Julie Eisenhower, oral history for "A Few Good Women," Penn State University Libraries, March 9, 1999.

272 *"I was involved in the planning"*: Barbara Franklin, email to the author, July 3, 2023.

272 *"There were a bunch"*: Ibid.

272 *Women's Surrogate Program*: President's Daily Diary, September 18, 1972, Appendix B. "Meeting with Women Republican Surrogates." https://www.nixonlibrary.gov/sites/default/files/virtuallibrary/documents/PDD/1972/084%20September%2016-30%201972.pdf. 11, 1972, Folder 12–11–72WH, Box 3, Hoover Archive, JDE Collection, White House, Washington, D.C.

272 *"legally it might open"*: Julie Eisenhower, oral history for "A Few Good Women," Penn State University Libraries, March 9, 1999.

273 *"billed as her"*: Ken Ringle, "'But Where Is the Real Pat Nixon?'" *Boston Globe*, September 29, 1972, sec. Living, 31.

273 *"carefully programmed"*: Ibid.

273 *"Are you concerned"*: David, *The Lonely Lady of San Clemente*, 166.

273 *"a cross between"*: Madeleine Edmondson, and Alden Duer Cohen, *The Women of Watergate* (New York, NY: Pocket Books, 1976), 62.

273 *Famed for years*: Edmondson and Cohen, *The Women of Watergate*, 32–62; Thomas, *Dateline: White House*, 227–42.

273 *"From the beginning"*: Edmondson and Cohen, *The Women of Watergate*, 37–38.

274 *In the fall of 1972*: David, *The Lonely Lady of San Clemente*, 167.

274 *"political prisoner"*: *The Martha Mitchell Effect*, Netflix, 2022.

274 *"they didn't really become"*: Chapin, *The President's Man*, 121.

274 *Chapin was not alone*: Lucy Winchester, phone interview with the author, June 17, 2022.

274 *"Unlike other political wives"*: Thomas, *Dateline: White House*, 242.

274 *"It worried her that"*: Eisenhower, *Pat Nixon—The Untold Story*, 349.

275 *"Haldeman was the enforcer"*: Bobbie Kilberg, interview with the author, April 11, 2022.

275 *"he treated me the just same"*: Ibid.

275 *"spent a fair amount of time"*: Ibid.

275 *"very cold and unwelcoming"*: Ibid.

275 *"Richard Nixon's son of a bitch"*: "The President's Palace Guard," *Newsweek*, Box 75.14, March 19, 1973, HRCWC.

275 *"He sits 100"*: Ibid.

275 *"very controlling, abrupt"*: Alexander Butterfield, interview with the author, December 8, 2022.

276 *"Bob Haldeman thought"*: Dr. Henry Kissinger, Zoom interview with the author, April 21, 2022.

276 *Kissinger recounted*: Ibid.

276 *On November 7*: Nixon, *RN*, 716.

277 *"I am at a loss"*: Ibid., 717.

277 *"For the Nixons"*: Truman, *First Ladies*, 200.

277 *"With pain and stoicism"*: Henry Kissinger, *White House Years, Vol. 1* (New York: Simon & Schuster, 1979), 1475.

277 *On January 27*: Lee, *League of Wives*, 234–35.

278 *"He was courteous"*: Nixon, *RN*, 745.

278 *"was the first First Lady"*: Anthony, "Pat Nixon, Stealth Feminist?"

278 *"I think abortion"*: David, *The Lonely Lady of San Clemente*, 153.

278 *"The Watergate case"*: *The Final Campaign*, exhibition text, 3, RNPLM, 1990.

278 *The five men were*: Ibid., 4.

279 *"there was a sense"*: Connie Stuart, oral history interview, August 15, 1988. NARA, 19.

279 *"By the time"*: Eisenhower, *Pat Nixon—The Untold Story*, 361.

279 *"only one person"*: Ibid., 354.

279 *The dueling interoffice*: Charles E. Stuart, *Never Trust a Local: Inside the Nixon White House* (New York: Algora, 2005), 133.

279 *"I've been campaigning"*: Connie Stuart, oral history interview, August 15, 1988, NARA, 19.

280 *Smith was the widow*: Walker, "Helen Smith—Protector and Publicist for Mrs. Nixon."

280 *Helen was a peacemaker*: Patti Matson, interview with the author, October 28, 2022.

280 *Helen kept Mrs. Nixon*: Ibid.

280 *"People trust Helen"*: Walker, "Helen Smith—Protector and Publicist for Mrs. Nixon."

280 *"She was not even informed"*: Bob Woodward interview with Helen McCain Smith, November 4, 1974, Box 75.14, HRCWC.

280 *"On many things"*: Ibid.

280 *"unlike the President's staff"*: Smith and Frank, "Ordeal! Pat Nixon's Final Days in the White House," 83–127.

281 *"a cancer"*: Thomas, *Being Nixon*, 436.

281 *It would turn out*: Ibid., 433.

282 *"She said she had been"*: Nixon, *RN,* 845–46.

282 *"Germans"*: Ehrlichman, *Witness to Power,* 389.

282 *"because I may not be alive"*: Haldeman, *The Haldeman Diaries,* 672.

282 *"crying uncontrollably"*: Ehrlichman, *Witness to Power,* 390.

282 *"he had prayed"*: Ibid.

282 *"two of the finest public servants"*: "President Nixon's First Watergate Speech," C, Accessed July 21, 2023, https://www.c-span.org/video/?299817-1%2Fpresident-nixons-watergate-speech.

283 *"the presidency should come"*: Ibid.

283 *"realize[d] that this"*: David Eisenhower, Zoom with the author, June 5, 2023.

283 *"a Nixon White House"*: Ibid.

283 *"I'm completely contrary"*: Ibid.

283 *"'She had more savvy'"*: Judy Bachrach, "Rosemary Woods: Facing Her Two Crises," *Washington Post,* July 7, 1974, H3.

27: GOOD AFTERNOON, MRS. FORD'S OFFICE

284 *"the White House dinner"*: Lucy Winchester, interview with the author, June 30, 2021.

284 *"Anyone who needs"*: Ibid.

284 *"of course they may bring"*: Pat Howard, interview with the author, May 20, 2021.

284 *"When a POW called"*: Ibid.

285 *"Pat was very much"*: Steve Bull, interview with the author, February 26, 2021.

285 *"I get this call"*: Steven Bull. Oral History Interview. June 25, 2007. NARA, 40.

285 *"After dinner"*: Mike Brazelton, email to the author, June 15, 2023.

285 *"The contrast between"*: Nixon, *RN,* 868.

285 *"And so the evening"*: Eisenhower, *Pat Nixon—The Untold Story,* 372.

286 *In mid-July*: Ted Widmer, "The Tapes That Doomed the Nixon Presidency," *Wall Street Journal,* July 22, 2023, Weekend Edition edition, sec. C4, https://www.wsj.com/articles/the-tapes-that-doomed-nixons-presidency-603ba648.

286 *"the right to maintain"*: *The Final Campaign,* exhibition text, 10.

286 *"private love letters"*: Eisenhower, *Pat Nixon—The Untold Story,* 380; "'Release of Tapes Displeased Pat,'" *Washington Post,* May 20, 1974, sec. A23.

286 *"a picture of her re-creating"*: Gary Brown, "The Monday After: Remembering Sebring's Rose Mary Woods and 'the Gap,'" Canton *Repository,* February 3, 2020, https://www.cantonrep.com/story/news/local/alliance/2020/02/03/the-monday-after-remembering-sebring/1781395007/.

286 *No charges were ever*: Eisenhower, *Pat Nixon—The Untold Story,* 389; Jonathan Aitken, *Nixon: A Life* (Washington, DC: Regnery, 1993), 512.

286 *"ridiculed publicly"*: Steve Bull, interview with the author, August 3, 2021.

286 *As if things*: Farrell, *Richard Nixon: The Life,* 521.

287 *"Nixon's decisiveness"*: Aitken, *Nixon: A Life,* 505.

287 *"Saturday Night Massacre"*: Thomas, *Being Nixon,* 473.

287 *"its impact on"*: Aitken, *Nixon: A Life,* 509.

287 *Acting Attorney General Bork*: Special, John Herbers "Nixon Names Saxbe Attorney General;

Jaworski Appointed Special Prosecutor," *New York Times*, November 2, 1973, https://www
.nytimes.com/1973/11/02/archives/nixon-names-saxbe-attorney-general-jaworski-appointed
-special.html?smid=em-share, accessed July 28, 2023.

287 *"She was fighting mad"*: Correspondence, Folder PN Correspondence, Clippings, Schedule VP
and Presidential years Helene notes 1973, Box 5, JNEC, RNPLM, 1–2.

287 *"Here it is"*: Ibid.

288 *"I'm not going to talk"*: Ibid., 2.

288 *"could rest, walk, read"*: Eisenhower, *Pat Nixon—The Untold Story*, 401.

288 *"For Mrs. Nixon"*: Smith and Frank, "Ordeal! Pat Nixon's Final Days in the White House."

288 *On March 1, 1974*: Eisenhower, *Pat Nixon—The Untold Story*, 402.

289 *"Brazilian soldiers formed"*: Donnie Radcliffe, "Winging Her Way Back Home," *Washington
Post*, March 16, 1974, B1.

289 *The First Lady had*: David, *The Lonely Lady of San Clemente*, 171.

289 *"her face glowing"*: Smith and Frank, "Ordeal! Pat Nixon's Final Days in the White House,"
129.

289 *"mixed signals"*: Eisenhower, *Pat Nixon—The Untold Story*, 404.

289 *Pat herself commented*: Swift, *Pat and Dick: The Nixons*, 328.

290 *"With its many omissions"*: Ted Widmer, "The Tapes That Doomed Nixon's Presidency," *Wall
Street Journal*, July 22, 2023, https://www.wsj.com/articles/the-tapes-that-doomed-nixons
-presidency-603ba648.

290 *"was shocked when"*: Stuart, *Never Trust a Local*, 88.

290 *"a place to flex muscles"*: Ibid.

290 *As the spring continued*: Eisenhower, *Pat Nixon—The Untold Story*, 391; David, *The Lonely Lady
of San Clemente*, 170.

290 *Exercise and the solace*: Eisenhower, *Pat Nixon—The Untold Story*, 407.

290 *"Pat, who had to sign"*: Brennan, *Pat Nixon: Embattled First Lady*, 161.

290 *"could sense her tightly"*: Nixon, *RN*, 963.

290 *"financial probity"*: Ibid.

291 *"Oh, that's for the birds"*: "Pat Pooh-Poos Jewelry Story," *San Francisco Chronicle*, May 16, 1974;
"Article on Jewels Is 'for the Birds,' Mrs. Nixon Says," *New York Times*, May 16, 1974.

291 *What worried the First Lady most*: Nixon, *RN*.

291 *"Julie and David eventually"*: Thomas, *Dateline: White House*, 207.

291 *"Julie and David had warmed"*: Correspondence, Folder PN Correspondence, Clippings,
Schedule VP and Presidential Kandie Stroud letter supporting PN, Box 5, JNEC, RNPLM.

291 *"Mother was the one"*: Eisenhower, *Pat Nixon—The Untold Story*, 408–9.

291 *"never wanted Julie out"*: Interview notes, Bob Woodward interview with Helen McCain
Smith, November 4, 1974, Box 75.14, HRCWC.

291 *"In the months since"*: Nora Ephron, *The Most of Nora Ephron* (New York: Alfred A. Knopf,
2013), 238.

292 *"have been around"*: Ibid., 238.

292 *"the Mystery Girl"*: Thomas, *Dateline: White House*, 174.

292 *"I don't think I'm"*: Ibid.

292 *"The staff were devoted"*: Joni Stevens, interview with the author, March 29, 2021.

292   *"We didn't want"*: Ibid.

292   *"Mrs. Nixon was always"*: Pat Howard, email to the author, August 4, 2023.

292   *"Mrs. Nixon"*: Susie Dolibois, email to the author, August 5, 2023.

293   *During the journey*: Nixon, *RN*, 1040–41.

293   *On July 12*: Eisenhower, *Pat Nixon—The Untold Story*, 415.

293   *Pat continued*: Philips-Schrock, *Nixon White House Redecoration*, 84, 151, 167.

294   *Pat showed Helene*: Eisenhower, *Pat Nixon—The Untold Story*, 416.

294   *Conger held a meeting*: "Lenox Meeting Memo," July 22, 1974, White House Office of the Curator, 08605.

294   *"As if a little puff of wind"*: Eisenhower, *Pat Nixon—The Untold Story*, 417.

294   *"I won't explain, Clem"*: Ibid., 418.

294   *"rocklike solidarity"*: Ibid., 420.

294   *"we all broke down"*: Nixon, *RN*, 1060–61.

295   *The taped Oval Office*: *The Final Campaign*, exhibition text, 28; Geoff Shepard, "Geoff Shepard: Author of the Real Watergate Scandal Book," June 21, 2023, http://shepardonwatergate.com/.

295   *"had entered a criminal conspiracy"*: Andrew Glass, "Watergate 'Smoking Gun' Tape Released, Aug. 5, 1975," *Politico*, August 5, 2018, https://www.politico.com/story/2018/08/05/watergate-smoking-gun-tape-released-aug-5-1974-753086.

295   *"Tuesday and Wednesday"*: Susan Dolibois, diary notes from August 6–8, 1974.

295   *"I needed her help"*: Nixon, *RN*, 1067.

295   *"Rose in tears"*: Ibid., 1068.

295   *"wait a week or so"*: Ibid., 1070.

296   *"The phones rang all day"*: Pat Howard, unpublished notes from August 8, 1974.

296   *"one call on 8/8"*: Joni Stevens, email to the author, August 6, 2023.

296   *"I had never been a quitter"*: "President Nixon's Resignation Speech," PBS, https://www.pbs.org/newshour/spc/character/links/nixon_speech.html, accessed August 8, 2023.

296   *"think about the reality"*: Pat Howard, email to the author, August 5, 2023.

296   *"We were writing envelopes"*: Joni Stevens, email to the author, August 6, 2023.

297   *During all this chaos*: Susie Dolibois, email to the author, August 5, 2023.

28: TRUE GRIT

298   *"Everyone's"*: Jack Brennan, interview by Brenda St. Hilaire, CSUF Oral History, 78.

298   *Passengers included*: Boyer and Boor, *Inside the President's Helicopter*, 360.

298   *David, Julie, Rose Mary*: Julie Eisenhower, email to the author, August 14, 2023.

298   *"the past but the future"*: Thomas, *Being Nixon*, 504.

298   *"Now she would not receive"*: Nixon, *RN*, 1086.

299   *"Both were totally drained"*: Eisenhower, *Pat Nixon—The Untold Story*, 429.

299   *When the flight landed*: Swift, *Pat and Dick: The Nixons*, 342.

299   *Pat instinctively reached out*: Ibid.

299   *"It was really"*: Bill Hudson, interview with the author, August 22, 2023.

299   *Though both Nixons*: Ibid.

299 *"Pat spent her first weeks"*: David, *The Lonely Lady of San Clemente*, 199.

299 *"Tricia and Ed"*: Eisenhower, *Pat Nixon—The Untold Story*, 432.

300 *On September 7*: "Walter Annenberg Embarked on His Successful Run as U.S. Ambassador to the United Kingdom 50 Years Ago," Sunnylands, May 20, 2022, https://sunnylands.org/article/walter-annenberg-embarked-on-his-successful-run-as-u-s-ambassador-to-the-united-kingdom-50-years-ago/.

300 *"The Nixons had visited"*: Sunnylands Guestbook, SA, Rancho Mirage, California, 2009.1.3252.

300 *"private dreamworld"*: Pat, letter to Leonore, May 5, 1970, SA, Rancho Mirage, California, 2009.1.2853.

300 *"When you're down"*: September 8, 1974, Sunnylands guestbook, SA, Rancho Mirage, California, 2009.1.3252.

300 *"A pardon for what?"*: Aitken, *Nixon: A Life*, 532.

300 *"She was obviously upset"*: Eisenhower, *Pat Nixon—The Untold Story*, 433.

300 *"This is the most humiliating"*: Ibid.

301 *Nixon suffered another attack*: Carter, *Richard Nixon: California's Native Son*, 257.

301 *Dick was released on*: Chapin, *The President's Man*, 353–57; "Revisiting Watergate: John Ehrlichman," *Washington Post*, https://www.washingtonpost.com/wp-srv/onpolitics/watergate/johnehrlichan.html, accessed September 1, 2023.

301 *"She gripped my hand"*: Thomas, *Being Nixon*, 507.

301 *"Of course you can"*: Ibid.

301 *"I think it's her"*: Lester David, "Pat Nixon's Golden Years," *McCall's* 114, no. 1 (October 1986): 135–41; Trude B. Feldman, "The Quiet Courage of Pat Nixon," *McCall's*, May 1975, 74.

302 *While Dick continued his slow*: Eisenhower, *Pat Nixon—The Untold Story*, 440–41.

302 *She and Dick enjoyed*: Carter, *Richard Nixon: California's Native Son*, 266.

302 *At Dick's insistence*: Eisenhower, *Pat Nixon—The Untold Story*, 441.

302 *In 1975*: Carter, *Richard Nixon: California's Native Son*, 266–67.

302 *In February 1976*: Jack Brennan, interview with the author, July 13, 2023.

302 *"distraught and even more underweight"*: Bob Woodward and Carl Bernstein, *The Final Days* (New York: Simon & Schuster, 1976), 166.

303 *No specific attributions*: Bob Woodward, interview with the author, Jan. 4, 2023.

303 *Bernstein initially*: Carl Bernstein, email to author, January 10, 2022.

303 *"I do or die"*: David, "Pat Nixon's Golden Years," 141.

303 *"Until the very end"*: Smith and Frank, "Ordeal! Pat Nixon's Final Days in the White House," 127.

303 *The claim that she was hiding*: Notes, Box 35, Gwendolyn B. King Collection, WHCF-SMOF.

303 *A sample calendar*: Ibid., Box 40.

303 *Only in the very last days*: Ibid., Box 42.

303 *"She kept up every day"*: Bill Hudson, interview with the author, July 28, 2021.

303 *"kept her normal"*: Ibid.

303 *"I was with her"*: Bill Hudson, email to the author, August 22, 2023.

304 *"reclusiveness"*: Bob Woodward, interview with the author, January 4, 2023.

304 *"May I come up"*: Lucy Winchester, interview with the author, June 26, 2021.

304 *"I was almost like"*: Steve Bull, interview with the author, August 3, 2021.

304 *"I do know that liquor"*: Smith and Frank, "Ordeal! Pat Nixon's Final Days in the White House," 127.

305 *"Absolutely not true"*: Alexander Butterfield, interviews with the author, December 8, 2022 and January 12, 2023.

305 *"Having held views"*: Wolfgang Saxon, "Nixon Sons-in-Law Accuse 2 Authors," *New York Times*, April 3, 1976, https://www.nytimes.com/1976/04/03/archives/nixon-sonsinlaw-accuse -2-authors.html.

305 *"distorted facts, rumors"*: Ibid.

305 *"His henchman called me"*: Edward Cox, interview with the author, August 29, 2023.

305 *"spun a story"*: Ibid.

305 *"She was just a wonderful mother"*: Ibid.

305 *"That's ridiculous"*: Ibid.

305 *"There are a lot of imaginings"*: David Eisenhower, Zoom interview with the author, June 5, 2023.

306 *Compounding the injury*: Don Roy King, "SNL Transcripts: Madeline Kahn: 05/08/76: Final Days," SNL Transcripts Tonight, January 3, 2019, https://snltranscripts.jt.org/75/75snixon .phtml, accessed August 19, 2023.

306 *Ford courageously*: Lisa McCubbin and Susan Ford Bales, *Betty Ford: First Lady, Women's Advocate, Survivor, Trailblazer* (New York: Gallery Books, 2019), 319.

306 *"I always had a lot"*: Bob Woodward, interview with the author, January 4, 2023.

306 *"despite my father's protests"*: Eisenhower, *Pat Nixon—The Untold Story*, 440–41, 447.

306 *The next morning*: Swift, *Pat and Dick: The Nixons*, 354.

307 *Fortunately, the stroke*: Eisenhower, *Pat Nixon—The Untold Story*, 440–41, 449–51.

307 *A frail-looking*: David, *The Lonely Lady of San Clemente*, 205–9.

307 *Family members*: Tricia Nixon Cox, email to the author, August 21, 2023.

307 *"visited Pat many times"*: Maureen Drown Nunn, email to the author, August 21, 2023.

307 *"She was a fighter"*: Ibid.

307 *"The scary intimations"*: Aitken, *Nixon: A Life*, 564.

307 *"I don't care what"*: Gulley and Reese, *Breaking Cover*, 242.

308 *In late 1978*: Winzola McLendon, "Pat Nixon Today," *Good Housekeeping* 190, no. 2 (February 1980): 129.

308 *"A very sensitive mouth"*: Ibid.

308 *The Nixons' first grandchild*: Aitken, *Nixon: A Life*, 565.

308 *"This is what life"*: Eisenhower, *Pat Nixon—The Untold Story*, 440–41, 457.

308 *The grandchildren*: Ibid., 457.

308 *In 1980*: Ibid., 458.

308 *In the fall of 1981*: David, "Pat Nixon's Golden Years," 137.

308 *In 1983*: Richard Pearson, "Pat Nixon, First Lady in 'Time of Turmoil,' Dies," *Washington Post*, June 23, 1993, http://www.washingtonpost.com/archive/politics/1993/06/23/pat-nixon-first -lady-in-time-of-turmoil-dies/2fadc435-a3e3-4e86-9cc9-7dfb91600f28.

309 *"They must wonder"*: Betsy Reimer, interview with the author, May 14, 2020.

309 *Pat Nixon gave up*: Nancy Sharkey, "Follow-up on the News; Nixon Guards," *The New York Times*, July 28, 1985.

309 *"After lunch President Nixon"*: Penny Adams, email to the author, August 22, 2023.

309 *"All three praised"*: Annette Haddad, "Nixon Library Dedicated by Four Presidents," UPI, July 19, 1990.

309 *"Resplendent in a green"*: Aitken, *Nixon: A Life*, 566.

309 *According to Dwight Chapin*: Dwight Chapin, interview with the author, January 29, 2021.

310 *"Every once in a while"*: Monica Crowley, interview with the author, April 30, 2021.

310 *"The little things"*: Ibid.

310 *Pat's last public appearance*: Swift, *Pat and Dick: The Nixons*, 283.

310 *"made the critical decision"*: Richard Nixon handwritten notes, May 8, 1993, JNEC, RNPLM.

310 *"Eisenhower told"*: Ibid.

311 *"Not just the beautiful people"*: Ibid.

311 *"heroic"*: Ibid.

311 *"when he was ready to give up"*: Ibid.

311 *He praised her*: Ibid.

311 *"never thought of her"*: Ibid.

311 *"Above all"*: Ibid.

311 *"For a record"*: Ibid.

311 *"be consoled by what you have"*: Letter, Jackie Kennedy Onassis to Pat Nixon when she becomes First Lady, Box 7, Folder VIP materials 1960–1978, JNEC, RNPLM; Nixon, *RN*, 254–55.

311 *"the tragedy of getting"*: Rick Perlstein, phone interview with the author, May 9, 2023.

311 *"greatest prize"*: Ibid.

311 *"Tell me about"*: "Mother's Last Two Days," handwritten notes, JNEC, RNPLM, 1–4.

311 *"I've just got to get well"*: Ibid.

311 *"No, not unless"*: Ibid.

311 *"Thank you"*: Ibid.

312 *"he broke down"*: Thomas, *Being Nixon*, 523.

312 *"remember the beauty"*: Funeral Program, Pat Nixon, June 26, 1993, Post-Presidential Materials, RNPLM.

312 *Pat's best friend*: Maureen Drown Nunn, email to the author, August 25, 2023.

312 *Richard Milhous Nixon*: Swift, *Pat and Dick: The Nixons*, 376.

312 *"For Patricia"*: Nixon, *Beyond Peace*, dedication page.

EPILOGUE: THE ROAD GOES ON. . .

313 *Thursday, March 16*: "Pat Nixon Park," City of Cerritos, http://www.cerritos.us/RESIDENTS/recreation/facilities/neighborhood_parks/pat_nixon_park.php, accessed August 7, 2023.

313 *Resolution 68*: "RESOLUTION CHAPTER 103, Senate Concurrent Resolution No. 68—Relative to the First Lady Pat Nixon Memorial Highway."

314 *"For her service"*: Senator Bob Archuleta, interview with the author, December 13, 2022.

314 *"I think that at the"*: Ibid.

314 *"We're also proud"*: Ibid.

315 *"She was independent"*: Jim Byron, remarks on March 16, 2023, dedication of the Pat Nixon Highway.

315 *"My mother loved to drive"*: Tricia Nixon Cox, remarks on March 16, 2023, dedication of the Pat Nixon Highway.

315 *"You are just Pat Nixon"*: Elizabeth Cloes, interview by Mary Suzanne Simon, May 29, 1970, OH #834, CSUF, Richard M. Nixon Project, 3; Carter, *Richard Nixon: California's Native Son*, 133.

INDEX

ABOUT THE AUTHOR

Hoa Jensen

Heath Hardage Lee is an award-winning historian, biographer, and curator. Lee's second book, *The League of Wives*, is being developed into a television series. Lee and her work have been featured on the *Today* show, C-SPAN, and the Smithsonian Channel's *America's Hidden Stories*. She also writes about history and politics for publications such as *Time, The Hill, The Atlantic,* and *White House History Quarterly.* She lives in Roanoke, Virginia, with her husband, Chris; her children, Anne Alston and James; and her French bulldog, Dolly Parton.